Narrating Complexity

Richard Walsh • Susan Stepney
Editors

Narrating Complexity

 Springer

Editors
Richard Walsh
Department of English and Related
Literature
University of York
York, UK

Susan Stepney
Department of Computer Science
University of York
York, UK

ISBN 978-3-030-09726-4   ISBN 978-3-319-64714-2   (eBook)
https://doi.org/10.1007/978-3-319-64714-2

This Springer imprint is published by the registered company Springer Nature Switzerland AG
The registered company address is: Gewerbestrasse 11, 6330 Cham, Switzerland

Contents

Contributors

Marco Bernini Department of English Studies, Durham University, Durham, UK

James Bown School of Design and Informatics and School of Science, Engineering and Technology, Abertay University, Dundee, UK

Leo Caves York Cross-disciplinary Centre for Systems Analysis, University of York, York, UK

Ana Teixeira de Melo Centre for Social Studies, University of Coimbra, Coimbra, Portugal

Jason Edwards Department of History of Art, University of York, York, UK

Alexey Goltsov School of Science, Engineering & Technology, Abertay University, Dundee, UK

Adam Lively Department of Media, Middlesex University, London, UK

Julian Miller Department of Electronic Engineering, University of York, York, UK

Federico Pianzola Department of Human Sciences for Education, University of Milan-Bicocca, Milan, Italy

Maria Poulaki Department of Music and Media, University of Surrey, Guildford, UK

Merja Polvinen Department of Modern Languages, University of Helsinki, Helsinki, Finland

Susan Stepney Department of Computer Science, University of York, York, UK

York Cross-disciplinary Centre for Systems Analysis, University of York, York, UK

Romana Turina Department of Theatre, Film and Television, University of York, York, UK

Emma Uprichard Centre for Interdisciplinary Methodologies, University of Warwick, Warwick, UK

Richard Walsh Department of English and Related Literature, University of York, York, UK

Interdisciplinary Centre for Narrative Studies, University of York, York, UK

Alan F. T. Winfield Bristol Robotics Laboratory, University of the West of England, Bristol, UK

Part I
Scene Setting

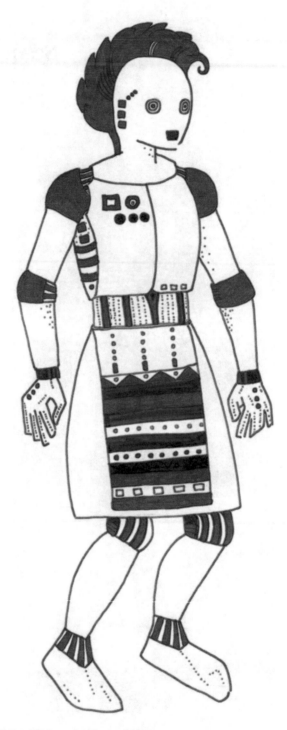

Chapter 1
Introduction and Overview: Who, What, Why

Richard Walsh and Susan Stepney

Abstract The introduction provides an account of the genesis of this volume. In particular, we sketch its prehistory in the dialogue cultivated by the NarCS network between complex systems scientists and narratologists, and introduce the fundamental questions animating that dialogue. It supplies the conceptual framework within which the network pursued those questions, and explains the interdisciplinary methodological assumptions we adopted from the outset, and which also inform this volume.

The scene: a YCCSA interdisciplinary seminar, with scones, circa 2012.

Narratologist:	Nice scones!
Complexity Scientist:	They are, aren't they? We find they're the most effective bait.
N:	I like the interdisciplinary environment you've got here around complex systems. I think narrative has a similar role to play in the humanities.
CS:	So your field is narrative—stories, you mean?
N:	More or less. Narrative theory is concerned with the kind of meaning, or logic, that characterizes stories. Narratives can be found in fictional and nonfictional discourses, in different media, in ordinary conversation. In the largest sense, narrative is a fundamental part of how we think.
CS:	So what's the connection with complex systems?

R. Walsh (✉)
Department of English and Related Literature, University of York, York, UK

Interdisciplinary Centre for Narrative Studies, University of York, York, UK
e-mail: richard.walsh@york.ac.uk

S. Stepney
Department of Computer Science, University of York, York, UK

York Cross-disciplinary Centre for Systems Analysis, University of York, York, UK

© Springer Nature Switzerland AG 2018
R. Walsh, S. Stepney (eds.), *Narrating Complexity*,
https://doi.org/10.1007/978-3-319-64714-2_1

N:	Well, one result of understanding narrative that way is that narratives turn out to be everywhere—
CS:	—just like complex systems—
N:	—so that the concept of narrative starts to seem so general that it risks becoming almost meaningless.
CS:	Yes, "narrative" has become a buzzword for political spin-doctors and people like that, hasn't it? I never know what they mean by it.
N:	Neither do I. It's an example of the way in which a concept can become so inclusive that its stops doing any real work. That's why I'm interested in defining the limits of narrative representation; and complex processes seem to present one, because they are non-linear.
CS:	Well, non-linearity is certainly a characteristic of complexity in systems—they don't generate nice straight line graphs. Complex systems have interesting properties like strong interactions between their parts, feedback, emergence, self-organisation, adaptation, growth, change. None of these is a "straight line" process. But why is that a problem for narrative?
N:	I think because narratives reduce complexity to linear sequence...
CS:	Ah—different senses of "linear," I think. One is linear *response*, and that's the usual complex systems meaning, and the other is linear *temporal sequence*, which I think is your narrative meaning. But for that matter, isn't there such a thing as a "non-linear" narrative, in your sense? "The Garden of Forking Paths," the film *Sliding Doors*, that kind of thing? How do they fit? Or is that something different?
N:	It's different, or perhaps just a misnomer. Narratives can explore non-linear temporality, but to be intelligible as narrative they still depend upon its essential linearity. The Borges story is *about* the idea of forking paths in time, it doesn't enact it; and even where narratives do present several incompatible sequences of events, as in *Sliding Doors*, they present each one as, precisely, a sequence—they haven't really evaded the linear logic of narrative at all. That's the problem I mean: if a complex system involves a network of interactions all going on together in reciprocal and recursive ways, a narrative might trace one or other sequence within that network, but it can't possibly capture the systemic nature of what is happening.

CS: That certainly captures something about the difficulty of understanding complex systems. Still, we can get a grasp upon them in other ways—we can construct models and run simulations, and these often show how systemic interactions can produce the emergent behaviour of the system.

N: Ok, so models and simulations show the operation of a system rather than telling it? The distinction between showing and telling has a history within narrative theory, so that's interesting. But how do you understand the idea of emergent behaviour?

CS: It's not at all well defined; there are several different definitions and descriptions. One that might be interesting here is the one that defines it in terms of needing two different languages. There's one language for describing the system at the micro-level where the action is, and another different language for describing the macro-level, where the emergence is seen. The emergent property is a different kind of thing, and so needs a different language for us to talk about it.

N: It seems to me that you might say emergent behaviour in a system is behaviour that becomes narratable at another level of representation?

CS: That sounds interesting. What's the difference between something being *narratable* and being *describable*?

N: Another opposition with a history in narrative theory! I'd say that any representation is broadly a form of description, but that narrative is our innate way of representing process—it's the form in which we make sense of stuff happening. So we seize upon patterns of emergent behaviour in systems because we can articulate them in narrative form; but the narrative we tell is oblivious to the systemic interactions actually producing the behaviour.

CS: I suppose it's generally true that the main interest of complex systems is what they do, how they behave; how to explain it, or predict it, or control it.

N: Yes, and our cognitive framework for representing behaviour is narrative; we're highly dependent upon it. Whenever we have to explain research publicly, we're told: "tell a story." But for complex systems—evolution by natural selection is a good example here—telling a story actually misrepresents what's going on. It's a problem for science communication, isn't it?

CS: Not just that; it's a problem of communication even between complex systems scientists—we're only human, after all!

N:	Right, even when we know that the mechanism of a process is systemic, there's a sense in which this doesn't amount to understanding until we can bring it into relation with narrative. We understand the way the world works through our narrative structures.
CS:	But if so, given we don't have any complex narratives, doesn't that mean we literally can't understand the complex world?
N:	Exactly! So what narrative theory needs to do is explore ways to complexify narrative...
CS:	And what complexity science needs to do is find new ways to narrate complexity!
Both:	To the Bat Cave!

And so it began. The dialogue above, or something like it, was the inaugural event of the collaboration that has led to this volume. It quickly became clear that narratologists and complex systems scientists had much to learn from each other, and potentially much to contribute to each other's research. We drew together an international group of interested researchers from both sides of the dialogue and from various disciplines, and formed the Narrative and Complex Systems network (NarCS). The nature of our collaboration immediately raised questions of interdisciplinary methodology. Its whole basis was the incommensurability between two frames of reference: what complex systems science shows us about how the world works, and the way narrative sets limits upon our ability to cognitively grasp that information. We did not want to presuppose the possibility of synthesis, either between objects of knowledge and modes of knowing, or between the disciplinary orientations that represented the two sides of the narrative-complexity problem. This encounter between disciplinary orientations looked a lot like that between the sciences and the humanities, in a kind of reprise of the "Two Cultures" debate of the 1950s and 1960s, with the social sciences occupying an interesting intermediate position to which their own internal methodological debates testify. Instead of a presumption of interdisciplinary synthesis and the consilience of knowledge, then, we adopted a model of interdisciplinary encounter—and dialogue. The reciprocity of dialogue, indeed, has informed both the process of collaboration within the NarCS network and the design of this book—and not just the decision to open it with a dialogue.

The activity of the NarCS network centred upon a series of workshops built around papers and presentations that articulated aspects of our common theme from different disciplinary perspectives. The principle was that we each brought our specific expertise to the exchange, and took from it the responses we elicited and the promptings of other members' presentations. Cumulatively, we began to map out a conceptual terrain that demarcated the several domains and levels on which the fundamental dialogue within the network was operating. We identified four quadrants, under the headings Communication, Culture, Conceptualization and Cognition (Fig. 1.1).

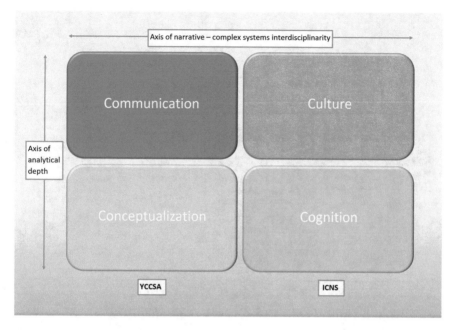

Fig. 1.1 A tale of four quadrants

The arrangement in two columns reflects the two sides of the dialogue at a basic level. Communication, in the left column, designates the problem presented by complex systems as, centrally, a science communication challenge of primary concern to complex systems scientists. Culture, in the right column, designates the efforts of elaborate forms of narrative, in various media (fiction, film, interactive digital media), to imagine and grapple with the representation of complexity.

The two columns, then, represent the home turf of, respectively, complex systems science and narratology; or the York Cross-Disciplinary Centre for Systems Analysis (YCCSA) and the Interdisciplinary Centre for Narrative Studies (ICNS).

The vertical axis distinguishes between the *level* of these public discourses and the theoretical level underpinning those manifestations. In the second row, Conceptualization refers to the ways in which complex systems science theorizes, models, and simulates the forms and behaviours of complex systems, while Cognition refers to the narratological theorization of narrative as an elemental cognitive mode of sensemaking, a specific logic intrinsic to the human understanding of processes.

It became apparent, though, that the dialogue between the narratological and complexity science perspectives was a layered phenomenon, and that within each of these quadrants we could distinguish orientations towards the topic that foregrounded its complex systems aspect or its narrative aspect (Fig. 1.2).

Here, nesting within the broad dialogue between the left and right of the diagram at the surface level and the deep level (that is, between Complexity Science and Narratology), there is a further dialogue between the left and right of each quadrant:

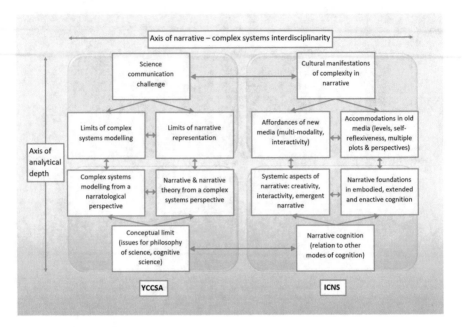

Fig. 1.2 Drilling down further

- Under **Communication**, the responsible public representation of complexity science calls both for a constructive appropriation of innovative narrative representations to complex systems modelling, for example through the hybrid, semiotic *and* experiential forms of interactive narrative; and for a critical perspective that foregrounds the limits of narrative representation and informs public awareness of these constraints.
- Under **Culture**, we can distinguish between the possibilities for innovative engagement with the representation of complexity afforded by digital media and interactive narrative on the one hand, and on the other hand the respects in which the most developed traditional cultural forms of narrative can be seen as highly reflexive, in the systemic sense that reflexive cycles of development underlie the elaboration of such narrative resources as genre, fictionality, vraisemblance and intertextuality, thematics, and levels of narration and focalization.
- Under **Conceptualization**, the theorization of staple complex systems ideas like emergence stands to gain considerably from the implications of its reciprocity with narrative; while even the most fundamental scientific practices of modelling, simulating and manipulating complex systems reveal implicit narrative assumptions that can animate narrative theory.
- Under **Cognition**, models of emergence offer a valuable approach to questions about the evolutionary and individual development of narrative competence, and the respects in which this development may be articulated in terms of reflexive

processes of abstraction from the particular, and recursive cycles of interpretative oscillation between the particular and the general. Likewise, emergence becomes of central interest to our conceptions of narrative sense-making as grounded in embodied cognition, in behavioural interaction and in systemic social contexts.

In short, the reciprocity inherent in a dialogic approach to interdisciplinarity also proves to be recursive in its operation, which gives great encouragement to our expectations that emergent effects can arise from the research process itself.

That being so, we decided early on that we wanted the same recursive dialogic process to inform the production of this volume, and that the process should still be visible in the volume's final published form. Each of the essays presented here is the outcome of several rounds of presentation and response, orally and in print, between members of the NarCS group. When the essays were in draft, we formalized this process by having each essay reviewed by members of the NarCS group, from both the complexity science and the humanities subcamps. The process was an instructive one with respect to the challenge of making ourselves intelligible to each other, and also genuinely provoked new thought and intellectual progress in the revised essays. At the end of many essays we have retained a selection of comments from their draft readers, along with responses from the authors; in the case of the essays by Adam Lively, Federico Pianzola and Romana Turina, we have appended a three-way exchange between them in response to each other.

The question of mutual intelligibility is not a trivial one when attempting inter-disciplinary dialogue of the breadth undertaken in this project. Incomprehension is the least problematic part of it; often, the appearance of comprehension turned out to be treacherous, and we discovered that we were using terms in quite different senses, or that we had assumed quite different unspoken premises. The sense of risk was tangible; often it felt as if the whole exchange might suddenly turn out to be based upon a misunderstanding, and crumble to dust. One of the prefatory tasks we have undertaken for this volume, therefore, is to present a reciprocal pair of introductory chapters: one offering an outline of key ideas in narrative theory with the needs of a readership of complex systems scientists primarily in mind; the other offering an outline of the central concepts of complex systems science with narratologists primarily in mind. We are fairly sure, however, that these chapters are of interest to a much broader audience than this specific brief might suggest.

Our editorial overview of the content of the chapters is reserved for Part III of the volume, where it forms part of the retrospective analysis of what we have learned. Readers seeking guidance on the topics and arguments presented in order to direct their reading may turn directly to Part III if they wish.

Chapter 2
Narrative Theory for Complexity Scientists

Richard Walsh

Abstract The aim of this chapter is to outline some of the key ideas and concepts in narrative theory, in order to make the field more accessible to those who have only a passing acquaintance with it (complexity scientists in particular). The chapter first gives an account of what narrative is, and then goes on to draw out some of the implications of that account for the way we think and understand in narrative terms. My discussion of these implications draws attention, as opportunity arises, to respects in which the form of narrative bears upon our ability to understand and communicate the way complex systems behave. The chapter does not survey the many facets of the problematic relation between narrative sensemaking and complex systems (that is really the work of the book as a whole), but it does provide a reasonably solid theoretical underpinning for the narrative problems, questions and possibilities taken up in subsequent chapters.

1 Introduction

The account of narrative offered here aspires to be recognizable and broadly acceptable to most narrative theorists, but it is not simply an exposition of the current state of knowledge about narrative; rather, it takes (and argues for) a particular view. Narrative theory, like most humanities-based discourses, is not a paradigm-based incremental science. It has a number of competing paradigms, some of which have gained some ascendency at certain periods, and all of which have roots in the broader history of the field. There is always scope for theoretical disagreement at every level, and consensus is as likely to be a manifestation of stale orthodoxy as a basis for the

R. Walsh (✉)
Department of English and Related Literature, University of York, York, UK

Interdisciplinary Centre for Narrative Studies, University of York, York, UK
e-mail: richard.walsh@york.ac.uk

© Springer Nature Switzerland AG 2018
R. Walsh, S. Stepney (eds.), *Narrating Complexity*,
https://doi.org/10.1007/978-3-319-64714-2_2

advancement of knowledge. In what follows I have tried to flag areas of substantial disagreement, but of course even the rhetoric of my qualifying statements should be viewed with suspicion.

2 Narrative

If we begin with the broad assumption that "narrative" means "story," we are somewhere close to the concept. However, the term "story" has a restrictive and skewed range of associations, suggesting (for example) a more or less extended, more or less conventionalized form of communication, often diverting, often fictional, sometimes artful. Also, as will become clear, within narrative theory the word also has more specific, technical senses (more than one, unfortunately). Most importantly, though, the sense of "narrative" with which we are concerned is somewhat abstracted from the sense in which "a narrative" is approximately synonymous with "a story," or even from the sense in which "narrative" is "the type of discourse characteristic of stories." Rather, we are concerned with narrative as a primary mode of thought, one that has a specific form and therefore constitutes a specific kind of logic.

Narrative, understood in these terms, is a basic way of making sense that is central to our ordinary engagement with the world and each other. While the logic of narrative is certainly deployed in stories, it is more fundamentally part of how we think. Nor is it simply an aspect of our linguistic ability (it is not dependent upon language, and may well be more primitive than language). Narrative is a mode of cognition, a distinct form of sensemaking with its own specific and limited range of affordances.[1] Narrative cognition is an essential and powerful means of understanding, and at the same time a significant constraint upon our ability to make sense of phenomena that resist its logic—notably, the behaviour of complex systems.

In order to clarify the implications of narrative for understanding, though, we need to define it more exactly. The following definition of narrative is my own, and by no means canonical, but it has the merit of delimiting the object of study whilst assuming as little as possible about it (without falling into metaphysics). It is therefore more abstract than most such definitions, though it allows us to arrive at the more common ideas of narrative subsequently:

Narrative is the semiotic articulation of linear temporal sequence

I go through this definition word by word below, but to get a preliminary grasp of it we might gloss it by saying that narrative is a way of meaning—"semiotic articulation"—not a kind of occurrence (something that happens is not, as such, narrative); and that it is concerned with a certain form—"linear temporal sequence"—not a certain subject matter, or a certain purpose. The definition leaves

---

[1]Essential sources for this view of narrative cognition are Bruner (1991), Turner (1996), and Herman (2002).

implicit some features of narrative that are taken as definitional in many other accounts, and I draw attention to these differences below. Many such features are really consequences of the nature of narrative cognition, rather than being intrinsic to it, and I address such consequences in Sect. 3, "Implications." The aim here, however, is to specify what is distinctive about narrative without saying too much and prematurely restricting the concept.

The core of the definition is its final term, which all the others premodify. For the sake of clear exposition, then, it makes sense to start at the end and work backwards through it.

2.1 Sequence

"Sequence" is the most neutral term possible for the specific formal relation that narrative articulates. It represents a bare transition from formlessness to a specific (total) order. What matters is this sequential form, not what it is that is sequenced. Accordingly, the definition leaves out things (such as consequence, events, or agency) that are certainly general characteristics of narrative, and might be thought definitional—are indeed definitional, according to some narrative theorists. In this definition, however, these characteristics do not define narrative, but result from the kind of order that narrative imposes upon phenomena. It is important to maintain a distinction between narrative thinking itself and the effects of such thinking.

"Consequence," for example, would have smuggled in the notion of causality, and so begged the question of whether causation is a condition for narrative representation or one of its conceptual products. This is not only a question for the philosophy of science but also a pragmatic caution: narratives frequently do impute causal connections without positively asserting them, and often in manifestly erroneous ways.

What about "events"? The event is the fundamental unit of almost every definition of narrative you're likely to come across, but that too seems to beg the question. Such appeals to the idea of "event" treat it as both a punctual and a durational concept. Some definitions assume that it is the link between two or more events that makes a minimal narrative, but an event can also be understood as something with internal structure and duration.[2] Such internal structure is explicit in definitions of narrative as minimally the articulation of a single event, but even the notionally punctual events that comprise two-event examples of minimal narrative can invariably be reconceived as durational: for example, consider the two events in E.M. Forster's minimal story, "the king died and then the queen died" (Forster 1962, p. 87). The narrative event is itself a product of narrative thinking, not its raw

---

[2]For a two-event definition of minimal narrative, see Prince (1982); for a one-event definition, see Genette (1988).

material; and it is itself an open question whether narrative thinking is adequate to the actual structure of processes, as this volume testifies.

Many narrative theorists would also want to insist that narrative is more specifically concerned with sequences of acts, that is, with agency; and I think it is, even where a particular narrative concerns entirely inanimate processes (a solar eclipse, say), for reasons that I discuss below. But if we want to consider a sequential account of a solar eclipse as a narrative—and I do—then agency too is better thought of as one of narrative's effects rather than a constituent element. This view also applies to a related and even more restrictive criterion for some definitions of narrative, which is "experientiality."[3] The essential quality being insisted upon here is not that narrative represents the action of agents, but that it represents experiencing agents; it is about their subjective experience, not just the action in itself. Again, this can't be literally the case unless the scope of narrative is restricted considerably. How much? Should there be no narratives without human agents? If not, how far should the criterion of experientiality extend, literally or figuratively? Narrative doesn't always deal in the human or human-like, but it does always bring its materials into relation with a human frame of reference, because that is what making narrative sense entails. In doing so it necessarily imposes a range of collateral ideas to some degree, including agency and experientiality.

2.2   Temporal

The sequential order narrative imposes is not spatial or conceptual, but temporal. Narrative is fundamentally about time, a quality which is distinct from the fact that expressing or producing it, as well as interpreting it, happens in time. In this respect, narration may be contrasted with description. Description is like narration in that it takes place in time, but unlike narration in that its own logic is spatial. This is to say that a description of a process either *is* a narrative, or is a conceptual spatialization of its temporality (the latter being an important alternative to narrative in the case of systemic processes). Conversely, a narrative may of course include spatial information (a substantial narrative may include extended passages of description, for that matter), but this is inessential to its logic as narrative. In this sense narrative and description are complementary, antithetical conceptual dispositions towards spatiotemporality.

Narrative, then, has a dual temporality, in that it both predicates temporal sequence and is itself articulated in temporal sequence. A narrative is *about* a certain temporal sequence, and its narration *has* a certain temporal sequence, and the two may not directly align. This quality has been a focus of enquiry in narrative theory, not least because the relation between these two temporalities, that of the told and that of the telling, is often exploited in the elaborate literary narratives that

---

[3]See especially Fludernik (1996).

narratological research has tended to favour. But such a circumstance is itself indicative of narrative's important capacity for reflexive elaboration. Just as it is possible to transform description into narrative simply by projecting, for example, the story of an act of looking onto its discursive movement from point to point, so it is possible for the temporality of a narrative's telling to become itself an object of narrative, giving us represented acts of narration. This reflexiveness is commonplace in more elaborate narrative forms, and it is often also recursive.

I have already rejected the idea that causal relations define the scope of narrative, but causality is often touted as a crucial feature taken to distinguish "narrative proper" from "mere" temporal sequence.[4] According to this definition, however, causality (or a certain notion of causality) is not a foundation for narrative sense but one of its contingent products. This view accords with a famous suggestion by Roland Barthes, that narrative is characterized by a systematic application of the logical fallacy, *post hoc ergo propter hoc* (Barthes 1975, p. 248). Accordingly, to define narrative by reference to causality would be to make one of the conceptual effects of narrative into a prerequisite for narrative. But might not a similar argument be advanced against defining narrative with reference to temporality? There is some force to this objection, and indeed approaches to narrative grounded in phenomenology have emphasized that our senses of time and narrative are dependent upon each other and mutually reinforcing.[5] If so, it would seem illegitimate to give conceptual priority to temporality and invoke it as part of a definition of narrative. But, on the one hand, our experience of temporality is broader and more fundamental (even if less coherent) than our narrative grasp of it; nor is narrative our only resource for thinking about time. And on the other hand, it is in any case folly to expect that an even more abstract definition would deliver more solid metaphysical foundations.[6]

2.3 Linear

The word "linear" in the definition serves to delimit the particular kind of temporal sequencing characteristic of narrative, and to exclude and contrast with the "non-linear," despite the fact that certain kinds of narrative—especially literary narrative—are often characterized as non-linear, and celebrated for that reason. There are two distinct senses of the non-linear at stake, however. The first, which is the sense that actually applies to narratives, refers to the various ways in which the articulation

---

[4]For example, Forster distinguishes between plot and mere story (in his own specific sense) on the basis of causality; so "The king died and then the queen died *of grief*," he says, is a plot (Forster 1962, p. 87). Causality also features prominently in White's distinction between annals, chronicle and narrative proper in his own, restrictive sense (White 1980); and causality is made the central feature of narrative in Richardson (1997), and in Kafalenos (2006).

[5]This is the central theme of Ricoeur (1984–1988).

[6]The philosophical background to the relation between narrative and time is nicely expounded by Currie (2007); see also the chapter on time in this volume ("Time Will Tell", Chap. 19).

of events in a narrative may not be given in a single consecutive sequence (i.e., non-linearity in narration), or the events narrated may not cohere as a sequence in principle (i.e., non-linearity of the narrated). Such narratives may simply narrate a non-chronological sequence of events or, more radically, they may fork down mutually exclusive paths, or form endless cycles or paradoxical strange loops. Even in the most extreme cases, however, "non-linear narrative" is strictly a misnomer, because these are not alternative forms of narrative so much as ways of impeding or subverting narrative. All these strategies are striking in part because they foreground the fact that narrative logic itself is always doggedly linear, requiring an inexorable progression from point to point, one by one, even when the narrative is structured in a way that exposes how pedestrian or inadequate this is.

The other sense of "non-linear" is the mathematical sense, in which the changes in two (or more) related variables are not directly proportional to each other. This sense applies only figuratively, at best, to "non-linear narratives." However, the centrality of non-linear systems to complex systems science does bear importantly upon narrative in two respects. Firstly, narrative is inadequate to the task of representing non-linear dynamical systems because of its limited ability to model multiple, simultaneous, reciprocal and recursive relations. The limitation is not just a practical matter of our finite cognitive resources, because our reliance upon narrative sensemaking (which is itself an adapted form of cognitive efficiency) makes it into a matter of principle. The narrative conception of temporality is linear in that it is founded upon an additive procedure (this particular, and then this, and then this; one damn thing after another), which gives narrative effective attentional focus, but at the cost of its synoptic grasp. Such a procedural constraint fails to address the quality of mathematical non-linearity captured by the phrase "solutions cannot be added together," and therefore cannot cope with complex systemic processes. Or, to frame the problem more generally, narrative is definitionally unable to account for the quality in *processes* that corresponds to the unity of complex *substances* as Aristotle conceives it; namely, in his much quoted phrase from the *Metaphysics*, the respect in which the whole is (according to various translations) "something beside," or "distinct from" or "over and above" the "mere heap" or "aggregate" or "sum" of the parts.[7]

Secondly, and antithetically, any given narrative may itself be considered to function as a system, in that its own coherence depends upon a network of significant relations within the medium in which it is told. The systemic discursive realization of a narrative may be part of a larger, prior system of meaning, such as a natural language, or it may establish its own signifying structure, as with a performative narrative. In either case, these systemic relations are internal to the narrative's operation as a way of meaning, and distinct from the temporal relations it attributes to its referent by giving narrative form to some actual or conceptual process. Meaning is a systemic phenomenon that narrative strongly coerces into the form

---

[7]From the *Metaphysics*, Book 8, 1045a. These are the translations of, respectively, Ross (Aristotle 1908), Tredennick (Aristotle 1933), and Bostock (Aristotle 1994).

of a linear logic. Even as a narrative imposes this logic upon its materials, its own dynamic production of meaning (the process of its articulation, or the process of any subsequent interpretation of it) is a manifestly non-linear process, involving a geometrical proliferation of significant relations with each meaningful unit that is introduced.[8] This important quality is particularly evident, for any extended narrative, in the gap that opens up between denotation and connotation; between what the narrative propositionally says (as the expression of a linear logic) and what it implies (through its elaboration within a system of meanings). Narratives, intriguingly, are themselves instances of the non-linear dynamic systems they are so ill-equipped to represent. This circumstance is crucial to the potential for cultural elaborations of narrative to transcend the limitations of narrative form. Not only does it offer a powerful conception of the history of narrative, it is also highly suggestive for the further potential of emerging forms of narrative in contemporary culture.

2.4   Articulation

The term "articulation," in this definition, serves to express the idea that narrative is indeed fundamentally a process, a meaning-making activity, both in production and reception. While a narrative *text* is a thing, narrative in the sense intended by this definition is neither that text itself, nor something transmitted by that text, but the basic cognitive mode of its creation and its interpretation. The word "articulation" has specific advantages in conveying this idea. It might seem that "communication" would be a more self-explanatory alternative, but that would limit the scope of narrative to its social manifestations, whereas we are seeking to characterize a kind of cognitive process. Although the conditions in which narrative cognition originated were very probably social, and possibly communicative, and indeed some kinds of narrative thinking might appropriately be described as forms of self-communication, even an internalized notion of communication doesn't capture the most elementary instances of narrative cognition.

Another alternative with less restrictive connotations than "communication" would be "expression," but there is a second objection to both of these terms. The problematic implication of both words is that there is something—some content, structure, meaning or intention—that exists prior to the narrative act, and is transmitted by it. Such a transmissive model of narrative looks plausible, perhaps, when the narrative concerned is taken to be a specific recounting of some prior conception, or "story," in another specific narratological sense of the word. In this view, a narrative's "discourse," the telling, is conceived as the transmission of its "story," the told.[9] A distinction of this sort seems plausible when interpreting the literary

---

[8] A unit of (narrative) meaning is a "seme" for Greimas (1983) and Barthes (1974); or a "narreme" for Dorfman (1969).

[9] The distinction between the telling and the told as "discourse" and "story" comes from Chatman; in the older terminology of the Russian Formalists, it is "syuzhet" and "fabula" (Tomashevsky 1965).

narratives on which narratology has tended to focus, not least because their narration often prominently deviates from chronological order or other kinds of perspectival coherence. Even in literary contexts, though, it is a problematic and contested idea, and one that I have argued against myself (Walsh 2007, Chap. 3). But in any case we are concerned here not just with the interpretation of extant narratives, but with narrative as a primary sense-making process in which meaning is created rather than merely transmitted, so we need a term with that connotation.[10]

"Articulation" works here because it can do the work that "expression" and "communication" do, and at the same time convey the required sense of "structuring, jointing; giving form to." To articulate, then, is both to *produce* significant form and, in doing so, to *express* it at the same time.

2.5 Semiotic

Semiotics, a field that was formalized by Charles Saunders Peirce in the late nineteenth century, is the study of signs and systems of signs and the production of meaning. The articulation of narrative is of a semiotic kind because it belongs to the realm of meaning and the use of signs, even where these signs are percepts, functioning within the mind's native perceptual systems. Narrative does not occur in the world, unmediated by the mind; rather, it is a cognitive process by which the mind makes the world intelligible, abstracting usable sense, pattern and order from it in some semiotic form. Narrative is only constituted as narrative in this conceptual abstraction from the immediacy of embodied experience to a semiotic domain.

This definition describes narrative as a semiotic process, rather than a more narrowly linguistic process, for more fundamental reasons than the evident fact that narratives can be told in media other than language. There are certainly many non-linguistic media that serve as vehicles for narrative, notably film (including silent film), visual arts such as comics, and performance arts such as dance, drama and mime; but this fact does not in itself preclude the possibility that we make cognitive sense of such narratives in linguistic terms. The more important consideration is that to characterize narrative cognition as linguistic would be to make it a much narrower concept than this definition intends. Peirce distinguishes between three types of sign: symbols, icons and indices.[11] While there is a loose sense in which any semiotic system can be called a language, linguistic signs in the strict sense are symbolic signs, those in which the relation between the sign's form and its meaning is purely conventional. In order to understand narrative cognition as a mental process operating most fundamentally at the level of perception, we also need

---

[10]My distinction here draws upon the one between "making sense of stories" and "stories as sense-making" in Herman (2003, pp. 12–14).

[11]For the first elaboration of these categories of signs, see Peirce (1982–, vol. 2).

to accommodate iconic signs, in which meaning involves resemblance, and indeed indexical signs in which meaning involves direct empirical connection.

It might be urged that narrative is not just semiotic but more specifically representational, and that the latter would be a more appropriate term. But it is at least plausible that the logic of narrative cognition can and should be understood in abstract terms distinct from its representational manifestations. There is, for example, some suggestive research on the connections between narrative and music (in an abstract rather than programmatic sense) that makes it worth keeping open this possibility.[12]

3 Implications

Narrative, then, is the semiotic articulation of linear temporal sequence; a basic cognitive mode of sensemaking that creates meaningful form with a specific temporal logic. It is the way in which we are cognitively disposed to discover **pattern** in processes, and to impose an order upon the flux of temporal phenomena. It is important to recognize that these patterns are in some sense there to be found, but also that their status *as* patterns is irreducibly relative to a view, to a specific cognitive stance informed by a set of assumptions about salience and relevance. These cognitive assumptions do not bear only upon the form taken by specific narrative representations, but also upon the form of narrative logic itself.

Narrative theory has always been a kind of **formalism**, but the drift of recent work in cognitive narratology is increasingly to locate the foundations of narrative's basic form in our cognitive architecture. One implication of this move is that the most fundamental features of narrative are evolved cognitive abilities, and no doubt adaptive to specific evolutionary pressures. The actual conditions in which narrative cognition emerged are open to speculation; what is certain is that they have little in common with the range of demands upon our narrative sense-making abilities today. In which case, the question is whether cultural forms of narrative, and the enculturation in narrative that is part of individual development, tend to perpetuate or mitigate the constraining features of narrative cognition. Is narrative sensemaking bound by the terms of its fundamental logic, or can it transcend them? (I think both.)

One of the most basic attributes of narrative cognition is that it is **perspectival**, in several senses. Because cognition is situated, narrative necessarily imposes order upon phenomena from a specific spatial and temporal point, which is that of the telling or articulation (the semiotic act) rather than that of the told. This perspective is intrinsically constituted in narration, and just as intrinsically adopted in the reception of narrative. Just as a narrative may concern circumstances abstracted from immediate experience, so its perspective of narration may be abstracted from the immediate site of cognition, and may in fact be abstracted from any embodied site of

---

[12]See Walsh (2011) and Almén (2008).

cognition whatsoever. What is striking, however, is that narration always remains spatiotemporally perspectival, even where it assumes the hypothetical privileges of omniscience, as in some forms of novelistic narration.

Sophisticated forms of narrative can also foreground and manipulate its perspectival qualities by representing the narrative act itself (character narration) or by partially aligning the narration with the perspective of a character (focalization).[13] Represented narrative acts draw attention to the potential for the perspective of narration to be itself extended in space and time, and hence the potential for significant change in that perspective, which may therefore have a narrative development of its own. Such elaborate explorations of the dual temporality of narrative, often compounded with a pointedly non-chronological relation between the time of the telling and that of the told, are a staple of modernist literary narratives by, for example, Virginia Woolf, William Faulkner, Joseph Conrad and Ford Maddox Ford.

The perspectival interest of such narratives is rarely just spatiotemporal. In most cases it is not the physical constraints upon the narrative subject position that matter, so much as the **evaluative** constraints associated with that position. In literary narrative theory these constraints tend to be explored in nuanced cultural terms, regarding the ways a narrative manifests the limiting assumptions of broad ideological or ethical attitudes, or the symptoms of a narrating character's psychological or intellectual profile, or the motivational context of such a character's interpretation of events. Where there is such a narrating character, the relevant narratological concept is unreliable narration, in which the evaluative limitations or biases of the narrator are foregrounded and themselves become central to the implicit authorial point of the narrative.[14]

The evaluative constraints upon narrative perspective run deeper than this, however. Every narrative is situated in a pragmatic context as well as a spatiotemporal context, and pragmatic considerations define its perspective because they determine criteria of **relevance**. Relevance is usually understood as a criterion of communicative pragmatics, so that the narrative form is influenced by circumstances of the context of telling.[15] This context will involve broad considerations, and often very specific ones too, that dictate the parameters of "tellability," or what is worth saying, for a given narrative act.[16]

In this sense, relevance may be understood as both a communicative consideration for the teller, and an assumption driving the interpretative effort of the receiver of a narrative. It is the answer to the standing question, what is the **point**? But a communicative context is only one aspect of the pragmatics of narrative, and not

---

[13]The concept of focalization was introduced in Genette (1980, Chap. 4).

[14]Unreliable narration, and the (partially) related concept of the implied author, were developed by Booth (1983).

[15]For relevance theory, see Sperber and Wilson (1995).

[16]On tellability, see Pratt (1977). A related concept is narrativity, which seems more specific, but also invites confusion between the qualities of the communicative act and those of its object. See Prince (1982).

even a necessary one. In the privacy of narrative cognition, the same sense of point orients the perspective of narrative sense making in relation to the subject's context of action, and indeed to the subject's current framework of understanding. The criteria of relevance that apply in narrative cognition can be wholly pre-reflective, but they strongly determine the narrative's identification of salient features in the object of its scrutiny.

Substantial implications follow in connection with a basic attribute of narrative, its **intentionality** regarding temporal phenomena, which is to say its "aboutness"; narrative articulates, in semiotic form, processes that are assumed to be actually or hypothetically independent of that articulation. The consequences of this intentional relation run in two directions simultaneously: from the cognizing subject towards the object, and (reflexively) back towards the subject. Features of narrative sensemaking activity are projected onto target processes, which are themselves then taken as the empirical ground for the logic of narrative itself. So, the sequential singularity of the narrative line is a feature of narrative's cognitive form, but one it attributes to its intentional object. Similarly, as already noted, the mere connectedness of narrative representations themselves inevitably implies **causal** connections in the represented processes. Forster made an explicit causal connection in "the king died and then the queen died of grief," but some implicit causal connection was already latent in "the king died and then the queen died," just to the extent that we take it as a narrative rather than some kind of list. The causal explanation is open to interpretation: it may be natural (a contagion?), social (a plot?), or supernatural (the Fates?); it may also be reflexively disavowed (paranoia?). All these possibilities share the assumption that some intimation of causality lurks in narrative coherence itself. While we may reflectively critique these attributions of causality, we can hardly avoid making them in the first place; and critique is not always vigilant.

Other consequences of the perspectival horizons of narrative cognition work in the same way. The pragmatic finitude of cognition demands that narrative seeks temporal wholes, an imperative that gives it a drive towards **closure** that is apparent at every scale of narrative unit from the minimal "narreme" to apocalyptic narratives, the function of which is to impose closure upon the history of time itself.[17] It is not just that closure is a representational imperative projected onto the object of representation; it is that this imperative is driven by criteria of relevance, or point, that are values of the representational perspective itself. Among the more elaborate forms of narrative there are many that make this quality of closure especially obvious. The sense of point at the end of a literary narrative, for example, really never reduces to finding out what happened; and some such narratives deliberately divorce the two. Raymond Carver's short stories, stereotypically, end before the end; Thomas Pynchon's *The Crying of Lot 49* ends, pointedly, just before the crying of lot 49. Yet that doesn't make these cases of incomplete, unresolved narrative; narrative closure is not ultimately about the resolution of an event, but the satisfaction of a semiotic demand for significance, for achieved relevance.

---

[17]On fictions of apocalypse as paradigms for narrative, see Kermode (1967).

The semiotic basis of closure has important consequences for narrative under-standing, precisely because its logic tends to get projected onto the represented events. As a semiotic discourse, narrative is oriented towards the end; its form, at every level, is given by the anticipation of closure, the ultimately achieved meaning that makes sense of the whole. But, inevitably, these qualities of the discursive form of narrative get attributed to its object of representation, giving narrative a strong disposition towards **teleology**. In fact the notion of teleology, or "final cause," as a principle of innate orientation towards an ultimate form, is the manifestation of a fundamentally narrative way of thinking.

Teleological thinking is an effect of narrative form, and distinct from any presumption of **agency** inherent in narrative. But narrative does strongly attribute agency, in the sense of a capacity for goal-directed action, for reasons that are probably intrinsic to its adaptive value as a cognitive tool in a social environment. Narrative theory has become very interested in narrative's role in theory of mind, or folk psychology, on the premise that the ability to attribute motive and intention to other people, and so anticipate their behaviour, is one of its basic affordances.[18] The agency attributed by narrative is a more inclusive concept than this, but any narrative representation of an agent strongly connotes such folk psychological attributions of motive and intention. Most substantial narratives are preoccupied with understand-ing the agency of others, whether real people or fictional characters, and much of the work in this field assumes that such understanding is a projection of our understand-ing of ourselves. However, it is at least as plausible to hypothesize that our under-standing of ourselves first arises from an internalization of our representations of others. The reflexive nature of such a move, to the extent that it also applies to other selves, means that this aspect of narrative sense-making is to some extent self-fulfilling, and its recursive nature ties it closely to the history of consciousness.

If narrative agency is understood as, at bottom, a direct consequence of narrative logic, then it helps to clarify one of the most obvious effects of narrative, which is its **anthropomorphism**. Definitions of narrative that restrict its scope to the experientiality of human agents can deal with the obvious fact that narratives often concern non-human agency by saying that they always treat their subject matter *as if* it had qualities of human agency. But while there are plenty of examples to support this idea, from beast fables to wildlife documentaries, they vary considerably in their degree of anthropomorphism, which suggests that it is an *effect* of narrative repre-sentation rather than a defining quality. On this view, human experientiality may itself be understood as contingent upon narrative sense-making. Narrative projects agency because it is the cognitive strategy of a social animal, and it does that much indiscriminately, but the more specific features associated with an experiencing human subject seem best treated as secondary effects of the development of narrative.

Another way of expressing this point is to say that narrative is not *about* the experiencing human agent, but *for* the experiencing human agent. That is, it is not in

---

[18]Key sources on narrative and other minds are Keen (2007), Palmer (2004), and Zunshine (2006).

essence an anthropomorphic form of representation, but an **anthropocentric** form of cognition. Fundamentally, this anthropocentrism is simply a pragmatist condition for knowledge as such, in that understanding something necessarily involves bringing it into an intelligible relation with a human point of view. If we consider narrative not as a subset of knowledge but as a form of knowledge, though, the significance of such a constraint is more pointed. On the one hand, narrative imposes a horizon upon understanding within its domain in just the way the general anthropocentrism of knowledge implies; on the other hand it is the legacy of a cognitive pre-history with imperatives quite different from the demands we place upon narrative today.

A further implication of this pragmatist view of narrative is worth bringing out. Its cognitive function, as I have formulated it, has an irreducibly heuristic character; it is good enough for current purposes. Narrative therefore always rests, not circumstantially but constitutionally, upon unexamined assumptions, so that the sense it produces remains, at its core, **implicit**. The limits of articulate sense in every narrative are in one respect just a pragmatic horizon to its endless capacity for elaboration, imposed by the finite resources of cognition or interpretation. But these limits are also the pragmatic limits of sense as such, in that narrative is not built upon some fundamental unit of meaning, but upon the embodied nature of cognition.[19] The roots of narrative logic necessarily spring from an empiricism beyond semiotics. The force of narrative is therefore always more bound up with what its form implies than with what it actually expresses, and the potency of the implicit has been evident throughout this discussion of narrative's effects.

At the same time, the territory of the implicit provides for narrative's most powerful feature, which is its **reflexiveness**. The vast capacity for elaboration that makes narrative such a ubiquitous presence in culture and daily life is accountable, in a rudimentary sense, to the way in which the implicit borderlands of every narrative invite further explanation, and our appetite for pursuing it is apparently insatiable. The implicit in narrative is itself a prompt to narrative cognition, making it the object of and occasion for more narrative. The impulse is manifest everywhere from the child's incessant "why?" in response to every narrative explanation, to the saturation of culture with sequels, prequels, series, spin-offs, adaptations, fan fictions and versions of all kinds. But more fundamentally, narrative's propensity for reflexiveness bears upon its own logic, not just the particulars of a given instance. Narrative sense-making's attention to itself does not only lead to its proliferation, but also its refinement. The cultural history of narrative traditions can be read as an extended series of such reflexive moves, in which the taken for granted becomes the focus of attention, or a particular meaning becomes a way of meaning, an instance becomes a trope. These reflexive moves occur on all scales, from local representational devices (the development of free indirect discourse, say) to global communicative purposes (the rhetorical possibility of fictionality).[20] I said earlier that I think narrative is both

---

[19]For approaches to narrative grounded in embodiment, see Turner (1996) and Fludernik (1996). For more specifically enactivist approaches, see Hutto and Myin (2012) and Caracciolo (2014).

[20]On fictionality as a rhetoric, see Walsh (2007); on the sense of narrative reflexiveness described here, see Walsh (2016).

bound by the terms of its own logic, and capable of transcending them, and this is why. Reflexiveness in one sense abstracts from given features of narrative and perpetuates them in grander form, but it can also be a critical abstraction, one that brings hidden assumptions into the light and pushes back the boundaries of narrative sense-making.

This account of the concept of narrative and its implications has touched upon many points of contact between issues of concern for narrative theorists and those of concern for complexity scientists. It has provided substantial reasons for the problematic nature of the relation between narrative and complex systems, and shown the extent to which this is a necessary state of affairs consequent upon the nature of narrative cognition. But it has also indicated several respects in which the relation has the potential to be reciprocally illuminating, and hints towards the possibility that, especially in narrative's more elaborate cultural forms and its new media manifestations, the incompatibility can be at least partially overcome. The explorations of these issues from diverse perspectives in various contexts is the business of the essays in the main body of this volume.

References

Almén B (2008) A theory of musical narrative. Indiana University Press, Bloomington

Aristotle (1908) Metaphysica. In: The works of Aristotle translated into English, vol 8 (trans: Ross WD). Clarendon Press, Oxford

Aristotle (1933) Aristotle in 23 volumes, vols 17, 18 (trans: Tredennick H). Harvard University Press, Cambridge

Aristotle (1994) Metaphysics books Z and H (trans: Bostock D). Oxford University Press, Oxford

Barthes R (1975) An introduction to the structural analysis of narrative. New Lit Hist 6(2):237–272

Barthes R (1974) S/Z (trans: Miller R). Hill & Wang, New York

Booth WC (1983) The rhetoric of fiction [1961], 2nd edn. University of Chicago Press, Chicago

Bruner J (1991) The narrative construction of reality. Crit Inq 18(1):1–21

Caracciolo M (2014) The experientiality of narrative: an enactivist approach. De Gruyter, Berlin

Chatman S (1978) Story and discourse: narrative structure in fiction and film. Cornell University Press, Ithaca

Currie M (2007) About time: narrative, fiction and the philosophy of time. Frontiers of theory. Edinburgh University Press, Edinburgh

Dorfman E (1969) The nareme in the medieval romance epic: an introduction to narrative structures. University of Toronto Press, Toronto

Fludernik M (1996) Towards a 'natural' narratology. Routledge, London

Forster EM (1962) Aspects of the novel [1927]. Penguin, Harmondsworth

Genette G (1980) Narrative discourse (trans: Lewin JE). Cornell University Press, Ithaca

Genette G (1988) Narrative discourse revisited (trans: Lewin JE). Cornell University Press, Ithaca

Greimas AJ (1983) Structural semantics: an attempt at a method (trans: McDowell D, Schleifer R, Velie A). University of Nebraska Press, Lincoln

Herman D (2002) Story logic: problems and possibilities of narrative. Frontiers of narrative. University of Nebraska Press, Lincoln

Herman D (2003) Introduction. In: Herman D (ed) Narrative theory and the cognitive sciences. CSLI, Stanford, pp 1–30

Hutto DD, Myin E (2012) Radicalizing enactivism: basic minds without content. MIT Press, Cambridge

Kafalenos E (2006) Narrative causalities. Theory and interpretation of narrative series. Ohio State University Press, Columbus

Keen S (2007) Empathy and the novel. Oxford University Press, Oxford

Kermode F (1967) The sense of an ending: studies in the theory of fiction. Oxford University Press, New York

Palmer A (2004) Fictional minds. University of Nebraska Press, Lincoln

Peirce CS (1982–) The writings of Charles S. Peirce: a chronological edition, 8 vols. In: Peirce Edition Project (eds). Indiana University Press, Bloomington

Pratt ML (1977) Toward a speech act theory of literary discourse. Indiana University Press, Bloomington

Prince G (1982) Narratology: the form and functioning of narrative. Mouton, Berlin

Richardson B (1997) Unlikely stories: causality and the nature of modern narrative. Associated University Presses, London

Ricoeur P (1984–1988) Time and narrative, 3 vols (trans: McLaughlin K, Pellauer D). University of Chicago Press, Chicago

Sperber D, Wilson D (1995) Relevance: communication and cognition, 2nd edn. Blackwell, Oxford

Tomashevsky B (1965) Thematics. In: Russian formalist criticism: four essays (trans: Lemon LT, Reis MJ). University of Nebraska Press, Lincoln, pp 61–95

Turner M (1996) The literary mind. Oxford University Press, New York

Walsh R (2007) The rhetoric of fictionality: narrative theory and the idea of fiction. Ohio State University Press, Columbus

Walsh R (2011) The common basis of narrative and music: somatic, social, and affective foundations. StoryWorlds J Narrat Stud 3:49–71

Walsh R (2016) The fictive reflex: a fresh look at reflexiveness and narrative representation. Neohelicon 43(2):379–389

White H (1980) The value of narrativity in the representation of reality. Crit Inq 7(1):5–27

Zunshine L (2006) Why we read fiction: theory of mind and the novel. Theory and interpretation of narrative series. Ohio State University Press, Columbus

Chapter 3
Complex Systems for Narrative Theorists

Susan Stepney

Abstract This chapter provides a relatively non-technical introduction to complex systems, from a scientific perspective, at a level useful to both scientists and narrative theorists. It covers several complexity science concepts: it discusses models and meta-models, and how these can be used to define the concepts of novelty, innovation, and emergence; it distinguishes the concepts of non-linearity of scale, and non-linearity in time; it introduces several concepts from dynamical systems theory, including trajectories through state space, deterministic behaviour, attractors, bifurcations, and the idea of "edge of chaos". It discusses how these concepts are used in their own domains, and how they might be applied metaphorically.

1 Introduction

This chapter provides a relatively non-technical introduction to complex systems, from a scientific perspective, at a level useful to both scientists and narrative theorists. It covers several complexity science concepts, including models, emergence, and dynamical systems. It discusses how these concepts are used in their own domains, how they might be applied metaphorically, and where, even in their own domains, they have inadequacies.

A **system** comprises interacting components and relationships that have higher level structure and behaviour, forming an integrated "whole". A **complex system** exhibits strong interactions between components, feedback between levels, emergence, self-organisation, openness, adaptation, growth, and change. Real world complex systems can comprise any combination of natural (e.g., physical, biological), artificial (e.g., engineered, computational), and social (e.g., individual,

S. Stepney (✉)
Department of Computer Science, University of York, York, UK

York Cross-disciplinary Centre for Systems Analysis, University of York, York, UK
e-mail: susan.stepney@york.ac.uk

© Springer Nature Switzerland AG 2018
R. Walsh, S. Stepney (eds.), *Narrating Complexity*,
https://doi.org/10.1007/978-3-319-64714-2_3

economic, political) parts, involving multiple stakeholders from multiple disciplines with differing requirements and goals.

Complexity science employs a variety of technical concepts and terms—such as dynamical systems and their attractors, emergence, self-organisation, "edge of chaos"—in its analysis of complex systems. As in any discipline, words in complexity science can have technical meanings that depart slightly, or even radically, from their everyday meanings. It is important to understand the technical meanings, or at least to realise where the meaning is not the everyday one, in order not to misapply complexity concepts.

These technical concepts can be applied in a variety of domains, such is their power. They can also be applied *metaphorically*, in domains where they are not technically applicable. In order to use a metaphor well it is important to understand the source domain, in order to understand the mapping underlying the metaphor. There is nothing quite as unhelpful as an explanation in terms of a metaphor, where the metaphor's source domain is equally ill-understood by the listener. A good understanding of the metaphor's domain allows a richer use of the metaphor, incorporating more of its properties and concepts.

2   Models and Meta-Models

All models are wrong, but some are useful
George E. P. Box, 1987

In science, a **model** is some abstract representation of a system, or class of systems, that can be manipulated and interrogated, to help understand the system of interest. A model might be expressed in natural language text, in cartoons, in formal diagrams, in mathematics, in computer code, or in combinations of these.

The more rigorous the model (mathematics, code, formal diagrams), the more the manipulations and interrogations can be formalised and mechanised. Mathematics allows general solutions; code when executed can help expose dynamical behaviours; diagrams help highlight relationships between components.

The system of interest is an **instance** of the model. It may be the only instance, in the case of a highly specific model, or there may be many actual and potential instances, in the case of a more generic model. Parts of the system are instances of parts of the model. For example, a model of an ecosystem might include the notions of animals, plants, foodwebs (who eats whom), and other classes of components. A particular population of animals and plants in the wild is an instance of the model.

More generic models, being more widely applicable, are somehow "better" models. But in order to make a model generic, more has to be abstracted and more details omitted, so it becomes less aware of specific system details. The art of modelling is a balancing act: general enough to be widely applicable, specific enough to be usefully applied.

A **meta-model** is a model of a model. In the way a model captures concepts in reality, a meta-model captures the concepts used in a model. So in the ecology example, the meta-model would have the concepts of entity (instantiated as animals and plants in the model) and of predation (instantiated as the connections of the foodweb in the model).

The meta-model gives the language for building the model. Three of the most common meta-models in complex systems analysis are those that underpin computational entity-based modelling,[1] mathematical differential equation modelling, and network-based modelling. An entity-based model is an instance of a meta-model that has discrete interacting entities, whereas a differential equation model (of potentially the same system) is an instance of a quite different meta-model that has continuous concentrations and rates of change. A network-based model focusses more on the relationships than the entities. The choice of meta-model affects the model, and therefore affects the manipulations and interrogations possible.

Complex systems need suitably complex models and suitably rich meta-models. They tend to combine concepts from the two common meta-models; for example, they are often hybrids of discrete entities and continuous components (some parts are best modelled as "things", some as "stuff"). This is part of what makes them mathematically and computationally intractable.

In many cases, the underlying model and meta-model being used might well be implicit. For example, I have never seen a formal description of the meta-model of differential equation models, although it is implicitly understood by all mathematicians. However, these models, implicit or otherwise, affect how we think about systems, what we perceive to be important, and what is deemed novel or emergent. Several of the concepts and metaphors of complex systems arise from different specific models and meta-models.

3   Novelty, Innovation, and Emergence

One of the features that makes complex systems interesting, and also difficult to capture and understand, is that they exhibit many kinds of change: they have complex structure and dynamics, they adapt and self-organise, they grow, they innovate, they have emergent properties.

The existence of emergent properties is sometimes used as a defining feature of complex systems, but emergence is itself a slippery concept to define. A summary of definitions from the literature can be found in Stepney et al. (2006). One way of understanding what comprises innovation and emergence in a system is in terms of the relevant model and meta-model used to capture the system (Banzhaf et al. 2016). If we define novelty as a state or situation we have not seen before, then we can define the following:

---

[1] Also known as agent-based modelling, and as individual-based modelling. Even when called "agent-based", there is not necessarily a requirement for the relevant entities to have "agency".

- Variation: novelty *within* the model
- Innovation: novelty that *changes the model*
- Emergence: novelty that *changes the meta-model*

So in an ecological system, a variation might be a change in population size of a particular species, an innovation might be the appearance of a new species or a species starting to predate on a different species from before, and an emergent property might be a population banding together to hunt in a pack where beforehand all predation was one-on-one. Whether these are actually examples of the particular classes depends on the exact form of the model and meta-model: innovation and emergence are (meta)model-dependent phenomena.

This ability of complex systems to move outside the model, and even outside the meta-model, is one property that makes them "complex". Most of our formal computational and mathematical tools analyse and explore the consequences of a pre-defined model, and work within a specific (if implicit) meta-model.

4 Linear vs. Non-Linear

An important meta-model for complex systems analysis is that of dynamical systems theory. Before describing that, this section discusses the meaning of *non-linear*, a core concept in dynamical systems. Non-linear contrasts with *linear*: in a straight line. There are different ways of not being a straight line.

4.1 Scale/Magnitude Non-Linearity

The term *non-linear* is used in a particular mathematical sense to mean how one property of a system (e.g., weight) depends on another property (e.g., height). If the graph of weight against height is a straight line, the relationship is linear. If it is not a straight line (curves up, or down, or oscillates), then it is *non-linear*.

The distinction between linear and non-linear is important in dynamical systems theory (and other branches of mathematics), because linear problems are (relatively) easy to solve. If I know the weights of two linear systems with given heights, say, then I can easily find the weight of another system that has the sum of their heights: it is simply the sum of their weights.[2] This is often phrased as "solutions can be added together". Because of this additive property, problems can be broken down into parts, solved individually, then added to get the overall solution. The whole is exactly the sum of its parts.

Non-linear systems do not have this property. Part solutions cannot be added in general. If the weight of a system scales as the cube of its height, say, then a system

---

[2]Provided zero height has zero weight. The more general case is slightly different, but the underlying principle holds.

Fig. 3.1 Lines *a* and *b* are linear and monotonic. Lines *c* and *d* are non-linear but monotonic. Line *e* is non-linear and non-monotonic

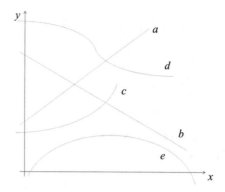

with double the height does not have double the weight (as it would if it were linear), but rather eight times the weight. In other cases, the relationship between properties of components and properties of the whole are even more obscure. The "whole is *something besides* the parts" (Aristotle 1908) [my emphasis].

Most real world systems are non-linear. Dynamical systems theory provides a formalism for analysing generic properties of such systems, without necessarily solving their detailed specific behaviour.

Sometimes a stronger distinction than non-linearity needs to be made: the line on the graph is not only curved, it increases and then decreases. The technical term for this property is *non-monotonic*. (All straight lines are monotonic.) In the non-monotonic case, we have a situation where for some values of *x*, an increase in *x* corresponds to an increase in *y*, yet for other values of *x*, an increase in *x* corresponds to a *decrease* in *y*. For example, if *x* is time and *y* is the height of the tide, then a little later the tide might be higher, but then later again it might be lower. See Fig. 3.1.

4.2   Temporal Non-Linearity

The term non-linear can also be applied, in a different way, to models of time; this is the meaning in "non-linear narrative", and needs to be clearly separated from the different mathematical use described above.

In the case of time ordering, *linear* means that the events that happen can be fully ordered in a line representing increasing time. For every pair of distinct instantaneous events *e* and *f*, event *e* either happens before event *f* or after it.

So here *non-linear* means that not all instantaneous events can be ordered in a single line. Events may be ordered in a branching tree-like structure, or in a general network, or in a circle, or in some other non-linear manner (Fig. 3.2). Branching time can be used to model alternative possible futures, as in Everett's 1957 Many Worlds interpretation of Quantum Mechanics. In fiction it is epitomised in Jorge Luis Borges' 1941 short story *The Garden of Forking Paths*, and used in the 1998 movie *Sliding Doors*, and Jo Walton's 2014 novel *My Real Children*.

Fig. 3.2 (**a**) linear time: there is a path from e to f along the time line; (**b**) branching time: there is no path from e to f along any time line; (**c**) partially ordered time: there is no path from e to f; (**d**) circular time: there is a path from e to f, and also a path from f to e

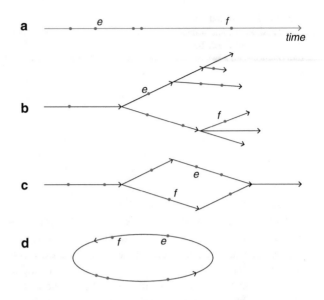

There is not much use of cyclic time in mathematics or computing, as it is difficult to form coherent and non-paradoxical models. Cyclic time could mean that e causes f *and* that f causes e, and would imply time travel, as you travel round the loop and find yourself in your own past, a favourite staple of science fiction, exploited with various degrees of success. General Relativity does allow "closed timelike curve" solutions (Tipler 1974), although it does not address the philosophical issues. Deutsch (1998) argues that such closed curves, and time travel, are incoherent concepts in the physical universe. An elegant fictional closed consistent time loop features in Robert A. Heinlein's 1959 short story "—All You Zombies—", where the protagonist is both his own father and own mother.

Cyclic time may be incoherent, but cyclic *causality* can be a useful concept. The graphical forms in Fig. 3.2 show which instantaneous events can have a causal relationship. If e is before f, then it can have a causal effect on f. If it is after, then it can be affected by f. If there is no path from e to f or *vice versa*, then neither event can have causal effect on the other. If instead of instantaneous events, we consider events that have duration, then such an extended event A can have a causal effect on B, which can later have an effect on A, and so on: there is **feedback** in the system. Consider the co-evolution of leopard and antelope populations: in some sense, each "causes" the other to become faster runners.

5 Dynamical Systems Theory

Dynamical systems theory is the name given to a mathematical approach that can be used to model and analyse certain restricted kinds of complex system. It is the source of many interesting and useful metaphors—including "attractor" and "bifurcation"—that can be used more widely. More technical detail can be found in (Stepney 2012; Strogatz 2014). Dynamical systems feature heavily (although with different terminology, for plot-important reasons) in Neal Stephenson's 2008 science fiction novel *Anathem*.

In a dynamical system, the **state** of the system is characterised by several variables whose values can change over time. For example, a simple pendulum might be characterised by the position x and velocity v of the pendulum bob, both of which have values that change as the bob swings back and forth.

5.1 Trajectories

The **state space** of the system is all the possible values the variables can take. If there are N variables, this abstract state space has N dimensions. Each possible state of the system is represented by a point in the state space. As the system evolves over time, the values of the state variables trace out a **trajectory** of points through that state space. This trajectory captures the history of the system. Different **initial conditions** (starting points; values of the variables at time zero) of the system give different trajectories.

How the values of the variables change over time is described by (generally non-linear) differential equations, one for each variable. Solving these *equations of motion* gives the relevant trajectory, defining the motion of the state through the state space. The state space and equations form the model. Dynamic systems theory assumes a predetermined and fixed state space: no new variables are needed to characterise a system at a later time. If the modelled complex system changes to need new variables, then such a model breaks down, and a new model needs to be formulated.

5.2 Determinism

Dynamical systems models are **deterministic**. That means at any point in the state space, there is a unique *next point* on the trajectory, determined by the equations of motion. (The modelling assumption is that the chosen variables are sufficient to completely capture the system's behaviour.) Consequently, trajectories can never cross; if they could, the point at which they crossed would have two different next points, one on each trajectory. However, in certain systems, trajectories may *merge*: two different starting points may have the same history later. If a system ever returns to a state it has previously encountered (if a trajectory loops around and merges with itself), then the consequence of determinism is that the system will follow the same behaviour as it did on the previous occasion: the system's history will repeat itself forever.

5.3 Attractors

A system may be started in any possible point in its state space. Dynamical systems theory classifies its subsequent history in terms of the **attractors** in the state space. An attractor is a region of state space that "captures" trajectories: once a system has moved into such a region, it never moves out again. The trajectory prior to capture describes the **transient** behaviour.

There are two main kinds of attractors: ordinary attractors and **strange attractors**. In an ordinary attractor (of which there are three distinct sub-kinds), the trajectory settles down to predictable behaviour: motion comes to a halt, or is periodic. For example, a simple pendulum with friction will eventually slow down and stop: whatever its starting point, it will end up at the unique point attractor, the single point in state space with $x = 0$, $v = 0$. Since many initial conditions can end in the same final state, we cannot *retrodict* such systems: seeing a stationary pendulum, we cannot say what its previous history was.

A strange attractor is a different sort of beast. It is also a region of state space, but trajectories within this space *diverge* from each other. Any two trajectories on the strange attractor, no matter how close together they are at some point in the state space, will be far apart (although still within the attractor) later on. This is **deterministic chaos**, also known as the **butterfly effect** (Lorenz 1972), and as **sensitive dependence on initial conditions**. In practice there is always some uncertainty in knowledge of the values of state variables. If the system has a strange attractor, the long term future of the system cannot be predicted: if the current state is x, the system will have one trajectory, but if the state is $x+\varepsilon$, then, no matter how tiny is ε, the eventual trajectory will be entirely different from that of x. The motion is chaotic, but it is not random. Ray Bradbury's 1952 short story "A Sound of Thunder" shows a small effect in the past, coincidentally the killing of a butterfly, having larger consequences in the future; James P Hogan's 1997 short story "Madam Butterfly" has the advantage of the new terminology allowing a punning title.

Probably the most famous strange attractor is the *Lorenz attractor* (Lorenz 1963), based on a system of three differential equations that are a highly abstracted model of the weather (Fig. 3.3). Trajectories loop around one lobe of the attractor, then pass to the other lobe and loop for a while there, before returning. Different initial conditions loop around different numbers of times, so after a while, trajectories that started arbitrarily close together will be on different lobes.

A science fictional use of a strange attractor features in Greg Egan's 1992 short story "Unstable Orbits in the Space of Lies".

5.4 Bifurcations

The equations defining a dynamical system may have one or more parameters: values that are constant within an instance of a model, but that can vary between models. Different values of the parameters can result in different properties of the

Fig. 3.3 The Lorenz "butterfly" attractor

attractor structure of the state space: different parameter values may result in different positions and numbers of attractors. In particular, changing a parameter value may cause an attractor to split in two, or **bifurcate**. This results in a qualitatively different behaviour of the system: where before it had one attractor (end point), now it has two (two possible long term behaviours, depending on initial conditions). In some cases, these two attractors may be far apart, so a small change in the parameter might result in a large change to the system's behaviour.

If a system is being influenced or controlled by a parameter, a crucial point is the relative timescales of motion to the attractor, and parametrical change of the attractor. The attractor becomes a moving target, and the system has a **meta-dynamics**: the dynamics of the attractor space itself. If the attractor moves slowly enough, then the system can track it, and move with it. But if the attractor moves quickly, or bifurcates and jumps, the system might lag behind, and find itself back in transient behaviour. If the changes are continually large, the system might never settle to an attractor, or might jump between attractors.

5.5   *Edge of Chaos*

One particularly interesting case where varying a parameter changes the attractor structure is when the attractor changes from an ordinary to a strange attractor. This means the observed behaviour changes from periodic to chaotic. This region of change is sometimes referred to as the **edge of chaos** (Langton 1990), and systems in this region can have particularly interesting behaviours, exhibiting complex structure on all scales, from fine grained to global scales, all caused by the same underlying mechanism. Systems at the edge of chaos seem to display a form of maximum complexity or maximum unpredictability: they are neither fully periodic (and hence readily predictable), nor fully chaotic (hence statistically predictable).

6 Concepts and Metaphors

The attractor is a powerful concept in dynamical systems analysis, and forms a powerful metaphor. The idea that a system might be perturbed, but then naturally move itself back to its attractor, and that attractors might drift, change, or split over time, has many potential applications.

The butterfly effect is another powerful metaphor. The idea that a system is governed by deterministic laws, but yet is unpredictable, has had a profound impact on science, firmly hammering another nail into the coffin of the Newtonian clockwork universe worldview.

Edge of chaos is another helpful concept when thinking about complex systems: that the most interesting place to be is somewhere between stultifying order and goldfish-brained chaos; instead, one is poised, ready to adapt and change, responsive and complex.

The references in this chapter give a few examples of the use of these metaphors in fiction. We also see many of these terms used throughout this book, giving us an opportunity to see these complexity concepts being used in a variety of different disciplinary contexts.

References

Aristotle (1908) Metaphysics (trans: Ross WD). Clarendon Press, Oxford

Banzhaf W et al (2016) Defining and simulating open-ended novelty: requirements, guidelines, and challenges. Theory Biosci 135(3):131–161

Deutsch D (1998) The fabric of reality. Penguin, London

Langton CG (1990) Computation at the edge of chaos: phase transitions and emergent computation. Phys D Nonlinear Phenom 42(1–3):12–37

Lorenz EN (1963) Deterministic nonperiodic flow. J Atmos Sci 20:130–141

Lorenz EN (1972) Predictability: does the flap of a butterfly's wings in Brazil set off a Tornado in Texas? AAAS. http://eaps4.mit.edu/research/Lorenz/Butterfly_1972.pdf

Stepney S (2012) Non-classical computation: a dynamical systems perspective. In: Rozenberg G, Bäck T, Kok JN (eds) Handbook of natural computing. Springer, Heidelberg, pp 1979–2025

Stepney S, Polack FAC, Turner HR (2006) Engineering emergence. In: 11th IEEE international conference on engineering of complex computer systems (ICECCS'06). IEEE, pp 89–97

Strogatz SH (2014) Nonlinear dynamics and chaos: with applications to physics, biology, chemistry, and engineering. Westview Press, Boulder

Tipler FJ (1974) Rotating cylinders and the possibility of global causality violation. Phys Rev D 9(8):2203–2206

Part II
Contributed Essays

Chapter 4
When Robots Tell Each Other Stories: The Emergence of Artificial Fiction

Alan F. T. Winfield

Abstract This chapter outlines a proposal for an embodied computational model of storytelling, using robots. If it could be built, the model would open the possibility for experimental demonstration and investigation of how simple narrative might emerge from interactions with the world and then be shared, as stories, with others. The core proposition of this chapter is that in such a system we would have a practical synthetic model of robot-robot storytelling. That model might then be used to experimentally explore a range of interesting questions, for example on narrative-based social learning or the relationship between the narrative self and shared narrative.

1 Introduction

The model set out in this essay has a surprising origin. It emerges from work toward making robots that can be safe in unknown or unpredictable environments (Winfield 2014). That work takes the idea of robots with dynamic, continuously updating, *internal models* (of themselves and their environment) and links that with Dennett's conceptual framework: the *Tower of Generate and Test*, leading to a new control system for safer cognitive robots. We then extend this schema, with the addition of a conceptually simple system for allowing robots to transmit and hence share parts of their internally modelled behaviour with each other. The core proposition of this chapter is that if we could build such a system, we would then have a model of robot-robot storytelling. That model might then be used to experimentally explore a range of interesting questions, for example on narrative-based social learning or the relationship between the narrative self and shared narrative.

A. F. T. Winfield (✉)
Bristol Robotics Laboratory, University of the West of England, Bristol, UK
e-mail: alan.winfield@brl.ac.uk

© Springer Nature Switzerland AG 2018
R. Walsh, S. Stepney (eds.), *Narrating Complexity*,
https://doi.org/10.1007/978-3-319-64714-2_4

39

2 Internal Models and Dennett's Tower of Generate and Test

An Internal Model is a mechanism for internally representing both the system itself and its current environment. An example of a robot with an Internal Model is a robot with a *simulation* of itself *and* its currently perceived environment, inside itself. A robot with such an Internal Model has, potentially, a mechanism for generating and testing what-if hypotheses; i.e.:

1. *what if* I carry out action x..? and, . . .
2. of several possible next actions x_i, *which* should I choose?

Holland (1992, p. 25) writes: "an internal model allows a system to look ahead to the future consequences of current actions, without actually committing itself to those actions". This leads to the idea of an Internal Model as a *consequence engine*—a mechanism for anticipating the consequences of actions. Dennett, in his book *Darwin's Dangerous Idea* (Dennett 1995), elaborates the same idea in what he calls the Tower of Generate-and-Test, a conceptual model for the evolution of intelligence that has become known as Dennett's Tower. Dennett's tower is a set of conceptual creatures each one of which is successively more capable of reacting to (and hence surviving in) the world through having more sophisticated strategies for generating and testing hypotheses about how to act in a given situation.

The ground floor of Dennett's tower represents *Darwinian creatures*; these have only natural selection as the generate-and-test mechanism, so mutation and selection is the only way that Darwinian creatures can adapt—individuals cannot. All biological organisms are Darwinian creatures. On the first floor we find *Skinnerian creatures*, a subset of Darwinians, which can learn, but only by generating and physically testing all different possible actions then reinforcing the successful behaviour—providing of course that the creature survives. On the second floor Dennett's *Popperian creatures* have the additional ability to internally model the possible actions so that some (the bad ones) are discarded before they are tried out for real. A robot with an Internal Model, capable of generating and testing what-if hypotheses, is thus an example of an artificial Popperian creature within Dennett's scheme. The ability to internally model possible actions is of course a significant innovation.

On the third floor of Dennett's tower, a sub-sub-subset of Darwinians, are *Gregorian creatures*. In addition to an internal model, Gregorians have what Dennett refers to, after Richard Gregory, as *mind tools*—including words, which they import from the (cultural) environment (Dennett 1995, p. 378). Conceptually therefore Dennett's Gregorians are social learners.

In the field of intelligent robots, specifically addressing the problem of machine consciousness (Holland 2003), the idea of embedding a simulator in a robot has emerged in recent years. Such a simulation allows a robot to internally try out (or 'imagine') alternative sequences of motor actions, to find the sequence that best achieves the goal (for instance, picking up an object), before then executing that sequence for real. Feedback from the real-world actions might also be used to calibrate the robot's internal model. The robot's embodied simulation thus adapts to the body's dynamics, and provides the robot with what Marques and Holland call a 'functional imagination' (Marques and Holland 2009).

Bongard et al. (2006) describe a 4-legged starfish-like robot that makes use of explicit internal simulation, both to enable the robot to learn its own body morphology and control, and notably allow the robot to recover from physical damage by learning the new morphology following the damage. The internal model of Bongard et al. models only the robot, not its environment. In contrast, Vaughan and Zuluaga (2006) demonstrate self-simulation of both a robot and its environment in order to allow a robot to plan navigation tasks with incomplete self-knowledge; their approach significantly provides perhaps the first experimental proof-of-concept of a robot using self-modelling to anticipate and hence avoid unsafe actions. Zagal et al. (2009) describe self-modelling using internal simulation in humanoid soccer robots; in what they call a 'back-to-reality' algorithm behaviours adapted and tested in simulation are transferred to the real robot.

All of the examples cited here describe robots capable of generating and testing what-if hypotheses using simulation-based internal models; in Dennett's scheme they are all Popperian robots.

3   A Generic Internal Modelling Architecture (for Safety)

Simulation technology is now sufficiently well developed to provide a practical basis for implementing the kind of Internal Model required to test what-if hypotheses outlined above. In robotics, advanced physics and sensor based simulation tools are commonly used to test and develop, even evolve, robot control algorithms before they are tested in real hardware. Examples of robot simulators include Webots (Michel 2004) and Player-Stage (Vaughan and Gerkey 2007). Furthermore, there is an emerging science of simulation, aiming for principled approaches to simulation tools and their use (Stepney et al. 2018).

Figure 4.1 outlines an architecture for a robot with an Internal Model in which the model is used to test and evaluate the consequences of the robot's next possible actions. Note that the machinery for modelling next actions is relatively independent of the robot's controller; the robot is capable of working normally without that machinery, albeit without the ability to generate and test what-if hypotheses. The what-if processes are not in the robot's main control loop, but instead run in parallel to override the Robot Controller's normal action selection if necessary; acting in effect as a safety governor by inhibiting unsafe actions.

At the heart of the architecture is the Internal Model (IM). The IM is initialised from the Object Tracker-Localiser and accepts, as inputs, candidate actions from an action generator. For each candidate action, the IM simulates the robot executing that action, and generates a set of model outputs ready for evaluation by the Consequence Evaluator. The Internal Model and Consequence Evaluator loop through each

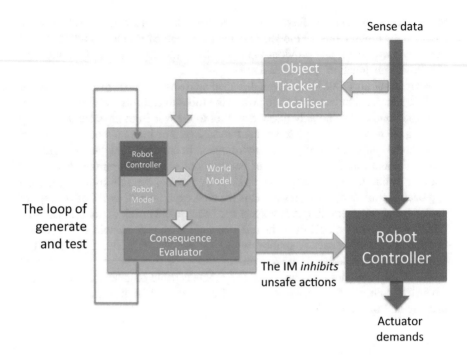

Fig. 4.1 A Control System Architecture for Safety. The Robot Control dataflows are shown in red (right); the Internal Model and its dataflows in blue (left)

possible next action; this is the loop of generate and test. The IM's simulator comprises three components: a World Model, Robot Model and Robot Controller; the latter is an exact duplicate of the real Robot Controller. The World Model is a simplified model of the robot's environment, including the robot's position and pose in it, at the present moment. Only when the complete set of next possible actions has been tested does the Consequence Evaluator send, to the Robot Controller, actions it assesses to be unsafe.

We have implemented the simulation-based internal model outlined here in a system of e-puck mobile robots and, with an additional logic layer demonstrated robots with simple ethical behaviours (Winfield et al. 2014), and robots with improved safety in dynamic environments (Blum et al. 2018). That system was able to generate and test 30 next possible actions every 0.5 second.

4   An Embodied Computational Model of Storytelling

Dennett's Tower describes an evolutionary drive toward internal modelling, allowing what-if generation and testing strategies for action. Let us explore the idea that these several what-if narratives are constructed fictions: they haven't

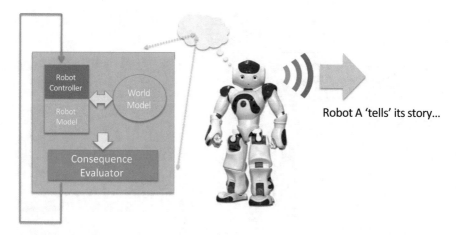

Robot A 'tells' its story...

Fig. 4.2 Robot A, the storyteller, 'narrativises' one of the 'what-if' sequences modelled by its generate-and-test machinery. First an action is tested in the robot's internal model (left), second, that action—which is not executed for real—is converted into speech and spoken by the robot

happened; most will never happen. Dennett's Popperian creatures thus, in principle, have the cognitive machinery for the creation of fictional narratives. If we allow them to 'tell' those stories then they become Gregorian creatures.

Assume that we have two robots, each equipped with the internal modelling machinery outlined above. Let us also assume that the robots are of a similar type, in other words they are conspecifics. Within Dennett's framework each robot is a Popperian creature; it is capable of generating and testing next possible actions. Let us now extend the robots' capabilities in the following way. Instead of simply discarding ('forgetting') an action that has been modelled and determined to be a bad action, the robot may transmit that action to another robot.

Figure 4.2 illustrates robot A 'imagining' a what-if sequence, then narrativising that sequence. It literally signals that sequence using some transmission medium. In practice we could make use of any number of signals and media: Morse code via wireless, or body movements intended to be visually interpreted, for instance. But, since we are building a model and it would be very convenient if it is easy for human observers to interpret the model, let us code the what-if sequence verbally and transmit it as a spoken language sequence. Technically this would be easy to arrange since we would use a standard speech synthesis process. Although it is a trivial narrative robot A is now able to *both* imagine and then literally *tell* a story, and because that story is of something that has not happened, it is a *fictional* narrative.[1]

Robot B is equipped with a microphone and speech recognition process—it is thus able to listen to robot A's story, as shown in Fig. 4.3. Let us assume it is programmed to 'understand' the same language, so that a word used by A signifies the same part of the what-if action sequence to both A and B. Providing the story has

---

[1]Here we assume a simple ontological approach to what is fictional narrative.

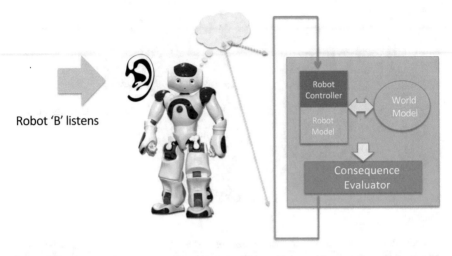

Fig. 4.3 Robot B, the listener, uses the same 'what-if' cognitive machinery to 'imagine' robot A's story. Here the robot hears A's spoken sequence, then converts it into an action which is tested in B's internal model

been heard correctly then robot B will interpret robot A's story as a what-if sequence. Now, because robot B has the same internal modelling machinery as A—they are conspecifics—it is capable of 'running' the story it has just heard within its own internal model. In order that this can happen we need to modify the robot's programming so that the what-if sequence it has heard and interpreted is substituted for an internally generated what-if sequence. This would be easy to do. But, once that substitution is made, robot B is able to run A's what-if sequence (its story) in *exactly* the same way it runs its own internally generated next possible actions, simulating and evaluating the consequences. Robot B is therefore able to 'imagine' robot A's story.[2]

In this model we have, in effect, co-opted the cognitive machinery for testing and discarding unsafe actions for imagining, or internally experiencing, heard stories. By adding the machinery for signalling and signifying internally generated sequences (narratives)—the machinery of semiotics—we have transformed our Popperian robots into Gregorian robots. Thus we have an embodied computational model of storytelling.

---

[2]Where is the meaning? It could be argued that when the listener replays the story in its IM (functional imagination) that *is* meaning.

5   What Could We Learn from This Model?

How does narrative emerge from interactions with the world? If we provide the robots outlined above with a context—a physical environment with physical features and, perhaps, safety hazards that they can move around in and explore—then, at a fundamental, level we are providing our robots with something they can tell stories about.[3] The physical act of moving through and exploring their environment, together with the cognitive act of running the internal model of Fig. 4.1, provide the robots with a rich set of 'imagined' what-if actions to share with each other using the model outlined above. There are practical details to resolve. For instance, how does a robot 'decide' when to tell a story? We might, for instance, trigger this action simply when the two robots find themselves in close proximity; if they are sharing a relatively limited space this could happen quite often. Another question is how does a robot decide whether to tell or to listen—the roles of robots A or B in Figs. 4.2 and 4.3? A simple mechanism might be to default to listening, but if a robot hears nothing for a randomly chosen number of seconds, then it switches to telling. A third question is how does a robot decide which of the several what-if actions tested in its internal model to tell? Here we could use the robot's evaluation of the consequences of those what-if actions; the one with the highest risk for instance might be the candidate for telling: "if I had continued to walk forward I would have fallen into a hole".

The 'robots gossiping' experiment outlined here would provide rich data for analysis. Perhaps most interesting would be to examine which simple stories are told and their relationship to the storytelling robot's current location in the world and the physical features in it. Equally interesting would be to look 'inside the head' of the listening robot and compare the way those heard narratives are 'imagined' from the different perspective[4] of the listener, given that its current position in the world is different. A simple extension to this experiment would be to provide robots with the ability to modify their internal models on the basis of heard stories so that, for example, the listener robot would add a 'potentially dangerous hole' to its world model. We would then have narrative-based social learning.

There are several further directions we could take these ideas.

First, consider the machinery for signalling and signifying narratives—the language. In the experiment outlined above this machinery is fixed and pre-programmed. If instead we introduce some plasticity so that robots can, for instance, either invent new signals or modify existing signals, for new features encountered in the environment, then we open the possibility for an emergent

---

[3]In the model set out here the context is the here and now. But of course the story could be used to create a different context for the listener, i.e., to initialize its World Model the story could begin: "Imagine you are standing by the . . ."

[4]Note that the listener's world model will be different to the storyteller's, since the objects and their locations in the world model are initialised by each robot's object tracker/localiser (Fig. 4.1) as it moves through the world.

robo-semiotics. While the idea of robo-semiotics is not new (Ziemke 2003) there are deep open questions on the cultural evolution of language (Steels 2011). The model outlined in this essay might allow us to address these questions in a new way by experimentally studying the transition from Popperian to Gregorian creatures.

Second, consider the potential for adding autobiographical memory structures to the robots. It would be relatively easy for a robot to build a memory of everything that has happened to it, but of much greater interest here is to integrate the autobiographical memory into the internal model, perhaps leading to what Conway (2005) describes as a self-memory system (SMS). Two experimental possibilities are of particular interest. One is that when an episode from the autobiographical memory is retrieved it is then rehearsed in the internal model, so memory recall becomes re-imagining. Another is that the autobiographical memory allows the storyteller robot to string together a series of recalled (and now re-imagined) actions into a longer narrative sequence.[5] Each robot, even though they are in a shared environment and with shared encounters, will have a unique personal narrative. Arguably each robot would then have, at least in some minimal sense, a developing narrative self.

Third, consider the relationship between the narrative self and shared narrative, i.e., the storytelling component of culture. In previous work the author has experimentally explored robots able to learn socially, by imitation. Because the imitation was embodied, imitation was imperfect and hence imitated actions—in this case short sequences of moves (dances)—mutated as they went through successive generations of imitation (Winfield and Erbas 2011). We call this noisy social learning. That work demonstrated behavioural evolution and the emergence of new behavioural 'traditions' in a robot collective; we also explored the impact of memory in the persistence of these traditions (Erbas et al. 2015). The robots of that work did not have simulation-based internal models.

Consider now the possibility that we allow several robots to learn socially from each other using the experimental models outlined in this essay, in particular narrative-based social learning and the narrative self. We then free run the experiment so that robots are able to gossip and re-tell heard stories, which then evolve and change over multiple successive retellings. We would then have an embodied computational model for exploring the emerging relationship between narrative self and shared narrative.

Acknowledgements The title of this chapter is a quote from the late Richard Gregory. In 2006 when discussing the possibility of emergent robot culture with the author, Richard Gregory declared: "when your robots start telling each other stories, *then* you'll really be onto something". The work of this chapter is partially funded by EPSRC grant reference EP/L024861/1.

---

[5]Note also that there is no reason that same machinery couldn't be used for the sharing of 'historical' narratives, rather than fictional, i.e., what actually happened to robot A, rather than what it imagines but didn't enact.

References

Blum C, Winfield AFT, Hafner VV (2018) Simulation-based internal models for safer robots. Front Robot AI 4:74

Bongard J, Zykov V, Lipson H (2006) Resilient machines through continuous self-modeling. Science 314(5802):1118–1121

Conway MA (2005) Memory and the self. J Mem Lang 53(4):594–628

Dennett D (1995) Darwin's dangerous idea. Penguin, London

Erbas MD, Bull L, Winfield AFT (2015) On the evolution of behaviors through embodied imitation. Artif Life 21(2):141–165

Holland JH (1992) Complex adaptive systems. Daedalus 121(1):17–30

Holland O (2003) Machine consciousness. Imprint Academic, Upton Pyne

Marques H, Holland O (2009) Architectures for functional imagination. Neurocomputing 72(4–6): 743–759

Michel O (2004) Webots: professional mobile robot simulation. Int J Adv Robot Syst 1(1):39–42

Steels L (2011) Modeling the cultural evolution of language. Phys Life Rev 8:339–356

Stepney S, Polack FAC, Alden K, Andrews PS, Bown JL, Droop A, Greaves RB, Read M, Sampson AT, Timmis J, Winfield AFT (2018) Engineering simulations as scientific instruments. Springer, Heidelberg (in press)

Vaughan RT, Gerkey BP (2007) Really reused robot code from the player/stage project. In: Brugali D (ed) Software engineering for experimental robotics. Springer, Heidelberg, pp 267–289

Vaughan RT, Zuluaga M (2006) Use your illusion: sensorimotor self-simulation allows complex agents to plan with incomplete self-knowledge. In: Nolfi S et al (eds) From animals to animats 9 (SAB 2006), LNCS, vol 4095. Springer, Heidelberg, pp 298–309

Winfield AF (2014) Robots with internal models: a route to self-aware and hence safer robots. In: Pitt J (ed) The computer after me: awareness and self-awareness in autonomic systems. Imperial College Press, London, pp 237–252

Winfield AF, Erbas MD (2011) On embodied memetic evolution and the emergence of behavioural traditions in robots. Memetic Comput 3(4):261–270

Winfield AF, Blum C, Liu W (2014) Towards an ethical robot: internal models, consequences and ethical action selection. In: Mistry M, Leonardis A, Witkowski M, Melhuish C (eds) Advances in autonomous robotics systems (TAROS 2014), LNCS, vol 8717. Springer, Heidelberg, pp 85–96

Zagal JC, Delpiano J, Ruiz-del Solar J (2009) Self-modeling in humanoid soccer robots. Robot Auton Syst 57(8):819–827

Ziemke T (2003) Robosemiotics and embodied enactive cognition. SEED – Semiotics. Evol Energy Dev 3(3):112–124

Chapter 5
Sense and Wonder: Complexity and the Limits of Narrative Understanding

Richard Walsh

Abstract This essay considers certain cognitive constraints upon the possibility of understanding complexity, as a first step towards identifying the most effective ways of negotiating with those constraints. Its premise is that our narrative understanding of systemic behaviour latches onto the system's emergent behaviour, at the cost of a disregard for how this emergent behaviour is actually being produced. This limit on narrative understanding points to a cognitive borderland, in which our cognitive engagement with complexity is felt as an "edge of sense" phenomenon. I pursue the qualities of this feeling in relation to the (rather surprising) attempts to define emergence in terms of surprise, and put the notion of surprise in narrative context by invoking Alfred Hitchcock's well-known distinction between surprise and suspense. Doing so provides a way to clarify the affective dimension of the observer's experience of emergence, and locates it in a certain double relation to knowledge in narrative. This double perspective clarifies the respect in which things may appear to make sense even while we are unable to make sense of them; an affective experience I equate with wonder. Wonder is, among other things, a religious feeling that conforms to this double perspectival structure by positing that the order of things, whilst eluding us, submits to omniscient cognition. I situate omniscience in relation to its literary analogue, omniscient narration, and contrast it with the position of the character narrator, in the middest—drawing upon Don DeLillo's *White Noise* as example. DeLillo's novel provides a suggestive link to *The Cloud of Unknowing* and a mystical tradition of understanding as a feeling, and even a relinquishing of knowledge. I end by relating this mystical sense of wonder to the unnarratable, and consider how it can help clarify our cognitive difficulties with emergence in complex systems.

R. Walsh (✉)
Department of English and Related Literature, University of York, York, UK

Interdisciplinary Centre for Narrative Studies, University of York, York, UK
e-mail: richard.walsh@york.ac.uk

© Springer Nature Switzerland AG 2018
R. Walsh, S. Stepney (eds.), *Narrating Complexity*,
https://doi.org/10.1007/978-3-319-64714-2_5

1 Introduction

I want to consider what it is to make sense of complexity, to bring it into a meaningful relation with our cognitive capacities, both for ourselves and for each other, and in doing so to scrutinize the parameters of narrative understanding as a cognitive and communicative resource. I propose to take a pragmatic view of cognition, in that I do not want to make a categorical distinction between understanding and other kinds of familiarity that might provide for use of an object, or for action within an environment. This view, which assumes a continuity between cognition and even very primitive kinds of response to stimuli, is a broadly enactivist approach to cognition, rather than a representational approach. I do not offer direct arguments for my preference here, but its relevance to the problem in hand will soon become apparent.

To bring complex processes into a meaningful relation with our cognitive capacities means bringing them into relation with narrative. Narrative, at its most elementary, is simply our primary cognitive model, albeit a tendentious model, of temporality; of change, or indeed persistence, over time. It is a premise of this essay that complexity resists the tendentiousness of narrative representation, so the ensuing question is, how can we characterize that resistance, from a cognitive point of view? To characterize a complex system as a system is already to have achieved some cognitive grasp of it: any system, understood as such, is a more or less well-defined whole, comprising a certain set of elements and the relations between those elements. It doesn't matter, for my purposes here, whether we are talking about a model of some real-world phenomena, or a system conceived in the abstract; in either case, to understand it as a system is already to have achieved a certain cognitive resolution. A system is something. All the interesting questions, though, have to do with what this something does.

In principle, a system may do absolutely nothing—that, we might say, is the extreme of order; or it might behave in ways exhibiting no pattern, no structure whatsoever—that is the extreme of chaos. In either case, there is nothing more to be said of the system; it is what it is. There is a continuum of cases in between, however, where the system's behaviour seems more or less intelligible, which is to say, accessible to narrative cognition. Many of these cases are orderly enough to be represented in a narrative form that is adequate for some purpose. Such narratives may be very simple or extremely elaborate, but they are successful just to the extent that narrative logic captures the represented behaviour. In all such cases we are able to progress from talk of what the system is to what it does; but for certain systems there is an important gap between our narrative talk of what a system does and how the system actually does it. In these cases, our narrative representation is not of the systemic behaviour of the system but of its emergent behaviour, and comes at the cost of a disregard for how this emergent behaviour is actually being produced.

Such systems, for which narrative understanding latches onto emergent behaviour in itself rather than in its relation to underlying systemic behaviours, are those we would want to call complex systems. This may seem a rather oblique approach to the question of complexity, but from a cognitive point of view (and therefore from a communicative point of view) it is fundamental. In the face of a complex system, we can make narrative sense of emergent behaviour only with a simultaneous awareness that our narrative logic is not really explanatory—or, worse, with a lack of such awareness. Mistakes of this sort can be pointed out to us, of course, but they are always liable to recur in subtler forms. Our cognitive need for narrative sense, then, needs to be kept in check by a meta-sense of its limitations. Must this negation of understanding result in a kind of collapse into incomprehension, or is there an inhabitable cognitive borderland here? I'm going to argue that there is certainly a borderland—and, much more tentatively, to consider the merits of inhabiting it.

Complexity has been characterized as an "edge of chaos" phenomenon (Crutchfield and Young 1990); however I want to consider the cognitive understanding of complexity as an "edge of sense" phenomenon. In our dealings with complex processes we can treat the bounds of this edge as, at one limit, the perception of pattern, and at the other, the cognitive resolution of narrative. The latter, for our purposes here, is sense. So how do we deal with the edge of sense?

2 Defining Emergence

Having invoked the concept of emergence, I need to consider a little more carefully what it means. My purpose in doing so is not primarily to define emergence, though, but rather to consider some of the implications of certain efforts to do so. A helpful survey of some of these attempts at definition can be found in Aleš Kubík's "Toward a Formalization of Emergence," which proposes a formal description of basic emergence in a multi-agent system. It does so on the basis of a distinction of levels common to many approaches to emergence, and consistent with the terms of my own reference to emergent behaviour here: emergence is a quality of the "macro behaviour" of a system, as opposed to the behaviour of its interacting system components, while the underlying behaviour of these components (which may include both agents and the system environment) is nonetheless what produces the emergent macro behaviour (Kubík 2003, p. 44).

One significant implication of such an approach is that emergence is "not primarily a matter of inexplicability" (p. 46). The definition is expansive enough to include very straightforward interactions within a system (Kubík cites direct co-operation between agents, for example). Just because a system exhibits emergent behaviour narratable at a macro level, it need not follow that interactions comprising the underlying component-level behaviour are intrinsically unnarratable. The crucial point is that these are discrete narratives, and the narrative of emergent behaviour is not explanatory at the level of the systemic interactions themselves. This rejection of inexplicability as a defining feature of emergence is also a rejection of previous attempts to define it in terms of surprise.[1] For Kubík, appealing to the observer's surprise is an unhelpful move:

> We believe the category of surprise obscures emergent phenomena. As a consequence there is a tendency to consider emergence as a property of the system that "cannot" be reduced to the lower level of description (i.e., properties of the agents and their interactions). Another consequence is that one can only describe as emergent those phenomena for which we lack a satisfactory notion of how they work. (p. 43)

More broadly, it is clear that for any reproducible emergent phenomenon, even the uninformed observer's surprise will not survive many repetitions. This seems so self-evident, though, that the most interesting issue is not whether surprise should be considered a defining feature of emergence, but why anyone might have ever thought that it could be. The very idea is extraordinary, and perhaps best taken as an expression of the perceived importance of something about our experience of emergent phenomena that it only approximates or gestures towards. Surprise, I suggest, is the wrong concept, but its place in the literature on emergence and its intuitive relevance to the cognitive challenge of complex systems make it a useful foil for my own discussion.

3   Surprise and Suspense

Perhaps the best way to flesh out the ideas at stake in the notion of surprise, from a narrative perspective, is to invoke Alfred Hitchcock's well-known distinction between surprise and suspense. In interview with François Truffaut, he explains it like this:

> We are now having a very innocent little chat. Let us suppose that there is a bomb underneath this table between us. Nothing happens, and then all of a sudden, "Boom!" There is an explosion. The public is surprised, but prior to this surprise, it has seen an absolutely ordinary scene of no special consequence. Now, let us take a suspense situation. The bomb is underneath the table and the public knows it, probably because they have seen the anarchist place it there. The public is aware that the bomb is going to explode at one o'clock and there is a clock in the decor. The public can see that it is a quarter to one.... In the first scene we have given the public fifteen seconds of surprise at the moment of the explosion. In the second we have provided them with fifteen minutes of suspense. The conclusion is that whenever possible the public must be informed. Except when the surprise is a twist, that is, when the unexpected ending is, in itself, the highlight of the story.[2]

For my purposes, there are three features of Hitchcock's account worth drawing out. Firstly, the distinction between surprise and suspense turns upon a matter of knowledge. The audience's lack of key information is the precondition for their

---

[1]For example, Ronald et al. (1999).

[2]Quoted in Truffaut (1984, p. 73).

surprise at a sudden reveal, whereas suspense *depends upon* the audience's knowledge, as distinct from that of the characters, as the basis for its tension between perspectives. The public must be informed. Secondly, Hitchcock's concern is with narrative affect—with the power of the story to enlist the audience's emotional engagement. His preference for suspense over surprise is justified by the quantifiable increase in affective power it offers to the storyteller (15 minutes instead of 15 seconds). Thirdly, this preference is ultimately a choice of genre. As his final comment acknowledges, there is a kind of narrative for which surprise is not only appropriate, but the main point, and that is the mystery story; whereas his choice of suspense aligns him with the thriller. And indeed he elsewhere contrasts the emotional quality of suspense with the intellectual quality of mystery (Hitchcock 1970). In generic terms, surprise coincides with the resolution of the mystery plot—the point when it finally makes sense, and the mystery is revealed to have been merely a puzzle with an intelligible solution. Surprise, in the mystery plot, is the affective response to unanticipated intellectual closure. Suspense, on the other hand, *precedes* narrative resolution; it is affectively constituted by an unresolved tension between two perspectives. In Hitchcock's example the tension operates between audience knowledge and character knowledge, but in fact this is a special case; more generally, it is a tension within the audience perspective itself. Suspense is the audience's anticipation of an as yet ambiguous outcome, an anticipation which itself assumes a disparity of knowledge between the current uncertain prospect and a future retrospect of what will have happened.[3] In life, too, we may feel suspense, to the extent that we project expectations—which is to say, engage in prospective narrative. But in our engagement with an extant narrative, the figure of the storyteller stands as guarantor for the anticipated retrospective knowledge. Narrative closure is a convergence of the perspectives of storyteller and audience, and a resolution of the emotional tension in the disparity between them.

It is not that the experience of trying to make sense of complexity is like a thriller, exactly. I am not arguing that the relation between narrative and complexity can be explained simply by replacing surprise with suspense. What Hitchcock's distinction helps us to see is that the association between emergence and surprise puts an emphasis upon its affective rather than cognitive impact which can be articulated in other ways; ways that can offer a more rounded idea of the experience while. avoiding the oddity entailed by the invocation of surprise. The notion of suspense retains that emphasis upon the affective dimension of the observer's experience of emergence, but also draws attention to other key features of this experience: a certain double relation to knowledge, and a state of unresolved engagement, in medias res, within a narrative in process rather than in response to the sudden coup of narrative closure. Narrative closure affords the cognitive satisfaction of a resolved, transcendent perspective upon the events or behaviour narrated; but if it is emergent

---

[3]See Sternberg (2003, p. 327) for a related tripartite distinction between suspense, curiosity and surprise as universals of narrative dynamics characterized, respectively, by prospection, retrospection and recognition.

behaviour, that satisfaction is achieved at a high price. The narrative coherence of emergent behaviour, and even the level of representation at which it coheres, are artefacts of the transcendent perspective itself. To remain in touch with the complexity of the systemic process requires us to forego closure and remain in some sense "in the middest."[4]

4   Knowledge and Understanding

By speaking in terms of "making sense," I am privileging the idea of the relational quality of the cognitive encounter with phenomena, and with emergent phenomena in particular. That is, we make sense of something to the extent that we are able to articulate its qualities in terms of our own representational or semiotic resources as cognitive subjects. But even the notion of "making sense" is ambiguous. On one reading, certainly, making sense is a cognitive activity like understanding, and so less about a state of affairs in itself than about your cognitive relation to it. You may understand more or less, and understanding is pragmatic in that it may be more or less sufficient for given purposes. On the other reading, however, something makes sense if it constitutes an actual or possible self-consistent state of affairs; if it is a legitimate object of propositional knowledge. Propositional knowledge does not admit of degree—you either know it or you don't. But what if there are legitimate objects of propositional knowledge in this sense which nonetheless elude our cognitive capacity to articulate them? What if there are phenomena that both do and do not make sense? This is how I want to take up the double perspective that Hitchcock's account of suspense introduces into the discussion. For him, that doubleness operates between the knowledge of the audience and the knowledge of the characters, and it is the superior perspective of the audience that provides for the affective quality of suspense. The situation when we attempt to understand emergence is somewhat closer to the general case of suspense, in which the doubleness operates between the current prospective view of an uncertain outcome and the expected resolution of what will have happened—in the "anticipation of retrospection" that Peter Brooks considers the master trope of narrative logic (Brooks 1984, p. 23). However, the suspense analogy does not apply to the logic of some particular narrative but, in a more abstract way, to the framework of narrative logic as such. We are aware of an order, an underlying logic, to the emergent behaviour, yet our cognitive representations of it in narrative form are unable to do justice to that order. Here the double perspective opens up a third space between sense and nonsense, a space in which things appear to make sense even while we are unable

---

[4]Kermode (1967, passim), who is himself invoking Sidney's *Apology for Poetry*: "a Poet thrusteth into the middest, euen where it most concerneth him, and there recoursing to the thinges forepaste, and diuining of things to come, maketh a pleasing analysis of all" (quoted p. 181). Kermode's reflections on the consolations of narrative closure are the foundation for my own here.

to make sense of them. The affective quality associated with this abstract cognitive experience is not suspense; I suggest that it is best characterized as wonder.

5 The Evocation of Wonder

What do I want from the concept of wonder, here? The word has a suggestive range of connotations, but for present purposes we can pick out the following from the *OED* as most pertinent. A wonder is "an extraordinary natural occurrence," which nicely evokes the double perspective I want. It is also "an astonishing occurrence, event, or fact; a surprising incident," confirming the affinity between wonder and surprise. Wonder is also "the emotion excited by the perception of something novel and unexpected, or inexplicable; astonishment mingled with perplexity or bewildered curiosity," which conveys the right blend of affect and cognition. Finally, *to* wonder is "to be struck with surprise or astonishment, to marvel," but also "to ask oneself in wonderment; to feel some doubt or curiosity . . . to be desirous to know or learn."[5]

Wonder, on this account, is the affective quality attached to that region just beyond the limits of understanding. It is the intuition of an order of things that exceeds my grasp. To wonder, we might say, is to imagine the possibility of understanding. It is not alien to scientific discourse; in fact it has always been a powerful affective driver for scientific curiosity, and it is very prominent in the rhetoric of contemporary science evangelists in popular media. The mention of evangelism, though, gestures towards a respect in which the attitude of wonder points to something other than just the *terra incognita* of the not yet known, as it does in the frontier model of the advancement of science. Wonder is also a religious feeling, precisely because it expresses a sense of the radically unknowable nature of a cosmos which *is* nonetheless known. In this case, the other, inaccessible perspective is that of an omniscient deity.

The distinctive feature of the religious sentiment of wonder is that it hypothesizes a perspective, that of an anthropomorphic yet inconceivably alien god, from which the order of things makes sense entirely. It imagines a perspective that transcends space and time and provides for absolute and final knowledge. So that while the premises of scientific advancement frame the wonderful as the not yet known, the premises of religious sentiment frame the wonderful as the known, but not by us. The religious perspective upon wonder adds to the double perspective with which we have been concerned the additional constraint that these two perspectives are radically incommensurable. Such a coincidence of contradictory perspectives is there, for example, in the status of the Catholic icon, and in the Eucharist; but also in the Protestant consecration of the Word, and especially its New World Puritan manifestations, in which the natural world, understood as both itself and the text of

---

[5]*OED*, "wonder" (n.) senses 2b, 4a, 7a; "wonder" (v.) senses 1, 2.

divine pan-semiosis, becomes the vehicle for an extraordinary proliferation of wonders.[6] The religious feeling of wonder as a powerful evocation of God, then, seems to be an ecumenical matter; it encapsulates a general intuition that the order of things, whilst eluding us, submits to omniscient cognition. But of course it follows that omniscience, the attribute of the deity, is itself necessarily unattainable.

6   Omniscience and Narration

The novel, as a narrative genre, has its own well-established analogue for divine omniscience, which is omniscient narration. This is the form of narration in which the authority of the storyteller's perspective underwrites the reader's "anticipation of retrospection," that double perspective I discussed earlier as the foundation of suspense. But while omniscient narration lays claim, if only in imagination, to the possibility of a transcendent perspective, it also at the same time foregrounds the inherent contradiction between "omniscience" and "perspective," and so the necessary unavailability of such a position. The heyday of such unquestionable authoritative narrators in the eighteenth- and nineteenth-century novel is long gone—the mode was a victim, crudely speaking, of the rise of modernism and the climate of epistemological scepticism in which it participated. Some critics have detected a resurgence of omniscient narration in the contemporary novel, although of course the terms of such a resurgence cannot be those of old; the lack of a homogeneous contemporary readership, for example, immediately exposes the culturally and socially relative nature of any position a novelist might adopt (Dawson 2009). Contemporary omniscient narration is necessarily much more aware of such problems than its nineteenth-century manifestations, yet the continuing attraction of the mode in spite of all is a significant dissent from the triumph of perspectivalism, of first-person narration and internal focalization, that we associate with modernism. I'm inclined to claim that one reason for this dissent is that contemporary literary fiction is wrestling with the challenge of narrating complexity. But since my concern here is not with the literary potential of omniscient narration per se, but with the problem of narration in general to which it testifies, I'll pursue the question negatively, by considering the limitations of first-person narration in Don DeLillo's novel *White Noise*. DeLillo is an author who has himself taken up the challenge of omniscient narration elsewhere, notably in *Underworld* (DeLillo 1997), where he arguably addresses the problems of complexity facing the contemporary novelist very directly.[7] In *White Noise*, however, he presents the narrative dilemma from the other side, through that novel's protagonist narrator Jack Gladney (DeLillo 1986).

Gladney, as narrator and as protagonist, is very much in the middest, and the affective state attached to his position is fear of death. In one respect, this fear is well

---

[6]See Hall (1990); for the Transcendentalist legacy of wonder, see Tanner (1965).

[7]In *The American* Mystery, Tanner (2000) has written very pertinently on *Underworld*.

motivated; he has been exposed to an "airborne toxic event," and his medical data now include alarming "bracketed numbers with pulsing stars" (DeLillo 1986, pp. 117, 140). But the fear is also a pervasive emotional response to mortality, shared with his wife Babette, who has resorted to the unlicensed drug Dylar in order to suppress the fear. Dylar's side effects include losing the ability to distinguish between words and what they represent. This loss of duality, or of the exteriority of representations to their objects, saturates the novel, which is preoccupied with the postmodern phenomenon of images that constitute their own immanent artificial reality. The consequent lack of any possible detached perspective comes together both with the issue of death and with that of narrative itself in Gladney's reflections upon plot. For him, "to plot is to die"; he sees himself as a death-bound *protagonist*. His academic friend Murray counters that "to plot is to live," offering Gladney the possibility (in theory) that he might transcend his fate by becoming the *narrator* of his own life (p. 291). This train of thought leads him to plot the murder of Willie Mink, the unscrupulous pedlar of Dylar; a plot which, in the event, farcically deviates from his own efforts to script it (pp. 304–313). Gladney, it seems, cannot gain a perspective beyond his own, and the novel ends inconclusively, his fate still unknown.

But in spite of this deflationary rhetoric there is another side to the novel. Throughout, the phenomena of postmodern society (from TV to the artificial sunsets caused by the airborne toxic event) have attracted a language of aesthetic awe, a register of religious affect. The religious subtext comes to a head in Gladney's encounter with some atheist nuns at the end of the novel, for whom it is not important that they believe, but only that people believe that they believe (p. 319). Their faux-naif painting of a cloudy heaven is an image that recalls the airborne toxic event itself, as well as its corporeal manifestation in the "nebulous mass" that may or may not be growing in Gladney's body (p. 280); but it also establishes a connection with the toddler Wilder, Babette's son who has yet to master language, who has no concept of death, and who is described by Murray as "a cloud of unknowing" (p. 290). The last substantial action of the novel concerns Wilder's apparently miraculous demonstration of his literal imperviousness to death, but I want to take up the paradoxical tradition of medieval mysticism to which *The Cloud of Unknowing* belongs. In particular, I want to consider this work's claim that to know God we have to relinquish altogether the idea of knowledge (Spearing 2001). The cloud of unknowing is a feeling, a kind of understanding that is not knowledge, nor even the fantasy of a higher knowledge, but actually the negation of knowledge. It is an exemplar of what Porter Abbott calls "the cognitive sublime," in the context of his important exploration of narrative negotiations with "the palpable unknown" (Abbott 2013, pp. 35–36). The pervasiveness of a quasi-religious register of wonder in DeLillo's novel is not, I suggest, an attempt to find redemptive aesthetic value beyond the opaque surfaces of postmodernity, but rather an expression of the palpable unknown. It is the intuition of—not a deity—but a secular order of things that makes sense even if we are unable to make sense of it.

7   Narrating the Unnarratable

Abbott's discussion of the palpable unknown in narrative leads him, as well, to the notion of wonder—which he affirms, but with due scepticism: "In the business of interpretation there are always words or phrases that serve as sufficient end-points, place-holders where the mind can rest, and certainly 'wonder' is one of them: as in, What's it about? Ah, yes, 'wonder,' or 'the capacity for wonder,' or 'the productivity of the imagination,' or 'the origins of the sacred'" (p. 51). Certainly the notion of wonder, in itself, does little to advance the project of grappling with the unnarratable in relation to the behaviour of complex systems or anything else; nor is *The Cloud of Unknowing* an especially encouraging precedent. But the unknowable God of medieval mysticism is a somewhat extreme case. There are degrees of inaccessibility to cognition and, by the same token, the limits of narratability are themselves also fuzzy. This fuzziness is inherent in the fact that narrative knowledge is in large part implicit knowledge: narratives do not state everything they mean. Recent work in cognitive narrative theory has highlighted the analogy between the function of inference from the "partial cues" of narrative and the function of cognition in the face of incomplete perception in everyday life (Auyoung 2013, p. 60). With due caution about the scope of the analogy, it might give us some licence to think about the relation between narrative's limitations and our ordinary cognitive abilities to transcend our own perspectivalism in perception. Here is a suggestive observation from Edward Branigan, who is himself invoking Marvin Minsky: "We know the object when we know how it may be seen regardless of the position from which it was actually seen. The object thus acquires an 'ideal' or 'abstract' quality. It should be mentioned that knowing how the object may be seen is very nearly imagining an object that is not in view at all."[8] That last sentence has a mystical, poetic quality that Branigan does not intend, since he is being entirely commonsensical in his distinction between imagining and viewing. Still, I think the idea of "imagining an object that is not in view at all" is a potent one if we transfer it to the domain of narrative understanding, because it is not just that narratives do not state everything they mean, but that they invite, through the open-ended process of inference, intuitions of sense *beyond* what they mean. In this sense the reach of narrative can extend into the periphery of understanding, by giving form to the affective quality of wonder precisely as the negative space of explanation. Narrative understanding, in other words, can mediate between explicit propositional knowledge, knowing *that*, and experiential knowledge by acquaintance, knowing *of*. Indeed this is not a marginal or supplementary feature of narrative, but the core of narrative logic, grounded as it must be in embodiment, in experience. Walter Benjamin, in his famous essay, "The Storyteller," gestures towards just such a conception of narrative logic when he mourns the demise of the storyteller's experiential authority in the face of the modern age of information: "Every morning brings us news of the globe, and yet we are poor in noteworthy stories. This is because no event any longer comes to us

---

[8]Branigan (1992, p. 15). Branigan's own footnote to this passage cites Minsky (1986, p. 114).

without already being shot through with explanation" (Benjamin 1970, p. 89). For Benjamin, "half the art of storytelling is to keep a story free from explanation," and for good reason. It is not just that the explicit literal mentality of explanation destroys the resonance of a well-told tale as it does the effect of a good joke, but that narrative logic is more fundamental than explanation—which is both dependent upon it and, pressed hard enough, reduces to it. Narrative sensemaking inhabits the borderland between cognition and affect, not circumstantially, but intrinsically. It is not so antipathetic to wonder after all.

Narratives of systemic processes need not be what they so often are, obfuscatory assertions of a cognitive mastery over the observed behaviour of a system, achieved by suppressing any recognition that the logic of narrative is alien to the phenomenon it is supposed to be explaining. Benjamin's storyteller knows that the force of a story is more powerful and primitive than explanation, and so keeps the latter at arm's length, holding sense in suspense. But if we apply the lesson reflexively, we can suspend the logic of narrative itself and narrate, as it were, under erasure—negating the imposition of narrative form in the act of resorting to it. Our narratives of systemic processes would then be in a mode of "as if," and their invocation of narrative logic would testify to our own cognitive need, not to any property of the systemic behaviour itself. The reflexive gesture is also recursive, so that by emphasizing the gap between the explicit narrative and the systemic behaviour, we also suspend our cognitive commitment to the implicit connectives of that narrative logic. To the extent that we bring those implicit connectives to consciousness, our negative intuition extends to the further implied assumptions that accompany them. While we do not overcome our need for narrative, in this way we make that need self-unravelling—and so prolong the encounter, and extend our acquaintance, with the complexity of the phenomenon itself.[9] To do this is to cultivate a secular kind of wonder, not as an affective end in itself but, quite pragmatically, as the proper empirical stance to adopt in the face of complexity.

References

Abbott HP (2013) Real mysteries: narrative and the unknowable. Ohio State University Press, Columbus

Auyoung E (2013) Partial cues and narrative understanding in Anna Karenina. In: Bernaerts L, Herman L, Vervaeck B, de Geest D (eds) Stories and minds: cognitive approaches to literary narrative. University of Nebraska Press, Lincoln, pp 59–80

Benjamin W (1970) The storyteller: reflections on the works of Nikolai Leskov [1955]. In: Illuminations. Jonathan Cape, London

Branigan E (1992) Narrative comprehension and film. Routledge, New York

---

[9]This is, I think, in tune with Shklovsky's thought when he explains the Russian Formalist concept of defamiliarization, or estrangement, as both the arch-literary artifice of "baring the device" (Shklovsky 1965b, pp. 26–30) and a way to "make the stone stony ... to increase the difficulty and length of perception" (Shklovsky 1965a, p. 12).

Brooks P (1984) Reading for the plot: design and intention in narrative. Knopf, New York

Crutchfield JP, Young K (1990) Computation at the onset of chaos. In: Zurek WH (ed) Complexity, entropy, and the physics of information. Addison-Wesley, Redwood City, pp 223–269

Dawson P (2009) The return of omniscience in contemporary fiction. Narrative 17(2):143–161

DeLillo D (1986) White noise [1984]. Pan Books, London

DeLillo D (1997) Underworld. Simon & Schuster, New York

Hall DD (1990) Worlds of wonder, days of judgment: popular religious belief in early new England. Harvard University Press, Cambridge

Hitchcock A (1970) AFI seminar. https://www.youtube.com/watch?v=-Xs111uH9ss

Kermode F (1967) The sense of an ending: studies in the theory of fiction. Oxford University Press, New York

Kubík A (2003) Toward a formalization of emergence. Artificial Life 9(1):41–65

Minsky M (1986) The society of mind. Simon and Schuster, New York

Ronald EA, Sipper M, Capcarrère MS (1999) Design, observation, surprise! a test of emergence. Artificial Life 5:225–239

Shklovsky V (1965a) Art as technique In: Lemon LT, Reis MJ (trans) Russian formalist criticism: four essays. University of Nebraska Press, Lincoln, pp 3–24

Shklovsky V (1965b) Sterne's Tristram Shandy: stylistic commentary. In: Lemon LT, Reis MJ (trans) Russian formalist criticism: four essays. University of Nebraska Press, Lincoln, pp 25–59

Spearing AC (trans) (2001) The cloud of unknowing and other works. Penguin, London

Sternberg M (2003) Universals of narrative and their cognitivist fortunes (I). Poet Today 24 (2):297–395

Tanner T (1965) The reign of wonder: naivety and reality in American literature. Cambridge University Press, Cambridge

Tanner T (2000) The American mystery: American literature from Emerson to DeLillo. Cambridge University Press, Cambridge

Truffaut F (1984) Hitchcock [1967], Rev edn. Simon & Schuster, New York

Chapter 6
Discussion and Comment (Sense and Wonder)

Adam Lively and Richard Walsh

Abstract Adam Lively and Richard Walsh in discussion on an earlier version of "Sense and Wonder."

AL: *"Narrative, at its most elementary, is simply our primary cognitive model, albeit a tendentious model, of temporality"*: Aren't there other ways of understanding the temporal apart from the narrative? What is distinctive about the narrative understanding of temporality? (Ricoeur as a point of reference here?)

RW: Yes indeed, we have other conceptual models of temporality. More specifically, there are both pre-narrative and post-narrative aspects to our experience of temporality. The premise is simply that the specific logic of narrative is the form of our basic cognitive articulation of temporality. The phenomenological orientation of Ricoeur's *Time and Narrative* (1988) is certainly consistent with this idea, though concerned with more elaborated cultural forms of narrative.

AL: *"To understand it as a system is already to have achieved a certain cognitive resolution. A system is something"*: Perhaps another way of saying this—see Niklas Luhmann (2013)—is that a system is something that is observed (from the point of view of another system).

RW: That is well put, and the congruence with Luhmann is a welcome consolidation of the point.

AL: The idea that suspense is in some way "open-ended" (like emergence) is interesting, but counter-intuitive (doesn't narrative suspense demand, and

A. Lively
Department of Media, Middlesex University, London, UK

R. Walsh (✉)
Department of English and Related Literature, University of York, York, UK

Interdisciplinary Centre for Narrative Studies, University of York, York, UK
e-mail: richard.walsh@york.ac.uk

© Springer Nature Switzerland AG 2018
R. Walsh, S. Stepney (eds.), *Narrating Complexity*,
https://doi.org/10.1007/978-3-319-64714-2_6

usually receive, consummation? (the bomb explodes—the viewer is not usually left dangling ...)

RW: The value of the idea of suspense here is to mediate between surprise and wonder, and its irresolution is certainly crucial to that. That is not quite the same as being open-ended; I agree that a craving for closure is an inherent part of the affective quality of suspense (that is part of my point), and of course narratives do typically provide resolution. But resolution dispels suspense; it is not part of it.

AL: "Retrospection" would seem to imply a form of (temporal) closure: is there dissonance here with the earlier contrast between suspense (as "process") and closure?

RW: No; the whole phrase is "the anticipation of retrospection," and that cognitive and affective situation, in the middest (as in my response to the previous comment), is exactly what I want to emphasize.

AL: It's interesting that the definitions of "wonder" attach it primarily to natural phenomena, but that it can be transferred to aesthetic phenomena (such as narratives) ... There is an interesting discussion of the manner in which we look at aesthetic phenomena as natural phenomena in Jan Mukařovský's essay "Intentionality and Intentionality in Art" in *Structure, Sign and Function: Selected Essays* (1977).

RW: Thanks for this reference—I agree that there is a strong association between attitudes of wonder and natural phenomena, and it is highly suggestive that aesthetic phenomena, including sophisticated forms of narrative, can attract the same response.

AL: I've recently come across a couple of references on the history of the concept of wonder that may (or may not!) be useful. I came across them in Crary (1999, pp. 17–18). Descartes has a discussion of admiration or wonderment in *The Passions of the Soul* (2015), and there is "a superb account of [the] tradition of admiration/wonderment" in Daston (1995). And see also Daston and Park (1998), especially pp. 311–328.

RW: I'm very grateful for these references, especially the last, which traces the relation between wonder as stimulus to inquiry, and wonder as a manifestation of dull ignorance. It gives a historical depth to the contemporary relevance of wonder as a mental state on the boundary between cognition and affect: "As theorized by medieval and early modern intellectuals, wonder was a cognitive passion, as much about knowing as feeling. To register wonder was to register a breached boundary, a classification subverted" (p. 14). The end point of their account is "the first half of the eighteenth century, when wonder was demoted from premiere philosophical passion to its very opposite, and once-frivolous curiosity took on the virtuous trappings of hard work" (p. 305). From this point onwards, they suggest, wonder lost its status as a stimulus to intellectual engagement to become the preserve of religious sentiment, and so served to set the bounds of science: "Wonder no longer set in motion feverish investigation but rather the argument from design" (p. 324). All of this resonates strongly with the tenor of my own argument, especially the idea that conceptual engagement with complexity requires a secularized re-incorporation of wonder within the epistemological scope of scientific understanding.

References

Crary J (1999) Suspensions of perception: attention, spectacle and modern culture. MIT Press, Cambridge

Daston L (1995) Curiosity in early modern science. Word Image 11(4):391–404

Daston L, Park K (1998) Wonders and the order of nature 1150–1750. Zone Books, New York

Descartes R (2015) In: Moriarty M (ed) The passions of the soul and other late philosophical writings. Oxford University Press, Oxford

Luhmann N (2013) In: Baecker D (ed) Introduction to systems theory (trans: P Gilgen). Polity Press, Cambridge

Mukařovský J (1977) Intentionality and intentionality in art. In: Burbank J, Steiner P (eds) Structure, sign and function: selected essays by Jan Mukařovský. Yale University Press, New Haven

Ricoeur P (1988) Time and narrative, 3 vols (trans: K McLaughlin, D Pellauer). University of Chicago Press, Chicago

Chapter 7
A Simple Story of a Complex Mind?

Merja Polvinen

> *The brain is a complex system, but that*
> *doesn't mean it's incomprehensible.*
> David Eagleman, *Incognito* (2012, p. 5)

> *We need a fable again.*
> Antonio Damasio, *Self Comes to Mind* (2012, p. 35)

Abstract The human mind has been described both as an emergent feature of dynamical neuronal networks, and as dependent on narrative structures. This chapter explores these two descriptions, and asks whether the irreducibly narrative representational techniques used both in popular science and literary fiction can accurately convey the systemic, nonconscious functions of the brainmind. Analysis of the use of narrative agency in David Eagleman's popular-science book *Incognito* and Peter Watts's science-fiction novel *Blindsight* suggests that, through the process of *enacting* a narrative representation, it might be possible for readers to gain a sense of the systemic functioning of their own brains, even when that systemic functioning is not being replicated in the representation as such.

1 Introduction

Among the many complex systems currently being studied, the human brain and the mind it generates are arguably among the most intractable. This chapter of the *Narrating Complexity* volume introduces the problems of trying to understand the

M. Polvinen (✉)
Department of Modern Languages, University of Helsinki, Helsinki, Finland
e-mail: merja.polvinen@helsinki.fi

© Springer Nature Switzerland AG 2018
R. Walsh, S. Stepney (eds.), *Narrating Complexity*,
https://doi.org/10.1007/978-3-319-64714-2_7

brainmind,[1] and does it from the perspective of the interdisciplinary field of cognitive humanities. Cognitive humanities aims to bring together the perspectives of the cognitive neurosciences and the humanities without conceding the former's priority over the latter, or losing the contextualising expertise developed within fields such as history, philosophy and literary and cultural studies. This joint perspective, it is hoped, will afford us a view of the brainmind that does not isolate the biological system from human experience and cultural practice, and that guides our focus to certain conceptual problems associated with the self-reflexive process of trying to understand the system of our brainminds with the kinds of brainminds we have.

At the same time, applying the premises of the humanities on the brainmind may cause more problems than it solves. One of those premises is that the most relevant part of cognition is the conscious mind as a generator and manipulator of meanings. Such a view is in contrast with the neuropsychological view of the brain, which takes the causally relevant parts of thought to happen below the level of consciousness or experience. This neuropsychological view of what Blakey Vermeule (2015) has called "the new unconscious"—in contrast to the Freudian psychoanalytic tradition—leads the humanities to the edge of what their methodology can reach, precisely because this new unconscious has "no ready-made phenomenology, no language in which to unfold its tales" (Vermeule 2015, p. 471). Instead of the "endlessly nattering unconscious of psychoanalysis" (p. 471), what the humanities are now dealing with is a split between conscious and nonconscious processes, where only the former are relatable in terms of narrative. Together with the cognitive sciences the humanities thus encounter the "hard problem", or the explanatory gap between brain states and mental states, and the question whether our scholarship should even try to grapple with nonconscious processes. Of course, various forms of art have for centuries tried to represent those processes and their consequences for conscious human experience, but the question remains whether it is at all worthwhile to represent and analyse, from a scholarly humanities perspective, processes that arguably do not enter that experience.

This debate keeps skirting the problems engaged by this volume: the incommensurabilities of systemic organisation and narrative representation. My focus here is, therefore, on a twofold problem: Firstly, the human mind has variously been described both as an emergent feature of the dynamical networks of neuronal activity and as a phenomenon that is inherently dependent on narrative structures. These models seem to do their best work by focusing on, respectively, the low-level neuronal and the high-level cognitive action of the mind, but the connection between them is still difficult to navigate. The second question then becomes whether the irreducibly narrative representational techniques used both by literary works and by scholarship in the humanities are able to convey anything about those functions of the brainmind that do not in themselves involve narrativity.

---

[1] The term derives from Jaak Panksepp's "BrainMind" (2005, Appendix C), originally introduced as a way of avoiding a mind-body dualism in talking about human cognition and consiousness.

In order to probe these questions, I analyse the rhetorical choices made in two texts that attempt to present—through narrative and without resorting to dynamical systems modelling—the idea of mind emerging from the system of the brain. David M. Eagleman's popular science book *Incognito* (2012) and Peter Watts's science fiction novel *Blindsight* (2006) both build on the dynamical systems approach in their understanding of the brainmind. It is also clear that both authors adopt specific narrative strategies in trying to convey to their lay readers the nature of those dynamics. These strategies include such traditional rhetorical tools as analogy and metaphor, as well as, in Eagleman's case, narrativising scientific discoveries into brief stories about the actions and experiences of the scientists involved, or in Watts's case, full-blown fictional—even fantastical—narrative. In addition, both writers take the further step of narrativising the functions of the object they try to talk about—that is, the nonconscious mental processes themselves.

I focus on one particular aspect in these texts: their presentation of agency. Which self is the one that self-organises in these narratives? Eagleman offers his readers various levels of the brain and mind as protagonists, and in doing so resorts to narrative means, even as the aim is to convey a sense of the systemic mind. In Watts's novel, narrative agency is given to a character whose sentience and selfhood are questioned by the events of the storyline—and indeed by the narrator himself. But in the process of imagining an alternative form of intelligent being for that narrator, readers make present for themselves forms of their own, lower-level cognitive processes. My reading of *Blindsight* leads me to suggest that a possible solution to the question of articulating the complex system of neural activity to our conscious narrative selves lies in the theory of enactive cognition.

2 Agency, Action and the Narrative Mind

Talking about agency and action from a complex systems perspective naturally carries some tensions. Agency can be looked at as an epistemic issue that determines whether someone or something is subject to outside forces or is an agent with self-determining force. This philosophical issue is shadowed by one of representation: even when the someone or something being represented is known to be without true agency and subject to outside forces, what representational forms are able to convey both temporal activity and lack of agency? Narrativity is traditionally understood to depend on events that can be presented as cause-and-effect structures, and the lack of linear causal structures in complex systems therefore limits narrativity. Thus H. Porter Abbott (2008, p. 233) has argued that the problem the human mind faces in trying to represent complex systems in a narrative form "is not simply the absence of centralized causal control, nor the operation of chance, but the absence of a narratable thread". Emergence, Abbott points out, is a form of action, but because of the "massive distribution of causal agents" typical to complex systems, it is "action without any discernible sequence of events, that is without a story. As such, emergent behavior is by definition unnarratable" (pp. 227, 233).

David M. Eagleman's *Incognito: The Secret Lives of the Brain* takes a systems view of consciousness as its starting-point, in the sense of presenting the self as an emergent feature of competing coalitions of decision-making networks in the brain.[2] For Eagleman the self as we experience it is a narrative constructed by those networks, a select pattern that gives cohesive directionality to the behaviour of the system as a whole:

> [Y]ou are made up of an entire parliament of pieces and parts and subsystems. Beyond a collection of local expert systems, we are collections of overlapping, ceaselessly reinvented mechanisms, a group of competing factions. The conscious mind fabricates stories to explain the sometimes inexplicable dynamics of the subsystems inside the brain. It can be disquieting to consider the extent to which all of our actions are driven by hardwired systems, doing what they do best, while we overlay stories about our choices (Eagleman 2012, p. 148).

This overlaying of stories is a way of making the systemic functioning of our own minds accessible to ourselves—an evolutionary quirk that gives us the particular advantage of being able to regulate the competing cognitive subsystems within. Thus Eagleman presents the tension between systemic and narrative processes as inherent to the lower-level/higher-level interaction.

However, in order to get across its message of brain-internal conflict, Eagleman's text draws on narrative conventions that give agency to the lower-level systems themselves. The book's opening chapter "There's Someone in My Head but It's Not Me" describes the results of a test measuring male attraction to pictures of female faces. The test showed that men were more attracted to females whose pupils were dilated—a result that did not correlate with the conscious reasons the men gave for their attraction. The choice, Eagleman explains, was not really made by the participants themselves, but by elements of cognition residing below the level of their consciousness. "In the largely inaccessible workings of the brain, *something* knew that a woman's dilated eyes correlates with sexual excitement and readiness. Their brains knew this, but the men in the study didn't—at least not explicitly" (2012, p. 5; emphasis original). In such passages, and in line with his subtitle, Eagleman presents the brain, rather than the self, as the protagonist, and the neural subsystems as the agents in cognition. Although Daniel Dennett wrote back in 1978 that the metaphor of neural subsystems as active "homunculi" would fade quickly and be replaced by more accurate forms of description (1981, p. 124), Eagleman still finds it necessary in 2011 to speak of "experts", "factions", "rivals" and "allies" to make his point (2012, pp. 107–109).

The same extension of agency also takes place when Eagleman creates an analogy between consciousness and the headlines of a national newspaper to point out how superficial our awareness is when compared to the deep layers of action conducted by the competing processes within the brain:

---

[2]Eagleman adds to Marvin Minsky's (1988) thinking the suggestion that rather than there just being a multitude of specialized "subagents" in the brain, those agents are in constant competition with each other for the "single output channel of your behavior" (Eagleman 2012, p. 107).

> Your brain buzzes with activity round the clock, and, just like the nation, almost everything transpires locally: small groups are constantly making decisions and sending out messages to other groups. [...] By the time you read a mental headline, the important action has already transpired, the deals are done (Eagleman 2012, p. 6).

And not only is the populace acting beyond the knowledge and control of the reader of headlines, that reader has lost awareness of the fact that the events occur without her influence:

> However, you are an odd kind of newspaper reader, reading the headline and taking credit for the idea as though you thought of it first. You gleefully say, 'I just thought of something!', when in fact your brain has performed an enormous amount of work before your moment of genius struck. [...] And who can blame you for thinking you deserve the credit? The brain works its machinations in secret, conjuring ideas like tremendous magic. It does not allow its colossal operating system to be probed by conscious cognition. The brain runs its show incognito (Eagleman 2012, p. 7).[3]

This disjunction between conscious, singular agency and the non-conscious, proliferating processes in Eagleman's presentation evokes the division between system and narrative, but does so in a way that assigns agency to the systemic processes. Eagleman has thus chosen narrativity over accuracy in this book, and even as he wants to present to his readers a mind that is subject to the determining forces of the systemic interactions of the brain (as opposed to being a self-determining subject), the demands of narrative structuring force him to (inaccurately) transfer the idea of intentional agency onto another level in the process.

One way out of this representational impasse could be the narrative view of the mind. This recursive solution suggests that rather than there being an explanatory gap between mental function and its narrative representations, our minds themselves are narrative in form, even though their neural underpinnings may be systemic. Jerome Bruner, in the 1990 volume *Acts of Meaning*, sets out to offer an alternative to the long-standing computational view of the mind. Whereas the computational model focuses on analysing human behaviour as the result of input, linear processing and output, Bruner's form of "cultural psychology" focuses on understanding consciousness through the concepts of action and agency. "A cultural psychology, almost by definition, will not be preoccupied with 'behavior' but with 'action', its intentionally based counterpart", Bruner notes. Furthermore, because Bruner focuses on "*situated action*—action situated in cultural settings, and in the mutually interacting intentional states of the participants" (Bruner 1990, p. 19; emphasis original), it is also central to his view that the action becomes what it is not only

---

[3]Eagleman also uses the second person pronoun as a central character in *Incognito*. In this he follows an established convention of popular psychology and self-help books, and the fluctuation between "the brain", "your brain" and "you" forms a rhythm which moves in accordance with whether Eagleman is discussing neural functions or the level of human experience. There is one further protagonist—"we"—which appears when Eagleman's discussion of human behaviour moves to failures of cognition (e.g., visual illusions on p. 18). Presumably the change occurs to avoid the implication that specific readers alone, and not humanity in general (or even Eagleman himself), fail in such a way: consider the rhetorical effect of "Why do you fail to perceive these obvious things? Are you really such a poor observer of your own experiences?" in comparison with the "we" used in the original on p. 21.

because of the intention of a single individual, but also because that individual's intention is part of a larger network of cultural information. Thus, in order to act meaningfully and intentionally, human beings make use of "folk psychology"—a pool of knowledge about human experience and action that is used not only to understand the actions of others, but also to make sense of our own experiences, and to guide our future actions. "Folk psychology", Bruner (1990, pp. 42–43) writes, "is about human agents doing things on the basis of their beliefs and desires, striving for goals, meeting obstacles which they best or which best them, all of this extended over time". Crucially, the organising principle of this pool of knowledge is "narrative in nature", not "logical or categorical" (Bruner 1990, p. 42).

Nearly 20 years later, Bruner's idea of folk psychology is being developed further by scholars combining his psychological and philosophical perspective with cognitive neuroscience. Daniel D. Hutto (2009), for example, takes up the idea of folk psychological narratives and argues that not only are they a crucial source of information for understanding ourselves and others, but also that our understanding of human beings and our understanding of narratives develop in a mutually dependent fashion. Folk psychology, Hutto suggests, "is essentially a narrative practice—its exercise, always and everywhere, invokes our capacity to construct or digest narratives of a special sort [...] that make explicit mention of how mental states (most prominently, beliefs and desires) figure in their lives" (Hutto 2009, p. 11). It must be noted, however, that neither Bruner nor Hutto claims a narrative structure for raw perception so much as "a readiness or predisposition to organize experience into a narrative form, into plot structures and the rest" (Bruner 1990, p. 45). Also, rather than the details of neuropsychology, Bruner is interested in the high-level operations of human minds as they negotiate interpersonal relationships and cultural contexts.

Roger C. Schank's *Tell Me a Story: Narrative and Intelligence*, originally published the same year as Bruner's *Acts of Meaning*, also uses an argument about the role of story as a way of organising information vital to the human being. But where Bruner sees human beings as users of the narratives of folk psychology, Schank leans towards locating agency in the narratives themselves. Human intelligence—and any artificial intelligence that would emulate it—Schank argues, consists of the application of narratives of what we have already experienced (or narratives of others' experiences) to a new situation. Such information is coded in our memories in the form of "scripts", or sets of "expectations about what will happen next in a well-understood situation" (Schank 1995, p. 7), and these scripts are "indexed" in such a manner as to be readily available in new but similar situations (Schank 1995, pp. 10–11). Schank's background in AI leads him to imply that human narrative intelligence is only an application of these pre-learned (or programmed) scripts, which are stored and retrieved in the brain in a way analogous to a computer. In Schank's argument, therefore, conscious intention concedes much of its agency to the stored scripts, and taken in its strong form, his hypothesis suggests that "scripts obviate the need to think" (Schank 1995, p. 8).

Arguably the most far-reaching argument about the narrative roots of human selves has been made by Daniel Dennett, who suggests that the practice of storytelling is so central to our social interaction and intelligence that it could be said to define our evolutionary niche: "Our fundamental tactic of self-protection, self-control, and self-definition is not spinning webs or building dams, but telling stories" (Dennett 1993, p. 418). In Dennett's idea of storytelling humans, agency is again given to the narratives themselves: "Our tales are spun, but for the most part we don't spin them: they spin us. Our human consciousness, and our narrative selfhood, is their product, not their source" (pp. 417–418). This self Dennett calls the "centre of narrative gravity" (1992, p. 103), a metaphor which draws on physicists' positing of a centre of gravity for an object, such as a chair. While that centre can be talked about as if were an object, it is "a theorist's fiction" (1992, p. 103):

> The physicist does an *interpretation*, if you like, of the chair and its behavior, and comes up with the theoretical abstraction of a center of gravity, which is then very useful in characterizing the behaviour of the chair in the future, under a wide variety of conditions (1992, p. 105; emphasis original).

Thus Dennett's formulation of the self is of a postulated unified agent which, in fact, only comes to be in the process of telling stories about itself, and although it can be talked about as an entity, it does not exist beyond the discourse that generated it.[4]

If Bruner, Schank and Dennett all have searched for ways in which our mental lives are dependent on narrative, none of them has a background in the study of narrative per se. On the narratological side of the fence, David Herman's work builds on Bruner's, and develops it towards a more analytical examination of the narrative structures involved. Herman understands the intersection of narrative theory and "the sciences of mind" to cover two interrelated questions:

> How do stories across media interlock with interpreters' mental capacities and dispositions, thus giving rise to narrative experiences? and How (to what extent, in what specific ways) does narrative scaffold efforts to make sense of experience itself? (Herman 2013a, p. 421)

Herman is thus focused on analysing the structures of stories as "models of action" (2009, p. 40), both in the sense of learned action-structures having narrative form, and in the sense of stories coding within themselves various action-structures that can then be examined—for the better comprehension of both the nature of human action and the nature of narrative. Stories, Herman suggests, are cognitive tools in the Vygotskian sense: they are "a primary technology for making sense of how things unfold in time [. . .], one that helps reveal how actions arise, how they are interrelated, and how much salience they should be assigned within a given environment for acting and interacting" (Herman 2013a, p. 431). As with Bruner, Herman's focus remains on the higher levels of cognition, and he explicitly steps away from claiming a role for narrative sensemaking on the nonconscious level (2013b, p. 73).

The paradigm of the narrative self thus argues that narrative can be an accurate form of representation for mind and consciousness, since those phenomena are

---

[4]Dennett's version of the narrative self has engaged the imaginations of many literary authors, such as the American novelist John Barth, who finds the idea to be in perfect concert with his own fascination with the figure of Scheherazade—a character who told herself into life and who is, for Barth, "the (fictionalistical, *as-if*ish) scenario-spinner that is the continuously auto-creating self of every one of us" (Barth 1995, p. 196; emphasis original; see also Polvinen 2008, pp. 141–186). For arguments against the idea of a narrative self, see Strawson (2004).

themselves narrative processes. At the same time, however, it does not fully take on the hard problem of the gap between conscious experience and the systemic neural level.

3   Mind as a Complex System

The roots of the dynamical systems approaches to cognition lie in the cybernetic revolution of the 1940s and 1950s, in the work of McCulloch, of Shannon and Weaver, and of von Neumann (Port and van Gelder 1995b, p. 36), as well as in the more "organismic" theories of biological systems in the 1960s and 1970s (Thelen and Smith 1994, p. xix). An initial split between two approaches—one focusing on computational models and another gravitating towards neural networks—eventually led to the latter developing in the 1980s into connectionism, and further into dynamical systems approaches (Port and van Gelder 1995b, pp. 36–39). Today, the view that at least at the neuronal level the best form of description for the brainmind is a dynamical one is widely shared, and the central metaphor of mind as a computer has been overtaken by that of mind as a living, interacting system.

The central tenets of the dynamical systems view of mind and brain are:

> The cognitive system is not a computer, it is a dynamical system. It is not the brain, inner and encapsulated; rather, it is the whole system comprised of nervous system, body, and environment. The cognitive system is not a discrete sequential manipulator of static representational structure; rather it is a structure of mutually and simultaneously influencing *change*. Its processes do not take place in the arbitrary, discrete time of computer steps; rather, they unfold in the *real* time of ongoing change in the environment, the body, and the nervous system. The cognitive system does not interact with other aspects of the world by passing messages or commands; rather, it continuously coevolves with them (Port and van Gelder 1995b, p. 3; emphases original).

The study of the brainmind from the perspective of dynamical systems theory has, accordingly, moved from symbol-based models and computational logic to studying rates of change and phase-space trajectories that are seen to correspond to some observable behaviours. For example, the methods used by the scholars published in Port and van Gelder's 1995 volume *Mind as Motion: Explorations in the Dynamics of Cognition* include both quantitative and qualitative modelling, as well as systems-theoretically informed description of the cognitive systems under study. With these tools the chapters examine issues such as language processing, the binding problem and the early childhood development of embodied cognition.[5]

If the dynamical view may now be said to be accepted as a description of interactions on the neuronal level, it is also possible to take it as a way of undermining the need for different approaches for lower-level and higher-level processes. Whereas the dominant model of computational cognitivism took

---

[5]Emotions have become much more central for the cognitive sciences since the 1990s, and emotional episodes have also been seen in terms of dynamical patterns (Colombetti 2014, pp. 53–82).

cognition to consist of two different processes—unconscious symbolic computation on the one hand, and conscious experience on the other—the dynamical view takes that distinction to be "a contemporary remnant of the traditional philosophical view that mind is somehow fundamentally distinct in nature from the material world (the body and the external physical world)" (Port and van Gelder 1995a, p. viii). Thus, "if we are interested in *cognitive* systems, then the behaviors of interest are their *cognitive performances* (perceiving, remembering, conversing, etc.), and it is *these* behaviors, at their characteristic time scales, that must unfold in a way described by the rule of [mathematical] evolution" (Port and van Gelder 1995b, p. 11; emphases original). Similarly, Esther Thelen and Linda B. Smith suggest that dynamical systems theory can break down the barrier between ways of understanding the lower-order processes of brain organisation on the one hand, and the higher-order processes of complex perception and cognition on the other. Abstract reasoning and metacognition, they argue, "are in principle no different from the less-abstract mental operations upon which they are ontogenetically based, and that, indeed, a common dynamic must unify all brain function as well as changes in brain and behavior" (Thelen and Smith 1994, p. 312).

However, Thelen and Smith also note the danger of thinking that just because the *dynamics* of the behaviour remains the same across various levels of cognition, the processes themselves repeat from one level to the next. An act such as that of weaving a fabric, and the act of thinking about weaving are different, Thelen and Smith insist, and should not be expected to consist of the same patterns:

> Thinking, like weaving, is a *behavior*, a product of the entire system's activity. However, the patterns of activity that are weaving and the patterns of activity that are thinking about weaving are not the same nor is one in any way contained within the other or 'raised up' to form the other (p. 337).

Also, and in accordance with the dynamical systems theory more generally, this model of mind separates the idea of "activity" from the idea of "action"—from intention and agency—and thus gives it a very different role than the narrative paradigm does. The presence of agency and intentionality in representations of dynamical systems, therefore, tends to give them a false sense of teleology—but at the same time our understanding of those systems depends on our ability to represent them in ways that make sense to us. So even if the dynamical systems view of the brain shows us all cognitive performance in terms of the same dynamics, the question remains how a narrative representation could articulate the agentless processes of nonconscious cognition.

4   Enacting Complexity

Peter Watts's science fiction novel *Blindsight* (2006) presents the problem of lower and higher-level processing in much the same way as Eagleman in his popular-science book. The novel takes the form of a classic first-contact story: an expedition of specialists is sent into deep space to intercept an alien vessel that has sent a group of probes to Earth. Among the technicians, military experts and linguists, the expedition includes the novel's narrator, Siri Keeton, a "Synthesist" or official observer. Due to severe epilepsy he suffered as a child, Siri has had half of his brain removed and replaced with an extensive computer databank and processor, making him uniquely able to analyse massive amounts of data for their large-scale patterns. At the same time, however, he has lost the ability to intuitively reflect on the relationship between himself and his environment, and is forced to rely on learned algorithms to interpret the actions and intentions of those around him. While his computer-assisted mind is able to analyse incredible masses of data on the surface behaviour of both the alien creatures and the people around him, as well as creating solutions on the basis of that data, Keeton is initially unable to properly access those levels of his own intelligence, which makes his sense of self muted and fragmented.

Keeton's mirror image in the novel is the alien the team encounters: a form of life that is massively intelligent but without sentience. Without a conscious self, the alien creatures, or "scramblers", embody the idea of multiple brain processes that do the actual work of cognising before consciousness has even an inkling of a decision needing to be made. "Imagine you're a scrambler", Keeton exhorts both himself and the novel's readers, in an attempt to understand what the team is facing. "Imagine you have intellect but no insight, agendas but no *awareness*. Your circuitry hums with strategies for survival and persistence, flexible, intelligent, even technologi-cal—but no other circuitry monitors it. You can think of anything, yet are conscious of nothing" (Watts 2006, p. 323; emphasis original).[6] The novel's storyline develops towards the predictable disaster, with Keeton the only survivor, and it does so by weaving together Keeton's voice and personality with the slow revelation of the scramblers' strange form of cognition. At the same time as readers' understanding of the nature of the scramblers' intelligence grows, Keeton gains an intuitive connec-tion to the processes of his modified brain. Initially, reflective awareness appears in his experience as moments of the blindsight the novel's title refers to: as fleeting visualisations in the corner of his eye that result from one part of his brain attempting to tell his conscious mind something by "passing notes under the table" (p. 319). By the end, Keeton's intuitive connection to his own subroutines is restored, making him able to tell the narrative he tells—a narrative that is much more than the surface data of the events he witnessed. "And now the game is over, and a single pawn stands on that scorched board and its face is human after all" (p. 360).

What makes Watts's novel particularly interesting in comparison to Eagleman's popular-science depiction is its choice of narrator and the consequent imaginative actions readers are asked to perform. Keeton frequently takes up second-person narration to command himself to imagine being something else—either the alien creatures or one of the crewmembers. For Keeton, the command to imagine is a way of bootstrapping himself towards human sentience, of creating the reflective layer that intelligence needs in order to become aware of both its own processes and of the

---

[6]For a detailed reading of the benefits of nonconscious cognition in Watts's novel, see Hayles (2017, pp. 96–111).

thoughts and intentions of other beings. The same command, however, also applies to the novel's readers, who, by actively imagining the characters and events of the fiction, exercise their own sentience: "Imagine you are Siri Keeton", begins the novel proper. At its end, the now fully cognitively human narrator reminds his audience that even in his restored state, they cannot just take his word as proof of sentience, but that like the Chinese room, he might just be "faking it", and that the readers' only access to his sentience is through empathetic imagination. "So, I can't really tell you, one way or the other. You'll just have to imagine you're Siri Keeton" (pp. 21, 362).

Blindsight creates an opportunity for readers to go through a cognitive process not otherwise available to them, and in this it partakes in one of the shared roles of all fictional narratives. What is unusual about it is its attempt to use the general toolbox of fiction to give its readers an intimation of nonconscious processing—to activate what Richard Walsh (this volume, Chap. 5) calls a "sense of wonder" about the systemic interactions that we otherwise find difficult to make sense of. Thus, while the narrative and dynamical systems models of the mind may both have their separate roles to play in our descriptions of the lower and higher levels of mental action, I also wish to examine the ways in which narrative might help the mind to make its own systemic elements present for the reflective, narrative consciousness. Is it possible for narrative representation to engage consciousness in systemic thinking—that is, is it possible for readers of Eagleman or Watts to gain a sense of the complex system of their own brains while having it represented to them in a narrative form, rather than through the system-based forms of thought made possible by mathematics and visual illustrations?

One description of how such a process might be possible is the theory of enactive cognition, which inherited the willingness shown in the 1990s in the works of Port and van Gelder, and Thelen and Smith, to engage dynamical systems theory and methods in the study of the higher levels of cognitive functioning. Francisco Varela and Evan Thompson, in particular, have been on the forefront of fashioning a model of enactive cognition on the basis of autopoiesis, connecting the physical properties of living beings with the organisational properties of life as well as those of mental processing. In this view, cognition is understood to mean simply all the activities of a biological system that can be defined as information processing, including the organismic regulation of the body and the sensorimotor coupling between the organism and its environment. In this sense, all life could be defined as cognition of some sort or another. The kind of cognition that humans practice—including intersubjective interaction and recognition of intentional action—is seen as an extension of, rather than a departure from, this basic kind of information exchange between an organism and its environment (e.g., Varela et al. 1993).

The three main points of enactive cognitive science have been formulated as follows:

1. [U]nderstanding the complex interplay of brain, body, and world requires the tools and methods of nonlinear dynamical systems theory;
2. traditional notions of representation and computation are inadequate;

3. traditional decompositions of the cognitive system into inner functional subsystems or modules ("boxology") are misleading, and blind us to arguably better decompositions into dynamical systems that cut across the brain–body–world divisions (Thompson and Varela 2001, p. 418).

Enactive cognition thus conceptualises the organisation of mind very differently from the traditional computational models, where the emphasis is on the interaction of processing units within the brain. Here the focus is on how large-scale brain activity emerges out of the transient integration of neural events, as well as on how the sensorimotor coupling of the embodied mind with its environment has to be understood as a feedback loop. So even if the idea of autopoiesis roots enaction in the very lowest levels of cognition, the enactive approach also aims to understand higher-level cognitive processing, as well as offer an explanation of the join between the two. This is because the autopoietic feedback loops between the organism and its environment also involve the concept of the enacting agent. As argued by Di Paolo, Rhode and De Jaegher in a seminal collection of essays on enaction, "[a]utonomous agency goes even further than the recognition of ongoing sensorimotor couplings as dynamical and emphasizes the role of the agent in the constructing, organizing, maintaining, and regulating those closed sensorimotor loops" (2010, p. 39). In doing so, a cognitive agent enacts a world for itself, even as its own being is determined by that world. Thus agency and the environment are tied together in a process that generates not only the agency itself (as a living, cognising being) but also the environment in which that agent operates. In the case of Watts's narrative, we enter a similar feedback relationship: one where the fiction as a cognitive environment is constituted by our mental actions, but also where that environment changes—both by limiting and by extending—the actions we can take.

Enactive cognitive science has not so far given much attention to narrative. Enaction is an approach mostly used in the study of sensory perception and sense-making, and even though it has recently been applied to the development of symbolic action in, for example, make-believe, this tends to be done in a way that ignores extended temporality.[7] However, the central role of narrative in human imagination makes it natural to seek further purchase between enactive cognition and narrative, and to elaborate the role of different forms of action in the enactive sense-making. What makes the enactive view relevant for the discussion on narrative and complexity in particular is, therefore, not only the way it connects these processes of autopoiesis all the way up to the level of conscious thought, but also the fact that enactment offers a way of conceptualising a form of conscious, narrative

---

[7]Thus, when Di Paolo, Rhode and De Jaegher speak of a child imagining a spoon to be a car, they focus on the embodied action of the play, rather than on the possibility of a storytelling frame for the action: "When a child skillfully supplements the perceptual lack of similarity between a spoon and a car by making the spoon move and sound like a car, he or she has grasped in an embodied manner the extent to which perception can be action-mediated. With his or her body, the child can now alter sense-making activity, both on external objects, as well as his or her own actions and those of others" (2010, p. 78).

access to our own systemic minds. Despite the fact that narrative descriptions may lose the specifically systemic characteristics of the complex system they try to depict, the enactive perspective suggests that through the process of participating in the sense-making encoded in a narrative we might still be able to gain access to those characteristics, and to inhabit what Richard Walsh calls "the edge of sense" (this volume, Chap. 5). Thus the mind might be able to constitute for itself—in the phenomenological sense of bringing to awareness—its own systemic functioning in the enaction of a narrative representation, rather than the systemic functioning being replicated in the representation as such.

5   Conclusion

It would be premature to claim that the problem of representing complexity in narrative is solved by the arrival of the theory of enactive cognition, as research into the interplay of narrativity and complex systems is only beginning. What enactive cognition does point us towards is the need to examine more carefully the uses of various structural, metaphorical and narrativising techniques within popular science and other texts that attempt to convey the idea of complexity to a non-specialist audience. This kind of research might be able to find new ways of discussing the rhetorical effects of such writing, as well as extend our existing understanding of the effects of narrative engagement with the help of the enactive paradigm. If it seems inescapable that narrative models of complexity do not share the specifically systemic elements, then perhaps mapping the thing represented and its representation on each other is, indeed, the wrong way to look at the problem at hand. Instead, the enactive view offers us a way of looking at what kind of combination of narrativity and metaphoric or symbolic representation is capable of triggering the imagining of complex systems in our minds.

As Marco Bernini also suggests in this volume (Chap. 17), even if the neural correlates of mental states cannot as such be accessed by the conscious mind, there is an argument to be made for seeing the enactment of a narrative as a method for the mind to explore not only its own narrative intuitions but also the systemic level of its functioning. The two descriptions of human cognition discussed in this chapter both attempt to make the systemic nature of the brainmind available to our human, narratively inclined form of cognition, and I am intuitively drawn towards the idea that the more complex and extended narrative enaction engaged by Watts's novel results in fuller sense-making than Eagleman's combination of description, argumentation and brief parables. In her essay "Making the Cut", N. Katherine Hayles (2000, pp. 145, 160) has argued that narrative is the necessary counter to systems theory precisely because it has the "loose bagginess" envisioned by Henry James—because it is "contextual" and "polysemous" and able to go beyond "the closures that systems theory would perform". In contrast with the minimalist, narratively confounding works that Bernini analyses, in this case it might be exactly the loose bagginess of extended narrative and fictional excess that allows for the fuller enactment. It thus seems that both minimalism and excess may achieve the desired result in different contexts.

On the other hand, it is true that narrative fiction in general steps into an area where it is difficult if not impossible to maintain many of the aspects of good science writing (such as the separation of fact and invention). It is an area where the needs of a good story may override the needs of accurate science, and where readers' attitudes toward the information offered is being directed by the rules of fictionality. Thus I do not suggest that popular science representations should abandon their own conventions and replace them with those of science fictional narratives; just that the benefits that come with enactive cognition may depend on the mixture of narrative and fictionality that is more easily available to novels than to science writing. However, we are only just beginning to understand the potential of the enactive frame for the analysis of narrative representation, and encountering such variety in the phenomena it reveals—as well as contextually variable and even mutually contradictory effects of the representational techniques involved—should not cause undue surprise.

References

Abbott HP (2008) Narrative and emergent behaviour. Poet Today 29(2):227–244

Barth J (1995) Once upon a time: storytelling explained. In: Further fridays: essays, lectures, and other nonfiction 1984−94 [1992]. Little, Brown, Boston, pp 181–196

Bruner J (1990) Acts of meaning. Harvard University Press, Cambridge

Colombetti G (2014) The feeling body: affective science meets the enactive mind. MIT Press, Cambridge

Damasio A (2012) Self comes to mind: constructing the conscious brain [2010]. Vintage, New York

Dennett DC (1981) Brainstorms: philosophical essays on mind and psychology [1978]. MIT Press, Cambridge

Dennett DC (1992) The self as the centre of narrative gravity. In: Kessel FS, Cole PM, Johnson DL (eds) Self and consciousness: multiple perspectives. Lawrence Erlbaum, Hillsdale, pp 103–115

Dennett DC (1993) Consciousness explained [1991]. Penguin, London

Di Paolo EA, Rhode M, De Jaegher H (2010) Horizons for the enactive mind: values, social interaction, and play. In: Stewart J, Gapenne O, Di Paolo EA (eds) Enaction: toward a new paradigm for cognitive science. MIT Press, Bradford, pp 33–87

Eagleman DM (2012) Incognito: the secret lives of the brain [2011]. Vintage, New York

Hayles NK (2000) Making the cut: the interplay of narrative and system, or what systems theory can't see. In: Rasch W, Wolfe C (eds) Observing complexity: systems theory and postmodernity. University of Minnesota Press, Minneapolis, pp 137–162

Hayles NK (2017) Unthought: the power of the cognitive nonconscious. University of Chicago Press, Chicago

Herman D (2009) Storied minds: narrative scaffolding for folk psychology. J Conscious Stud 16 (6−8):40–68

Herman D (2013a) Narrative theory and the sciences of mind. Lit Compass 10(5):421–436

Herman D (2013b) Storytelling and the sciences of mind. MIT Press, Cambridge

Hutto DD (2009) Folk psychology as narrative practice. J Conscious Stud 16(6–8):9–39

Minsky M (1988) Society of mind [1985]. Simon & Schuster, New York

Panksepp J (2005) Affective neuroscience [1998]. Oxford University Press, Oxford

Polvinen M (2008) Reading the texture of reality: chaos theory, literature and the humanist perspective, English Department Studies 6. University of Helsinki, Helsinki

Port RF, van Gelder T (1995a) Preface. In: Port RF, Van Gelder T (eds) Mind as motion: explorations in the dynamics of cognition. MIT Press, pp. vii–x, Cambridge

Port RF, van Gelder T (1995b) It's about time: an overview of the dynamical approach to cognition. In: Port RF, Van Gelder T (eds) Mind as motion: explorations in the dynamics of cognition. MIT Press, Cambridge, pp 1–44

Schank RC (1995) Tell me a story: narrative and intelligence [1990]. Northwestern University Press, Evanston

Strawson G (2004) Against narrativity. Ratio 17:428–452

Thelen E, Smith LB (1994) A dynamic systems approach to the development of cognition and action. MIT Press, Bradford

Thompson E, Varela FJ (2001) Radical embodiment: neural dynamics and consciousness. Trends Cogn Sci 5(10):418–425

Varela FJ, Thompson E, Rosch E (1993) The embodied mind: cognitive science and human experience [1991]. MIT Press, Cambridge

Vermeule B (2015) The new unconscious: a literary guided tour. In: Zunshine L (ed) The Oxford handbook of cognitive literary studies. Oxford University Press, Oxford, pp 463–482

Watts P (2006) Blindsight. Tor, New York

Chapter 8
Discussion and Comment (A Simple Story of a Complex Mind?)

Marco Bernini, Susan Stepney, and Merja Polvinen

Abstract Marco Bernini, Susan Stepney and Merja Polvinen in discussion on an earlier version of "A Simple Story of a Complex Mind?"

MB: *"Together with the cognitive sciences the humanities thus encounter the "hard problem", or the explanatory gap between brain states and mental states, and the question whether our scholarship should even try to grapple with precognitive processes"*: I see what you are aiming at, and it is a very important point (i.e., "how can literature have something to say on what happens only at the brain level?"); it is also an issue underlying my essay in this volume. However, I am not sure that Kahnemann's distinction is the kind of distinction you need or are referring to. It seems to me you are pointing at a distinction of level (mental vs. neuronal events) whereas Kahnemann is pointing at a distinction of agency or conscious experience of an action (thinking, moving, perceiving). Literature can easily represent what is beyond the threshold of agency or consciousness (showing non-attentional moments of a character who is about to get hit by a bus, for instance) but might have some serious problem in representing what happens in the brain at that moment; or am I getting something wrong?

MP: I dropped Kahnemann—it was a bit of a last-minute addition to the previous version anyway. But my point here was not so much to talk about what literature can do, but about what literary studies can do in terms of analysing

M. Bernini
Department of English Studies, Durham University, Durham, UK

S. Stepney (✉)
Department of Computer Science, University of York, York, UK

York Cross-disciplinary Centre for Systems Analysis, University of York, York, UK
e-mail: susan.stepney@york.ac.uk

M. Polvinen
Department of Modern Languages, University of Helsinki, Helsinki, Finland

© Springer Nature Switzerland AG 2018
R. Walsh, S. Stepney (eds.), *Narrating Complexity*,
https://doi.org/10.1007/978-3-319-64714-2_8

the patterns of experience that are represented in texts, but also recreated by readers.

SS: *"Emergence, Abbott points out, is a form of action, but because of the 'massive distribution of causal agents' typical to complex systems, it is 'action without any discernible sequence of events, that is without a story. As such, emergent behavior is by definition unnarratable' (2008, pp. 227, 233)"*: Interesting perspective. Richard [Walsh] and I originally started discussing that what made a particular complex system behaviour *emergent* was that it *was* narratable—we "notice" it, conceptualise it, because we can narrate it—e.g., flocking is narratable, surely?

MP: I think what Abbott means is that, for example, flocking is describable, but only narratable in the sense of it being a phenomenon that can be observed and the observation could then be narrated. But it is not narratable in the sense that the cause-and-effect relations within that behaviour could be put in a narrative form (imagine trying to tell the story of bird A turning left and then bird B and then ... doesn't work).

SS: *"An act such as that of weaving a fabric, and the act of thinking about weaving are different, Thelen and Smith insist, and should not be expected to be the same patterns of activity"*: The physical body movements are different, but many of the mental processes are the same (mirror neurons, etc.), so it isn't simply a category difference.

MP: The idea of mirror neurons has come along after the dynamical view, and I admit I don't know whether it has been incorporated in some sense. But on the other hand, the idea of mirror neurons itself (as well as mental representations in general) has received a lot of criticism, and the point here is to draw attention to the differences between the dynamics and the behaviour on the one hand, and activity and intentional action on the other.

SS: *"In this view, cognition is understood to mean simply all the activities of a biological system that can be defined as information processing, including the organismic regulation of the body and the sensorimotor coupling between the organism and its environment"*: That's a rather peculiar weak definition of "cognition", literally making it synonymous with information processing. I think I prefer Irun Cohen's definition:

> *A cognitive system is one that has three properties:*
> ** it contains internal images of its environment*
> ** it self-organises by updating its internal images based on its experience*
> ** it makes decisions based on its internal state*

Crucially—because decisions are based on an internal state that reflects the environment—if the environment or state changes, the decisions can change (it can *learn*).

MP: The point of enactive cognition is to move towards seeing cognition as interaction with environment *without* brain-internal representations. But rather than have the full debate here, I just brought some of these points out more towards the beginning of the chapter to guide readers' expectations better.

MB: *"The kind of cognition that humans practice—including intersubjective interaction and recognition of intentional action—is seen as an extension of, rather than a departure from, this basic kind of information exchange between an organism and its environment (e.g., Varela, Thompson and Rosch 1993)"*: Since this is the kind of bridge/path linking complex neuronal interaction with their mental counterpart you are (rightly) looking for to support your argument, I would spend a couple of more lines around the nature of this fractal hypothesis of enactivism, where small-scale and large-scale cognition are unified under the same principles.

MP: Agreed—I have tried to bring this up more in the current version.

SS: *"The two descriptions of human cognition discussed in this chapter both attempt to make the systemic nature of the brainmind available to our human, narratively inclined form of cognition, and I am intuitively drawn towards the idea that the more complex and extended narrative enaction engaged by Watts's novel results in fuller sense-making than Eagleman's combination of description, argumentation and brief parables"*: I've read *Blindsight*, yet I missed quite a lot of what you talk about here. So it was not more sense-making for me!

MP: On the other hand, literary works are rarely meant to be one-off 'downloads' of information into their readers' minds, but instead this kind of 'fuller' sense-making often comes out only after repeated readings. And not necessarily to every reader—half of this comes from my particular brainmind having done a certain kind of work with the stuff offered to me by the matrix of the text.

Chapter 9
Closure, Observation and Coupling: On Narrative and Autopoiesis

Adam Lively

Abstract This chapter outlines three themes that it takes to be central to the conception of narrative fiction as an autopoietic system: closure, observation and coupling. Closure refers to the processes by which a system such as a narrative distinguishes itself, through its own internal operations, from its environment. Observation refers to the emergence and vicissitudes of linguistic function in the artistic text, function being dependent on the proliferating, recursively embedded perspectives at stake in narrative fiction (perspectives of readers, narrators, characters). Coupling refers to the constraints that interacting autopoietic systems impose on one another, and how this process should be understood in relation to narrative—either in terms of interactions between reader and text, or between broader autopoietic systems of perception and communication. These themes are explored with reference to Aristotelian narrative theory, the functionalist semiotics of Jan Mukařovský and the systems theory of Niklas Luhmann.

1 Introduction

In his *Introduction to Systems Theory*, Niklas Luhmann recounts a conversation in which Humberto Maturana explained to him how he hit on the term *autopoiesis* for his theory of self-reproducing systems. A philosopher colleague had been explaining to him Aristotle's distinction between *praxis* (an action that is self-sufficient in the sense of being of a certain value in itself) and *poiēsis* (a "making"—an action that is intended to produce something outside itself, a "work"). "Maturana found a bridge between the two concepts," Luhmann writes. "He spoke of *autopoiesis*, a poiesis that is its own work [. . .] the system that is its own work" (Luhmann 2013, pp. 77–78). There is an irony here. For Maturana would come to contest Luhmann's application of the concept of autopoiesis to social or communicative systems. Yet *poiēsis* is the title of Aristotle's treatise on the "making" of works of art (especially dramatic

A. Lively (✉)
Department of Media, Middlesex University, London, UK
e-mail: a.lively@mdx.ac.uk

tragedy), and throughout that work he repeatedly has recourse to the analogy between, on the one hand, the way that works of art like tragedies are constructed and, on the other, the way that organic forms are constructed.

In this chapter, I pursue this question of how narrative fiction can be thought of in autopoietic terms. This is not an approach that has yet made much impact in narrative theory, though Luhmann (2000) has written at length on autopoiesis and the "art system" and Bruce Clarke (2014) on the post-humanist ideological implications of thinking about narrative in systems-theoretical ways. My intentions in relation to this new field, then, are modest and exploratory. I draw on three principal sources, and identify three themes that, I suggest, should be central to a worked-through theory of autopoiesis and narrative.[1] Two of the sources I have already mentioned—firstly Aristotle's *Poetics*, his defence (against the attacks of his former teacher Plato) of the cognitive and ethical value of the arts; and secondly, Luhmann's account of art as a special instance of an autopoietic "social" or "communicative" system. The third source is the writings on aesthetics of the Czech semiotician and literary scholar Jan Mukařovský. Mukařovský was writing in the 1930s and 1940s in the wake of the emergence, in the linguistics of Saussure and in Russian Formalism, of perhaps the first modern ideas of "system" in relation to language and literature.[2] Yet the "Czech structuralism" of which he was a prominent representative took a view of "system" quite different from that which had been presented by Saussure (and which would be pursued by the structuralism of the French school in the 1960s). One of my concerns is to show how Luhmann's concepts of operative closure and autopoiesis in relation to artworks are foreshadowed both by Mukařovský's concept of the "contexture" created by the "aesthetic function" and by Aristotle's account of the internal organization of an artwork or "mimetic representation". In all three cases, it will be noted, narrative is understood in the context of a general aesthetic theory. Yet for all three, as we shall see, narrative constitutes, on account of its explicitly temporal and constructional quality, a paradigmatic case.

The connections between these three disparate sources coalesce around the three ideas that I suggest should be central to a theory of narrative and autopoiesis. Section 2 is on *closure*—or, to use terms that I explain below, the "operative closure" by which a system distinguishes itself, through its own internal operations, from its environment. (Here, as far as Aristotle is concerned, I am concerned in particular with the extrapolations from the *Poetics* of two neo-Aristotelian narrative theorists, Paul Ricoeur and Meir Sternberg.) From my treatment of this first idea emerge the key issues of perception and recursion. Section 3, on *observation*, takes up these

---

[1]I am writing here about narrative fiction—that is, narratives that distinguish themselves as "made" in the sense of "made up": they involve artistry and constitute works of "art". This raises the question of the use of narrative forms in non-artistic and non-fictional contexts. There is not space in this paper to address this question directly, but I take it that it could be handled in terms of the poly-functionalist view of language set out in Sect. 3 of this paper.

[2]Luhmann acknowledges Saussure as a source for his "difference-theoretical" approach to systems—that is, the notion that the operations of social systems are based (like Saussure's *langue*, or language-system) on *difference* (Luhmann 2013, pp. 44–45).

themes in relation to function and what Luhmann terms "second-order" observation. Section 4, on *coupling*, considers the constraints that interacting autopoietic systems impose on one another, and how this process should be understood in relation to narrative. Here I contrast the views of Aristotle and Mukařovský, which are rooted in the notion of the unified subject, with that of Luhmann, according to which the productive mutual constraints at work in narrative are those not between subject and object (e.g., reader and text), but between autopoietic systems of perception and communication.

2   Closure

Tragedy, Aristotle writes, is "an imitation [*mimēsis*] of an action that is complete in itself, as a whole of some magnitude":

> Now a whole is that which has beginning, middle, and end. A beginning is that which is not necessarily after anything else, and which has naturally something else after it; a middle is that which is by nature after one thing and has also another after it; and an end is that which is naturally after something itself, either as its necessary or usual consequent, and with nothing else after it (Aristotle 1941, p. 1462 [1450b]).

Aristotle is using "action" in a particular sense here. There is a general sense of an action as seen from the point of view of an agent—that is the things s/he does, the actions that s/he performs. And there is the sense of an "action" as seen from a broader, external perspective (such as that of an audience in a theatre), which encompasses origins and consequences of which the agent may be unaware. It is the latter sense that Aristotle is using when he refers to "an action that is complete in itself" (Rorty 1992a, pp. 7–8). Tragedy represents this unity of an action (in this strong sense) through its *muthos*, which Aristotle defines as its "organization of events" (*ē tōn pragmatōn sustasis*)—or, as Paul Ricoeur parses the term *sustasis* in his commentary on Aristotle's *Poetics*, its "organizing the events into a system" (Ricoeur 1984, p. 33). In Aristotle's account, a well-constructed "complex plot" (Sophocles' *Oedipus* is his favoured example) crucially includes elements of "discovery" and "reversal of fortune" for the protagonist: these elements hinge on the disparity between the two senses of action—on the one hand, discrete actions from the perspective of the agent, and, on the other, "whole" actions from a point of view taking in origins and consequences.

Paul Ricoeur (1984) and Meir Sternberg (1992) have drawn from Aristotle parallel conclusions concerning the temporality of narrative. Both have highlighted how Aristotle's concept of discrete events making up a single temporal whole, the representation of a "single action" (in the strong sense), implies a simultaneity of two different ways of experiencing the narrative—one "chronological" or "episodic", the other "teleological" or "configurational". The chrono-logic of succession drives forward from beginning to end, while the "grasping together" of teleo-logic looks back from the end to the beginning (Ricoeur 1984, pp. 66–68). Sternberg highlights how the differentiation and phasing of these two streams produces such narrative effects as curiosity, suspense and surprise (Sternberg 1992, pp. 474–479). The important point here about the reinterpretations of Aristotle by Ricoeur and Sternberg is that they share an insistence that the unity or closure of narrative cannot be conceived purely in (mono)linear terms, in terms of the beginning- and end-points of a single line. The non-linear differentiation outlined above, whereby actions are seen simultaneously as causes of effects and as functions of a whole that is oriented towards the perceiver, creates what one might term a bi- or multi-linearity in the perception of narrative.

For Jan Mukařovský, the key term for the temporal whole of narrative is "contexture". In line with the neo-Aristotelianism of Ricoeur and Sternberg, he characterizes contexture in dynamic and constructional terms, as "a sequence of semantic units (e.g., words, sentences), a sequence unalterable without a change in the whole, in which the meaning accumulates successively" (Mukařovský 1977, p. 73). And we find, too, the same differentiation between two phases—a phase of linear succession and a phase of retrospective configuration from the point of view of a projected or achieved endpoint. A narrative presents itself as a succession, but simultaneously "the semantic intention tending toward the wholeness of the contexture accompanies its perception from the first word" (Mukařovský 1977, p. 74).

Mukařovský's distinctive contribution to this discussion of narrative's closure lies in the way his focus on function clarifies two points that we see emerge from Ricoeur's and Sternberg's accounts: the gearing of the temporal whole to the *perception* of the reader/audience, and the generation of a recursive, non-linear structure whereby textual elements are seen simultaneously according to different functions. In order to appreciate this contribution, it is necessary to give a brief account of his polyfunctionalist semiotics.[3] Mukařovský constructs a typology of linguistic functions on the basis of two distinctions. The first is a distinction between, on the one hand, uses of the sign that are directed immediately at reality, and, on the other hand, uses of the sign that take the mediating role of the sign as itself the object of the sign. The former uses are either "practical" functions, which directly interact with reality (an instruction, for example, or an expressive cry of pain or alarm), or "theoretical" functions, which aim to represent reality in the mind (scientific language being a prime example). The latter uses—those which take the mediating role of the sign as their object—are either "symbolic" functions, which have as their object the association or mediation between the sign and reality (Mukařovský gives the example of a national flag), or "aesthetic" functions, which take as their object the mediation between the sign and the perceiving subject. The second distinction, which forms the basis of the sub-categories listed above, is a distinction as to whether the language is oriented towards the subject or the object. Thus the practical function is oriented towards its object (reality) in the sense that here the language interacts directly with reality, seeking to change or express it, whereas in the case of

---

[3]Mukařovský was influenced by the functionalist semiotics of Karl Bühler (1990): I discuss the significance of this influence in the following section.

Table 9.1 Matrix of basic functional possibilities

	Immediate (Sign as "instrument")	Semiotic/mediated (Sign as "object")
Orientation to subject	Theoretical	Aesthetic
Orientation to object	Practical	Symbolic

the theoretical function the language is oriented towards the subject in that it is aimed not at changing or directly expressing reality but at constructing an image of reality in the mind of the subject. The "symbolic" function is said to be oriented towards the object because the mediation at stake is that between sign and object, whereas in the case of the "aesthetic" the mediation that forms the object of the sign is, as we have said, that between sign and perceiving subject. Mukařovský combines these distinctions to form a matrix of basic functional possibilities (Mukařovský 1977, pp. 39–45; Steiner 1977, pp. xxvii–xxix), see Table 9.1.

These possibilities and interrelations should be seen in terms of a simultaneous polyfunctionality: "As a rule, several functions are not only potentially but actually present in an act or creation, and among them there may be some which the agent or creator did not think of or did not even desire. No sphere of human action or human creation is limited to a single function. There is always a greater number of functions, and there are tensions, variances, and balancing among them" (Mukařovský 1977, p. 37). An innumerable variety of hierarchical interrelations between these functions is possible—in advertising, for example, one finds a subordination of the aesthetic function to practical functions (Mukařovský 1977, p. 32). A fictional narrative will contain language used for many different functions, belonging to any of the practical, theoretical and symbolic (or indeed aesthetic) categories set out above: but these functions will themselves be the object of the overarching aesthetic function.

Thus the aesthetic function, for Mukařovský, involves an orientation with two aspects. It is an orientation towards the sign itself—that is, in a work of art, towards the *whole* of the work of art as a sign—but more specifically, it is an orientation towards the subject's response or attitude towards the sign (a response that is in principle open-ended rather than determined by a particular relation to reality). One might take as an example Jasper Johns' famous Pop Art painting *Stars and Stripes*. Mukařovský, as we have seen, cites a national flag as being a prime example of the symbolic function: it is geared to the identification of the sign with a particular portion of reality (the country, the nation, the people).[4] In Johns' painting, this symbolic function is not erased: rather, this function becomes itself a sign that is the object of the aesthetic function, thus orienting it towards the open-ended, indeterminate response of the perceiver. In general, according to Mukařovský, when the aesthetic function is dominant—that is, in an artistic work such as a fictional narrative—subordinate functions will tend to proliferate: the aesthetic function is characterized "by the fact that it adds a facet to the acting individual's functional

---

[4]This identification can be seen in the idea that an insult to the one is an insult to the other—hence laws against "desecrating" the flag in, for example, the United States.

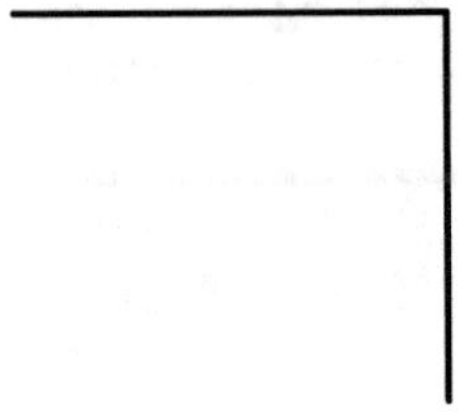

Fig. 9.1 A distinction

diversity in some way" (Mukařovský 1977, p. 38). These two aspects of the aesthetic function lead to a seemingly paradoxical situation whereby the work of art is oriented both towards maximal closure and unity (because all the functions are oriented towards the *whole* of the work of art as a sign) and simultaneously towards maximal internal differentiation and diversification (because the orientation is simultaneously towards the *whole* of the subject's existence).[5]

This relation between perception, recursion and closure is central to Luhmann's concept of "form". Luhmann's systems theory is based on a "differential or difference theoretical approach" that draws on British mathematician George Spencer-Brown's calculus of distinctions, presented in his book *The Laws of Form* (Spencer Brown 1969). Spencer-Brown begins with an injunction: "Draw a distinction!" (In the context of the preceding discussion of polyfunctionality, one might take the example of a distinction between two linguistics functions.) On the "unmarked space" of the blank sheet of paper, he marks the distinction with the form shown in Fig. 9.1 (Spencer-Brown 1969, p. 4).

This form is a unity that is, paradoxically, also a difference—the difference between the distinction proper (the vertical line), which has two sides, and the indication of the distinction (the horizontal line), which marks only one side of the distinction. The indication of a distinction is internal to the distinction and marks only one side of a two-sided form: every distinction has an "unmarked" space that is the choice of *this* (as opposed to any other) distinction: "When handling a distinction, you always have a blind spot or something invisible behind your back. You cannot observe yourself as the one who handles the distinction. Rather you must make yourself invisible if you want to observe" (Luhmann 2013, p. 104).[6]

Luhmann follows Spencer-Brown in using the term "form" for the boundary articulated by a distinction. A form is asymmetrical because, although it has two

[5]Mukařovský's argument that the aesthetic function tends to generate polyfunctionality can be compared to Meir Sternberg's "Proteus Principle" concerning narrative—the idea that narrative is characterised by a many-to-many correlation between form and function (see Pianzola, Chap. 8 in this book).

[6]A different formulation of the same point, from a phenomenological perspective, can be found in Mikhail Bakhtin's essay "Author and Hero in Aesthetic Activity", where he describes the asymmetric relation between a self that is the unique origin of a subjectivity and a self that presents itself as an object to that subjectivity: there will always be an "excess" of the one over the other, whereby the "horizon" of the subjectivity exceeds that of the self that it encompasses as object (Bakhtin 1990, pp. 22–23).

sides, at any one time only one of the sides is indicated. Thus a system distinguishes itself from its environment through its internal operations. An artwork is such a form, for it strives towards just such a "double-closure": "A work of art must distinguish itself externally from other objects and events, or it will lose itself in the world. Internally, the work closes itself off by limiting further possibilities with each of its formal decisions" (Luhmann 2000, p. 29). Narrative is exemplary in this respect: "A narration opens with the phrase 'once upon a time ...,' which demarcates an imaginary space for the unfolding of the narration at the exclusion of everything else" (Luhmann 2000, p. 32). Taken as whole, "the sequence of operations closes itself off and in doing so excludes other things" (p. 33). Luhmann invokes in this context the same term, "contexture", employed by Mukařovský: "Every choice of contexture generates a surrounding space, the unmarked space of Spencer-Brown's formal calculus" (Luhmann 2000, p. 33).

In drawing a boundary, as we have indicated, the sequence of operations limits itself to internal operations. These internal operations that articulate a form are recursive, since any crossing into the unmarked space of a distinction presupposes the original distinction: the form, in Spencer-Brown's formulation, "reenters" the form (Luhmann 2000, p. 139). In terms of narrative, such recursion guarantees connectivity within the narrative and justifies describing the narrative as a form of autopoiesis, in that

> the elements of the system are produced within the network of the system's elements, that is, through recursions. A communication cannot occur as an isolated phenomenon, as a singular event brought about by a combination of physical, chemical, living, and psychic causes. Nor can it proceed through simple replication, merely by substituting disappearing elements for one another (Luhmann 2000, p. 49)[7].

Thus Luhmann's difference-theoretical approach clarifies at a high level of abstraction how the sequential series of successive "distinctions" of which the narrative is composed is simultaneously a recursive unfolding of that which is given at the beginning—provided, that is, that one understands that "given" in terms of the initiating articulation of a form (in Mukařovský's terms, an orientation of the sign to the whole of the aesthetic sign of which it is an element).

It also helps to clarify the linkage between this recursive dynamic, on the one hand, and, on the other hand, the polyfunctionality that Mukařovský points to as the basis of narrative's non-linear dimension. "A function," as Luhmann writes, "is nothing other than a focus for comparison. It marks a problem [...] in such a way that multiple solutions can be compared and that the problem remains open for further selections and substitutions" (Luhmann 2000, p. 138). Functions are also

---

[7]In narrative fiction, Luhmann's stricture concerning the "isolated phenomenon" or "singular event" can be applied even to those features that Barthes (1986) groups together under the term "reality effect"—that is, "realistic" details or specifications that are deliberately inconsequential to the plot or theme: here, as Barthes points out, the apparently "singular event" authenticates the "realism" (the "referential illusion") of the narrative considered as a totality, as a singular, whole aesthetic sign: these details "say nothing but this: *we are the real*; it is the category of 'the real' (and not its contingent contents) which is then signified" (Barthes 1986, p. 148).

available, as we have seen in our earlier discussion of Mukařovský, for recursive operations. In a narrative, an action or use of language that serves one particular function can simultaneously serve (or can subsequently come to be seen to simultaneously serve) a quite different function. On the other hand, functionality emerges from what Luhmann calls "second-order observation":

> Unlike purpose, function does not serve the orientation of first-order observers—of the actor himself, his advisors, or his critics. An operation needs no knowledge of its function; it can substitute a purpose [. . .] (p. 137).

Thus the consideration of functionality raises the issue of observation (including that of what Luhmann means here by "second-order observation). It is to this issue that I now turn.

3   Observation

The function of art in the modern world, according to Luhmann, is to bring to consciousness the interaction of perception and communication: in non-artistic contexts "communication captivates perception and thereby directs awareness", whereas "[a]rt seeks a different kind of relationship between perception and communication—one that is irritating and defies normality—*and just this is communicated*" (Luhmann 2000, p. 23). Art deals in meanings (including linguistic meaning), but it is also something that is perceived, a "quasi-object" whose operative closure (as we have seen in Sect. 2) distinguishes it from everything else in the world. Above all, art is a prime example of a "second-order" observation system—a system constituted not just by "first-order" operations of observation and distinction-making (as outlined in Sect. 2), but also by second-order "observations of observations".

Before turning to Luhmann's account of art as a second-order observation system—and its particular application to narrative—I will draw out how versions of its basic conceptual linkage between perception and communication can be found, too, both in Aristotle and in Mukařovský's concept of the aesthetic function. In Aristotle, the key term is *mimēsis*.[8] Aristotle's concept of *mimēsis* should be distinguished, in the first place, from the Platonic idea that a representation is a degenerate third-hand copy (coming after the object it represents, which itself comes after the Ideal Form of which the object is a partial realization). Aristotle comes at the question of representation, by contrast, from the point of view of human development. Mimetic representation, for Aristotle, is natural to children and is one of the primary features that distinguishes humans from animals: it both increases the scope for learning and is inherently pleasurable (Aristotle 1941, p. 1457 [1448b]).

---

[8]*Mimēsis* is often given in English as "imitation", which has somewhat belittling connotations that don't do justice to the key role that he saw it playing in human cognition and development. Here I follow Stephen Halliwell (1986) in preferring the term "mimetic representation", in which an iconic or imitative aspect is understood.

Although it is a form of iconicity, an imitative relation whereby a similarity is perceived between the representation and what it represents, Aristotle gives *mimēsis* a surprisingly wide scope, taking in not just visual art and drama, but also dance and even music. Written narrative is also a mimetic representation, and not just at those points where the author (through "direct speech") "impersonates" or "takes on" the voice of characters: the narrative as a whole is also a mimetic representation in that in narrating the author is "taking on" the voice a fictive narrator. Aryeh Kosman's commentary on the *Poetics* provides a useful gloss on this point:

> A poet [. . .] is not primarily a creator of things that imitate: it is the poet himself who is an imitator in that she makes imitation things. It is not, in other words, that the poet is an imitator because she creates a piece of discourse that imitates a non-discursive reality; she is an imitator because she imitates a speaker speaking about reality, though it is not her reality, but the reality of that fictional speaker's fictional world. It is this relation between the poet and the speaker that is the primary imitative relation. The poet creates an imitation speaker who makes real speeches in the imitative world, 'imaginary gardens with real toads in them' as Marianne Moore once put it, not imaginary toads in gardens that are real (Kosman 1992, p. 57).

Mimetic representation then is an imitative *action* by the author, and its reception by the audience is similarly constructional.

An artistic representation, according to Aristotle, has the sensible qualities of an ordinary object, but *qua* representation these qualities take on for the perceiver an additional function in that they are perceived also in terms of their relation to the object represented: it is through contemplation of this extra dimension, Aristotle argues, that we are able to take pleasure in representations of objects distasteful in themselves, such as a painting of a corpse (Aristotle 1941, p. 1457 [1448b]). In her commentary on the *Poetics*, Elizabeth Belfiore provides the following gloss on *theōria* or "contemplation", the term that Aristotle employs for the perception of the mimetic, representational object:

> by means of *theōria* we learn and reason about a representational relationship between the imitation and the object imitated. *Theōria* is nonpractical. *Theōria* alone, Aristotle writes in *Nicomachean Ethics* 10.1177b 1-4, "is loved for itself. For nothing results from it except contemplating, but from practical things we acquire something, to a greater or lesser degree, in addition to the action." (Belfiore 1992, p. 67)

Aristotle works out this relation to the experience of the contemplator in terms of his notion of the "cathartic" response: I return to catharsis in the Sect. 4, where I consider the role of constraint.

As we saw in Sect. 2, Mukařovský conceives the "aesthetic function" as focussed on the open-ended perception by the reader of the sign's contexture. But there is another level at which Mukařovský's functionalism integrates perception and communication, which can be seen if we draw out its indebtedness to Karl Bühler's instrumentalist theory of language (1990/1934). Bühler's starting point is the close interconnection between language and perception: language, according to this view,

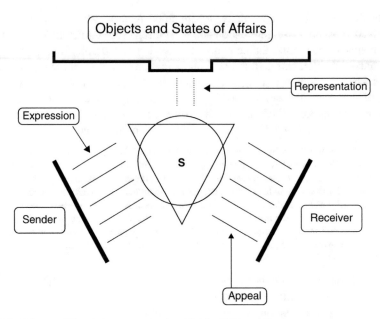

Fig. 9.2 Schema of linguistic communication (Bühler 1990, p. 35)

is a *mediation*, something *through* which things are revealed, or *by means of which* (as an *instrument* or *tool*) people are guided to look at them.[9] His schema of linguistic communication presents what psychologists today would call the "joint-attentional situation" (Tomasello 1999; Eilan et al. 2005); see Fig. 9.2.

In Fig. 9.2, the sign (indicated by the circle S) encompasses three facets or "semantic functions", depending on the pole of the triad to which it is oriented. Particular instances of language-use are "phenomena of dominance, in which one of the three fundamental relationships of the language sounds is in the foreground" (39). To this schema Mukařovský's aesthetic function adds another phenomenological layer: the perception inherent in the (joint attentional) sign itself becomes an object of perception, since everything, under the aesthetic function, is referred back to the perception of the viewer or artist. In narrative, for example, the perception of the manifold different ways in which language can be used—its various simultaneous possible functions—itself becomes, by a recursive operation, the object of perception.

Once again, Luhmann's difference-theoretical account of communicative systems—and in particular his concept of second-order observation—helps clarify the recursion at stake here. For Luhmann, as we saw in Sect. 2, the act of observing

---

[9]Bühler points out that the etymology of common Indo-European words for "sign" (e.g., *Zeichen* (sign), σῆμα (sign), δείξις (pointing), *signum*, etc.) characteristically refers to "a showing (or a revealing) of things to the viewer, or the other way round, leading the viewer (the viewing gaze) to the things" (Bühler 1990, p. 44).

involves making a distinction in which only one side, the "marked" side, is visible in indicating the distinction. There remains an "unmarked space"—that is, the space from which the observer makes the distinction. "At the same time," Luhmann continues, "the observer—in drawing a distinction—makes himself visible to others. He betrays his presence—even if a further distinction is required to distinguish him" (Luhmann 2000, p. 54). In second-order observation, where one "observes an observer", one "pays attention to how they observe" (Luhmann 2013, p. 111) and in doing so, in distinguishing the distinction they are making, one reveals the unmarked space of the original distinction: "Second-order observation is observation of an observer with a view to that which he cannot see" (p. 112). At the same time, a second-order observation is also a first-order observation, it is not a free-floating, God-like omniscience: "the second-order observer remains anchored in the world (and accordingly observable). And he sees only what he can distinguish" (Luhmann 2000, p. 56).

But it is a mistake, according to Luhmann, to think of observation merely in terms of "subjects". From a difference-theoretical perspective, observation is an operation that is carried out by a communication in making a distinction: "One speaks about something specific and thematizes what one is speaking about. Thus, one uses a distinction; one speaks about *this* and nothing else" (Luhmann 2000, p. 105). Modern societies, according to Luhmann, have developed, through their increasing functional differentiation and complexity, "communicative systems" that are based on this kind of second-order observation. The "art system" is only one example of such systems: other examples he cites includes the law, science, education and politics (Luhmann 2000, pp. 63–65; 2013, pp. 115–116). To elaborate on just one of these examples: scientists carry out first-order observations in their laboratories, but the autopoiesis of the scientific system occurs at the level of second-order observation, when these first-order observations, mediated by publication in peer-reviewed journals, are subjected to the scrutiny of other scientists, who are now able to observe the mode of observation of the original scientists (Luhmann 2000, p. 63).

What distinguishes the art system from these other second-order systems is that it produces perceptible objects or events marked by the kind of operative closure outlined in Sect. 2. The distinct boundary, the form, marked out in each of the recursive operations by which the artwork is constructed, presents an object for the joint attention of artist and perceivers: the art system in general has developed "the specialised function of orchestrating second-order observations" (p. 67) in the form of perceptible events/objects. In narrative fiction the observation of observation is particularly explicit and thematised—for in this case, as I explore further in Sect. 4, the reader is constantly invited to observe the mimetic representation of narrators and characters. "Narratives," as Bruce Clarke writes, "beckon us to reconstruct their virtual structures as the actual traces of other observers, to experience those narrations as observing systems and not just as sequential semiotic structures" (Clarke 2014, p. 96).

4   Coupling

My starting-point was that Aristotle's *Poetics* is about *poiēsis*—making. It is framed as a practical guide to making tragedy (and, as a subsidiary topic, epic—a second part of the treatise, on comedy, was lost). A large part of the book is concerned with practical, prescriptive advice on the construction of the tragic plot (*muthos*), which Aristotle regards as the most important aspect of making a tragedy. The definition of tragedy which Aristotle gives near the beginning is highly specific:

> A tragedy [...] is the imitation [*mimēsis*] of an action that is serious and also, as having magnitude, complete in itself; in language with pleasurable accessories, each kind brought in separately in the parts of the work; in a dramatic, not in a narrative form; with incidents arousing pity and fear, wherewith to accomplish its catharsis of such emotions (Aristotle 1941, p. 1460 [1449b]).

Thus tragedy, for Aristotle, has an end or purpose that is located in the reaction of the audience—it is the function of tragedy to produce that particular interaction with the audience. And "catharsis" is not merely an emotional spasm, a response to a stimulus, but a process with important cognitive and ethical dimensions.[10] Amélie Rorty identifies three sources for Aristotle's use of the term: a medical usage, referring to a therapeutic cleansing or purgation; a religious usage, referring to the ritualized expression of dangerous emotions; and its use as "a cognitive term referring to an intellectual resolution or clarification that involves directing emotions to their appropriate intentional objects" (Rorty 1992a, b, p. 14). She goes on to put forward a modern analogy in terms of the psychotherapeutic notion of "working through":

> Like a therapeutic *working through*, catharsis occurs at the experienced sense of closure. In recognizing and re-cognizing the real directions of their attitudes, the members of an audience are able to feel them appropriately; and by experiencing them in their clarified and purified forms, in a ritually defined and bounded setting, they are able to experience, however briefly, the kind of psychological functioning, the balance and harmony that self-knowledge can bring to action (Rorty 1992a, b, p. 15).

The role of the Aristotelian audience is thus an enactive one in which the audience brings to the encounter with the mimetic representation emotional responses which have cognitive dimensions and which are also expressions of ethical or social norms.[11] It is the function of tragedy to fulfil the end or *telos* of this particular interaction, which lies at the juncture of, on the one hand, the tragedy's *poiēsis*, its

---

[10]"Aristotle conceives of the tragic emotions not as overwhelming waves of feeling, but as part of an integrated response to the structured material of poetic drama: the framework for the experience of these emotions is nothing other than the cognitive understanding of the mimetic representation of human action and character" (Halliwell 1986, pp. 173–174). The "Poetics" should be read in the context of Aristotle's wider views about the positive role played by the emotions in cognition (Belfiore 1992, pp. 181–225).

[11]Elizabeth Belfiore has drawn attention, in particular, to the role of the notion of *philia*—roughly "kinship", though extending to other relationships of mutual obligation and respect (Belfiore 1992, pp. 70–81): "*Philia* is of primary importance in Aristotle's theory of tragedy. Because the individual

design and crafting, and, on the other hand, the normative emotional response of the audience.

The relationship between *poiēsis* and catharsis is thus one of mutual constraint: the tragedian is constrained by the end of catharsis to adopt a particular approach to plot-construction, and the audience, as we have seen, is constrained by the *poiēsis* of the mimetic representation to make particular actions and events the object of its emotional response. Both sides of the interaction are systems. On the *poiēsis* side, running through Aristotle's account of the construction of tragedy is an analogy with the way different parts and functions are co-ordinated towards a unified end in a living organism (Belfiore 1992, pp. 56–57). The key term here is *sustasis,* variously translated as "structure", "organization" or "system".[12] On the other side, too—the side of the audience as opposed to the mimetic representation—we find, rather than a unitary, elemental response, a complex interaction of cognitive, emotional and normative aspects.

From the perspective of twentieth-century views on art, what is striking about Aristotle's *Poetics*, what makes it distinctly "classical" in its outlook, is its insistence on a single norm guiding the work. Jan Mukařovský's essay "The Aesthetic Norm" (1937) gives us, by contrast, a characteristically modern, pluralistic picture. In the art of any period, he writes, "we can always distinguish the simultaneous activity of several different systems of norms" (Mukařovský 1937, p. 51). Furthermore, in a single work a "complex tangle of norms" may contend for attention, some positively endorsed, others making their presence felt in a "negative" way, through their deliberate and conspicuous violation (p. 52) Yet this important difference—attributable, in Luhmann's terms, to the autopoietic internal differentiation of the modern "art system"—should not blind us to the commonalities between, on the one hand, Mukařovský's view of the relationship between norm, function and system, and, on the other hand, that of Aristotle. For Mukařovský, the significance of a norm is that it implements the "realization" of a function (one might say, in the terms we used in Sect. 3, that it "observes" the function). This realization of the function is characterized in Aristotelian, teleological terms, and also in terms of its operating as a constraint:

> Because such a realization [of the function] presupposes an activity tending towards a specific goal, we must admit that the limitation by which this activity is organized has in itself the character of energy as well (Mukařovský 1937, p. 49).

---

parts of the plot and the plot structure as a whole involve *philia*, it determines in large part the emotional response of the audience" (p. 70).

[12]One of the key benefits, for Aristotle, of mimetic representations is that experience of their *sustasis* helps us better appreciate the systems and structures found in the natural world and in ourselves (Belfiore 1992, pp. 68–70). As Belfiore summarises Aristotle's perspective: "We understand systematically, and this know ourselves, through contemplation of the natural 'systems' (or 'structures': *sustēmata, sustaseis*) in nature that are imitated in craft products" (Belfiore 1992, pp. 69–70).

A norm is a limitation, a constraint, that provides "energy" for the realization of functions—it is a "regulating energetic principle" (p. 49). It is to be distinguished from a rule, in that it may resist codification: the limitations it imposes may not be expressible in words (pp. 49–50).

In Aristotle and Mukařovský, then, we find, in embryo, the notion of a non-causal relationship of mutual constraint between systems. But the systems here are seen in terms of the traditional opposition of subject and object (the audience/reader on one side, the artwork (e.g., the fictional narrative) on the other), either in the form of Aristotelian catharsis and *poiēsis*, or, as we saw above, of Mukařovský's interface, set into operation by the "aesthetic function", between the "whole" of the aesthetic sign and the "whole" of the subject's existence. Luhmann goes beyond this by supplanting the subject/object dichotomy with the "structural coupling" of perception and communication.

Luhmann adapts the notion of "structural coupling" between systems from Humberto Maturana (Luhmann 2013, pp. 84–85). Coupling involves a reduction of complexity, since it is highly selective with regard to the environment of the system (p. 85). The brain, for example, is coupled with the external environment via the "narrow bandwidth" of the sense organs, especially eye and ear (p. 86). Particularly important and productive for human beings are the constraints generated by the coupling of consciousness and communication, both of which are autopoietic systems, but which only occur in the form of this structural coupling (p. 86). [In this case, Luhmann suggests, the original coupling mechanism—the "narrow band-width" that constrains both sides—is language (p. 87).] The artwork serves the specific function of systematically coupling consciousness (perception) and communication ("psychic and social systems"):

> Art makes perception available for communication, and it does so outside the standardized forms of a language (that, for its part, is perceptible). Art cannot overcome the separation between psychic and social systems. Both types of system remain operatively inaccessible to each other. *And this accounts for the significance of art.* Art integrates perception and communication without merging or confusing their respective operations. Integration means nothing more than that disparate systems operate simultaneously and constrain one another's freedom (Luhmann 2000, p. 48).

Art, Luhmann writes, "makes perception available for communication", but he could as well have written "makes communication available for perception". In Sect. 3 I outlined how, for Aristotle, mimetic representation makes a communication (language, for example) available for perception as an observable and reproducible event or object (language becomes a narration). Another way putting this is that among the objects we can perceive are (communicative) signs. But at the same time, those signs stand for objects (Marianne Moore's "real toads in an imaginary garden"), so that (as we saw with Bühler's joint attentional approach to language) communication and perception are tightly coupled at this level too. We have entered the realm of recursive second-order observation, the observation of observation, where the "form re-enters the form". It is in this sense, that, as we have said,

Luhmann, in his formulation, could have entered the cycle of perception and communication at any point.[13]

It is through this process of mutual constraint as between perceptual and communicative systems (superseding the subject/object dichotomy) that "communication through art tends towards system formation and eventually differentiates a social system of art" (Luhmann 2000, p. 49). Our concern here is how this model can be seen to manifest itself in narrative fiction. Elsewhere (Lively 2014, pp. 36–111) I have explored how the development of narrative fiction can be described in terms of the affordances it offers (especially with the transitions to written and printed forms) for a process of recursive embedding, whereby signs standing for joint attentional communication themselves become the objects of joint attention. In medieval tale collections (*Scheherazade*, Boccaccio's *Decameron*, Chaucer's *Canterbury Tales*), for example, the narrator is personified and observed (pp. 70–83). In Cervantes' *Don Quixote*, narrators and characters become nodes in a labyrinthine network of recursive joint attentional perspectives (pp. 84–99). In the late nineteenth- and twentieth-century use of Free Indirect Discourse we find the development of an oscillatory cycle of perception and communication (utterance) to evoke, at the level of discourse itself, the phenomenology of experience (Lively 2014, pp. 238–253). All these cases can be seen as recursive, autopoietic elaborations ("ornaments", to use a term of Luhmann's (2000, p. 120)) of that original moment of mimetic representation when the actor playing Oedipus stood before his audience and spoke his line—when communication was perceived and perception communicated.

5   Conclusion

This chapter has outlined three themes that I take to be central to any autopoietic approach to narrative. In Sect. 2 I discussed narrative as a form of communication that, through its own internal operations, closes itself off in order to present itself as an object (a mimetic representation, in Aristotle's terms) for perception. In Sect. 3 I outlined how operations that produce this closure take the form of recursive observations of observations (or observations of observations of observations etc.) whereby, as Mukařovský's concept of "contexture" clarifies, the narrative constitutes what one might think of as a continuously morphing but closed "state space" of potential and actualized functions. According to this perspective, actualization of functions (any particular path through the state space, if you will) will depend, in Luhmann's terms, on the constraints of an observing system such as a reader. But

---

[13]This is not to imply that there is a stable "symmetry" to the coupling of perception and communication in art: indeed, there may be a "runaway" gearing towards perception in the art system—hence modern art in which the demands of perception test the limits of communication (Umberto Eco's "open work"—e.g., James Joyce's *Finnegans Wake*) (Luhmann 2000, p. 77).

this coupling itself is dependent (it is impossible to say which comes "first") on the coupling whereby the narrative makes itself available simultaneously as communication and object of perception: it is this constraint that has been particularly productive in the development of narrative fiction, and that has determined narrative fiction's particular fulfilment of Luhmann's stipulation that "a work qualifies as art only when *it employs constraints for the sake of increasing the work's freedom in disposing over further constraints*" (Luhmann 2000, p. 35; emphasis in the original).

References

Aristotle (1941) Poetics (trans: I Bywater). In: McKeon R (ed) The basic works of Aristotle. Random House, New York, pp 1453–1487

Bakhtin M (1990) Author and hero in aesthetic activity (trans: V Liapunov). In: Holquist M, Liapunov V (eds) Art and answerability: early philosophical essays. University of Texas Press, Austin, pp 4–256

Barthes R (1986) The reality effect (trans R Howard). In: The rustle of language. Blackwell, Oxford, pp 141–148

Belfiore ES (1992) Tragic pleasures: Aristotle on plot and emotion. Princeton University Press, Princeton

Bühler K (1990) Theory of language: the representational function of language [1934] (trans: DF Goodwin). John Benjamins. In: Amsterdam

Clarke B (2014) Neocybernetics and narrative. University of Minnesota Press, Minneapolis

Eilan N, Hoerl C, McCormack T, Roessler J (eds) (2005) Joint attention: communication and other minds. Oxford University Press, Oxford

Halliwell S (1986) Aristotle's poetics. Duckworth, London

Kosman A (1992) Acting: drama as the mimēsis of praxis. In: Rorty (ed.), pp. 51–72.

Lively A (2014) Mediation and dynamics in the experience of narrative fiction. PhD Thesis, Royal Holloway, University of London. https://mdx.academia.edu/AdamLively

Luhmann N (2000) Art as a social system (trans: EM Knodt). Stanford University Press. In: Stanford

Luhmann N (2013) Introduction to systems theory (trans: P Gilgen). In: D Baecker (ed) Polity Press, Cambridge

Mukařovský J (1937) The aesthetic norm. In: Mukařovský, vol 1977, pp 49–56

Mukařovský J (1977) Structure, sign and function: selected essays by Jan Mukařovský (trans: J Burbank, P Steiner). Yale University Press, New Haven

Ricoeur P (1984) Time and narrative (trans: K McLaughlin, D Pellauer). University of Chicago Press, Chicago, p 1

Rorty AO (1992a) The psychology of Aristotelian tragedy, in Rorty (1992b). pp 1–22

Rorty AO (ed) (1992b) Essays on Aristotle's poetics. Princeton University Press, Princeton

Spencer-Brown G (1969) The laws of form. Allen and Unwin, London

Steiner P (1977) Jan Mukařovský's structural aesthetics. In: Mukařovský, vol 1977, pp ix–xxxix

Sternberg M (1992) Telling in time (II): chronology, teleology, narrativity. Poet Today 13(3): 463–541

Tomasello M (1999) The cultural origins of human cognition. Harvard University Press, Cambridge

Chapter 10
Looking at Narrative as a Complex System: The Proteus Principle

Federico Pianzola

Abstract I am here proposing a strategy of consolidation for narrative studies. Disciplines and paradigms have their own specificities, which implicitly shape how we approach narrative phenomena. To make explicit such processes of selection and contextualization is an act of intellectual honesty and I suggest how to do it in three simple steps: (i) adopting a systemic perspective, (ii) distinguishing between logical levels, (iii) employing the Proteus Principle in the formation of theories. Narrative is seen and used in many different ways that can be conceived as systems, i.e. considering that the properties of narrative cannot be studied in isolation but are interconnected in a network of relations where all the components are influencing each other.

1 Introduction

In every scientific inquiry definitions are important because they determine what aspects of the defined phenomenon are to be considered necessary for the phenomenon to occur, and which of them are to be subjected to analysis and theorization. For instance, if we define narrative as a sequence of events, then narrative theory should be concerned with how other aspects of the discourse and context are related to its sequentiality. Whereas, if we base our definition on "experientiality" (Fludernik 1996; Caracciolo 2014), then matters of agentiality, perspective, perception and cognition become relevant and crucial for the description of narrative phenomena.

Nowadays the increasing complexity and variety of narratives is challenging narratologists to reconsider many of the concepts and tools elaborated so far, since their applicability and descriptive power is facing serious troubles due to some interesting changes in the semiosphere, like the popularity of transmedial narratives, the interactivity allowed by digital media and not least the growing audience's awareness of the strategies used to tell a story. Here I argue that looking at narrative

F. Pianzola (✉)
Department of Human Sciences for Education, University of Milan-Bicocca, Milan, Italy
e-mail: federico.pianzola@unimib.it

© Springer Nature Switzerland AG 2018
R. Walsh, S. Stepney (eds.), *Narrating Complexity*,
https://doi.org/10.1007/978-3-319-64714-2_10

as a complex system can help to grasp the richness of this domain of research and also help to adapt to the changing landscape the most useful instruments elaborated by narratology. My hope is to contribute to the consolidation of narrative studies making the efforts of different researches and disciplines toward the same object of study converge.

I want to suggest a way for interdisciplinary collaboration in narrative studies, inspired by systems theory, but in order to do so I need to preliminarily extend systemic thinking to the object of study itself. Therefore, before talking about interdisciplinarity, I focus on how to define narrative in systemic terms.[1]

The basic assumption of the present volume is that narrative is "the semiotic articulation of linear temporal sequence" (Walsh, Chap. 2). The premises in this definition are that (i) all our experiences occur in a temporal dimension and (ii) time is usually simplified in a linear model. The crucial point is that in some cases (in narratives) we interact with this linearity articulating it in a semiotic way, i.e., giving meaning to it. Although Walsh does not further specify the qualities of this semiotic articulation, I maintain that looking at narrative as a complex system means conceiving the semiotic articulation as a non-linear phenomenon:

> *Definition 1.* Narrativity is a property emerging from the organisation of a system constituted by interdependent components interacting over time in non-linear ways.

More specifically, I claim that narrativity is an *emergent behaviour* of a system coupled to certain contexts, i.e., a property which is only present when the scope of the system under scrutiny is expanded to include its environment as well (Bar Yam 2004; Ryan 2007). In the case of narrative, the environment typically includes the audience. This kind of approach is promoted by systems theory, a worldview that shifts the emphasis of theoretical description from individual parts to the organiza-tion of parts, conceiving the interactions and correlations between the properties of a system not as static and constant but as dynamic processes (Bánáthy 1997).

In this volume, Merja Polvinen (Chap. 7) summarizes different ways in which cognition has been described and the approach presented in her Sect. 4, "Enacting Complexity", is inspired by systems theory: "understanding the complex interplay of brain, body, and world requires the tools and methods of nonlinear dynamical systems theory" (Thompson and Varela 2001, p. 418). I think that narrative can be conceived in the same terms, considering the nonlinear interactions between brain, body, discourse and environment.

Many of the contributions in this volume deal with the problem of representing complex systems and emergent behaviours through narrative, that is, they are concerned with what we can do with narrative: can we use it to represent emergent behaviour? However, in this chapter I am also focusing on what narrative is,

---

[1]In light of the interdisciplinary orientation of this volume, I am here focusing on scientific conceptions of complexity and system. Cf. Steiner (1984, pp. 99–137) for an historical overview of philosophical influences that led Russian formalists (especially Tynjanov) to develop a systemic view of literature and narrative. And cf. Pier (2017) for a more recent attempt at understanding narratology in terms of systems and complexity.

claiming that it is narrative in the first place that is to be characterized in terms of emergent behaviour. To say that narrativity is emergent does not directly affect what we can achieve with it, because the two are matters concerning systems of different scope, as I will show.

I focus in particular on how the same attitude at the base of systemic thinking is already shaping some narrative theories. Namely, it can be found in Meir Sternberg's work (1992, 2010) about narrative universals (suspense, curiosity and surprise): systemic thinking informs Sternberg's Proteus Principle (PP), the many-to-many correlation between forms and functions (1982), an operative rule that makes his narrative theory radically different from the majority of other theories.

In Sect. 2 I deal with an implicit assumption of narrative theories, namely how we select our object of research; in Sect. 3 I explain how the PP is put into work in the formulation of theories; and in Sect. 4 I suggest how the PP can be used to compare narrative theories of different kind and scope, granting operative interaction between concepts, models and theories developed and used in different paradigms and disciplines.

2   Theoretical Premises

2.1   What Is a Theory?

"Narratologies aren't empirical generalizations but more or less systematized schemes of conceptual stipulations. Such (schemes of) concepts cannot be validated empirically; rather, they have to be evaluated with regard to criteria like, for example, applicability, simplicity, coherence, unity, etc." (Kindt 2009, p. 42). With this claim Kindt is stressing that our knowledge of a phenomenon is at least partly shaped by the framework adopted in our observations, thus throwing into relief the rhetorical and constructive aspect of every theory. According to this view, in formulating and evaluating a theory our attention should be directed toward how we "systematize" and "stipulate" our knowledge of a phenomenon. As stated by Antonio Gramsci:

> what interests science is not so much the objectivity of reality but people, who elaborate research methods, who continually rectify the material instruments that reinforce their sensory organs and logical instruments for discrimination and verification—that is, culture, that is, world-view, that is, the relationship between people and reality mediated by technology (Gramsci 1975, p. 1457; quoted by Suvin 2010b, p. 88).

The PP has its roots in this kind of scientific attitude: what is required for its adoption is a widening of focus, from the phenomenon to the role we have in its occurrence and in its description. That is, a shift from an epistemology of representation to an epistemology of construction (von Glaserfeld 1990). What matters for the sake of my reflections is the framework within which we exercise our theoretical activity, rather than the different ontological positions that can be associated to a constructivist epistemology. Namely, I am interested in understanding on which basis we assume a theory to be correct and informative: on what ground do we say we know what narrative is? What criteria do we use to judge the effectiveness and accuracy of our theories? I am talking about how we map the territory of narratives, although I am aware that the map is often mistaken for the territory (Bateson 1987, pp. 458–461).

Formulating a theory is like mapping a territory and, in this respect, adopting a constructivist epistemology means taking into account in our theoretical activity the process of designing the map, be it a mental model or an explicit theory. A map is a model produced in a relationship between the observer (a system able of cognitive and aesthetic processes, and equipped with tools for observations) and the territory (a system composed of many parts organized in a dynamic network of relations), it is not a mere representation of the territory. To such extent, "theories are not true or false but good or bad instruments for research. Reality is in principle prior to human thought, yet it is co-created by human understanding, in a never-ending feedback" (Suvin 2010b, p. 80). Every theory is constructed by an observer who tries to understand and synthesize her experience, thus a theory which tries to map narrative only on the basis of its discursive components is overcoming the role of the observer, who is anyway always involved in the co-creation of the observed phenomena.

2.2 Narrative Organization and Narrative Structure

In this light, the phenomenon to be subjected to our theoretical activity should be a system composed by some 'elements' in interaction with the environment, and thus with the observer too. The focus of the theory then will be on the relations between the selected elements and the environment—the discourse–audience relations[2]—and on the parts–whole relations (von Bertalanffy 1968), i.e., the relations between discursive elements and their effect on the audience's experience of the discourse as a whole. An example of this attitude is the following:

> Definition 2. I define narrativity as the play of suspense/curiosity/surprise between represented and communicative time (in whatever combination, whatever medium, whatever manifest or latent form). (Sternberg 1992, p. 529)

This definition assumes the discourse's environment to be crucial for the perception of narrativity, since suspense, curiosity or surprise are not properties of the

---

[2]I am here assuming that the audience's experience of a discourse is always situated in a certain context, thus I use the term *audience* synecdochically, referring to a situated cognitive and aesthetic experience. Moreover, I would like to specify that I am using the terms *audience* and *discourse*—drawn from the rhetorical tradition—because I think they sound more familiar in the context of narrative studies. However, if narrative is conceived as a mode of cognition (Hutto 2008; Herman 2013) *agent* and *stimuli* might be more adequate terms, general enough to be used in every context, like, for instance, when I imagine a tiger jumping on my desk interrupting my writing (cf. Caracciolo 2014, pp. 93–109).

discourse, rather they emerge in interaction with the audience, namely in those kind of interactions occurring between the perception of represented and communicative time.

Theories adopting this framework approach their object of study describing our processes of cognition, our aesthetic experiences and our construction of knowledge, i.e., our interactions with an 'object,' not the 'structure of an object.' What emerges from the encounter between two entities (the system under scrutiny and the environment, another system) is a certain kind of *organization* of the discursive system in relation to a certain kind of environment; whereas the *structure* is the actual configuration of components by which a specific system reaches that kind of organization (Maturana and Varela 1980, p. 77). For instance, *Definition 2* specifies what the narrative *organization* of a system is, whereas the following definition describes a specific kind of narrative *structure*:

> *Definition 3.* A narrative (Fr. *récit*; Ger. *Erzählung*) is a representation of a possible world in a linguistic and/or visual medium, at whose centre there are one or several protagonists of an anthropomorphic nature who are existentially anchored in a temporal and spatial sense and who (mostly) perform goal-directed actions (action and plot structure). (Fludernik 2009, p. 6)

Definition 3 specifies what elements a discourse must necessarily represent in order to be identified as a narrative, hence it focuses on the structure of the discursive system, because it lists the properties of the components and not the relations between them. Although it is formulated by a different author, this definition could be part of a specific actualization of the narrative organization indicated in *Definition 2*. That is: under certain conditions, the play of suspense/curiosity/surprise between represented and communicative time is achieved by representing a possible world, at whose centre there are one or several protagonists of an anthropomorphic nature who are existentially anchored in a temporal and spatial sense and who (mostly) perform goal-directed actions. However, according to *Definition 2* this condition is not sufficient, since it does not specify either the interdependence between the system elements or their relation to the environment.

In order to take into account the role the context and the audience play in the co-creation of the observed phenomenon, a theory whose aim is to identify the constitutive properties of a specific kind of system should focus on the organization of the system, i.e., on how audience and discourse interact. To put it bluntly, the specificity of narrative should be searched in the way the discourse–audience system is organized.[3] This is the key of the shift from an epistemology of representation to

---

[3]A similar attitude is shown by Gilbert Ryle (1949) and Ludwig Wittgenstein (1953) when they claim that the phrase "the meaning of something" is not referential and does not pick out any object as a meaning, it simply points out the way in which we use something (a term). The focus is upon our relationship to the term, upon our act of relating it to a state of the world, not on the state of the world itself. Referentiality is just one aspect of that relationship. In a similar way, a theory is just one way of knowing what a narrative is: unavoidably it is the most relevant in academia, but in other contexts we can claim to know what narrative is on the ground of some practice or beliefs that do not have a conceptual form (cf. Wittgenstein 1969).

an epistemology of construction: the basis on which narrative is perceived/defined is a network of dynamic relations, not a group of objects or their properties. In this light, as anticipated in *Definition 1*, in the present work I use the term *narrativity* as indicating the degree of narrative organization of a system.

An important aspect of this kind of approach is that the distinction between *organization* and *structure* is seen as a choice instrumental to the description of the system, not as something intrinsic to it. That is to say, in formulating a narrative theory we identify what is peculiar to all and only the discourse–audience interactions that we usually call narratives, i.e., a specific kind of organization among all the possible kinds of interactions between audience and discourse. Once we have that model, we should be able to use it in the description of various phenomena in which that specific kind of organization occurs. In other words, we should be able to understand how that kind of organization is achieved through different structures in different contexts: how narrativity emerges in novels, dramatic performances, video games, oral conversations, etc. In brief, once we have a model of the system organization we can use it to understand the structures of various systems, what we need is just to develop an ability to perceive that organizational pattern. I say more about this in Sect. 3.3.

When we put theories at work we should bear in mind that the distinction between organization and structure is linked to the scope of our observations. For instance, if we believe that some discursive elements (events, agents, storyworld, etc.) are crucial for the narrative organization of a certain system, we are focusing on their role as individual components of the whole discourse–audience system we are observing, not as components of the smaller discursive system. That is to say, for the purpose of understanding the narrativity we experience, we are deliberately conceiving them as structural elements of the narrative organization of the discourse-audience system, not for the role they have as structural elements of the discourse organization alone. From this perspective, if we maintain, for instance, that the representation of time is necessary for narrativity to emerge, then we will take into account temporal markers (tenses, adverbs, etc.) for the role they have in shaping the discourse–audience relations, and not for the role they have in, let's say, discursive cohesion. These are processes of abstractions that inevitably occur in every theorization, and to be aware of that is of great importance in order not to mistake the map for the territory. This is quite clear in cases like *Definition 2*—no one would think that suspense, curiosity or surprise are elements immanent to the discourse—but can be trickier if we are working with concepts like those used in *Definition 3*, because we could be heuristically induced to think that some structural elements are indeed necessary and sufficient for narrative organization, whereas it might be the case that they only occur under certain conditions, not having any direct and linear correlation to the narrativity of the system. For instance, the spatial anchoring to a possible world of a protagonist and her performance of goal-directed actions also occur in argumentative and descriptive texts: e.g., Venice is in Italy, I am writing this chapter in Venice, therefore I am writing in Italy.

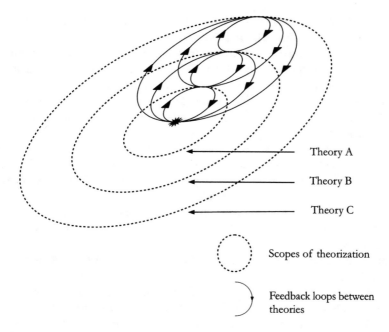

Theory A

Theory B

Theory C

Scopes of theorization

Feedback loops between
theories

Fig. 10.1 Bateson's typology arranged in a spatial model (Tosey et al. 2012, p. 300, modified)

2.3   Theories: Scope and Logical Types

What I am trying to underline is that for the purpose of our descriptions we distinguish concepts of different logical type. Gregory Bateson applied Bertrand Russell's Theory of Logical Types to the concept of *learning* (Bateson 1987, pp. 284–314) and I think it can be usefully applied to the processes of theory formation as well. A theory is a conceptual model of how we organize our experiences, and as there are different logical types of organization—systems and sub-systems of different scope, like the experience of an event, the experience of a narrative or the experience of a breach of the canonical (Bruner 1990)—so there are theories of different logical type. Figure 10.1 displays how they interact in a systemic framework.

In Fig. 10.1, different theorizations are arranged "as concentric circles to represent the idea that each successive level extends beyond the boundary of, and includes, the previous level. Learning at 'higher' levels means that new premises with a successively wider scope are involved" (Tosey et al. 2012, p. 299). In a similar way, the choice to focus on the discourse–audience system is a premise of wider scope than the choice to describe the components of the discourse system only.

Figure 10.1 also introduces feedback loops from each level to all of the prior levels, and vice versa. These loops represent the central principle of recursion, which is that causality flows from cause to effect and back again, [. . .]. The diagram looks complex, which is precisely our point; recursion involves greater complexity than, and is more dynamic than, a linear hierarchy (p. 299).

The frame we choose for our theories is never hermetically isolated: information of different logical types interacts and our knowledge is recursively shaped at every level, e.g., our knowledge of the components of discourse affects our knowledge of the discourse–audience interactions, and in turn our knowledge of those discourse–audience interactions that we call narratives affects our perception and description of the discourse components.

The levels are not to be considered as having actual extent: this is a model of our activity of knowledge construction and theorization. For instance, looking at the narrativity of a system we are imposing a certain conceptual hierarchy onto the system, considering its narrative organization more relevant than other aspects; but if we look at the argumentative organization of the system it might be that narrative organization intervenes *as* part of the argumentation. The scope of every system is postulated by our observation, and the distinction of logical types is "exclusively a feature of the description and pertains to a frame of reference defined by the observer" (Maturana and Varela 1980, p. 110). In Sects. 3 and 4 I show how a distinction between logical types is crucial both to the application of the Proteus Principle and to my proposal for a dialogue between narrative paradigms, but now I would like to briefly clarify what are the implications of focusing on the discourse–audience interactions.

According to Bateson, "communicators always live in a forked universe of being both participants and observers" and "they must be able to handle the very different perspectives that this situation engenders" (Harrier-Jones 2004, p. 150). Focusing on the relations between audience and discourse is a way to acknowledge the impossibility to transcend our role as participants that somehow co-construct the phenomena that we observe. We formulate theories that describe ourselves as part of the system, but distinguishing between logical types does not mean that we are taking a privileged perspective on the phenomenon—a God's-eye theory (Putnam 1981). This is because we are constrained "to reflect on our concepts and beliefs from the internal perspective of having to use them even as we investigate them. There is no external point from which we can view our conceptual scheme" (Grayling 2010, p. 771). Distinguishing between logical types and focusing on the discourse–audience system are ways to cope with these epistemological boundaries, making explicit the scope, aim, limits and possibilities of each theory, and thus trying to be aware of them.

In the face of this complexity, the effort of complexity science is directed toward a normative definition of a system's organization, in order to have a model that could also be used for a formalised study of it. One solution proposed to do that is to define an emergent property of a system (e.g., narrativity) as constituted in relation to a certain scope: "Rather than just describing what emergent properties are like, our definition prescribes the conditions whereby a property should be formally considered to be emergent" (Ryan 2007, p. 76). I now show how this choice has been adopted in narrative studies by Meir Sternberg, even though no reference to complexity science can be found in his work.

3   The Proteus Principle: A Pattern for Many Theories

3.1   The Proteus Principle in the Light of Systems Theory

The PP—introduced in narrative studies by Meir Sternberg (1982)—states that there is a many-to-many correlation between forms and functions, i.e., different forms can serve the same purpose (e.g., to be necessary for narrativity, like events are often considered to be) and a form can serve different purposes (e.g., to participate in both narrative and argumentative organization, like the *post hoc ergo propter hoc* linking of propositions; Pier 2008). Using Maturana and Varela's terminology: narrative organization can be realized by many different structures, and those same structures can also participate in other kinds of organization.

A theory describing the organization of a system does not specify the properties of the components which realize the actual system, it only specifies in which ways the components must interact to constitute the system as a unity. Therefore, the organization of a system is independent of the properties of its components, which can be any, and a given kind of system can be constituted in many different ways by many different components, as far as they organize themselves following a certain pattern (Maturana and Varela 1980, p. 77).

Maturana and Varela's epistemology is not too different from that of Bateson since the concepts of *structure, organization, system, context* and *domain* are hierarchically distinguished in a logical typology and can refer to different 'things' depending on the scope of our observations. Similarly, Sternberg's terms *form* and *function* refer to roles that can be attributed to elements of different logical type according to the scope of the theory.[4] For instance, both a represented event and a sequence of sentences can be *forms*, although they concern parts of discourse of different scope. And both generating suspense about the outcome of an event and "finding an intentional state that mitigates or at least makes comprehensible a deviation from a canonical cultural pattern" (Bruner 1990, pp. 49–50) can be *functions*, although the respective effects concern contexts of different scope. *Form* and *function* are not fixed concepts, they are relational concepts (cf. Steiner 1984, p. 87): they can be applied to different things (elements, properties, strategies, effects) depending on the scope of our observations and on the context to which the object/process under scrutiny is coupled.

A systemic approach to narrative focuses on the discourse–audience system and is ruled by the following principles:

- depending on the context, different structures (forms) can have the function of generating a specific kind of organization (narrativity);

---

[4]Alternative schemes of concepts where a similar logical distinction is made are: "form–device–material" or "frame–device–form," used respectively by the Russian Formalists and Skalin (2008, p. 209).

- narrativity is a form that can have many functions (aesthetic, cognitive, social, educational, etc.).

Let us consider how the PP actually works in the formulation of a narrative theory. The starting hypothesis is that *narrative* is the name we give to a specific kind of relations between audience and discourse; thus, we set the scope of our theory to the discourse–audience system. The second step is to identify the network of relations that generate narrative organization, i.e., what interactions of the system's components are constitutive of narrative organization. At this point we have a basic theory of narrative, thanks to which we should be able to identify narrative organization in every discourse–audience system we consider.

For example:

> *Definition 4*. Narrative organization is the semiotic articulation of a linear temporal sequence. That is, the relation the audience has with a discourse whenever they are experiencing (giving meaning to) it with regard to its linear unfolding in time (cf. Walsh, Chap. 2).

In this case, the discourse–audience relation is semiotic in kind, more specifically we can talk of narrativity whenever the audience interaction with a discourse is organized according to a linear temporal sequence and it generates meaning by virtue of this interaction. It should be noted that, even though the linear unfolding in time of discourse is crucial for the emergence of narrativity, nonetheless the relations the audience develops with this linear temporal sequence are non-linear:

> [a narrative's] own dynamic production of meaning (that is, the process of its primary articulation, but also the process of any subsequent interpretation of it) is a manifestly non-linear process involving a geometrical proliferation of significant relations with each meaningful unit that is introduced (Walsh, Chap. 2).

Two things are noteworthy in such a framework: (i) the scope of the theory is limited to a description of how the relations between system components are organized as narrative, without requiring any subspecific property of the components (it is not required that the discourse represent something specific, or that the audience have a specific attitude or knowledge); (ii) the contexts and functions of narrative organization are not specified either, acknowledging that narratives can be used with different purposes, and allowing the theory to be tested with different sorts of discourses. Furthermore, this kind of theory can potentially be enriched, integrated, contextualized by various disciplines and applied to different fields of research. The Proteus Principle can be used as a rule for the formation of theories with different scope and can help avoiding confusion between logical types, which can hinder the viability of a theory and possibly lead to misguiding results. Regarding (i), for instance, if we want to specify what properties are more likely to enable the system components to interact and generate narrative organization, then we should reduce the scope of our theory and consider those interacting components as a system whose organization we are then going to describe. That is to say, we have to reframe the theory focusing on the relations between the properties of the components.

Definition 4 is an example of a narrative definition proposed for the first time in this book, so for the sake of clarity I am going to illustrate another theory, explicitly developed in compliance with the Proteus Principle.

3.2   Meir Sternberg's Narrative Theory[5]

Meir Sternberg's narrative theory (1978, 1992) goes as stated in *Definition 2*:

Definition 2. I define narrativity as the play of suspense/curiosity/surprise between represented and communicative time (in whatever combination, whatever medium, whatever manifest or latent form). (1992, p. 529)

Or, in another formulation:

Definition 2bis. Narrativity lives between the processes uniquely run together by the genre: actional and communicative, told and telling/reading sequence. This interplay between temporalities generates the three universal effects/interests/dynamics of prospection, retrospection, and recognition—suspense, curiosity, and surprise, for short. (2001, p. 117; emphasis mine)

In order to understand how it is informed by the PP let us have a look at its basic pattern. The named system components are: represented time (actional process, told sequence), and communicative time (telling/reading sequence). These components are necessary but not sufficient, and in fact the theory specifies their reciprocal relations, i.e., their organization: represented and communicative time interact and such relation generates dynamics of prospection (suspense effect), retrospection (curiosity effect), and recognition (surprise effect). This is a basic theory of narrative informed by the Proteus Principle.

Sternberg's theory seems more complex than the pattern I have outlined and it might be confusing to read of components that generate effects from which narrative organization is emerging. But the point is that organization is defined by a network of relations, not by specific elements, and relations within a system are complex: recursive causality (feedback loops) is an operative rule within the system itself—between components of the same logical type—just as it is operative between systems of different logical type (Bateson 1987, pp. 411–412). Thus, although it is true that action is represented in the discourse—and in formulating a theory it is much easier to start from 'objective data'—nonetheless, "the sense comes before the surface, operationally as well as hierarchically speaking, because it alone has the power to shape the data into the appropriate narrative design" (Sternberg 1992, p. 520). The narrative organization of the system "is not given in representation—much less in any predetermined form—but (re)constructed in communication to produce the generic interplay between times" (p. 521). This

---

[5]Other scholars who showed this epistemic attitude are, for instance, Francesco Orlando (1978) for literary theory, Darko Suvin (2010a, 1979) for theories of science fiction and utopia, and Nielsen et al. (2015a, b) for fictionality.

might seem a fallacious example of circular reasoning but it is not so in the framework of a constructivist epistemology, since evidential priority is given to the effects perceived by the observer—to our relationship to the discourse. That is to say, the foundation of the theory lies on a pragmatic condition (Passalacqua and Pianzola 2016; Grayling 2010).[6]

The Protean pattern at the core of Sternberg's theory is that narrativity is identified as a kind of organization, and such organization can be generated by many different structures. That is to say, it is not specified through which means the discourse–audience relations constitutive of narrative are generated—though in his works Sternberg gives various accounts of the possibilities offered by rhetoric and poetics for the achievement of narrative organization. For instance, regarding the audience's cognitive processes that can be involved in dynamics of recognition: "rather than being confined to any particular mental aspect or faculty singled out by this or that aesthetic—or method of analysis—surprise freely ranges over the entire mind brought into narrative play" (Sternberg 1992, p. 522). Overall,

> [a]long with its affective force, it may therefore play on such axes of response to discourse as the formal, the perceptual, the referential, the otherwise semantic or semanticized, the psychic, the aesthetic, the logical, the ideological, all variously interpenetrating. Or, given that our impressions and inferences are always in the making and can always be overtaken along the sequence by the unpredictable, the operation of surprise cuts across the boundaries of pattern-making, world-making, address-making, theme-and-judgment-making, and sense-making at large. Once unsettled, for example, continuity reveals itself behind time as discontinuity, the whole as at most a part, the univocal as ambiguous, the premise as a problem, the established fact as an open gap covered with or in error, the flat-looking agent as a mixture or a riddle, the straight face as an ironic mask, the omnicommunicative teller as suppressive or himself limited, ontological well-formedness as an epistemological trap and lesson for the subject caught in it. (pp. 522–523)

And specifically with respect to the properties of discourse:

> the distinctiveness of surprise relates to the manner and point of disordering, not (like catharsis) to the matter disordered into surprise-sequence. Accordingly, it subsumes and brings together all of the elements that make for retrospective enlightenment—for some hidden deformation of time and understanding, with a view to their belated reformation under the pressure of unforeseen (dis)closures. (p. 523)

Thus, for example, among the discursive elements that can cause an interplay between represented and communicative time leading to surprise there are: motive, character, perspective, interpersonal relations, a picture of society, the text's entire reality-model, deferred and piecemeal exposition, impressions made only to be unmade or remade in the sequel, etc. (p. 523).

---

[6]I subscribe to Wittgenstein's argument (1969, §204) that the epistemic regress problem is overcome by the assumption of transcendental conditions of experience that are *reasonable*—founded upon our *forms of life*—not logical. We do not doubt to know what narrative is—in Wittgenstein's terms: we know how to use the word *narrative*—and this is a ground solid enough to support our theoretical activity.

In complex systems, even with only three variables, not knowing the initial condition of one variable can lead the system to outcomes that are unpredictable. Imagine what this means for semiotic processes, where the most unknown variable is the audience. The relations between discursive properties and audience attitudes that can generate the three narrative dynamics are huge in number, since there are many possible discursive properties and audience attitudes, and consequently the number of possible interactions (structures) is exponentially bigger. Given such a number of possible initial conditions it cannot be predicted with certainty which discursive properties and audience attitudes generate the interplay between temporalities and the narrative dynamics. Nonetheless, it surely can be explored how frequent certain discursive properties and audience attitudes occur in the processes from which narrative organization emerges. But how should such an enterprise be undertaken with the purpose of enriching our activity of mapping the domain of narrative without getting lost between all the potential structures? And without mistaking one specific structure for the organization that defines all narratives?

3.3 How to Use the Proteus Principle

Aiming for a theory with good explanatory and predictive force, we can select the kind of system that we are going to take into account and adjust the frame of our theory according to our research goals. This can be done by setting a broader scope for the observed phenomenon to which we are applying the theory, i.e., by selecting a specific kind of context where narrative organization occurs, a corpus of discourse–audience systems which we are going to explore. For instance, within the frame of high-school contexts, by which means are dynamics of prospection (suspense) usually generated? What correlations are there between the educational setting and the emergence of suspense? Or, how can a recreational attitude affect the dynamics of prospection in comparison to an information-seeking attitude? That is, if I have read thousands of detective stories and in reading a new one I am obsessively looking for the traces of the murderer's identity, does this attitude shape the suspense I experience (and, consequently, its narrativity)?

The same process of theory formation works the other way round, namely we can narrow the scope of our observation, selecting a kind of discursive property and exploring its intervention in the broader narrative organization. For example, what role does the representation of a sequence of events have in generating suspense in narratives?[7] And of course we can shape the scope in both ways simultaneously, e.g., exploring the role of future tenses in narrative organization in high-school contexts. Or more selectively: the role of future tenses in the representation of a sequence of

---

[7]As seen in Sect. 3.2, according to Sternberg, the representation of a sequence of events is only one among many other ways for generating suspense, curiosity or surprise.

events in narratives produced in educational contexts by teenagers writing about their future lives.[8]

This is how we can change the scope of our observations and formulate theories of different logical type within a framework characterized by a constructivist epistemology and by the adoption of the Proteus Principle. However, in doing so we should bear in mind that we are framing contexts and discursive properties always within the domain of narrative theory. That is to say, we are considering contexts and discursive properties with respect to the processes that generate narrative organization, a phenomenon emerging from interactions within a different scope. Thus, reframing our theory we will notice the relations between certain discursive properties inasmuch as they participate in narrative organization, and we will tend to look for the relations occurring between narrative organization and other elements of a set of contexts. However, it is crucial to be aware that the 'nature' or 'functioning' of none of the parts can be reduced to the kind of organization we are exploring. E.g., in general, future tenses are not necessary for narrative organization, and narratives do not necessarily have an educational function. A similar remark with respect to a more commonly invoked element could be: are *events* necessary and sufficient for narrative organization? Apparently no, but the question is thorny and I do not have the space to address it here.[9]

Given a theory that identifies narrative within a certain scope, theories of different scope describe the narrative organization of the discourse–audience system under certain conditions, namely in a subset of the domain of narrative phenomena. However, a theory of broader scope is not more important or better than a theory of narrower scope. The strength of a theory should be evaluated according to a combination of various parameters: accuracy, scope, fruitfulness, consistency, simplicity (Kuhn 1996) and falsifiability (Popper 1963). In this light, I can say that the PP is very strong, since it displays: *unity,* "consist[ing] of just one problem-solving strategy [. . .] that can be applied to a wide range of problems;" *fecundity,* "rais[ing] new questions and presum[ing] those questions can be answered without giving up its problem-solving strategies;" and allowing auxiliary hypotheses to be tested independently (Kitcher 1982, pp. 45–48).

The PP is a strategy that can be used for every scope, inviting us to focus on the relations between forms and functions, on what cognitive and aesthetic processes

---

[8]A similar kind of scoping was done by Gérard Genette investigating the role of the tense *imparfait* in Marcel Proust's narrative, a research that brought him to readdress the issue of narrative sequentiality and to use the concept of *syllepsis* for those events whose order cannot be established (1980, p. 155).

[9]Is there any event in the so-called "shortest story ever written:" "For sale: baby shoes, never worn"? (Wright 2014, p. 327). I guess this example is problematic because it requires at least Hühn's concept of "non-event" (2016) (a baby has not worn the shoes), and reference to some cognitive construction of hypothetical events that are not told. (A miscarriage? A stillborn baby? A shoemaker who ran out of business?) Perhaps we can consider events necessary for narrative organization, but we should acknowledge that events are not necessarily represented, they are constructs, whose source is not only discourse but also imagination, past experiences, etc. Thus, events too emerge from the audience–discourse interaction.

intervene in the discourse–audience relations. Given the complexity of the system and of the interactions between theorizations of different scope, we cannot reduce a theory to the description of the parts of which a system is composed, nor the specificity of the system (the cause of its organization) is localized in some specific part of it, rather it is distributed between the parts and emerging from their interaction (Maturana and Varela 1980). Therefore, for every theory we are going to formulate in the narrative domain, we should ask ourselves: within what scope is that discursive element functional to narrative organization? And within what scope does context play a determinative or partly effective role? And not: is this element functional or is it accidental? (Bateson 1987, p. 312). For instance, we could address the following questions: within what scope is the syntax of a language functional for narrative organization, i.e., put constraints upon or affect the narrativity of the system? And which is the narrower scope for which it still makes sense to consider how culture, i.e., our commitments to beliefs, desires, social rules, etc., imposes patterns that intervene in the constitution of our narratives?

The Proteus Principle is a pattern that can help answer these and other questions, connecting different narrative theories and models of different scope concerning the domain of narrative phenomena. And I think that this will facilitate our work to enrich the map of that domain.

4   One Pattern for Many Theories (Looking at Narrative Studies as a Complex System)

If we want to explore the relations between fields of research interested in narrative, however diverse such interest may be, it would be desirable for scholars working in different fields to be able to compare and possibly benefit from insights coming from different sources. However, in order to do so, theories need to be commensurable, that is, we need a common 'unit of measurement': e.g., epistemology, theoretical assumptions, methods of inquiry, meaning of concepts, scope of the investigated domain (Feyerabend 1975).

Many ways can be followed in order to achieve commensurability between theories but I argue for the adoption of a common strategy for the positioning of each theory within the domain of narrative studies: the Proteus Principle. In footnotes 3 and 4 I have highlighted homologies between different theories by applying the PP: although the terms used in each theory are different I have noted similar kinds of relations, and similar kinds of form–function combinations. The main reason why I am arguing in favour of the PP is that it enables commensurability between theories while allowing us to choose other variables: ontology (realist or constructivist) and within what scope to ontologically define individual elements; meaning given to concepts (e.g., *form* can be different from or homologous with *structure*); scope of inquiry (e.g., fictional novels, imperfective aspect of verbs); methods of analysis, etc. Accordingly, rather than talking of rival *scientific paradigms* (Kuhn 1996) within the domain of narrative studies it would be possible to conceive of a *research programme* (Lakatos 1990) that broadly focuses on the phenomenology of narrative systems, and of many *auxiliary hypotheses* having different scopes of inquiry within the domain.

In the light of the logical typology I have outlined, each research can extend its inquiry on a single scope, spread over systems with different scope, or focus on the coupling of the system with a specific kind of context, but, according to the Protean pattern, concepts and theories belonging to different disciplines are commensurable as long as they are considered with respect to the appropriate scope. For the same reason, research methods can integrate with each other as long as they avoid conflicts between logical types, like, for instance, importing a concept from another theory and applying it to a system with different scope without considering that a change of the systemic relations consequently changes its meaning. In this sense the PP can be seen as a heuristic to be applied systematically for the formation, extension and rearticulation of theories (Ballerio 2010, p. 188).

Considering a narrative theory through the lens of the PP leaves open two directions for auxiliary theories: (i) there can be different structures that generate narrative organization; (ii) narrative organization can be used with different functions. Beside the quoted example from Sternberg other scholars showed a similar attitude in defining the topic of their researches: for instance, Fludernik (1996) and Bortolussi and Dixon (2003) focus on the correlations between mental processes and discursive properties, and Herman explicitly states that his research has two extents: "at the level of *persons* and *person–environment interactions*" (Herman 2013, p. ix), i.e., how narrative organization intervenes in discursive worldmaking and how stories serve as means for making sense of experience. Moreover, in Herman's theory it is also evident how systems of different scope are linked by feedback loops, both in the reading process and in our theoretical activity.[10]

In our explorations of narratives, we encounter complex networks of correspondences between forms and functions, and if our efforts of comprehension are oriented by a theoretical pattern that we can recursively apply in every analysis and context, then it is easier to synthesise data, ask new constructive questions, formulate hypotheses and try to build explanatory theories. In these processes, the PP helps to bear in mind that "no amount of rigorous discourse of a given logical type can 'explain' phenomena of a higher type," and that in analysing a certain element or relation we should be "automatically excluding from explanation phenomena beyond its logical scope" (Bateson 1987, p. 300). Seeing different logical types and understanding the scope of the concepts and theories we use will help us understand how the mutual feedbacks between theories can be fruitful both to confirm the validity of our syntheses and to correct their flaws.

So far in this section I have talked about the possible intersections between disciplines and between theories, but what about the relations between state-of-

---

[10]But not only cognitive approaches adopt the PP: see Skalin (2008) for an example of aesthetic perspective.

the-art narratologies and older paradigms? The PP can be a guide for a diachronic dialogue too, since identifying on what scope a theory focuses is a precious piece of information to orient our understanding of its commensurability with earlier theories. And programmatically adopting the PP would make this confrontation easier in the future.

The narrative domain keeps evolving, its boundaries are moving and new structures appear thanks to linguistic and literary experimentations, deployment of new media, changes in cultural and cognitive affordances, etc. The contexts in which we use narrative are different from those of a century ago, the audience keeps evolving and so do the properties we encounter in discourse: modifications of the environment require adaptations, and neither the structures generating narrative nor the effects achieved in/through narrative can be packed in fixed forms and moved between contexts. Organization and its effects emerge through systemic relations. The uses of narrative modify the context and in turn the environment (a literary tradition, the psychoanalytic setting, marketing strategies, etc.) intervene to shape the discourse–audience system. Narratives occur and have occurred in a wide range of contexts across a huge time span because they adapted by changing their components and structures, not their systemic relations: everywhere and every time narratives are able to organize the discourse–audience relations in meaningful and effective ways.

Theories, being models of the phenomena they describe, should reflect such adaptability, thus concepts and paradigms need to change in order to be considered useful over time and across contexts. Otherwise, if changes in the environment are too drastic and a particular structure cannot contribute to the emergence of narrative organization anymore, then a theory describing that particular structure of the phenomenon—rather than its organization—would lose its explanatory force. Whole 'narrative species' can be exterminated in the evolution of a domain, and so can the instruments we use to map the domain: concepts, hermeneutic strategies, typologies, etc. More often the evolution of bodies of knowledge is not that fierce and they can co-evolve with the environment, healing themselves and achieving a new internal consistency (Bateson 1979, p. 206). For example, the effacement of French Structuralism does not mean that such a paradigm cannot generate theoretical or analytical knowledge anymore, it is simply a 'natural' evolutionary process of the narratological research programme in response to modifications of the narrative domain: with the appearance of new conditions the quantity and quality of knowledge generated by French Structuralism has been reshaped. Thus, we need to put it into perspective and reconceptualize it, being aware of the scope of this paradigm. Like Newtonian gravitation theory vis-à-vis Einstein's relativity: classical mechanics is easy to apply and allows satisfactory approximations in many circumstances, but relativity theory has a wider scope and is more accurate, enabling us to grasp more details of the systemic relations we observe in the domain of its applicability.

Neither a rigid conservatism nor a craving for change is healthy; an antagonism between the two attitudes would probably be better. But, like in any scientific field, there is always the risk that the narratological research programme be ruled by the 'strength' of the competitors rather than by the strength of their theories and arguments (Bateson 1979, p. 223). In using theories, however flexible they might be, we always employ multiple parameters for the evaluation of their strength and such criteria may conflict with each other and/or with our practical goals (Goodman and Elgin 1988, pp. 11–23). In order to overcome such difficulties, we should adopt a wider perspective on the paradigms we foster, and bring our theories on a ground where they can be tested, possibly falsified, compete with other theories and eventually be modified for the sake of a greater explanatory force. The Proteus Principle provides exactly that ground.

5 Conclusions

"We are the inheritors of categorized knowledge; therefore we inherit also a world view that consists of parts strung together, rather than of wholes regarded through different sets of filters" (Beer 1980, p. 63). We get so used to the perspective we inherit that we often forget that it is only a mental habit—an interface through which we organize knowledge—and an obsolete one, since it is an obstacle to the acknowledgment of different points of view that can describe the same phenomenon in different ways. "As long as the phenomena are integrally respected, they can be most lawfully explained in multiple ways" (Suvin 2010b, p. 76), but pluralism does not mean freedom from any constraint, it is also a matter of recognizing the appropriateness and validity of different perspectives. Therefore, our critical skills need to be always alert and, in order to be used properly, we need to develop an ability to see patterns of parts–whole relationships (i.e., correlations between discursive elements/attitudes /effects and narrative organization), so that we can confront theories and evaluate the scope and accuracy with which they describe a phenomenon.

> What is in that sense, say, the truth of the atom bomb? Depending on the categories and interests chosen, it may (among a multitude of other possible answers) be the instantaneous liberation of a given high quantity of energy for a destructive purpose, or the proof for a given inter-atomic structure of matter, or, finally, the effect on the lives of hundreds of thousands of inhabitants of Hiroshima and Nagasaki. The first answer is military, the second pertains to 'objective' theoretical physics [...] the third to the horizon of a not yet existing humanised science. The formal difference between them is that each succeeding answer has a larger scope: the physical one can envision the military one, but only the humanised one may envision all of them. [...] We are here faced with the necessity for a dialectics between systems and openness, in brief the necessity for open-ended systems or indeed provisional and historical totalities. The openness is both formal and historical, it pertains to viewing a subject(-matter) within different situations and by different appraisers with differing value-systems. (Suvin 2010b, p. 72)

Many narratological paradigms already show a similar attitude and traces of it can also be found in the works by the Russian Formalists and Bakhtin (Steiner 1984; Sini 2010), Jakobson and Lotman (Grishakova 2008), and in the later Barthes (van Ooijen 2012). The need to understand the evolution of narrative studies is clearly expressed in the theme of the 2013 ENN Conference—"Emerging Vectors of Narratology: Toward Consolidation or Diversification?"—subscribed to by many scholars and perfectly epitomised in the words by Paul Dawson:

> The most important aspect in the pursuit of consolidation is to avoid homogenizing consensus, to attend to the specificities of individual disciplines and different objects of study, to recognize that 'narrative' itself is a contingent and changing construct of specific disciplinary methods. To clarify the distinctions and relations between narrative as mode of thought, a social practice and a cultural artefact, before asserting that there is a common ground between scholars across the disciplines, beyond the fact that they use the same 'keyword' in their abstracts for journal articles and research interests. (Dawson 2013, p. 110).

It is from such a perspective that I am here proposing a Protean strategy of consolidation for narrative studies. Disciplines and paradigms have their own specificities, and in approaching narrative phenomena they implicitly shape them. To make explicit such processes of selection and contextualization is an act of intellectual honesty that can enhance the dialogue between scholars, and I suggest to do it in three steps: (i) adopting a systemic perspective, (ii) making explicit the scope of our observations, (iii) employing the Proteus Principle in the evaluation of theories. Narrative is seen and used in many different ways that can be conceived as systems, i.e., considering that the properties of narrative cannot be studied in isolation but are interconnected in a network of relations where all the components are influencing each other. We are interested in narrative, therefore it is in first stance us as observers using concepts, theories and instruments that modify the phenomenon that we study, since we correlate to narrative organization all other aspects and relations of the phenomenon. Moreover, not every property of the system has the same status with respect to narrative: some properties intervene in narrative organization only inasmuch as they are related to other properties, namely as sub-systems of narrative, and distinguishing between logical types can help us to account for this complex network of relations. The PP is the tool through which we can grasp the interactions and build models of them. Setting narrative studies (and any semiotic analysis) free from categorized knowledge may raise its status with respect to science.

> One can *analyze* a situation one moment, seeking to divide it into relatively independent claims or suggestions, and then *synthesize* it the next, seeking the common meaning or significance of the parts. Analysis and synthesis can be used as phases of recurring cycles of inquiry rather than as static, warring orientations. (Bredo 2009, p. 440)

The scope of our inquiries can change at every observation but it is our responsibility to manage perspectives and paradigms acknowledging their diversity and limiting their applicability to what is pertinent.

Narrative studies are an evolving domain, therefore the Proteus Principle cannot be adopted as an absolute truth but only as a working hypothesis that may or may not turn out to be viable (von Glaserfeld 1990, p. 22). Given the magnitude of the narrative turn and its growing trend in the last thirty years, it is probable that in the future narrative will be a protagonist in many fields of research. In the light of possible cooperation, the viability of the Proteus Principle for narrative studies lies in its being fit for the environment in which narrative analysis and inquiry are being used. That is, it allows us to easily export ideas into new contexts—thus increasing the interest in narrative studies—and can facilitate the interdisciplinary sharing of ideas, which eventually feed back into the specific research fields of those involved in the dialogue.

References

Ballerio S (2010) Neuroscienze e teoria letteraria. I – Premesse teoriche e metodologiche. Enthymema 1:164–189

Bánáthy BH (1997) A taste of systemics. The first international electronic seminar on wholeness. December 1, 1996; to December 31, 1997. http://www.newciv.org/ISSS_Primer/asem04bb. html

Bar-Yam Y (2004) A mathematical theory of strong emergence using multiscale variety. Complexity 9(6):15–24

Bateson G (1979) Mind and nature: a necessary unity, Advances in systems theory, complexity, and the human sciences. Hampton Press, New York

Bateson G (1987) Steps to an ecology of mind. In: Collected essays in anthropology, psychiatry, evolution, and epistemology [1972]. Aronson, Northvale

Beer S (1980) Preface to Autopoiesis and cognition. In: Maturana HR, Varela FJ (eds) The realization of the living. Reidel, Dordrecht

Bortolussi M, Dixon P (2003) Psychonarratology: foundations for the empirical study of literary response. Cambridge University Press, Cambridge

Bredo E (2009) Comments on howe: getting over the methodology wars. Educ Res 38(6):441–448

Bruner JS (1990) Acts of meaning. Harvard University Press, Cambridge

Caracciolo M (2014) The experientiality of narrative. An enactivist approach. De Gruyter, Berlin

Dawson P (2013) Emerging vectors of narratology: toward consolidation or diversification? (A response). Enthymema 9:109–114

Feyerabend PK (1975) Against method. Outline of an anarchistic theory of knowledge. New Left Books, London

Fludernik M (1996) Towards a 'natural' narratology. Routledge, London

Fludernik M (2009) An introduction to narratology. Routledge, London

Genette G (1980) Narrative discourse: an essay in method (trans: JE Lewin). Cornell University Press, Ithaca

Goodman N, Elgin CZ (1988) Reconceptions in philosophy and other arts and sciences. Hackett, Indianapolis

Gramsci A (1975) Quaderni del carcere [1971] (trans: Q Hoare, G Nowell Smith). In: Gerratana V (ed) Selections from the prison notebooks. Einaudi\International Publishers, Torino\New York

Grayling AC (2010) Transcendental arguments. In: Dancy J, Sosa E, Steup M (eds) A companion to epistemology, 2nd edn. Chichester, Wiley-Blackwell, pp 768–771

Grishakova M (2008) Literariness, fictionality and the theory of possible worlds. In: Skalin L-Å (ed) Narrativity, fictionality, and literariness: the narrative turn and the study of literary fiction. Örebro University, Örebro, pp 57–76

Harrier-Jones P (2004) Revisiting angels fear: recursion, ecology and aesthetics. SEED J 4(1):143–165

Herman D (2013) Storytelling and the sciences of mind. MIT Press, Cambridge

Hühn P (2016) The eventfulness of non-events. In: Baroni R, Revaz F (eds) Narrative sequence in contemporary narratology. Ohio State University Press, Columbus, pp 37–47

Hutto DD (2008) Folk psychological narratives: the sociocultural basis of understanding reasons. MIT Press, Cambridge

Kindt T (2009) Narratological expansionism and its discontents. In: Heinen S, Sommer R (eds) Narratology in the age of cross-disciplinary narrative research. De Gruyter, Berlin, pp 35–47

Kitcher P (1982) Abusing science: the case against creationism. MIT Press, Cambridge

Kuhn TS (1996) The structure of scientific revolutions [1962], 3rd edn. University of Chicago Press, Chicago

Lakatos I (1990) Falsification and the methodology of scientific research programmes. In: Lakatos I, Musgrave A (eds) Criticism and the growth of knowledge [1970]. Cambridge University Press, Cambridge

Maturana HR, Varela FJ (1980) Autopoiesis and cognition. The realization of the living. Reidel, Dordrecht

Nielsen HS, Phelan J, Walsh R (2015a) Ten theses about fictionality. Narrative 23(1):61–73

Nielsen HS, Phelan J, Walsh R (2015b) Fictionality as rhetoric: a response to Paul Dawson. Narrative 23(1):101–111

Orlando F (1978) Toward a Freudian theory of literature, with an analysis of Racine's 'Phèdre' [1973] (tran: C Lee [Italian]). Johns Hopkins University Press, Baltimore

Passalacqua F, Pianzola F (2016) Epistemological problems in narrative theory: constructivist vs. objectivist paradigm. In: Baroni R, Revaz F (eds) Narrative sequence in contemporary narratology. Ohio State University Press, Columbus, pp 195–217

Pier J (2008) After this, therefore because of this. In: Pier J, Landa JÁG (eds) Theorizing narrativity. De Gruyter, Berlin, pp 109–140

Pier J (2017) Complexity: a paradigm for narrative? In: Hansen PK, Pier J, Roussin P, Schmid W (eds) Emerging vectors of narratology. De Gruyter, Berlin, pp 533–566

Popper KR (1963) Conjectures and refutations. Routledge, London

Putnam H (1981) Reason, truth and history. Cambridge University Press, Cambridge

Ryan A (2007) Emergence is coupled to scope, not level. Complexity 13(2):67–77

Ryle G (1949) The concept of mind. University of Chicago Press, Chicago

Sini S (2010) L'intero irrequieto: sulla poligenesi dell'idea strutturale nel pensiero russo del primo Novecento. Enthymema 1:191–228

Skalin L-Å (2008) 'Telling a story'. Reflections on fictional and non-fictional narratives. In: Skalin L-Å (ed) Narrativity, fictionality, and literariness: the narrative turn and the study of literary fiction. Örebro University, Örebro, pp 201–260

Steiner P (1984) Russian formalism. A metapoetics. Cornell University Press, Ithaca

Sternberg M (1978) Expositional modes and temporal ordering in fiction. Indiana University Press, Bloomington

Sternberg M (1982) Proteus in quotation-land: mimesis and the forms of reported discourse. Poet Today 3(2):107–156

Sternberg M (1992) Telling in time (II): chronology, teleology, narrativity. Poet Today 13 (3):463–541

Sternberg M (2001) How narrativity makes a difference. Narrative 9:115–122

Sternberg M (2010) Narrativity: from objectivist to functional paradigm. Poet Today 31:507–659

Suvin D (1979) Metamorphoses of science fiction: on the poetics and history of a literary genre. Yale University Press, New Haven

Suvin D (2010a) Science fiction and the novum [1977]. In: Defined by a hollow: essays on Utopia, science fiction and political epistemology. Peter Lang, Bern

Suvin D (2010b) On the horizons of epistemology and science. Crit Q 52(1):68–101

Thompson E, Varela FJ (2001) Radical embodiment: neural dynamics and consciousness. Trends Cogn Sci 5(10):418–425

Tosey P, Visser M, Saunders MNK (2012) The origins and conceptualizations of 'triple-loop' learning: a critical review. Manag Learn 43(3):291–307

van Ooijen E (2012) Notes on the conceptualization of style as embodied idiolect in French structuralism. In: Rossholm G, Johansson C (eds) Disputable core concepts of narrative theory. Peter Lang, Bern, pp 269–278

von Bertalanffy LK (1968) General system theory: foundations, development, applications. George Braziller, New York von Glaserfeld E (1990) An exposition of constructivism: why some like it radical. In: Davis RB, Maher CA, Noddings N (eds) Constructivist views on the teaching and learning of mathematics. National Council of Teachers of Mathematics, Reston, pp 19–29

Wittgenstein L (1953) Philosophical investigations. Blackwell, Oxford

Wittgenstein L (1969) On certainty. Blackwell, Oxford

Wright FA (2014) The short story just got shorter: Hemingway, narrative, and the six-word urban legend. J Pop Cult 47(2):327–340

Chapter 11
Narrative Experiences of History and Complex Systems

Romana Turina

> *Historical distance emerges as a complex balance that has as*
> *much to do with the emotional or political uses of the past as*
> *with its explanatory functions or its formal design.*
> (Phillips 2013, p. 5)
> *The 'before now' doesn't have in it a shape of its own.*
> (Jenkins and Munslow 2004, p. 3)

Abstract This chapter considers elements at play in the establishment of our current historical knowledge. Looking at past events as complex adaptive systems, it demonstrates why the current mediation of history is oversimplified. By formulating the possibility of a complex narrative matrix (environment), it explores its potential in offering both an archive of evidence drawn from multiple agents, and presenting the evolving relationship between them in time. This matrix aligns itself with a simulation of a CAS, the primary interest being the VR matrix's ability to be both an interactive interface enabling exploration of the evidential material from different points of access, and a construction able to reveal its procedural work; a dynamic that elicits the creation of meaning by including the reasoning behind the chosen archival material, the product of the process, and the process itself.

1 Introduction

The scope of historical investigation has widened considerably in the last 50 years. Historians compile studies on political events, social structures, economic conditions, relationships between genders, material culture, the image of the body through

R. Turina (✉)
Department of Theatre, Film and Television, University of York, York, UK
e-mail: rt748@york.ac.uk

© Springer Nature Switzerland AG 2018
R. Walsh, S. Stepney (eds.), *Narrating Complexity*,
https://doi.org/10.1007/978-3-319-64714-2_11

123

time and more, which often cross into different disciplines as testified in the *Journal of Interdisciplinary History*, among others. Keen on a sense of historical distance, scholars base their work on the idea that a genuine encounter with the past needs to recognise its alterity to the present, but investigation can create the condition for an objective understanding, able to offer some answers to their desire to abbreviate this same distance. Periodisation helps the discipline to function, as it furnishes historians with ideas about periods, their characteristics qualities and offers possible tropes of historical explanation (Jordanova 2012, p. 96). In this effort, many historians try to grasp the 'reality' of the past by detaching themselves from the present, as Erwin Panofsky (1955) advocated. However, often the struggle reveals a far more challenging adversary than distance, the openness of the past to conflicting narratives deriving from the same set of archival material, physical items or assumptions. This openness of the 'before now' to variable forms of appropriation is sustained both by the impossibility of accessing the correspondence of the narrative to the past and the impossibility of finding closure in an exhaustive context because the possibility to find another set of circumstances that gives context to the past is always open. Historical narratives are therefore evolving and start to look into a viable new form of exploration, understanding and explanation of the past with the aid of new technology.

In this chapter, I look at past events as complex adaptive systems because this angle of enquiry enables an explicative reading of the current mediation of history that is oversimplified. Also, it permits us to consider social interactions that happened in the past as sharing the quality of a layered network, where parallel and interconnected decisions influence groups of actors and the synergy created, the whole system. This kind of continuously changing interaction, based on feedback and subject to linear and non-linear causality, reveals qualities that need to be tackled with new narrative tools if we wish to explain them. New technologies might offer some potential solutions in the form of game-engines employed to create narrative systems, which open space to think about narrative matrices. Narrative matrices, as narrative environments, would be potentially able to offer a pre-processed archive of evidence, sources and information, which inform on what they are and the relationship between them, as a start. If we grant to this hypothesis the status of the horizon on which traces of the past are dealt with, the theoretical questions a narrative matrix built using a game engine brings to the surface might start to find answers in discussing two theoretical claims on the ontological quality of such an environment. A first claim implies that the interaction with such an interface would enable us to make personal choices about what is the important narrative within the system, by exploring the evidential base and constructing a purposeful interpretation and narrative reading of the event. Also, it would have an educative value in the sense that it draws attention to the openness of the past to different narrative interpretations. However, this claim is an already established educative practice, which accepts the confines of narrative explanation, and can be observed in the educative employment of games to learn. The second claim, which is central to this chapter, is that such a narrative matrix would offer something more. It would give proof that the experience of negotiating the archive isn't separate from interpretation; as such narrative would reveal the work of a process that creates meaning by including the product of the process, the material of the process, and the process itself. And in this sense, if the attention remains suspended in the process, there is space for an understanding of the material, and the logic behind the creation of *mythos* (in the Aristotelian meaning of plot) before it becomes crystallised into a narrative. Granting this strong claim would open an investigative space not dissimilar to models in the sciences, where different choices produce different results. More importantly, this reflective and reflexive side to the process would also be indicative of the presence of a pre-reflective stage where experience, the experiential dimension that the game engine offers, might reveal how perception and emotion influence our understanding of the sources and the construction of meaning in the making of history.

In considering narrative matrices, the chapter hopes to foster additional discussion on the status of historical knowledge, on paradigms of historical understanding and narrative solutions able to picture the complex, generative and adaptive systems that past events are. To make the discussion as clear as possible, in the next three sections, I cover the conceptual frame enabling the understanding of the theoretical proposal that follows.

2 The 'Situatedness' of Understanding

We need to be aware that political processes affect historical practice and its methodology, which with each ideological change becomes oriented by a different set of assumptions, a newly defined sense of distance, and a new epistemological horizon.

> Every successful revolution darkens the achievements of previous generations, and the more successful the revolution, the more damage is done to the memory of earlier times (Phillips 2013, p. 21).

Consequently, for example, the classical historical writing was conceived as an educative body of work for heirs of a certain rank, who had little to do with trivial day-to-day matters and needed elevated images and life-lessons able to prepare them for service in politics. Modernity learned to write history according to different principles, the typical and repeatable and grew wary of overarching ideals. Between these two orientations, the Italian Renaissance offered a mixture of idealisation and attention to details, where brief historical narratives were accumulated in a list of cases able to form patterns of instruction that educated in a comparative mode rather than in the coherence of a single subject or story—like in the case of Machiavelli who wrote historical accounts "to uncover the larger designs governing success and failure" (Phillips 2013, p. 46). Accordingly, the understanding of past events is always framed by the seeker's purpose, social status, ideology and historical location. Similarly, our understanding of such interpretations of events is also framed, as the objectivity we seek is equally related to time and space. The point of view and the set of arguments accepted in debating the objectivity of any study makes of the investigation into the past an analysis of multiple social interactions that we approach from a specific angle, and prevent us from 'seeing' it omnisciently. Consequently, the analysis of the social interactions we call history presents similar issues to the analysis of complex adaptive systems in other fields, as they defy our understanding in similar ways. For example, social agents are enmeshed in a web of connections and survive adapting, often navigating through the system, interacting with other agents to their own benefit. Similarly, the behaviour of many complex systems emerges from the activities of agents that operate on their lower level, which overcome systemic changes and manage to affect the superior levels. Complexity enters the social system also in the necessity that social agents have to predict and react to the actions or predictions of others, which are complicated if agents are coupled to one another due to any kind of bond. In such situations, their interactions become nonlinear, and the social system becomes "difficult to decompose, and complexity ensues" (Miller and Page 2010, p. 10).

Another element to consider is that each version of historical accounts, and each political orientation of the historical practice, carries a stance in relation to narrative. The spectrum varies according to the narrative relationship to idealisation, realism and the account of details employed. For example, details can offer frankness and clarity but the intensification of their use can slip into emotionalism. Yet, intensification permitted a close look at lives never recorded before, as in the case of the 1960s' interest in microhistory,[1] which provoked a 'realignment' of historical investigation and engaged with a very effective exploration of personal experience in all its particularity—but at the expense of a foreshortening of historical perspective. Consequently, the historical narrative is always 'on a mission' because the historical understanding guiding the narrative is impregnated by a point of view that influences the cognitive process at work while compiling the historical account. A point of view that even if not necessarily evident hinders the effort for a whole encompassing objectivity. Multiple efforts have been made to address the issue by narrating the past from different points of view. In cinema, noticeable attempts are found in films like *Rashomon* (Kurosawa 1950) or in simultaneous narratives that use split screens, where examples include very early experimentation like *Napoléon* (Gance 1927). These attempts addressed what can be considered a two-dimensional approach to the complexity of the human experience. They look into events through the prism of memory and the search for the truth. However, they do not tackle the effects of a certain transmission of experience. A tridimensional approach seems to be a more adequate proposition to the narration of past events, as it takes into consideration time as a prolific and echoing narrative space. Such narrative would account for the effects of the transmission of the historical knowledge. For example to the generations that followed the witnesses, considering how specific historical interpretations affected their decisions in life. As a result, the narrative process would take into account the evolution of affect, and the impact of contrasting interpretations when coming into contact. Such impacts on the social system resonate on multiple levels, as explored

---

[1]See Marc Bloch (1965, 1967), and Lucien Febvre (1925, 1929).

among others by the multidisciplinary study of postmemory[2] and post-memory[3] in literature and film. Research in these fields made apparent how

> Our concern with history is a concern with preformed images already imprinted on our brains, images at which we keep staring while the truth lies elsewhere, away from it all, somewhere as yet undiscovered (Sebald 2001, p. 72).

Thus, the narration of history needs to take into account memory's relationship to history, which continues to be a challenge (Kansteiner 2002, p. 184).

3   Interpretation and Priming of Past Events

The communication of experience exists in relationship to language and correspondence. In the case of the past, the communication of experience involves the recovery of traces, materiality and specificity sufficient to infer a sense of correspondence that, however, is not possible to access. The past is gone, and to narrate it we mostly engage with some form of reference that reflects its temporal, material and cognitive distance from us. As Hans-Georg Gadamer suggested,

> Historical consciousness no longer listens sanctimoniously to the voice that reaches out from the past, but in reflections on it, replaces it within the context where it took root to see the significance and relative value proper to it. This reflexive posture towards tradition is called interpretation (1979, p. 111).

However, this engagement is guided at each attempt by our specific, actual, immanent, question; the one reason we are looking into the past to understand it, or to make sense of it at all. In so doing, we obtain not an objective 'knowing' of the past but a 'reading' of the past through a speculative filter that brings our world to it. To understand this issue, it might be useful to consider the initial challenges filmmakers face when aiming to portray a specific historical figure or an event of historical significance. The most common levels of enquiry into the traces of the past follow one or multiple of the following processes: the filmmakers collect documents and the acts of witnesses. The filmmakers collect multiple narratives regarding the event, which have been already put together by different narrators. The filmmakers collect every point of view on the event by people who witnessed it, experienced the consequences of it, and studied the event without any involvement in it. Also, the filmmakers might discover an unknown source of knowledge and put together a novel narrative version on the event, which was previously alien to the academic enquiries or public discourses. Finally, the filmmakers decide where to focus their

---

[2]Postmemory is a concept established by Marianne Hirsch (2012), which is positioned within the study of the trauma derived from the experience of the Holocaust. It is related to Eva Hoffman's conceptualization of the second generation as a 'hinge generation' (Hoffman 2004).

[3]Post-memory indicates an expansion of Hirsch's concept, as in Löschnigg and Sokołowska-Paryż (2014). It represents the study of how and why subsequent postmemory generations come back to the representation of specific historical moments.

interest and produce their narrative on the event; a process not far dissimilar to the work of scholars, which varies according to the academic rigour exercised.

Within the organisation of the traces of the past, as done by archival classification, news, books or films, there is an important element to take into consideration, priming. Relevant especially in the political debate, priming is a process in which the media attend to some issues while ignoring others, and in so doing alter the perception of the importance of certain events (Severin and Tankard 1997). The 'priming effect' is specifically important in the case of little-known history, as such events can be cast out of any historical narration accessible to the public. Also, they can be presented in the context of a historical narrative with a connotation able to negate a diverse interpretation of it, because the first description obtains the effect of setting the event in a certain frame of understanding—and hinders further possibilities to make primary in relevance a different aspect of the same event.

Priming is 'the invisible hand' of any historical narrative, as its effects reverberate in time and affect each following interpretation of this event. These are either a point of departure toward new mediations or a deepening of the same kind of understanding, which focuses on bringing to the surface additional findings corroborating the public narrative. The effect of priming on the audience is severe because the associations and cognitive patterns created by the first set of assumptions we accept on an event can be salient and long lasting (Bargh et al. 1996, pp. 230–244). Also, as priming is an implicit memory effect, it influences the response to the related stimulus. Accordingly, people are faster in deciding when a word follows an associatively or semantically related word (Schvaneveldt and Meyer 1973, pp. 395–409) and to these decisions can be associated specific behaviour. The behaviour differs according to different priming, which can occur following perceptual, semantic or conceptual stimulus repetition (Meyer et al. 1975, pp. 98–118). Scholars are not immune to priming that occurs in their field of studies. Academic historiography attempts to narrate the past by confronting the effects of priming. By negotiating the set of assumptions to follow, it tries to allow a satisfactory level of objectivity to the representation of the events the historian put together. However, this is not an easy task because the affect of priming is often not directly recognisable, and the way we decide what seems objective is also the result of our mindset—as discussed above. Consequently, to offer a narrative of a historical event, academic historiography would ideally be able to penetrate and recognise various levels of experience, interpretation, cultural conditioning, ideology and priming before obtaining an understanding of the event that attempts a satisfactory level of 'objectivity' in explaining it.

4 Multiplicity of Point of View and Complex Adaptive Systems

As demonstrated by the French Annales school, the British neo-Marxist school (Poirrier 2008, p. 189), and the 'new history from below' (Lyons 2010, Sect. 59.1), reality and the past are 'felt' differently according to each person/group socio-cultural position in time and space. As discussed, the past operated on different mind sets than the present. The cognitive distance that divides the historian from this past is temporal and spatial, as well as perspectival, technological, sociological. Scholarly work is also biased by a characteristic culture of causation the scholar is ingrained in, which is distinctively different from what would be in place in the past. Consequently, each research in the understanding of the past is destined to go as close as possible to its truth as the researchers' cognitive horizon permits, and to fail in capturing an exhaustive understanding of what is gone. This is not a negative element, as it plays as an agent of continuous irritation able to produce more and more research. Also, it stands as a clear indicator of our ever evolving distance from what 'was before', which can guard us against attempting any grand interpretative closure that does not take into account the situatedness of our understanding. The similarities of past events to complex adaptive systems start to come to surface especially in the study of the networks created by affects of priming and simultaneous, preceding or following reactions against them. For example, negative feedback loops to specific interpretations of a past event might make the other people sharing the interpretation less likely to speak up, or act. In the case of positive feedback loops, they might make others more likely to come forward and support the interpretation. In some cases, a positive loop can hinder further expressions of support, as the way feedback loops work is not necessarily linear. For example, heterogeneity in the understanding of an event often coagulates around decentralised opinion leaders. Accesses to the media vary as their commitment to establishing their interpretation of the event as 'the truth' varies, and they deliver it to any form of public record. Media theory offers a variety of models to study misrepresentation, opinion leaders, influence patterns and affect. However, the fluid motion of feedback present in any social system is tough to translate into comprehensive narratives able to portray it. Subsequently, history often appears as a list of well-recorded micro-events building up to a major event that the narrator tries to reconstruct. Priming and divergent interpretations of the event are not considered, as well as the network of reciprocal feedback loops, self-feeding narrative echoes, or decentralised narratives.

A significant example can be found in the disputed narration of history in the northeastern part of present-day Italy, specifically in the city of Trieste. The northeast in Italy carries a distinct importance because the events that led to its annexation to Italy in 1918 saw the nation united by the power of the media, which created the cognitive environment able to promote the annexation of Trieste. Subsequently, the event was subjected to a process of priming able to affect the following interpretations of the city's history, and identity, to the present. Accordingly, the initial priming favoured the acquisition of a set of assumptions on the Italianity of Trieste

as advocated by the wealthy Italian mercantile minority, a position that has continually been re-established during the twentieth century. As during the Cold War,
when Trieste's location on the edge of the Iron Curtain offered to the Italian media
plenty of opportunities to proclaim the need to 'save' the Italian city from a
Communist-Slav invasion. Simultaneously, this cluster of assumptions negated
narrative space to events testifying to the presence of an enmeshed multi-ethnic
population and a predominantly dual culture, Italian and Slav. Priming, iteration and
deepening of a singular interpretation of events, and the negation of representative
space to other versions of historical memory created a phenomenon of 'silenced
history'. The memory of this silenced history was retained in the city as a residual
cultural well, key to the survival of the indigenous Slovenian community. Also, it
affected the internal dynamics of the social interactions for the last 70 years, posing a
challenge to the understanding of the social network in place, as well as to the official
mediation of Trieste's culture and past.

Thus, a narrative matrix able to display this complex system of social history
would have to take into account the silenced history as well. Display its affect on the
social network and the net of feedback springing from the clashes between the
official historical memory, Italian, and the residual historical memory denied visi-
bility, Slav. Accordingly, such a matrix would give space to a multiple-viewpoint
narration of the Italian anti-Slavism, as prompted by the actions of the *Voluntary
Militia for National Security* (Milizia Volontaria per la sicurezza nationale), commonly known as *Blackshirts* (Camicie nere), or Fascist Squads (Squadristi), whose
'punitive missions' against socialists, communists and the 300,000 Slovenians and
100,000 Croatians indigenous of the territory became frequent in Trieste after 1918.
It would take into account the 'Fascism of the border', as advocated by the proto-
fascist *Triestine Combat league* (Fascio Triestino di combattimento) from 1919,
which presents a distinctively ethnic overtone in comparison to the policies applied
in central Italy. Finally, it would give voice to the acts of public violence that
intensified on 3 April 1920 when hundreds of Slav shops, clubs, and houses were
attacked, and culminated with the *Narodni Dom/National Hall* of the Slovenians
being burnt down on 13 July (Hametz 2005, pp. 20–22). It would offer data on the
existence of 14,756 members of the Fascist party in Trieste, representing more than
18% of the overall membership of the movement (Bosworth 2006, pp. 153–159),
which confirmed that in 1922 when Mussolini gained political power in Italy,
Fascism had already triumphed in Trieste with a clear anti-Slavic connotation
(Vinci 1998, p. 100). It would testify to the controversial aspects of the *Gentile
Reform* (1923), which is remembered in Italy solely on the basis of its importance in
establishing a modern educational system, but also forbade the public use of any
other language than Italian in any public places (Verginella 2008, p. 19) and closed
the Slovenian schools. Finally, it would reveal and explore the establishment of
Italian concentration camps for the Slav population, which are rarely mentioned in
any academic studies.

The historical process taken into account is an example of the fairly straightforward juxtaposition of a dominant narrative of national consolidation and of counter-
narrative, which managed to survive within the same social system that tried to

delete it. However, its apparent simplicity enables some consideration on how a narrative matrix engaged in the explanation of the metahistory (White 1973) of historiographical productions and receptions of these opposed discourses would benefit by the application of complex system theories. First, the feedback loops produced by clashes between the hegemonic historical discourse and silenced residual history, within the social system, affected several generations of social actors, and actants[4] (classes of actors), causing the emergence of a variety of minor and major changes in the system, which are not always understandable by linear causality. Similarly, the ways each level of the system, between actors and actants, absorbed and reacted to the imposed historical interpretation of certain events elicited a process of interaction and mutual influences that defy conventional linear descriptions. Such interaction seems to have been rich, as recent emergent phenomena demonstrate how actors in the system have affected its permeability to the silenced history of the Slavs. As of 2015, one of such phenomena is the resurfacing of historical memory regarding artistic events memorialising a culture deeply rooted in its past. Simultaneously, the establishment of new social venues testifies to the current rising of the Slovenian cultural power in Trieste—with at a micro level a dramatic increase in the number of Italian children enrolling in the few Slovenian kindergartens—when Italy declares Trieste's population as predominantly Italian.

5   Virtual Reality and Narrative Engines

To clearly understand how new technologies might serve the narration of historical events, read as complex adaptive systems, it is necessary to see how these technologies present an entirely different, but familiar on many levels, method of communication. On this occasion, I consider the narrative potential of virtual reality (VR). As a narrative medium, VR presents characteristics that are directly related to its interactivity, which is both dependent on time and space and to its sphere of representation which is immersive. The concept of immersion in this section is considered in its diversity to the experience it offers in comparison to reading a book, where the narrative representation is mental, or other forms like cinema and theatre, where the representation is visual. In VR, immersion is embedded in the narrative quality of the medium, which 'by doing' offers the real-time experience of circumstances, environments and conflicts. However, as a narrative medium, VR is still in its infancy, as the forms and means of narrative/communication that are distinctive to it are not clearly identified, yet. More importantly, the role and potential of the users' agency, which is not relegated to the position of spectators as in the case of the audience, needs continuous exploration. This is due to the complex relationship users experience due to interactivity, which here I consider as

---

[4]See A. J. Greimas (1966, 1979), Lucien Tesnière (1966), Mieke Bal (1985).

An expression of the extent that, in a given series of communication exchanges, any third (or later) transmission (or message) is related to the degree to which previous exchanges referred to even earlier transmissions (Rafaeli 1988, pp. 110–134).

If we consider such a system as a narrative environment, where multiple elements affect each other, the users can assume the role of the authors of stories or the role of participants in an already established mesh of plot. Consequently, the system can interact with the users via a character-driven narrative or a plot-driven narrative. Accordingly, the narrative can be already determined by the system, with a high level of authoring if plot-based, or lower level if it is character-based. So far stories have been represented in interactive environments in four general modes. The linear story structure that mirrors cinema; the 'tree' story structure that employs branching story lines able to offer multiple endings; a generative story structure where interaction triggers the unfolding of the story; and a more universal approach where the story elements are coded, and each decision is taken according to the availability of those elements to the users. Early on specific attention has been given to systems focused on character-based narrative models, where the role of the users is critical (Cavazza et al. 2001a, pp. 145–154, 2001b, pp. 156–170; Porteous et al. 2013, pp. 595–602; Szilas and Mancini 2005, pp. 115–125), and lately it has been given to how generative digital media is reshaping narrative (Ronfard and Szilas 2014), as there are today models able to implement a 'story logic' that triggers the occurrence of certain events according to different algorithms. These narratives could become instrumental in the creation of interlaced narrative matrices able to explain complex systems, from which also the explanation of history could benefit.

At the present, the most powerful VR narrative engines we create are employed for the production of commercial computer games. Some games can come close to an implementation of some of the characteristic dynamics of complex systems. Examples include games like *SimCity* (Maxis 1989) or *No Man's Sky* (Hello Games 2016). *SimCity* is based on research on methods of city planning. The city emerges from the interaction of specific agents loaded with some properties and some feedback abilities, mostly implemented by the featured independent agents. *No Man's Sky* creates planets, stars, life forms and ecosystems through random procedural generation—which uses *deterministic algorithms*[5] and a *seed number*[6] able to give the impression of an open system. Also, most recently the game *Never Alone* (Upper One Game 2014), which uses the medium to transmit the cultural tradition of a little represented group, the Alaska native community. Games set in historical times are very popular, and some are used to teach history in schools, constituting a valuable aid in learning principles of game mechanics, determinism and contingency, economics, environmental issues, and periodization in history (Wainwright 2014; Lieberman 2010). In these cases, historical simulations are interpretations of the past, which for game purposes are designed as a 'problem space'. The player is

---

[5]A deterministic algorithm produces the same output, given a particular input. Examples include Turing machines.

[6]A *seed number* is a number that is used to start a pseudorandom generation of numbers.

an agent in a physical world and needs to achieve some goals that are contextualised in this space. The outcome of each effort to achieve a goal is shaped by a specific level of access to resources, which vary in quality and quantity, and by constraints, as also according to the space/time/culture and social system the game is situated in. Each constraint, quality, and motive is translated in the metric system that conforms to the 0s and 1s by which a central processing unit (CPU) can receive orders. Consequently, no matter how abstract the concept in the real world is, in the game it becomes a matter of quantification. As a result, so far historical simulations produced by games engines are 'teleological in their focus' as "the quantifiable gameplay elements and mechanics all, in a tightly designed game any way, factor directly into whether the player achieves their goals" (McCall 2012).

When considering the game engines for the creation of a narrative matrix able to offer 'descriptions' of complex adaptive system—here focusing on historical events as complex, generative, social systems—central to the status of this form of expression is the epistemological framing of the 'encounter' with this medium. The exploration of what games' narratives are reveals that they certainly are a mode of representation but also something entirely different, a procedural medium that makes them subject to different modes of narration from film and novels (Murray 1997). Firstly, they are a system of procedurals able to convey a play-rhetoric and contributing to the player's construction of meaning—similarly to other narrative forms. Examples of such mechanics are found in early games: "the people have a game called *weiqi*, which is a kind of 'art of war'" (Halter 2006, p. 21). According to the author the game functioned as a military guide. The traditional game was then interpreted in the board game *Go*, known as the 'encircling game' and displaying the most traditional Chinese war technique (Shotwell 2003, p. 134), which constituted an interesting translation of traditional military philosophy and strategies into the procedural of the game. Also, the ability of games to transmit certain values, which might clash with the hegemonic cultural power of the moment, is testified by banned games displaying no violent or sexual content. Early examples include the board game *Monopoly* (1935) that in Hungary during the Communist period was translated into the game *Economize Wisely* (1960), which substituted the accumulation of capital with politically correct goals like getting a job, an apartment, and a saving account (DiMaggio 2001, p. 102). This development is particularly poignant as the game was invented as an educational device by Elizabeth Magie (Economic Game Company 1904) to demonstrate how rents enrich the landlord—hence the name of the original board game *The Landlord's Game*. The game, however, became particularly popular because it made explicit the rules of monopolistic societies and not because it was a proof of the unfairness of the system (Orbanes 2006). Thus, values in games are transmitted on two different levels: on the *text level*, where signs are interpreted in many ways and according to the player's cultural background; and on the *ergodic level*, where the player's performance generates new signs that are subjected to interpretation as well. Computer game procedurals, coded by the team creating the game, enable the paths on/between which the player can experience the game and generate content. In some cases, as early studies in computer games demonstrate, the values transmitted by the game's structure can be negotiated between the players and the team, like in the case of Massively Multiplayer Online Games (MMOG) (Jacobson and Taylor 2003). However, in most cases, the designers, who convey more or less intentionally a determined set of values through their games, exploit the rhetorical potential of the computer game.

Historical simulation games are especially interesting for their procedurals because

> Simulation acts as a kind of map-in-time visually and viscerally (as the player internalises the game's logic) demonstrating the repercussions and interrelatedness of many different social decisions (Friedman 1999).

The 'authors', in this case, the designers, select an interpretation of the past and make it playable. The choice of a specific 'problem space' bonds the game to a specific level of the portrayal of the past—not much different to a linear story where the point of view is dictated by a person, or group, whose predicaments take place within a specific social stratum. This limitation, however, is one of the problems historical simulations created with game engines can solve better than other media, as a player can 'enter' and 'exit' the lives of multiple agents and therefore acquire a sense of their limitations, interrelationships, different goals, fears and points of view. The problem, however, is that commercial games commit to small sets of agents and rules, to function smoothly and to connect to every part of the system harmoniously. Consequently, so far, they failed in offering an articulate enough representation of any historical period.

6 Complex Narratives

So far complexity science has been applied only to the study of war (Solvit 2012), as a complex adaptive system, and human communication (Corman et al. 2006), as resonance analysis. It also seems applicable to the development of multidimensional historical narratives with the use of game engines able to reproduce events as complex adaptive systems (CAS) and look at the responses/reactions of different agents to various elements in time, one of which would be priming. Such a narrative matrix would demonstrate the pertinence of a CAS based approach and explore possibilities in the evolution of historical studies beyond the reductionist philosophy that flattens out past events to a fixed moment, whose causality is completely manageable.

If specifically applied to the study of disputed history or silenced history, as in the example offered above, such narrative matrices of historical simulation would add levels of investigation to the current scholarly research. Specifically, they would offer simultaneousness, speed and access to experience and multiple points of view, in time. Also, they would offer the chance to experience the effects of priming, the consequences of identification with various interpretations of events and the impact of residual historical memory. Similarly, they could produce an arena for the study of the metahistory of historiographical narratives. Complex narratives of such nature need to be based on a set of notions able to offer a basic narrative theory for VR. This would consider narrative as a process and comprehend both mimetic narratives, based on showing (through the use of character and plot), and diegetic narratives, based on telling (as in the Greek chorus, and oral history). The mimetic sphere of influence would take into account recent theories of neo-Aristotelian drama (Nelson and Mateas 2005; Cavazza and Pizzi 2006), which consider the user as a character within the system. This would testify to the possibility immersion offers to the users, as they can experience the constraints the historical period put on people in matters of economic, social and ideological limits. The micro activity could be secured by the presence of branching plot points able to offer an upgrade to the characters' ability to cope with the environment and the events investing them, which would also function within the advancement of the overarching historical simulation in place. 'Experience' then would become *the story* in the micro-universe of the user, as the result of the users' interaction with the system would be experienced as a personalised path of actions, which face the 'reaction' of the narrative system in the person of the AI characters. In this way, the user would be exposed to the complex system, which might present the emergence of unexpected phenomena due to the players' actions. The result would be a simulation open to trial, which would secure the presence of as many limitations, by procedurals, and opportunities for actions as possible, in a mimetic application of the historical knowledge. Accordingly, it would be sensitive to the 'human factor' and the unexpected, able to reveal relationships within the narrative matrix that were not necessarily visible. Consequently, the Aristotelian categories would be applied but read in accordance to the new medium; most importantly *character* would comprise AI characters and users; *mythos* (plot) would evolve according to the action of the users but within a set of possible events, according to the historical data. Thus, this narrative matrix would regard character as an active narrative element but also base historical understanding on the emotional impact of the matrix on the users. They would experience and interpret the historical circumstances where specific events took place—according to the users' ability to avoid them from happening, to elicit their passing, or producing different events. Such an experience would be possible only if a good level of believability would be put in place, as underlined in research on virtual worlds and interactions has established (Magnenat-Thalmann et al. 2005, pp. 2–9; Alkawaz et al. 2015, pp. 1–10).

To narrate within this kind of environment, we would accept the narrative matrix as a summing up of more than the system's parts, where by understanding the behaviour of the individual actors, and actants, we would not be able to understand the system as a whole. For example, by understanding and following the activity of Trieste's average citizen between 1915 and 1918, it would be impossible to understand how a small number of wealthy mercantile people assured its annexation to Italy, when the vast majority of its population was both not Italian and not interested in being part of Italy (Purini 2010). However, by observing the loops of feedback and emergence produced within the system, we would be able to explore the status of our historical knowledge. Accordingly, such a complex narrative system would take into account the initial dominant priming and the whole interpretative spectrum that evolved from this initial set of assumptions. In such a system, the possibility to

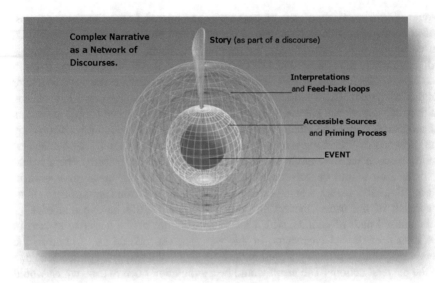

Fig. 11.1 Complex narrative as network of discourses

translate truthfully some aspect of the micro-processes operating in it is open, as is the experimentation on the history of the matrix, because the history of the evolution of the system itself would be responsible for its reactions. Finally, this narrative matrix would be of interest in the study of the delicate equilibrium offered by the actors' response to information available to them locally and their ignorance of the system as a whole.

Thinking of a possible graphic representation of such a narrative matrix, I conceive of a narrative system able to produce a multiplicity of access, where the users would try to reach the truth about the event. Consequently, stories would function as an experience of both 'moments' in the production of multiple discourses on the same event, and as receptions that each interpretation receives in time by the interested public, actors and actants, in a flow of feedback loop. The offered graphic (Fig. 11.1) presents a map of the possible system on a micro level, where the story inhabited by the player would partake in the discourse related to the event. The story would ideally share in the understanding of the event, and the user would try to reach truth and understanding beyond the layers of interpretation following the priming effect, but it is not a pre-requisite of the system as such an accomplishment is unlikely to happen. Understanding would remain locked to the cognitive ability of the seeker, as discussed in the previous sections.

However, a variety of experiences offered by multiple points of entrance into the event, reactions to priming, and related subsequent interpretations, and the narration of the metahistory of the historical representation would be specifically important, as their complex multiplicity can bring to surface a space where the networks of activities can be perceived as a whole. Also, as a tool for the academic research, it

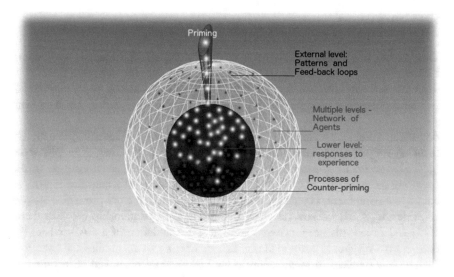

Fig. 11.2 Priming and counter priming

could indicate relationships between activity and past actions/expressions, like the resurgence of historical memory. If applied, for example, it could indicate links between actants able to explain the current Slovenian cultural resurgence in Trieste, because the system could show how silenced history affected the descendants of specific actors, induced them to adapt and survive in unsuspected ways, and influence the system.

To implement such a matrix, procedurals could be used to reveal an identity, situatedness, a discourse, and priming politics. A vast multiplicity of playable agents could account for the heterogeneous list of agents surviving in a social CAS. Similarly, on another level of diegetic enquiry, users could find insight into why and how certain historians interpreted one event by preferring a certain set of evidence over another—translating and unveiling the long term social effects of priming, as Fig. 11.2 simplifies.

As a result, a different set of roles and goals would offer a different experience, maybe eliciting a desire to 'enter' the system and experience it from different perspectives. I can see how such a laborious system of interrelated levels of activity in which to plant elements would offer a venue for the utilisation of game engines for multiple scientific purposes—one of which could serve academic historiography.

7   Conclusions

This chapter has considered elements at play in the establishment of our current historical knowledge. Looking at the past events as complex adaptive systems, it demonstrated why the current mediation of history could be felt as oversimplified. By the continuously changing interactions in human society, fed by feedback and subject to linear and non-linear causality, I have considered the qualities that need to be tackled within new narrative tools for the explanation of historical events. By focusing on VR, I debated the value of new technologies, which might show applicable solutions to a new concept of historical narrative, specifically in media operating on game-engines. By formulating the possibility of a narrative matrix, as narrative environment, I considered its potential in offering a pre-processed archive of evidence, which informs on what they are and the relationship between them. However, I read this pre-processed archive as a simulation of a CAS, where the narrative matrix should bring to the surface answers about the ontological quality of such an environment in relationship to the historical event looked at in time and space. The primary interest being, the matrix's ability to be not only an interactive interface enabling the exploration of the evidential material and the construction of individual interpretation and narrative of the historical event—which nonetheless would enable personal choices about what is the important narrative within the system. The matrix should draw attention to the openness of the past to different narrative interpretations by giving proofs of how the experience of negotiating the archive isn't separate from interpretation itself, and how it changes in time. The narrative medium would reveal the work of a process that creates meaning by including the product of the process, the material of the process, and the process itself. This would involve the creation of a complicated narrative matrix able to offer multiple points of entry into the system. However, such a narrative environment would be of high value in suspending the attention to a pre-narrative stage, giving space to experiencing conflicts and ideological acculturations, social interactions and influences from different points of view, times and ideological positions. Thus, it would offer a space for an understanding of the material, and the logic behind the creation of historical *mythos* before it becomes crystalized into a given narrative. This kind of knowledge would share characteristics of the knowledge acquired by 'doing' and 'living', which in the case of historical explanation bears a value. Accordingly, game engines could constitute the technology enabling such complicated computational models to create 'history-labs on the desk'. They could play patterns of behaviours, and go deep into issues surrendering specific agents; they could offer narrative experiences able not only to make us observe the emergence of the historical event, but to viscerally learn how multiple simultaneous processes could have made 'it' happen. Also, we could do more. We could experiment. This would be the place where the 'openness of the past' to multiple interpretations would be activated by the intention to put the system out of balance and see how the system's reaction might reveal internal laws, influences or relationships.

Finally, it has to be noticed that this would not be a perfect representation of the past event; the impossibility of accessing the correspondence of the narrative to the past would still be looming over the matrix. However, such a system could reduce the level, or the connotation, of the problem. Similarly, it would be a historical narrative 'on a mission', as we would clearly look for certain answers, built it out of a specific selection of historical sources we consider objective and exhaustive. There is no escape from the situatedness of the historical understanding. Powerful engines processing the procedurals of the narrative matrix could open new angles of investigation in the metahistory of reception, interpretation and effect. It would be as if 'traveling in time' with insight on each sub-level of the system. The irritating feeling remains present, as in so doing we would obtain not a 'knowing' of the past but another 'reading' of some aspects of it, mediated by our technological framework and limited speculative understanding. Yet, everything is impossible until it is done.

References

Alkawaz MH, Dzulkifli M, Basori AH, Saba T (2015) Blend shape interpoliation and FACS for realistic avatar. 3D Res 6(1):6

Bal M (1985) Narratology: introduction to the theory of narrative. University of Toronto Press, Toronto

Bargh JA, Chen M, Burrows L (1996) Automaticity of social behavior: direct effects of trait construct and stereotype activation on action. J Pers Soc Psychol 71(2):230–244

Bloch M (1965) Feudal society 1: the growth of ties of dependence. University of Chicago Press, Chicago

Bloch M (1967) Seigneurie française et manoir anglais. Armand Colin, Parigi

Bosworth RJB (2006) Mussolini's Italy – life under the fascist dictatorship, 1915–1945. Penguin Press, New York

Cavazza M, Pizzi D (2006) Narratology for interactive storytelling: a critical introduction. In: Gobel S, Malkewitz R, Iurgel I (eds) IDSE 2006, LNCS 4326. Springer, Heidelberg, pp 72–83

Cavazza M, Charles F, Mead SJ (2001a) Characters in search of an author: AI-based virtual storytelling. First international conference on virtual storytelling. Avignon, France

Cavazza M, Charles F, Mead SJ (2001b) Agents' interaction in virtual storytelling. In: Proceedings of the international workshop on intelligent virtual agents, Madrid, Spain. Springer, Heidelberg, pp 156–170

Corman SR, Kuhn T, McPhee RD, Dooley KJ (2006) Studying complex discursive systems – centering resonance analysis of communication. Hum Commun Res 28(2):157–206

DiMaggio P (2001) The twenty-first century firm: changing economic organization in international perspective. Princeton University Press, Princeton

Febvre L (1925) A geographical introduction to history. Trubner, London

Febvre L (1929) Martin Luther: a destiny. Dutton, New York

Friedman T (1999) The semiotics of simcity. First Monday. http://www.firstmonday.org/ojs/index.php/fm/article/view/660/575. Accessed 2 Jan 2016

Gadamer HG (1979) The problem of historical consciousness. In: Rabinow P, Sullivan WM (eds) Interpretive social science: a reader. University of California, Berkely, pp 103–160

Gance, Abel, Director (1927) Napoléon. [Napoléon vu par Abel Gance (original title)] Produced by Abel Gance, Henri de Cazotte, Wengoroff, Hugo Stinnes, France

Greimas AJ (1966) Sémantique structural. Larousse, Paris

Greimas AJ (1979) Sémiotique. Dictionnaire raisonné de la théorie du language. Hachette, Paris

Halter E (2006) From Sun Tzu to Xbox: war and video games. Thunder's Mouth Press, New York

Hametz M (2005) Making Trieste Italian, 1918–1954. Boydell Press, Martlesham

Hirsch M (2012) The generation of postmemory: visual culture after the Holocaust. Columbia University Press, New York

Hoffman E (2004) After such knowledge: memory, history, and the legacy of the Holocaust. Public Affairs, New York

Jakobsson M, Taylor TL (2003) The Sopranos meets Everquest: social networking in massively multiplayer online games. FineArt Forum 17(8):81–90

Jenkins K, Munslow A (2004) The nature of history reader. Routledge, London

Jordanova L (2012) The look of the past – visual and material evidence in historical practice. Cambridge University Press, Cambridge

Kansteiner W (2002) Finding meaning in memory: a methodological critique of collective memory studies. Hist Theor 41(2):179–197

Kurosawa Akira, Director (1950) Rashomon. Produced by Minoru Jingo, Japan

Lieberman M (2010) Four ways to teach with video games. In: Gaming across the curriculum. http://currents.dwrl.utexas.edu/2010/lieberman_four-ways-to-teach-with-video-games. Accessed 28 Dec 2015

Löschnigg M, Sokołowska-Paryż M (2014) The great war in post-memory literature and film. De Gruyter, Berlin

Lyons M (2010) A new history from below? The writing culture of ordinary people in Europe. Hist Aust 7(3):59.1–59.9

MacCall J (2012) Historical simulations as problem spaces: criticism and classroom use. J Digit Humanit 1(2) Spring. http://journalofdigitalhumanities.org/1-2/historical-simulations-as-problem-spaces-by-jeremiah-mccall/. Accessed 3 Jan 2016

Magnenat-Thalmann N, HyungSeok K, Egges A, Garchery S (2005) Believability and interaction in virtual worlds. In: MMM 2005, Proceedings of the 11th international multimedia modelling conference, IEEE Computer Society, Washington, pp 2–9

Meyer DE, Schvaneveldt RW, Ruddy MG (1975) Loci of contextual effects on visual word recognition. In: Rabbitt P, Dornic S (eds) Attention and performance V. Academic Press, London, pp 98–118

Miller JH, Page SE (2010) Complex adaptive systems – an introduction to computational models of social life. Princeton University Press, Princeton

Murray JH (1997) Hamlet on the holodeck: the future of narrative in cyberspace. The Free Press, New York

Nelson M, Mateas M (2005) Search-based drama management in the interactive fiction anchorhead. Proceedings of artificial intelligence and interactive digital entertainment (AIIDE 2005), Marina del Rey, June

Orbanes P (2006) Monopoly: the world's most famous game – and how it got that way. Da Capo Press, Boston

Panofsky E (1955) The history of art as a humanistic discipline. In: Meaning in the visual arts. Doubleday Anchor Books, New York, pp 1–25

Phillips Salber M (2013) On historical distance. Yale University Press, London

Poirrier P (2008) L'histoire Culturelle: Un 'Tournant Mondial' dans L'Historiographie? Presses Universitaires de Dijon, Dijon

Porteous J, Charles F, Cavazza M (2013) NetworkING: using character relationships for interactive narrative generation. In: Proceedings of the 12th international conference on autonomous agents and multiagent systems (AAMAS), Saint-Paul, MN, USA, May, pp 595–602

Purini P (2010) Metamorfosi Etniche – I cambiamenti di popolazione a Trieste, Gorizia, Fiume e in Istria (1914–1975). Kappa Vu, Udine

Rafaeli S (1988) Interactivity: from new media to communication. In: Hawkins RP, Wiemann JM, Pingree S (eds) Sage annual review of communication research: advancing communication science: merging mass and interpersonal processes, vol 16. Sage, Beverly Hills, pp 110–134

Ronfard R, Szilas N (2014) How generative digital media is reshaping narrative. In: International conference on narrative, 27–29 Mar 2014, Cambridge, USA

Schvaneveldt RW, Meyer DE (1973) Retrieval and comparison processes in semantic memory. In Kornblum S, (ed) Attention and performance IV. Academic Press, New York, pp 395–409

Sebald WG (2001) Austerlitz (trans: Bell A). Modern Library, New York

Severin WJ, Tankard J (1997) Communication theories: origins, methods, and uses in the mass media. Longman, New York

Shotwell P (2003) Go! more than a game. Tuttle Publishing, Massachussets

Solvit S (2012) Dimensions of war. Understanding war as a complex adaptive system. L'Harmattan, Paris

Szilas N, Mancini M (2005) The control of agents' expressivity in interactive drama. In: Subsol G (ed) Proceedings of the international conference of virtual storytelling, ICVS 2005, LNCS 3805, Strasbourg, France, Nov–Dec, pp 115–124

Tesnière L (1966) Éléments de syntaxe structural. Klincksieck, Paris

Verginella M (2008) Il confine degli altri: la questione giuliana e la memoria slovena. Donzelli Editore, Rome

Vinci A (1998) Il Fascismo di confine. I viaggi di Erodoto 34:100–105

Wainwright AM (2014) Teaching historical theory through video games. Hist Teach 47(4): 579–612. http://www.societyforhistoryeducation.org/pdfs/A14_Wainwright.pdf. Accessed 29 Dec 2015

White H (1973) Metahistory: the historical imagination in nineteenth-century Europe. John Hopkins University Press, Baltimore

Chapter 12
Three-Way Dialogue (Closure, Proteus, History)

Adam Lively, Federico Pianzola, and Romana Turina

Abstract Adam Lively, Federico Pianzola, and Romana Turina in conversation on earlier versions of each of their essays, "Closure, Observation and Coupling," "The Proteus Principle," and "Narrative Experiences of History and Complex Systems."

1 To Adam, on "Closure, Observation and Coupling"

FP: Adam, you showed how Aristotle, Luhmann and Mukařovský in their theories are paying attention to three issues: the function of narrative (aesthetic, reflective), the distinctness of narrative (operative closure) and the coupling of narrative (its relation to the environment). That is: what a system does; what are the operations that enable it to do so; and in what conditions it operates and achieves its functions. I think this way of approaching narrative is very important for the soundness of every theory.

But you also showed how to conceive of narrative in autopoietic terms. I just have a remark to make about the concept of "operative closure." That's the way in which a system differentiates itself from the environment, i.e., through its own internal operations. Well, a discourse in itself doesn't have any internal operation, it can only be operated by a semiotic agent (person, or even machine; cf. Winfield, Chap. 4). Thus, I think operative closure pertains to the discourse-audience system. A discourse is not a complex system in itself because it exists only in relation to a semiotic agent. For instance, a garden comes into being thanks to the interaction of a gardener with the environment,

A. Lively (✉)
Department of Media, Middlesex University, London, UK
e-mail: a.lively@mdx.ac.uk

F. Pianzola
Department of Human Sciences for Education, University of Milan-Bicocca, Milan, Italy

R. Turina
Department of Theatre, Film and Television, University of York, York, UK

© Springer Nature Switzerland AG 2018   143
R. Walsh, S. Stepney (eds.), *Narrating Complexity*,
https://doi.org/10.1007/978-3-319-64714-2_12

but then it can live and change beyond such interactions (cf. Caves and Melo, Chap. 13). On the contrary, a discourse exists only when it is perceived by a semiotic agent, that is, when discourse and agent interact. What do you think?

AL: This is a pivotal question. The answer that Niklas Luhmann would give is that discourses do indeed constitute autopoietic systems: indeed, when he talks of autopoietic "social systems" he means systems of discourse. As he discusses in his *Introduction to Systems Theory*, this marks the parting of the ways between him and Maturana, for whom autopoietic systems are by definition biological. For Luhmann, there are biological systems, such as consciousness or perception, but there are also systems of communication that share the same systemic characteristics as these biological systems. It is true—as you point out, and as Luhmann acknowledges—that there can be no communication without consciousness: a discursive system has to have a biological realization. But at the same time, there can arguably be no consciousness without (some form of) communication: the two kinds of system are in a relationship of "structural coupling." (In *Art as a Social System* Luhmann characterises the artwork (of which, as I explain in my chapter, narrative forms something of paradigmatic instance) as a quasi-object whose purpose is a particular synchronization of perception and communication.) While one may, of course, continue to talk, at the level of personhood, of the "response" of the individual reader to the text, Luhmann's systems theory—admittedly radical in its scope—offers a way of thinking of such interactions in terms of the coupling and constraints operating between systems (biological or discursive). The radical thought is that our conventional ideas of perception and what constitutes a "subject" obscure the manner in which it is systems that observe each other—indeed, a system is only a system from the point of view of another system. (Is there a sense in which a text "observes" its reader just as much as the reader observes the text?!)

2   To Federico, on "The Proteus Principle"

RT: Federico, you speak of "consolidation of narrative studies." Can a consolidation leave space for a certain freedom? Your chapter supports the Proteus Principle, can any consolidation leave space for the exercise of such a principle?

FP: With the term "consolidation" I mean a deeper awareness of what each theory and model do in their description of narrative, and also an awareness of the epistemological ground on which each theory is based. Such awareness can help us better understand how we can combine theories or whether we can transfer them to a field that is different from the one in which they originated, like applying Labov's sociolinguistic model to the study of written fiction. Yes, there is space for freedom, since every discipline will continue to pursue its own research interests. Working for a consolidation means finding a way to avoid superficial analogies between disciplines, which "are useless in science and harmful in their practical consequences" (von Bertalanffy 1950, p. 142).

The PP is the strategy I suggest to use with the aim of consolidation. It doesn't mean that we all have to do theory in the same way: e.g., among other things, psychology will be interested in how narrative intervenes in the construction of our identity, whereas unnatural narratology will be interested in describing how a narrator can represent the thoughts of a zombie. But we can use the PP to see whether any anti-mimetic "unnatural" narrative strategy can be used in a personal narrative and how it can affect the construction of our identity.

RT: Thank you, Federico. I can see how your interest in consolidation could be a valuable solution to misunderstandings caused by those superficial analogies you refer to. Also, it would be interesting to apply such a model to the idea of a narrative matrix I refer to. To know, exactly, the epistemological ground on which each narrative is based seems to be an essential part of my proposed approach to the study and interpretation of history and metahistory.

AL: Federico, you present two complementary arguments, both of which are highly pertinent to the question of the relation between narrative and systems theory. The first of these concerns the scope of narrative analysis, and here you draw a distinction between, on the one hand, purely discursive elements ("structure"), and, on the other hand, the systemic interaction between discourse and audience (narrative "organization"). In the second part of the essay, you argue that Meir Sternberg's "Proteus Principle" (which finds in narrative a many-to-many correlation between form and function) constitutes an important starting-point for a systems-based narrative theory.

While expressed in different terms, this second argument is congruent, I think, with the polyfunctionalism that, as I discussed in my chapter, one finds in the work of Jan Mukařovský (and which is taken up subsequently by Wolfgang Iser in *The Act of Reading*).

FP: You are right about the congruence of the PP and polyfunctionality. Sternberg is not the first narratologue to adopt a kind of systems thinking: if we go back to Russian Formalism, there we find a conception of the work of art as a complex system: "Literature is a speech construction perceived precisely qua construction, i.e., literature is a dynamic speech construction" (Tynjanov 1929, quoted by Steiner 1984, p. 104). And "the unity of a work is not a closed symmetrical whole but an unfolding dynamic integrity; among its elements stands not the static sign of equation and addition, but always the dynamic sign of correlation and integration" (Tynjanov 1924, quoted by Steiner 1984, p. 116). Of course you mentioned Iser, who said that "effects and responses are properties neither of the text nor of the reader; the text represents a potential effect that is realized in the reading process" (Iser 1978, p. ix).

AL: I'd like to focus on the distinction between "structure" and "organization,"
        because it seems to me that the making of this distinction raises some
        interesting and problematic questions (which echo, perhaps, long-standing
        debates both within narratology and, more generally in literary criticism and
        history, between textualist and contextualist, or "intrinsic" and "extrinsic,"
        approaches). The question is whether, and if so how, a distinction can be
        drawn between the two scopes—on the one hand, the realm of the purely
        discursive or textual, and, on the other, the realm of the text–audience
        interaction.

        The difficulties involved in making this distinction are highlighted in the
        second paragraph of Sect. 3.3 ("How to use the Proteus Principle"), where
        you discuss the process of "selecting a kind of discursive property and
        exploring its intervention in the broader narrative organization." As an
        example of this process, you cite the investigation of "[the] role [that] the
        representation of a sequence of events [has] in generating suspense in
        narratives." But as cognitive narratology has shown us, the representation
        of a sequence of events is never a purely textual phenomenon, but invokes
        mental constructions, through the enaction of "frames" or "scripts." Even at
        the seemingly most "structural" level of grammatical cohesion, as Ronald
        Langacker has demonstrated, different constructions invoke the enaction of
        different imagistic schemata.

FP: I think I've chosen a misleading example to show the structure/organization
        distinction. These concepts do not have different scope. Let me quote directly
        from Maturana and Varela in order to make it clear: "The organization of a
        machine (or system) does not specify the properties of the components which
        realize the machine as a concrete system, it only specifies the relations which
        these must generate to constitute the machine or system as a unity. Therefore,
        the organization of a machine is independent of the properties of its
        components which can be any, and a given machine can be realized in
        many different manners by many different kinds of components. In other
        words, [. . .] a given machine can be realized by many different structures"
        (1980, p. 77). However, I am aware that in the case of narrative, it makes
        sense to talk about structure as a set of discursive elements or properties,
        because these are the variables we can better observe and describe. Only in
        some cases have extra-discursive elements been taken into account as
        constitutive elements of the narrative: e.g., the role of intertextuality and the
        historical context in the progression of a covert plot described by Dan Shen
        (2014), or the role of the repertoire in Iser's theory (1978).

AL: Alternatively, one might question the structure/organization distinction from
        a quite different, post-structuralist perspective. From this perspective, the
        important point is that any manifestation of the interaction between
        discourse and audience (any interpretation or reading) will take the form of
        more discourse, more "text," and this new text is generated by discursive
        systems transcending any putative origin in the subject ("audience"/"reader"/

"interpreter") just as much as is the original text: the distinction between subject and object cannot hold. Here one could note the congruence (acknowledged by Luhmann himself) between, on the one hand, Luhmann's radical application of autopoietic systems theory to social and discursive systems, and, on the other hand, Derrida's "grammatology."

So the problem is: How does one make distinctions between, on the one hand, what is "intrinsic" to the text, and, on the other, what pertains to the interaction with the audience, without falling into precisely the kind of subject–object paradigm that is brought into question by systems theory?

FP: The discourse–audience interactions do not generate more discourse, more text, because in principle there is no discourse prior to the interaction of some 'linguistic material' with an agent capable of semiotic processes. However, this doesn't mean that the subject is the origin of the discourse, there is no deterministic or linear causality in this, it is only the encounter between a stimulus and an agent that can originate the emergence of a certain discursive organization. The point is that the discourse is constituted in this process of emergent organization. It is in this sense that I can accept the claim that "discursive systems transcend any putative origin in the subject."

Furthermore, I'd like to specify that the discourse–audience interactions are not just interpretations or readings of the discourse: as I just said, they are constitutive of the discourse. This is called autopoiesis, but I avoided the term because I think it's very difficult to grasp and to describe it correctly. I decided to use the subject–object (audience–discourse) distinction in an attempt to make systems theory more understandable for those not familiar with it, but I am aware that this might not be the best choice. After all, this is just the beginning of this line of research and much can be improved.

3   To Romana, on "Narrative Experiences of History and Complex Systems"

FP: Romana, you introduce the terms "narrative matrix" and "narrative system," which seems to be a sort of stage previous to the composition of a narrative. Do they pre-exist the narrative? If so, how are they composed? Or are they constructed with data deriving from narratives?

RT: I can see a stage of pre-narrative in which the structure is determined to offer space for multiple narratives, to be organised in layers of relational influence and borderline zones, where there is space for the evolution of content. To compose a matrix, the purpose of the narrative has to be clear: the function the narrative has and the audience it means to address. Similar to each narrative utterance, the matrix exists to fulfil its function. The same historical event could be narrated on the basis of different matrices. However, the ultimate matrix, the one I refer to in the chapter, is able to offer a view on multiple constructs, each serving a specific narrative function related to one historical event. If the construction of the narrative has to be derived from the available data—archival and acts of witness. In this matrix, the collection of data goes beyond this level of interest and maps also the different interpretations—and the functions they served—throughout the ages, effectively offering a meta-history of the history we try to observe via the intergenerational relationships of the agents at play. Not to forget that these narratives cannot escape the imprint of their time, as every narrative system is the result of the time and location it is built in. I consider this interesting as well, and clearly useful to remember, go back to, and use for additional elaborations of historical matrices, in time.

FP: What is a narrative system?

RT: This question can be address on multiple levels. We can build narrative systems in different media, which might address different needs and purposes. The matrix I have in mind, ideally, would function utilising multiple media and use the specific quality of each medium to offer insight into history on multiple levels, one of which is self-reflection on the relationship in time between media and history. Again, a narrative system would be highly influenced by the society that is creating it. Therefore there is no correct answer here, it is a matter of functionalism and constructivism.

References

Iser W (1978) The act of reading: a theory of aesthetic response. The Johns Hopkins University Press, Baltimore

Maturana HR, Varela FJ (1980) Autopoiesis and cognition: the realization of the living. Reidel, Dordrecht

Shen D (2014) Style and rhetoric of short narrative fiction: covert progressions behind overt plots. Routledge, London

Steiner P (1984) Russian formalism. A metapoetics. Cornell University Press, Ithaca

von Bertalanffy L (1950) An outline of general system theory. Br J Philos Sci 1(2):134–165

Tynjanov J (1924) Problema stichotvomogo jazyka. Leningrad

Tynjanov J (1929) Literaturny j fakt. Archaisty i novatory. Leningrad

Chapter 13
(Gardening) Gardening: A Relational Framework for Complex Thinking About Complex Systems

Leo Caves and Ana Teixeira de Melo

Abstract For positive outcomes to be achieved in the management of change in complex systems, our modes of thinking need to be congruent with the complexity of the targeted systems. In this chapter, we draw inspiration from the concept of gardening, conceived as a systemic activity of managing relations or the process by which a gardener relates to the relations of a complex system, to develop a relational thinking framework for complex thinking applied to change in complex systems. This framework is based on a relational worldview of interventions, as systemic activities aimed at change in complex systems. We propose a heuristic, in the form of a recursive relational thinking method, which can be used to explore different configurations of relations that represent abstract entities within a *modelworld*. Further we suggest that these configurations of relations can be the base for a corresponding *storyworld*, to assist in the narration of change in complex systems. We present this general abstract framework and apply it (recursively) to gardening itself as an example of a domain of change. This exercise illustrates how the proposed relational framework can be used to generate different models of change and supporting narratives, as well as the fitness of different modes of intervention in relation to desired outcomes. The result is, in itself, a basic relational framework or meta-model to guide the planning, evaluation and communication of interventions in complex systems.

L. Caves (✉)
Independent Researcher, Sao Felix da Marinha, Portugal

York Cross-Disciplinary Centre for Systems Analysis, University of York, York, UK

A. T. de Melo
Centre for Social Studies, University of Coimbra, Coimbra, Portugal

© Springer Nature Switzerland AG 2018
R. Walsh, S. Stepney (eds.), *Narrating Complexity*,
https://doi.org/10.1007/978-3-319-64714-2_13

1 Clearing the Ground: Introduction

Cybernetics is the science or the art of manipulating defensible metaphors; showing how they may be constructed and what can be inferred as a result of their existence (Pask 1975)

What is our capacity for affecting change in our complex world? How can we relate to a complex system in a way that brings about a positive or desired change? This chapter emerges from a need to know how we could organize our thinking and acting regarding change in complex systems.

Academics, policy makers and practitioners face the challenges of tackling systems that are complex and, therefore, not readily predictable or controllable (Sterman 2006). Change in these systems is not linear and is dependent on a multitude of factors, including the history of the system. Commonly, interventions have been designed using forms of thinking and practice that were developed from simplistic, reductionist and mechanistic worldviews and applied to a world that is ... not (or is only in restricted circumstances) (Capra 1997). Consequently, the outcome of change is often not the one that was aimed for and unexpected behaviours may emerge, sometimes as negative side effects (Sterman 2006). In light of this, we believe the way we think and the way we conduct interventions needs to be congruent with the nature of the systems we seek to influence: we need complex thinking for complex systems.

In this chapter, we do not review theories of complex systems nor even core concepts (Kelso 1997; Érdi 2007; Mitchell 2009). Instead, we focus on a *framework of thinking* that has a pragmatic focus and supports the exploration and general practices of those who seek effective ways of relating to the complex world. Rather than focusing on specific systems, we develop an abstract systemic *framework* and consider general questions, inviting the reader to think (i) "what are the things I need to think about when I think of change in my system of interest?", and (ii) "how do I need to think about these things, and the relations between them?" The application of the framework requires system-specific content that must be built for a particular system or class of systems. We hope that this framework will be applicable to different types of systems and we invite the reader to try to explore it in their own settings. We believe this framework is capable of supporting a sufficiently complex thinking to guide effective action in different kinds of systems, but also to provide a common basis for the evaluation of interventions. We also believe it can provide a simple and familiar language to facilitate interdisciplinary dialogue. We invite the reader for an exploratory *mindwalk* (Capra 1990) into the terrains of complex thinking while keeping a focus on their own systems of interest.

2   Laying Out the Gardening: A Relational Framework for Complex Thinking About Complex Systems

A new knowledge of organization is capable of creating a new organization of knowledge (Morin 1992)

In the tradition of thinkers concerned with developing forms of complex thinking (e.g. Whitehead 1929; Bateson 1979; Morin 2005, 2008) we sought to explore the relations implicated in change in complex systems in a way that reflects aspects of their systemic organisation and properties. We looked for a way of thinking that captured the relations from which a whole emerges and transforms and that could be applied to different kinds of systems.

2.1   Gardening as an Inspiration for Thinking About Complex Systems

Gardening provided us the inspiration for *how to think* about interventions in complex systems (i.e., process). We view gardening as a *systemic activity of managing relations* or the process by which a gardener *relates to the relations of a complex system* (e.g., the plants to the soil, the different plants to each other, the garden to its surroundings, the capacity of the gardener in relation to the kind of garden envisaged).

It is also a good example of interventions in nature—the archetype of a complex system. Therefore, it should provide us with relevant information to understand *what* we need to think about when we think of interventions in complex systems (i.e., content).

Is gardening a domain of activity for change in complex systems that is sufficiently rich to offer insights that are applicable to a broad range of other complex systems? Is the analogy appropriate? Control in behaviour of (complex) systems is the central concern of cybernetics (Wiener 1961). The requirement for an effective (model of a) controller is captured in the *Law of Requisite Variety* (Ashby 1958),[1] which states that any controller for a system needs to be at least as rich as the aspects of the dynamical behaviour of the system that we wish to explore or influence. In principle, a controller that is rich enough (in terms of the numbers of states it can generate) can absorb the essential complexities of the system, as experienced by a given observer, and will support an understanding of the capacity for system changes, and the possible effective modes of change, even if it does not provide a clear vision of what it changes into. However, if the controller is relatively

---

[1]The Law of Requisite Variety has different forms: "The larger the variety of actions available to a control system, the larger the variety of perturbations it is able to compensate." or "Variety destroys variety", or as Stafford Beer (1979) rephrased it: "Variety absorbs variety".

impoverished, it will fail in these respects and this may lead to misunderstanding, inappropriate interventions and unexpected or even damaging outcomes.

2.2   A Relational Worldview

We adopt a *relational wordview* as a way to build models of complex systems through the essential relations that sustain them and that are implicated in change. In a relational worldview, all of the components exist in relation to one another, i.e., they are *relata* (Whitehead 1920). Any entity is defined in a relationship with something else (Varela 1976; Cassirer et al. 1923; Kelso and Engstrom 2008). The thing to which it is related will confer it a different identity or add a new perspective to it. All visions regarding any entity are, therefore, relative to the choice of the position of an observer, and the properties that are highlighted will change according to the particular relative position adopted (Goguen and Varela 1979). Systems are relational entities and they have to be understood with a focus on those relations that build and transform them. This relational perspective aligns with that of Bateson (1979), who defined relationship as a product of *double description* arising from complementary perspectives (e.g., how binocular vision arises from the interaction of monocular views from each eye). Different types of interaction give rise to different relationships, allowing for a variety of descriptions, depending on one's point of view. Due to their richness, complex systems require a plurality of descriptions and each part of the system will appear in a different way depending on what it is being compared or related to.

2.3   A Recursive Relational Thinking Process

Relating concepts and ideas through comparison has long been used in the social sciences as a way of producing meaningful information regarding certain phenomena or for building theories (Glaser and Strauss 1967). One of the difficulties of analysing a complex system is that there is often a myriad of elements to be considered and a multitude of relations between them, all of which are implicated in the system's form and capacity for transformation. To address this, we needed a feasible way to explore this (potentially vast) space of relations in order to be able to identify the critical ones—those on which change could depend.

To this end, we looked to the characteristics of complex systems themselves. Complex systems have ways of compressing information through self-organisation (Haken 1987). The enormous variety of behaviours and elements at the lower levels of the system are synergetically coupled into new coordination variables (patterns, forms, structures, etc.) that reduce the number of parameters needed to understand the behaviour of the system (Haken 1984; Kelso 1997). In our case, we were looking for the emergence of new patterns of ideas about the system at hand that would provide understanding and suggest actions for effective intervention.

We tried to mimic the behaviour of a complex system not just by exploring and coordinating the relations between the important elements, but by going further and exploring relations of relations in a way that allowed for the compression of information and the emergence of novel patterns of ideas about how to manage change in that system. Detailed phenomena at one level, requiring explicit consideration of multiple interactions, are implicitly subsumed by a reconceptualised description at another.[2]

We aimed to develop a method based on systematically relating the core relata that, according to our worldview, we considered necessary to understand the system and the intervention. Therefore, we developed a *recursive relational thinking process* that allowed for a systematic exploration of relations within and around our system of interest. We explored our worldview, its constituent elements and relations, using this method to build up configurations of relations that provide insight into a complex system and its capacity for change.

We needed to distinguish between the base relata of the system before exploring their relations. Then, the build-up of new levels of description of a system through relating relata provides higher order concepts that, themselves, can be related both within and between levels. In so doing, we aimed to produce meaningful information and eventually assist the emergence of some degree of novelty (e.g., perspective, insight).

To be able to deal with the diversity of relata and their richness we assumed that we could not just compare relata, but had to compare relations themselves—that thereby become relata in a recursive fashion. In doing so, we aimed to compress information into new levels of description without having to cover all possible combinations of individual relata.

By systematically comparing relata we build different trajectories or pathways leading to a higher order perspective leading to new insight. Because the relata of the system are interconnected, in principle, we could start with any two relata and explore their connection with any other individual relata or their relations and similar patterns would eventually emerge [*equifinality* (von Bertalanffy 1971)]. Nevertheless, different routes could produce different nuances that could be relevant for different purposes [*multifinality* (Wilden 2013)]. By comparing relations, novel (higher order) relata emerge that can then be further related. Due to their emergent character, understanding of these higher order relata may not be reducible to their component relata in simple ways.

Considering the different base relata of the system (Fig. 13.2, later), we could conduct multiple iterations of relating (relations) at different levels until we reach

---

[2]For example, the different languages accounting for micro-, meso- or macroscopic phenomena in physics, or the individual, group, or population level descriptions in the social sciences. Although these examples relate to emergence of new levels of description related to (a hierarchy of) spatial scale, we consider the more general case of the emergence of novel concepts at new levels of relating relations.

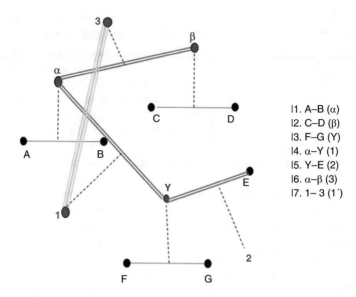

Fig. 13.1 Graphical representation of the relational thinking process on a hypothetical domain, starting with 6 base (zeroth-order) relata (A–G) showing the construction of a relational configuration through a relational pathway of 7 iterations (I1-I7). Each iteration relates relata at one level, to form higher order relata at another level: zeroth order (base): A–G; first order: α–γ; second order: 1–3; third order: 1'

either a perspective that we consider to be sufficiently meaningful to provide insight, allow experimentation or inform practice, or some form of saturation is achieved (Glaser and Strauss 1967; Miles and Huberman 1994).

Although some pathways are possibly more laborious or slow to lead to meaningful information, we should be able to start anywhere and, by moving towards higher-order patterns, find similar patterns of properties or types of information. The choices of the starting point, of the relata to be considered and of the relational pathways to explore, are dependent on the observer's previous knowledge of the field and their preferences. The important point is that that the exploration is systematic and that the observer tracks the trajectory of iterations so they can rebuild or revisit the trajectory at particular points to experiment with different routes. A visual representation of the building of the relational pathway can be of assistance. In the end, the observer should be able to see a web of connections covering almost all the relata that were set up.

In Fig. 13.1 we present an abstract representation of a relational pathway. The pathway represents a trajectory of relating relata to each other to build up new levels of relata. The process moves towards a configuration of relations that forms the entities within a hypothetical relational world. The process starts by laying out the initial relata represented by black dots and Roman letters. The observer starts at one given point and attempts to relate to relata. Once a relation is established, it is taken as if it is a new relatum. In Fig. 13.1, we used the dotted line to transform a given relation into a new relatum (dot on the figure) to be then related. The pathway may continue from that relatum, or new individual relata can be connected before moving on to a point of establishing a relation between relations. In our example, in Iteration 1 (I1) relata A and B are transformed into relation α. In iteration 2 we choose to explore the relation between C and D from which a new point β is created. Only in Iteration 4 (I4) do we start to relate relations. The relation of relations is taken to be of a different order and is represented by Arabic numerals. For example, in Iteration 4 the relation between α and γ construct the higher order relata 1. These second order relata can also be built by comparing one base relata with one second order relation, as in Iteration 5 (I5). Finally, at iteration 7 (I7) a third order relation is built that relates two relations of relations. If the observer finds it easier to see how many of the relata have been covered, triangles can be built by using the points that include the two relata plus the point created to represent their relation.

We are not proposing a mechanical procedure or algorithm, but a flexible, accessible process for a principled recursive comparison of relations that is explicitly dependent on the cognitive capacities of the thinker and their choices (Mauthner and Doucet 2003). In the proposed framework, relata at different levels can be related in recursive loops. Ideally, after several iterations, the thinker would have covered, through consideration (and selection) of individual relata and their relations (and relations of relations, etc.), most of the relational landscape could be explored. The important point is to track the trajectories so they can be rebuilt if new insight is necessary or if the evaluation of a trajectory reveals poor outcomes and new alternatives need to be explored.

2.4   A Relational Framework (or Meta-Model)

Together, the relational worldview and the recursive relational thinking result in a meta-model in the form of a *relational framework for complex thinking about complex systems*. Using this framework, different models can be built that support different narratives. These can be used to describe and explain potential interventions and their effects, and to support case study evaluations (Yin 2013).

2.5   Relational Modelworlds

The result of using the framework on a particular domain (e.g., in this chapter, that of gardening) is a set of configurations of relationships from which different higher-order concepts or perspectives can emerge that provide insight into the system in relation to change processes. These concepts emerge from the recursive relational thinking process and provide useful abstract entities that can be used to build models of change processes in a given domain. As these entities can be generated and combined in different ways, to create different models, they provide the basis for a *relational modelworld.*[3]

2.6   The Roles of the Meta-Observer

In this chapter, we adopt the perspective of a meta-observer who aims to understand and evaluate action and change in a complex system. This observer, presenting the properties of observers as defined by Varela (1976) (capacity for indication, capacity for time, capacity for agreement) is implicitly part of our model. The observer is not 'neutral' but necessarily guided by our own preferences (von Foerster 2007).

In this chapter, the authors take the role of a meta-observer. In other contexts, this meta-observer could be, for example, a consultant, a supervisor, or an advisor. An element of the world that is being explored could also take a meta-stance or a reflexive position and adopt this role. The role may also be distributed among different elements of an internal or external system. Different relative positions of this meta-observer will likely present different capacities, and provide different insights, leading to different types of interventions and evaluations.

3   Planting the Gardening: Foundations for the Construction of a Modelworld for Gardening

> *I think this is what hooks one to gardening: it is the closest one can come to being present at creation.* (In Demakis, 2012)

3.1   A Relational Worldview for Gardening as an Archetype of Interventions in Complex Systems

Gardening provided the inspiration and analogy for our thinking and the development of our framework. Additionally, it offers rich illustrations of the theory and practice of managing relations in nature and a common familiar language to which readers from different disciplinary cultures can relate.

We needed a model capable of informing us about what were the minimal number of components needed to describe and explain change in complex systems, as well as the core relations between them. The selection of the core components is grounded in systemic and ecological models that call attention to processes of mutual causality,

---

[3]We use the term *modelworld* for the results of the meta-modelling framework that can create a range of models.

and co-evolution in living systems (Bateson 1972; Capra 1990; Macy 1991), as well as to the active role of the observer in shaping the reality they seek to address (Varela and Maturana 1987; von Foerster 2007).

If we want to understand gardening as an analogous to interventions in complex systems, we need to be able to explore how different configurations of relations (sets of relations between relations) within our worldview sustain certain types of outcomes (e.g., particular types or purposes of gardens).

3.2   Base Relata

When thinking of our worldview for gardening, the first step was to identify our base relata,[4] i.e., the basic constituents of our world that were to be explored in relation to each other. The choice of the base relata is dependent on the meta-observer's knowledge and intuition and/or could be the result of a principled modelling methodology, e.g., Andrews et al. (2011). We believe the relata we consider below are a general starting point for the exploration of scenarios relating to affecting change in a variety of complex systems.

Figure 13.2 presents the base relata that form the foundations of the modelworld for gardening.

The core relata are a trinity of Garden, Environment and Gardener (more generally the System, Environment and Intervenor[5]). To these base relata we add relations of *coupling* between them. In addition, for the Gardener, we consider their *reflexivity* in relation to both the Garden and the Environment. *Time* is an essential relatum for change processes and is largely implicit in our scheme (Sect. 13.4.1); we explicitly consider time in the relation between the Current Garden and Future Garden.

For these relata, we needed to identify and consider which characteristics are important. For the Garden and the Environment, we focused on their *Complexity*. For the Gardener, we focused on both their *Pragmatic and Theoretical Systemicity*[6] and Resourcefulness. The quality of the characteristics of the relata (e.g., high, low) also needs to be considered. More details about these relata and their characteristics are provided in Sect. 13.4 below.

---

[4]Note that the relata we start with can be both objects and relations, reflecting our relational stance.

[5]The name "Intervenor" may conjure up notions of an external agent of change, but as we take a meta-position, we explicitly include it *within* our (meta-)model as part of the worldview (a meta-system). Depending on the distinction being made by an observer, the intervenor can come from outside or inside the system. It is the particular type of relation (e.g., intention) in respect of the possibility of change that provides the distinction for this role.

[6]"Having the property of system-characteristics" (Checkland 2000).

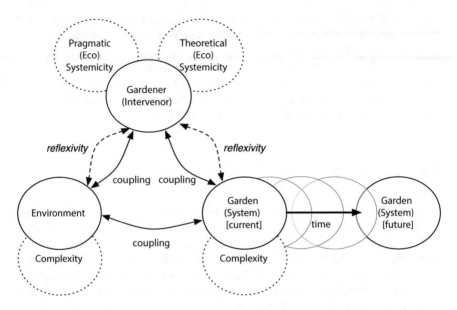

Fig. 13.2 The configuration of base relata for building a modelworld for gardening indicating the process of change from current to future garden

---

Invitations for Reflection

- What are the base relata to build a relational modelworld for exploring change in your system of interest?
- To what do the relata correspond?
- How much do you already know about the relata and their relationships?
- What other similar models have been built and explored and in what ways do they relate to yours?

3.3   Applying the Relational Thinking Framework to Gardening

Figure 13.3 represents the development of the relational thinking applied to the worldview of gardening as we explored it, at different stages. We decided to start with the garden from our base (zeroth order) relata and selected a property of the garden to explore, namely its complexity. By comparing the complexity of the current garden and the complexity of our future garden, we created a relation corresponding to the complexity of change as our initial first order relation.

We then progressively moved to other individual relata, relating them, until we started to relate either relations with individual base relata (elements or relations) or

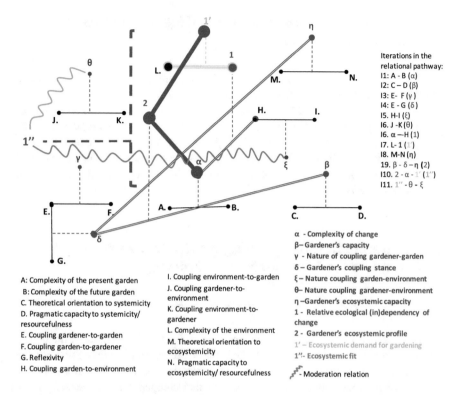

Iterations in the relational pathway:

I1: A - B (α)
I2: C – D (β)
I3: E- F (γ)
I4: E - G (δ)
I5: H-I (ξ)
I6. J -K (θ)
I6. α —H (1)
I7. L- 1 (1′)
I8. M-N (η)
I9. β - δ – η (2)
I10. 2 - α - 1′ (1″)
I11. 1″ - θ - ξ

A: Complexity of the present garden
B: Complexity of the future garden
C. Theoretical orientation to systemicity
D. Pragmatic capacity to systemicity/resourcefulness
E. Coupling gardener-to-garden
F. Coupling garden-to-gardener
G. Reflexivity
H. Coupling garden-to-environment

I. Coupling environment-to-garden
J. Coupling gardener-to-environment
K. Coupling environment-to-gardener
L. Complexity of the environment
M. Theoretical orientation to ecosystemicity
N. Pragmatic capacity to ecosystemicity/ resourcefulness

α - Complexity of change
β– Gardener's capacity
γ - Nature of coupling gardener-garden
δ – Gardener's coupling stance
ξ – Nature coupling garden-environment
θ– Nature coupling gardener-environment
η –Gardener's ecosystemic capacity
1 - Relative ecological (in)dependency of change
2 - Gardener's ecosystemic profile
1′ – Ecosystemic demand for gardening
1″- Ecosystemic fit

🌿 - Moderation relation

Fig. 13.3 Representation of the configuration of relations resulting from the relational thinking pathway used to explore the modelworld for gardening

relations with relations progressing to higher orders until we felt that the map of relations was significantly covered.

In the following sections we trace the path we used in this process of exploring our relata and creating and relating relations. In exploring each relation, we asked: "What is it that emerges?", "How do the individual relata interact?", "What is represented by the interaction and what new entity emerges from this configuration of relations"? We explored each new individual relatum and its interactions, trying to understand "What does this mean? To what does this correspond in the world of gardening?" In this process, and by reflecting on the interaction of prototypes of relations or states, we started to identify *patterns* (fuzzy relational prototypes or conceptual categories) corresponding to different expressions of those relations. When transforming a relation into a new relatum we sought to condense information by abstracting the extreme positions of the emergent characteristics and using these "polar" prototypes to explore the following interactions, in order to facilitate reasoning. Although there is necessarily some loss of richness, we tried to keep the previous level in the background to assist us in identifying important nuances of the new interactions.

3.4 A Relational Framework for Thinking About Change in Complex Systems

We have developed a relational framework (or meta-model) for thinking about change in complex systems, using gardening as an example. In summary, playing with the recursiveness that defines many complex systems, we applied a gardening-informed complex thinking framework to a relational worldview of gardening as an intervention in a complex system. We explored *gardening* as an example of an activity that is generally familiar and that provides a rich setting in which to consider what *kinds of elements,* in what *kinds of relations,* in *what conditions* are related to *what kinds of outcomes.*

4 Cultivating Gardening: Using the Relational Framework to Explore the Modelworld for Gardening

A society grows great when old men plant trees whose shade they know they shall never sit in. Greek proverb

Our framework was built to understand change in complex systems. Change is a transformation from one state to another state in time. Our starting point for the exploration of gardening was a comparison between the state of the current garden and that of the future garden (Fig. 13.2). For that comparison, we focused on the property of complexity of the garden. However, before we explore this, we offer some considerations about time.

4.1 Time, Relative Timescales, Timeliness and History

Gardening is an exercise in thinking about and managing relations (and relations of relations). An important consideration is how these relations change in time. This brings in considerations of relative timescale, and the notion of *timeliness.*

Driving Oscillations Many aspects of gardening are driven by the natural tempo of our planet's orbit around the sun. This celestial relation drives and entrains many environmental processes such as the progression in the expression of nature, at two coupled timescales: (i) the annual seasons: winter, dormant and fallow; spring, awakening and budding; summer, resplendent and blossoming; autumn, decay and decline; and (ii) the diurnal cycle with its 24-hour period.

Relative Timescales and Coupling Between Timescales Gardening naturally provides a context for the consideration of multiple relative timescales that need to be understood for effective management. Different practices are appropriate at different timescales. For example, the common gardening rituals occurring: (i) *daily*, such as watering, pest-vigilance, dead-heading; (ii) *weekly*, such as pruning, weeding, mowing; (iii) *monthly*, such as transplanting, thinning-out; (iv) *seasonally*, such as planting, harvesting; (v) *annually*, such as plant rotation, soil rotovation/tilling; and (vi) *longer term*, such as a transition to organic, establishing microenvironments/services, e.g., a new pond; maturation/achieving balance.

A key feature of these interventions at multiple timescales is the way in which they are coupled: practices at each level support or facilitate actions at other levels. For example, the seasonal production of fruits and vegetables is supported by annual preparation of the soil, but also the daily ritual of watering and watching for pests, that in turn supports weekly selective harvesting of the produce.

Timeliness Another important aspect of gardening practice is that of knowing *when* is the right time for a particular action or practice. Within the rhythm of the seasons, there are particular beats that are associated with different kinds of actions. For example, the seasonal dependence of particular rituals: in winter, pruning of plants; in spring, sowing of seeds; in summer, harvesting of produce; in autumn, digging over the soil (and so on). The timing of these actions/interventions are organised in the form of a Gardener's Calendar which guides the gardener as to what should they be doing, when.

One ritual exemplifies timeliness, weeding. Weeding needs to be done often and in a timely fashion. It is best to remove weeds before they become established (putting down stronger roots, making them more difficult to remove, and more prone to recurrence). It is often better to weed in the morning or after rainfall, when the soil is moist, as this aids their removal. There can be grave consequences to not attending to these gardening rituals. Any temptation to skip weeding must be set against the aphorism *"One year of seed; seven years of weed".*[7]

History In gardening, we generally don't start from a clean slate. The garden, environment and gardener all have a history that may need to be considered in relation to other relata. These histories may impact upon such things as couplings, complexity, etc. For example, a previous use of pesticides in the neighbouring environment will impact on the timescales for a change towards an organic garden.

Invitations for Reflection

- What are the intrinsic timescales of the system you are relating to?
- How do the different timescales relate to each other?
- Are there key external drivers that impose a rhythm upon the system?
- Is it possible to characterise different phases of activity within the system rhythms?

(continued)

---

[7]That is, if you don't deal with your weed and it goes to seed and multiplies, you are going to have a lot of additional work in future to eradicate the problem ...

- Do different phases suggest particular kinds of activities? When is the best time to intervene?
- Can you envisage strong sequential dependencies of any these activities? Can you use these to order/prioritise the activities?
- Is it possible to set up a calendar to orchestrate these activities?

4.2   The Complexity of Change

4.2.1   Relation in Time: Complexity of the Current Garden ×
Complexity of Future Garden

When starting to think about gardening, one of the first issues to be considered is the characteristics of the garden as you find it (the Current Garden). What are the elements present, how diverse are they, how are they connected, what structures exist, what have they been used for? These may (or may not) combine into a particular *type* of garden. When you think of the structure of the garden you may want to think in terms of:

- **Diversity (heterogeneity) of its elements**: Gardens varying from low(er) to high (er) diversity (e.g., herb, flower, orchard, vegetable gardens, kitchen, cottage).
- **Nature or type of elements**: Gardens with plants that need particular conditions (e.g., light, shade, humidity) with particular categories of elements (e.g., with water or rocks) or combinations of elements of a different nature, such as the proportion of organic to non-organic elements (e.g., gardens mainly with flowers or grass vs. gardens mainly with sand or rocks).
- **Density of elements**: Gardens varying from low(er) density to high(er) density (e.g., market garden).
- **Boundary conditions**: The degree and nature of the connection and differentiation from the surrounding environment (e.g., open gardens, walled gardens).
- **Internal organisation (specific properties of the relations between the elements)**: The different types of layout of gardens and different zones within the layout; gardens within gardens (subsystems), the degree of connectedness (plants in large beds or spread vases) (e.g., Chinese, Zen, radial gardens).
- **Function/purpose**: The different functions or purposes supported by the garden (e.g., utilitarian/productive, aesthetic/sensual, conservation/diversity, social/leisure). This will necessarily be dependent on the perspective being adopted.

The structure of the garden itself will create constraints (Varela and Maturana 1987) regarding the type of change to be achieved and the demand of resources to support the desired transformation. The gardener then needs to think about what kind of garden is aimed for (the Future Garden[8]). Different gardens will present different types of *complexity*.[9] The elements above relate to the structural complexity. Other expressions of complexity may need to be considered, such as the degree to which the garden changes and how it changes through time (*dynamical complexity*). For example, does the garden stay approximately the same or does it change throughout the year with elements that operate on different timescales?

Types and Levels of Change When thinking about gardening or managing the relations with a complex system, we necessarily need to think of a dynamic process, which unfolds through time, and about some degree of change. The management of complexity is about managing the relations that underlie or express change, both within the system and in regard to its coupling with the environment (cf. Sect. 13.4.6). We focus, for now, on the internal relations within the garden. Often intervenors are frustrated with the failure to achieve a certain type or level of change and also frequently we hear reports of unintended and unpredictable changes. In some occasions, this relates to a mismatch between the type and level of change aimed for, and the type and level of change achieved in the given targeted system. It can also relate to a mismatch between the level of change induced and the level of change needed considering the internal structure of the system or the structures and dynamics implicated in the maintenance of a type of problem or solution (Watzlawick et al. 1974; Meadows 2008).

When thinking about gardening and change one necessarily needs to attend to the complexity of the change that is aimed for, but also for the potential transitions between different kinds of changes that may be enacted as a result of the self-organisation of the system in response to the perturbations induced by the gardening. This means that although we may be working for minor changes, aiming, for example, at maintenance, there is a possibility of inadvertently driving the system to a point of transition (Guckenheimer 2007) where deeper *transformations* may occur leading to a different *kind* of system (with different structures and rules).

Watzlawick and collaborators (1974) differentiated *changes of first order* and *changes of second order*. The former can be defined as more superficial changes, or quantitative changes, that operate within or for the maintenance of a general internal structure or rules. The latter correspond to qualitative changes, changes of kind, or changes in the rules of the underlying logic of the system.

Degrees of Complexity The complexity of change emerges as a relation of difference between the complexity of the Current garden and the complexity of the Future garden, which we consider as varying from low to high. The variations of complexity can occur within the same order of change or correspond to a change of order. For

---

[8]We acknowledge a distinction between the gardener's intended garden (Target Garden) and that actually achieved through the gardening process (Future Garden). This deserves more attention, outside of the scope of this chapter.

[9]There are many definitions and measures of complexity that are reviewed elsewhere (Manson 2001; Ladyman et al. 2013). The reader should carefully consider the definitions and measures that are most suitable for a given situation.

Table 13.1 Patterns extracted regarding the complexity of change

		Complexity of the future garden	
		Low	High
Complexity of the Current garden	High	High to low transformative change (second order)	High to high transformative change (second order)
		High control maintenance (first order)	High routine maintenance (first order)
	Low	Low to low transformative change (second order)	Low to high transformative change (second order)
		Low-routine maintenance (first order)	Nurturing maintenance (first order)

example,[10] a gardener may want to increase the structural complexity of the garden, by increasing the number and diversity of flowering plants, but not change its topology. It may happen that one of the new species proliferates within the flowerbeds and outcompetes the other flowers, leading to a state of lower complexity, within the existing topology of the garden (first order). Alternatively, the new species may change the overall soil balance (e.g., pH, moisture, microbiota) which has a knock-on effect on the rest of the garden, e.g., promoting unanticipated growth of adventitious species, resulting in a drastic change in the character of the garden (second order).

In scenarios involving transformation, i.e., changes of kind, ethical considerations may be appropriate.

4.2.2 Patterns of the Complexity of Change

By roughly conceptualizing the complexity of a garden on a continuum varying from low to high, and comparing the Current garden with that of the Future garden, we identify eight broad fuzzy prototypes or patterns of the complexity of change as presented in Table 13.1.

We then classified the patterns extracted according to the degree of the complexity of the change, considering three levels, low, moderate and high, and defined them as described below:

High Complexity of Change

- **Low to high (complexity) transformational change (second order):** transformation into a different, more complex, kind of system.
- **High to high (complexity) transformational change (second order):** transformation into a different kind of system with similar complexity.

---

[10]Although dependent on the measure of complexity considered, we offer illustrative examples without reference to the particular technical measures that could be adopted.

- **High to low (complexity) transformational change (second order):** transformation into a different kind of system with lower complexity.
- **High to low (complexity) control maintenance (first order):** controlling the complexity of a system, lowering it, with no change of kind.

Moderate Complexity of Change

- **High (complexity) routine maintenance (first order):** promoting changes that maintain the high levels of complexity of a system while preventing deeper transformations.[11]
- **Low to low (complexity) transformational change (second order):** transformation into a different kind of garden with lower complexity.
- **Low to high (complexity) nurturing maintenance (first order):** promoting changes that increase the complexity of the system, without changes of kind.

Low Complexity of Change

- **Low (complexity) routine maintenance (first order):** promoting changes that maintain the low level of complexity of a system.

Staging Change Some of these changes are more likely to facilitate others, depending on the history of the system and the particular conditions in which gardening occurs. For example, nurturing maintenance may intentionally (or inadvertently) lead to second order change from low to high complexity, while control maintenance could lead to second order, high to low changes. This may lead to strategies where larger changes occur through a number of intermediate stages, analogous to the multistage developmental processes of some biological systems (Ryan 2011). The gardener may need to monitor the change process closely in circumstances where transitions between different types of change are likely to occur. Change can take many forms. While in some cases change may be catastrophic, with drastic qualitative transformations, in other cases change is more incremental or quantitative (Lerner 2001).

As the gardener explores the possibilities of their garden, it may be useful to consider its history, i.e., the types of changes it has experienced. The history may inform the gardener about the responsiveness of the garden and its preferences in terms of states. This may help to anticipate the possibilities of future change, while keeping attentive to the *adjacent possible* (Kaufmann 2000).

---

[11]A highly complex system may be poised for transformation. Therefore, maintaining high complexity without change of type requires a more intensive and complex form of maintenance that we distinguish from regular routine maintenance.

Invitations for Reflection

- What is the difference between the current state of the system and the desired one? How necessary is that change and how viable does it seem to be?
- What does the intended change mean in relation to the original (or current) state of the system (or past state when doing a retrospective evaluation)? What are the possible implications (gains and costs) of such transformations?
- How likely is it that the aimed transformation could convert into a different kind of transformation (as could easily happen when attempting low to high nurturing maintenance changes), and to what extent is it possible to anticipate what that could be? What could be the consequences?
- How compatible/fit and/or complex do the aimed transformations seem in the face of the history of the particular current state of the system and the known history of transformations in similar systems? What is known that may provide hints on the type of changes possible or its expression?

4.3 Gardener's Capacity

4.3.1 Relation: Theoretical Orientation to Systemicity × Pragmatic Capacity/Resourcefulness for Systemicity

You should rather be grateful for the weeds you have in your mind, because eventually they will enrich your practice Shunryu Suzuki (1973)

The gardener is central to gardening. We think of the gardener's capacity as encompassing their ability to understand and/or explain the behaviour of the garden, in particular the complexity of the organization of relations that sustain it (i) as it is; (ii) as it was; and (iii) as it could be. Therefore, when exploring gardening one must conceive of the gardener's orientation or theoretical capacity to systemicity: their theoretical, conceptual, descriptive and/or explanatory framework, and the extent to which they apprehend the complexity of the system and its systemic properties. On the other hand, we must consider the pragmatic aspects of gardening and the gardener's resources to act in a way that is congruent with and informed by their understanding of the garden's complexity. The gardener's capacity is therefore a relation between their orientation to systemicity and their pragmatic capacity, including the available resources. For example, the gardener may have a good understanding of the disease transmission among plants, but have a limited knowledge of techniques to treat it systemically, rather relying on limited, symptom-focused treatments: this relates to high systemic orientation, but low pragmatic capacity/resourcefulness. By contrast, take a gardener with a lot of tools and resources that could be used to affect the internal relations of the garden but, without the systemic understanding, their very pragmatic capacity may actually cause harm.

Theoretical Capacity A gardener needs a model to approach their garden that provides some understanding of the system and its main organizational and operational processes. This model may have been theoretically or empirically driven. It may have been developed for a particular garden and result from the observation of such a garden for prolonged periods of time, or rely on more general knowledge regarding the class or kind of garden to which it belongs.

The theoretical orientation of a gardener to systemicity can be understood as an indicator of the gardener's readiness or preparedness for gardening. There are different ways a gardener can learn about a system or a class of systems in order to understand the possibilities of change. Learning about a general class of gardens can be done independently or with assistance. A gardener may be self-taught (e.g., through gardening books, or TV programs) or have received formal education (e.g., gardening courses). Some gardeners learn by their own experience. However, in gardening there is a long tradition of apprenticeship, learning at the elbow of a more experienced gardener. A gardener may be more or less specialised in a particular type of garden. A broader knowledge base may be useful in situations that have not been well studied or when the gardener needs to problem solve and deal with unexpected events. However, the knowledge available may not be applicable to their particular garden and new investigations are needed, often in relation to practice. Therefore, the gardener is also necessarily a researcher.

Pragmatic Capacity The pragmatic capacity includes (i) materials used in gardening; (ii) the tools available; and (iii) the specific techniques available for gardening and for intervening at multiple and different relational levels of the organisation of the garden, as required by a systemic conceptualisation. Many of the techniques of gardening are inherently systemic and can be regarded as different means of moderating the coupling between the garden and the environment (or at a different scale, a plant and its local environment within the garden). Depending on the type of coupling and moderation required, a number of different tools and techniques can be utilised, that may employ different types of approaches and technologies.

An example of a moderation technique is the *promotion of tighter coupling of system elements to enhance transfer of energy.* There can be moderation of plant nutrient intake by plants through remodelling of the structure of the soil and interfering with the activity of its micro-organisms and the relation to plants. This can be performed through mechanical means (e.g., rotavator, spade, fork, hoe) which in turn promotes the soil ecology. Alternatively (or in combination), the application of fertilizer or compost uses chemical means to alter soil composition that will provide energy to plants.

Another example pertains to the *reconfiguration of the spatial relations within and between elements of a system to promote their growth.* There can be an influence on the spacing between plants, by cutting away overlapping (or overshadowing) foliage and, thereby, affect plant growth. For an individual plant, pruning can be used to stimulate new growth, for example, towards increasing the yield of fruit trees. This is typically performed by mechanical means through such tools as the axe, saw, mower, etc.

Table 13.2 Patterns extracted regarding the gardener's capacity

		Theoretical orientation to systemicity	
		Low	High
Pragmatic capacity/resourcefulness for systemicity	High	Moderate "pragmatic"	High
	Low	Low	Moderate "theoretical"

Gardening Philosophies Different approaches to gardening combine particular theories (or conceptions) with associated (e.g., dictated, preferred, forbidden) pragmatics. Examples of such *gardening philosophies* are: *organic*, working without artificial agrochemicals, e.g., Bradley et al. (2010); *permaculture*, working in harmony with natural principles, e.g., Hemenway (2009); *hydroponics*, substituting soil for water as the growing medium, e.g., Nicholls (1990); and *slow gardening,*[12] a no-stress approach to gardening.

4.3.2 Patterns of Gardener's Capacity

By relating the theoretical orientation to systemicity and the pragmatic capacity of the gardener, and considering these characteristics as varying from high to low, we were able to identify four broad profiles of gardeners as illustrated in Table 13.2.

The patterns or fuzzy prototypes extracted regarding the gardener's capacity can be defined as follows:

- **High capacity**: Systemically prepared and resourceful gardener
- **Moderate "pragmatic" capacity**: Systemically unprepared but resourceful gardener
- **Moderate "theoretical" capacity:** Systemically prepared but unresourceful gardener
- **Low:** Systemically unprepared and unresourceful gardener

Invitations for Reflection

- How much knowledge is available regarding the systemic features of the system (type of system) of interest?
- How much knowledge is available regarding the complex features of the particular system that is being targeted?
- How capable is the intervenor?

(continued)

---

[12]http://www.slowgardening.net/

- How viable is it for the intervenor to improve its theoretical or pragmatic capacity?
- If the intervenor is theoretically or pragmatically unprepared how viable is it to couple him or her with others with greater theoretical or pragmatic capacity?
- How much information/knowledge is needed to initiate an intervention aiming at change? How much can novel information be produced as the intervention develops? What are the advantages and disadvantages/risks?
- What resources are available for the intervention and to what extent do they address the degree of systemicity and a congruent conceptualisation of the system?

4.4 The Nature of Coupling

4.4.1 Relation: Coupling Gardener-to-Garden × Coupling Garden-to-Gardener

It is difficult to think about gardening without thinking of the gardener. In our own experience, we may recall cases where people repeated established procedures carefully or tried to "follow" a Master's instructions, only to realise a very different outcome of gardening from the one expected. Gardening is not purely mechanical; it requires some kind of *feel* for the system (the notion of "green fingers").

When interacting with each other both the garden and the gardener are coupled, meaning they will change and adapt their behaviours, to different extents, as a function of each other (Kelso 1997). Here we consider coupling strength as how much the garden and the gardener change as a function of the other or how reactive they are. The nature of the coupling will influence the nature of the transformations that are possible in the garden but also the process of change and, consequently, the type of strategies adopted for gardening.

The degree of mutuality and strength of coupling may impact upon the choice of strategies for gardening, or its efficacy, in different ways. For example, if a gardener is closely and strongly coupled to the system they will be able to make timely adjustments in the strategies used, correct courses, anticipate the unfolding of certain behaviours and of the transformations of the landscape of possibilities. If, for example, the gardener is closely and strongly coupled with the system, but not otherwise, they may be able to have sufficient information about what other systems are relevant to the change that could be approached to indirectly influence the system in focus.

Table 13.3 Patterns extracted regarding the nature of coupling

| | | Coupling gardener-to-garden | |
		Low	High
Coupling garden-to-gardener	High	Engaged garden (with gardener)	Mutual strong coupling
	Low	Mutual weak coupling	Engaged gardener (with garden)

4.4.2 Patterns of the Nature of Coupling[13]

When considering the relation of how much the gardener changes as a function of a garden and how much the garden changes as a function of the gardener we can extrapolate four broad patterns or fuzzy prototypes of coupling, relating to the degree of strength and mutuality of coupling (Table 13.3).

We define the four fuzzy prototypes as follows:

- **Mutual strong coupling:** Symmetric coupling—both gardener and garden are mutually engaged and changing as a function of each other.
- **Engaged garden (to gardener):** Asymmetric coupling—low gardener-to-garden/ high garden-to-gardener.
- **Engaged gardener (with garden):** Asymmetric coupling—high gardener-to-garden/ low garden-to-gardener.
- **Mutual weak coupling:** Symmetric coupling—both gardener and garden are disengaged and hardly change as a function of each other.

Invitations for Reflection

- What information is being exchanged that informs the intervenor of the state of the system? What triggers change in the intervenor's behaviour and *vice versa*?
- To what information is the system more responsive?
- What are the implications of the intervenor changing as a function of the system and *vice versa,* and how much would that condition the choice of efficacy or available strategies for promoting change?

---

[13]In building up the relational configuration (Fig. 13.3), we decided not to integrate all dimensions of the nature of coupling, choosing instead to focus on the perspective of the gardener. Nevertheless, when reaching higher relational levels, we returned to relate to the dimension of coupling. The relevance of this dimension then became clear, as a moderator of other relations: the specific nature of the coupling corresponds to variations in those relations, lowering or increasing the levels of fit.

4.5 The Gardener's Coupling Stance

4.5.1 Relation: Gardener-to-Garden Coupling × Reflexivity

The garden suggests there might be a place where we can meet nature halfway Michael Pollan (2007)

Traditionally, the specific contributions of a particular intervenor have been largely ignored as they were assumed to be "objective" or neutral, provoking changes or interfering with the system without being changed by it. This is the case in the original conception of cybernetics (First-order) (Wiener 1961).

Second-order cybernetics called attention to the active role of the observer and the impossibility of separating the one who observes (or intervenes) and that which is being observed or subject to intervention (von Foerster 2007). When the intervenor/observer is highly structurally coupled with the system they aim to inspect or change, it is likely that they will also be subject to change, and changes in the target system are identified as changes in the gardener's reactions to it (Varela and Maturana 1987).

Constructivist theorists acknowledged the uniqueness of the contributions of the individual intervenor to the system and to the construction of the understanding of it, as well as the impossibility of a completely detached objective or neutral stance (von Glasersfeld 1984; Hoffman 1993). As Maturana (1987) states, "anything said is said by an observer". While in complex systems science the role of the observer is still frequently ignored, thinkers such as Morin (2005) have stated that a science informed by complex thinking should be able to bridge the subjective and the objective, the participant and the observer, as complementary facets of a complex world.

Reflexivity In this context, we understand reflexivity as the extent to which intervenors are capable of taking the position of observer themselves (Kegan 1982; Marks-Tarlow et al. 2002), allowing them to reflect on their contributions to the coupling as well as on the process implicated in their relation to the system (Hoffman 1993). Additionally, the reflexivity may facilitate the creation of new knowledge regarding the system, by transforming the relations of the garden and gardener in the coupling into meaningful information about the processes regulating both. Reflexivity thus becomes a central component of a gardener's *coupling stance*. If we assume the role of intervenor as an essential part of thinking about change in complex systems, reflexivity will necessarily be *implicit* in any dimension implicated in gardening. Nevertheless, we believe it must be brought forth *explicitly* as the *degree of reflexivity* that a gardener is capable of.

4.5.2 Patterns of Coupling Stance

By relating the gardener's degree of coupling to the garden and their degree of reflexivity in that coupling we derived four fuzzy patterns of coupling stance as illustrated in Table 13.4.

Table 13.4 Patterns extracted regarding the gardener's coupling stance

| | | Reflexivity | |
		Low	High
Gardener-to-garden coupling	High	Impulsive	Adaptive
	Low	Disconnected	Intellectual

The patterns are defined as follows:

- **Adaptive stance:** The gardener is strongly coupled and highly reflexive
- **Impulsive stance:** The gardener is strongly coupled but poorly reflexive
- **Intellectual stance:** The gardener is weakly coupled, but highly reflexive
- **Disconnected stance:** The gardener is weakly coupled and non-reflexive

Invitations for Reflection

- What does the intervenor need to know about the behaviour of the system in order support and monitor its change?
- How can the intervenor obtain the relevant information regarding the states and operations of the system?
- How aware is the intervenor of their influence on the system and *vice versa*? How aware is the intervenor of what factors contribute to shape the vision (e.g., assumptions, expectations, models, explanations, goals) that guides the coupling to the system?

4.6 Nature of Coupling Garden-Environment

4.6.1 Relation: Coupling Garden-to-Environment × Coupling Environment-to-Garden

What defines a garden is a distinction between what is considered inside it and outside it. This distinction is dependent on an observer (Goguen and Varela 1979; Maturana 1988) and based on several criteria that can include physical, biological, legal, psychological or other. To some extent, some gardens also define themselves by integrating into their own operations and feeding in the products of their own self-referential activities (Maturana and Varela 1991). On the other hand, the garden and all that is considered its environment define each other in a relation of mutual dependence. Therefore, the garden's emergence and transformation needs to considered in relation to its eco-self-organization (Morin 2005).

A garden is connected to and embedded within other systems that constitute its environment (encompassing physical, biological and social factors) that, together with their relations, define an ecosystem (the community of organisms in relation to the environment) (Begon et al. 2009).

Table 13.5 Patterns extracted regarding the coupling of garden- environment

		Coupling garden-to-environment	
		Low	High
Environment-to-garden	High	Engaged environment (with garden)	Mutual high coupling
	Low	Mutual weak coupling	Engaged garden (with environment)

Not all other systems or their elements are equally important for all the activities or existence of the garden. There will be relative degrees of dependence and autonomy of the garden in relation to the environment. Some will have larger effects due to their proximity, their degree of connectedness, or their relations to other systems to which the garden is more closely connected. Their importance (relative degree of coupling) is indicated by their mutual response to perturbation (Varela and Maturana 1987). The same can be said about the elements and system that constitute the environment and their relation to the garden.

4.6.2 Patterns of Coupling Garden-Environment

We can think of coupling in terms of strength and directionality (garden-to-environment; environment-to-garden), and their relations result in the nature of coupling for which we have abstracted four general fuzzy prototypes or patterns (Table 13.5).

The patterns encountered are defined as follows:

- **Mutual high coupling:** Symmetric coupling—garden and environment are mutually coupled and changing as a function of each other.
- **Engaged environment (with garden):** Asymmetric coupling—the garden is poorly coupled to its environment and changing little as a function of it, while the environment is strongly coupled to the garden and changing as a function of it.
- **Engaged garden (with environment):** Asymmetric coupling—the garden is highly coupled to its environment and changing as a function of it but the environment is poorly coupled with the garden and changing little as a function of it.
- **Mutual weak coupling:** Symmetric coupling—both garden and environment are poorly coupled and changing little as a function of each other.

4.7 Nature of Coupling Gardener-Environment

4.7.1 Relation: Coupling Gardener-to-Environment × Coupling Environment-to-Gardener

Just as the garden has a certain degree of coupling to the environment and *vice versa*, so the relation between the gardener and the environment can be thought of in similar

Table 13.6 Patterns extracted regarding the coupling of gardener to environment

		Coupling gardener-to-environment	
		Low	High
Environment-to-gardener	High	Engaged environment (with gardener)	Mutual high coupling
	Low	Mutual weak coupling	Engaged gardener (with environment)

terms. The degree of coupling of the gardener to the environment may be particularly important in cases when the garden is poorly responsive to the gardener. When this occurs but the garden is highly responsive to the environment, the gardener may use approaches that affect the garden indirectly by perturbing its environment or its relation to it (cf. gardening philosophies in Sect. 4.3). In other situations when the environment is poorly responsive to the gardener there are constraints posed on the type of strategies available.

4.7.2 Patterns of Coupling Gardener-Environment[14]

We have abstracted four fuzzy patterns related to the coupling of the gardener to the garden's environment, as presented in Table 13.6.

The patterns extracted are defined as follows:

- **Mutual high coupling:** Symmetric coupling—gardener and garden's environment are mutually coupled and changing as a function of each other.
- **Engaged environment (with gardener):** Asymmetric coupling—the gardener is poorly coupled to the garden's environment and changing little as a function of it, but the environment is strongly coupled to the gardener and changing as a function of it.
- **Engaged gardener (with environment):** Asymmetric coupling—the gardener is highly coupled to the garden's environment and changing as a function of it, but the environment is poorly coupled with the gardener and changing little as a function of it
- **Mutual weak coupling:** Symmetric coupling—both gardener and garden's environment are poorly coupled and changing little as a function of each other.

---

[14]cf. Sect. 4.4.1

Table 13.7 Patterns extracted regarding the ecosystemic (in)dependency of change

		Coupling garden-to-environment	
		Low	High
Complexity of change	High	Moderate "Watch coupling"	High
	Low	Low	Moderate "Watch environment"

4.8 Relative Ecosystemic (In)dependency of Change

4.8.1 Relation: Coupling Garden-to-Environment × Complexity of Change

The type of change aimed for may involve different degrees of freedom that can be related to the nature of the coupling of the garden to its environment. In other words, some changes are more or less (in)dependent of the environment, due to the nature of coupling, and its structural and dynamic conditions. Depending on its nature, such coupling may assist or resist change; it may even derail, or reroute the attempted changes.[15]

4.8.2 Patterns of Ecosystemic (In)dependency of Change

By relating the degree of complexity of change with the degree of coupling of the garden to its environment we abstracted four patterns or fuzzy prototypes of the degree of ecosystemic (in)dependency of change, as illustrated in Table 13.7.

The moderate positions represent situations that could, depending on the circumstances, result in a change of the degree of coupling, as described below:

- **High dependency of change:** The garden is highly coupled to the environment and the complexity of change tends towards being high. The unfolding and outcome of change will be highly dependent on characteristics of the ecosystem.
- **Moderate "watch coupling":** The garden is poorly coupled to the environment and the complexity of change is high, but as the garden increases in complexity the nature of the coupling may change, lowering or increasing the dependency on the environment. Therefore, monitoring changes in the garden-environment coupling, as the complexity of the garden changes, may be important.
- **Moderate "watch environment":** The garden is highly coupled to the environment and the complexity of change tends towards being low. In principle, change could occur in a relatively independent way. However, if the environment is

---

[15]The independence or interference of the system operation with respect to environmental coupling can be related to the concepts of "orthogonality" and "crosstalk" concerning signal transmission in electrical engineering (and synthetic biology).

subject to significant changes, then the nature of the coupling to the garden may also change, lowering or increasing the dependency of change. Therefore, monitoring changes in the environment may be important.

- **Low dependency of change:** The garden is loosely coupled to its environment and the targeted change is of low complexity.

In situations where (or when) the coupling is low, and the change is not complex, one could imagine that the changes would be relatively independent of the environment. Nevertheless, in complex changes (cf. Sect. 4.2), the transformations of kind (or the increased probability of transitions to transformations of kind) may imply changes in the relations with the environment which may implicate a different kind of coupling. Therefore, there is still, to some degree, a relative dependence of the change on the environment which calls for some attention.

> **Invitations for Reflection**
>
> - What are the relata of the environment to which the system is more closely and strongly coupled? What are the factors and processes in the environment that most contribute to sustain or influence change in the system's behaviour?
> - What are the information, the factors and processes that sustain the coupling with the environment?
> - What are the relata and processes that, at the boundary of the system, mostly support and/or moderate the coupling with the environment? What is the information exchanged and/or transformed through these relata or processes (and where does this happen)?
> - How can the intervenor identify which environmental factors and processes are most influential on the system? How can the intervenor produce this information?
> - What timescales do these influential processes operate and how frequently should the intervenor update information about them? When should this information be gathered?
> - How strong is the coupling to the environment and how complex is the change? To what extent are the changes in the garden or their maintenance dependent on the environment?

4.9 Ecosystemic Demand for Gardening

4.9.1 Relation: Ecosystemic (In)dependency of Change × Complexity of Environment

The ecosystemic (in)dependence of change offers an indication of how much the gardener needs to attend to the characteristics of the environment, in its relation to the garden, when aiming for a given type of change. The complexity of the environment

Table 13.8 Patterns extracted regarding the ecosystemic demand for gardening

		Complexity of the environment	
		Low	High
Relative ecological (in)dependency of change	High	Moderate 'Watch garden"	High
	Low	Low	Moderate "Watch environment"

can be thought of as using the same relata as the complexity of the garden (cf. Sect. 4.2). Highly complex environments are likely to be adaptive and change through time which may impact on the garden and its possibilities of change.

The relation of the ecosystemic (in)dependence of change to the degree of complexity of the environment will provide us with indications of how much the gardening needs to be integrative and include some gardening with/of the ecosystem (or selected aspects of it). It will also provide an indicator of how much gardening can be performed in a relatively focused way, with more or less attention dedicated to monitoring the impact that the changes in the garden have on the environment or *vice versa*.

4.9.2   Patterns of Ecosystemic Demand for Gardening

By comparing the complexity of the environment with the ecological (in)dependency of change, we have abstracted four patterns or fuzzy prototypes of degree of ecosystemic demand for gardening, as illustrated in Table 13.8.

The four patterns are defined as follows:

- **High ecosystemic demand for gardening:** The environment is highly complex and there is a high ecological dependency of change, demanding an integrative ecosystemic approach to gardening.
- **Moderate "watch garden":** The environment has low complexity but there is a high ecological dependency for change. This suggests a focused approach to gardening, as long as there is a monitoring of the ecosystemic (asymmetric) changes in the garden, that may impact the environment (thus potentially changing the relevance of its complexity to the change process).
- **Moderate "watch environment":** The environment is complex and there is a low ecological dependency for change. This suggests a focused approach to gardening, as long as there is monitoring of ecosystemic (asymmetric) changes in the environment, which may impact on the garden (thus potentially changing the relevance of its complexity to the change process). For example, an assimilation of the garden by the environment, if the garden is insufficiently complex to match the environment's complexity.
- **Low ecosystemic demand for gardening:** The complexity of the targeted change is low, and there is low ecological dependency, suggesting the suitability of a focused approach to gardening without the need for high ecosystemic monitoring.

When the ecosystemic demand is high the gardener may need to develop articulated interventions that focus not just on the garden but also work on changes in its environment and their relation. For example, a gardener may build a recreational garden along a coastline while collaborating with local authorities to augment and preserve the areas of dunes. This integrative intervention may be necessary to avoid the degradation of the coastline while preserving the integrity and viability of the new garden.

In the case of moderate demand, a gardener may wish to create a kitchen garden near a wooded area, realising that there is no need for an integrative approach. Nevertheless, the gardener may need to monitor the extent to which the garden is unbalancing the flora and fauna of the wood, e.g., due to pesticide runoff or an imbalance, or a proliferation of non-native plants in the wood due to seed dispersion.

Invitations for Reflection

- Considering the dependency of the system of the environment, and the complexity of the change aimed for, how viable it is to develop focused interventions (restricted to the system) and how much does the intervenor need to work towards changes in the environment or in the relation system-environment (e.g., interventions at the boundary)?

4.10   Gardener's Ecosystemic Capacity

4.10.1   Relation: Theoretical Orientation to Ecosystemicity × Pragmatic Capacity/Resourcefulness for Ecosystemicity

We previously discussed the gardener's capacity for systemicity (theoretical and pragmatic, cf. Sect. 4.3). Following what has been said about the need to include the garden's environment and the coupling of the garden with the environment (ecosystemicity) in our preparation for gardening, we should expand the definition of the gardener's capacity to include their theoretical (or conceptual) ability to understand the ecosystemic relations of the garden as well as the degree to which the gardener has the resources, tools and techniques to act congruently with that ecosystemic understanding.

(Ecosystemic) Pragmatic Capacity In this context, a necessary extension of the gardener's consideration of moderating relations is to the coupling of the garden to its environment. An example of an ecosystemic moderation technique is *safeguarding system integrity through reinforcing system boundaries* (or *compartmentalisation*). There can be moderation of organism-plant coupling, for example, by reducing the influx of large "pests" (such as foxes, rabbits, birds, neighbouring children) through the use of *barriers* or *deterrents* via mechanical means (e.g., fencing, netting, traps); for small "pests" (such as insects or weeds) different mechanical barriers might be used (e.g., polythene, mulch), or chemical measures (e.g., herbicides, insecticides) for

elimination or deterrence, which may also be used in combination with mechanical extraction (e.g., hand, trowel, hoe, etc.).

A variant of the above is *safeguarding system integrity through harnessing synergistic system-environment interactions* where measures are taken to harness ecosystemic services to effect changes in the garden. For example using *incentives* (such as water, food, shelter) to attract organisms (e.g., birds) that are natural predators for "pests" (e.g., insects) in the garden.[16]

Another example is *moderating environment-system interactions to promote system operation/change.* The moderating physical factors (e.g., moisture, air, light, heat) of the environment in relation to garden elements can be used to promote the introduction / establishment of new plants. This can be done through establishing micro-environments (e.g., greenhouse (hothouse, cold frame), "cloche", rock garden, grow-bag, pot) or macro-environments (e.g., pond, wooded area, clearing), through a combination of mechanical/ecological means.

4.10.2   Patterns of Gardener's Ecosystemic Capacity

We extended the abstracted patterns of the gardener's capacity (Sect. 4.3.1) to include the consideration of ecosystemicity. The patterns are similar to the ones presented in Table 13.2 for the gardener's capacity.

The four patterns are defined as follows:

- **High:** The gardener is ecosystemically prepared and resourceful in that domain.
- **Moderate "Eco-pragmatic":** The gardener is ecosystemically unprepared but resourceful to potentially intervene in that domain.
- **Moderate "Eco-theoretical":** The gardener is ecosystemically prepared but unresourceful to intervene in that domain.
- **Low:** The gardener is ecosystemically unprepared and an unresourceful gardener.

Invitations for Reflection

- To what extent does the intervenor understand the relata of the system and its environment and their characteristics? To what extent does the intervenor have models that afford an understanding of how the changes in the system or the environment affect one another?
- How much do the models, theories, hypotheses or ecosystemic understanding of the intervenor allow them to understand the extent to which changes in the system are ecosystemically supported and/or viable?
- To what extent does the intervenor have the resources to effect the necessary changes in a way that is congruent with the ecosystemic relations?

---

[16]We note that within the garden a similar ecological strategy is employed in *Companion Planting*: proximal planting of different plants for synergistic effects that promote plant growth/health via control of pests, pollination, etc. See, for example, Little (2008).

4.11 Gardener's Ecosystemic Profile

4.11.1 Relation: Gardener's Systemic Capacity × Gardener's Coupling Stance (× Gardener's Ecosystemic Capacity)

So far, we have addressed the gardener from different perspectives. By relating the characteristics of the gardener's contributions (systemic and ecosystemic capacity and coupling stance), themselves representing other relations, we can identify different profiles of gardeners that will interact in different ways with different gardens and their ecologies, with different impact on the possibilities of change.

4.11.2 Patterns of the Gardener's Ecosystemic Profile

As we progress in the thinking process the different configurations of relationships gain form, as more general patterns of gardening that have some correspondence with "real world" gardening; see Fig. 13.4.

We abstracted 16 different profiles of gardeners by relating the gardener's systemic capacity and coupling stance, which we organised into 5 broad categories and defined, according to the following:

Professional Gardeners

- **Master**: High capacity and adaptive stance.
- **Professor**: Moderate "theoretical" capacity [systemically prepared but unresourceful], adaptive stance.
- **Engaged Practitioner**: High capacity, impulsive stance.

Intuitive Gardener

- **Tinkerer**: Moderate "pragmatic" capacity [systemically unprepared, resourceful], adaptive stance.

Technical Gardeners

- **Techno-intellectual gardener**: Moderate to high pragmatic capacity, moderate theoretical capacity, intellectual stance.
- **Technician**: Moderate to high pragmatic capacity, moderate theoretical capacity, disconnected stance.
- **Theoretician**: Moderate to high theoretical capacity, intellectual stance.

Apprentice Gardeners

- **Eager apprentice**: Low capacity, adaptive stance.
- **Impulsive apprentice**: Low capacity, impulsive stance.
- **Impulsive advanced apprentice**: Moderate "theoretical" capacity, impulsive stance.

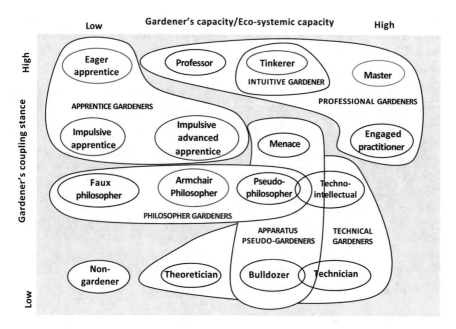

Fig. 13.4 Gardener's profiles and categories

Philosopher Gardeners

- **Armchair philosopher**: Moderate "theoretical" capacity, intellectual stance.
- **Pseudo-philosopher**: Moderate "pragmatic" capacity, intellectual stance.
- **Faux-philosopher**: Low capacity, intellectual stance.

Apparatus Pseudo-gardeners

- **Menace**: Moderate "pragmatic" capacity, impulsive stance.
- **Bulldozer**: Moderate "pragmatic" capacity, disconnected stance

  Non-gardener: Low capacity, disconnected stance.

Gardener's Ecosystemic Capacity If we consider these profiles together with the gardener's ecosystemic capacity, we have a clearer idea of the gardener's specific contributions to the relations with the gardens and their ecologies. A gardener's ecosystemic profile would indicate an additional ecosystemic capability. We have not listed them to avoid a redundancy of terms, but they are considered below.

Gardeners Within Gardening Culture It is acknowledged that you cannot become an effective gardener as a purely theoretical pursuit: you need *practice* to gain experience. As a practitioner, there are various stages of development, such as the archetypes: novice, amateur, professional and "expert" (or Master) gardener. Becoming a Master may take decades of practice. Different types of garden (or gardening) will have their own experts. Even a Master gardener is unlikely to have expertise that spans a wide array of different types of garden, plants species, or widely different environmental conditions. Thus, in the gardening community, advice is often sought from "Expert Panels"[17] where a given question will elicit a variety of opinion from a range of different gardening experts.

> **Invitations for Reflection**
>
> • How many intervenors are there and what is their profile? How do they complement each other?
> • How viable is it for an intervenor to change their profile? In which characteristics (reflexiveness, coupling, theoretical systemicity, pragmatic systemicity)? What is the likely timescale for those changes? What conditions are needed for that change?

5   Contemplating the Gardening: Constructing and Evaluating Narratives of Change

5.1   Relation: Gardener's (Eco-)systemic Profile (Systemic Profile × Ecosystemic Capacity) × Complexity of Change × Ecosystemic Demand

I appreciate the misunderstanding I have had with Nature over my perennial border. I think it is a flower garden; she thinks it is a meadow lacking grass, and tries to correct the error.
Sara Stein (2000)

The outcomes of gardening, as a complex activity, are emergent products of the configurations of the relations involved. Thus they are associated with the congruence (different degrees of fit) of the properties of the different relations involved in gardening. As Guerrero et al. (2015) state: "*problems of fit arise from challenges related to the connectedness and interdependence between ecological and social systems*" and the "*ability to effectively manage environmental change is contingent on the degree to which a governance system fits, or aligns with, the characteristics of the biophysical system*".

---

[17]For example, *Gardeners' Question Time* is a long-standing program on BBC Radio 4, where a panel of experts provides advice on the audience's gardening problems.

5.2 From Modelworld to Storyworld: Narratives of Gardening

Using the relational framework, we have a way of developing different models of interventions in complex systems. Each model corresponds to different configurations of relations and/or their combination within the relational modelworld. Each model supports the development of different narratives of change of a given complex system, as their rich multi-level relationships lead to the emergence of contexts, characters, actions, plots and timelines that constitute the basic elements of a narrative. Thus the modelworld provides the basis for a *storyworld*.[18] Narratives, as natural communication devices, will assist in communicating the often difficult and counterintuitive issues relating to complex systems.

5.3 Evaluating the Fitness of Gardening: Fitness Landscapes

The narratives arising from the different models can be used for the evaluation of interventions, as the fitness of the model can be gauged with respect to different types of outcomes. Thus, the models and their narratives can, on the one hand, guide the planning and development of interventions and, on the other hand, guide their evaluation.

Different categories of gardeners present different capacities and profiles that make them more or less suited to manage the relationships underlying a range of changes in the garden, from very simple to highly complex. The profiles of these different gardeners (based on their systemic capacity and coupling stance) will contribute in unique ways to the degree of systemic fit of the focused gardening activity.

Each category and type of gardener will be more or less suited to contribute effectively and to support particular kinds of changes, as well as to deal with unexpected events during the course of change. A poor fit can result not in only in a failure to achieve the proposed goals but also in unintended side effects that may risk the integrity of the system and/or of its ecology.

We systematically related the gardener's profile (character(s)) with the complexity of change (event), under different conditions (contexts) of ecosystemic demand and ecosystemic capacity (ecosystemic profile) for gardening (action), in order to hypothesise about the degrees of fit in terms of outcome (finale) of change (time) that would result from the different configurations of relationships. Each configuration of relations supports the construction of different narratives. The emergent fit of how these different configurations of relations behave through time, in enacting a type of change, can be represented graphically in what we call conceptual fitness landscapes

---

[18]"the shared universe within which the settings, characters, objects, events, and actions of one or more narratives exist" (von Stackelberg 2011).

(Pigliucci 2012). In Figs. 13.5, 13.6 and 13.7 we illustrate the different conceptual fitness landscapes that we have explored. We considered degrees of fit varying from positive fit (optimal to sufficient) and also negative (potentially harmful), considering that in some situations one could be inefficient (cases of positive fit, with a potential excess of resources or capacities).

In cases of *high complexity of change* (Fig. 13.5a), the Professionals and the Technical gardeners are the ones more likely to exhibit good fit in gardening. Although the Professor has theoretical capacity, and an adaptive coupling stance, without resources they are unlikely to be able to support changes in the garden. By contrast, the Tinkerer, although lacking the theoretical capacity for systemicity, has resources or pragmatic capacity and is not only highly coupled with the system, but also reflexive, which gives them the capacity to learn with the system, thereby increasing their possibilities of a positive fit.

However, in conditions of *high ecological demand and high ecosystemic capacity* (Fig. 13.5b) the Professor, due to their knowledge of ecosystemicity and their resourcefulness at this level, may, through indirect ecological interventions, be capable of supporting the change in the system, therefore increasing fit. On the other hand, in these more difficult conditions the Tinkerer's more intuitive mode of learning may not be sufficient, except perhaps in situations where there is strong coupling with the environment, which would allow them to learn through it. In that case the fit could be sufficient. The Pseudo-gardeners (Philosopher and Apparatus) are likely to cause damage due to their high resourcefulness being associated with little knowledge and either low coupling or reflexivity, which inhibits their adaptive capacity. Because the Professional is not reflexive, in situations of unexpected events they may have more difficulties adjusting to them. Therefore, their fitness is not as high as that of the Master.

Due to the high ecological demand in cases of *moderate ecosystem demand, but "pragmatic" ecosystemicity capacity* (Fig. 13.5c), the fitness of the Master may decrease. However, both the Master and the Professor, due to their reflexiveness and coupling, may see their fitness increase when they are also highly coupled with the environment (which gives them an opportunity to develop knowledge by experience). The poor reflexiveness of the Engaged Practitioner and the poor coupling of the Technicals limit the fitness of their gardening.

In situations of *high ecosystemic demand but moderate "theoretical" capacity* (Fig. 13.5d) the fitness is significantly reduced as the gardeners are limited in their response to the demand of integrative ecosystemic interventions. Nevertheless, the more reflexive and coupled gardeners, as long as they have systemic capacity, may be able to use their knowledge regarding the systemic fit between the garden and the environment to support their change (e.g., by working with the garden so it induces changes in the environment or working with the garden to minimize the impact of factors that may impede change).

In situations of *moderate ecosystemic demand but moderate capacity* (Fig. 13.5e) the degree of coupling of the gardener to the environment may be important, and act as moderator of the ecosystemic fit, as it may increase the degree of fitness in cases of environmental monitoring demand ("watch environment") for most gardeners. In

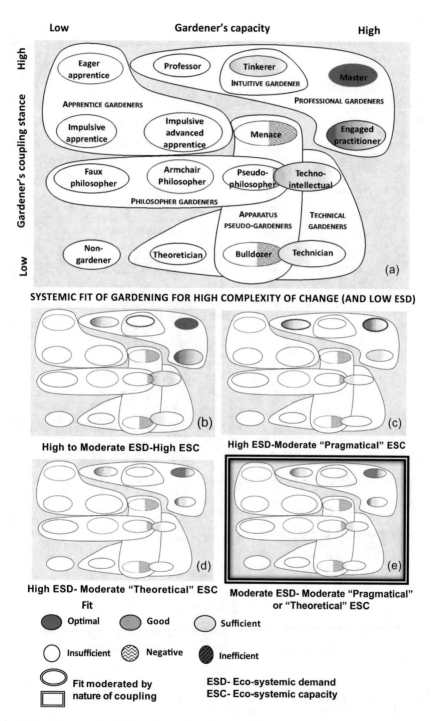

Fig. 13.5 Conceptual landscape of variations of systemic fit of gardening for different gardener profiles in conditions of high complexity of change, under different conditions of ecosystemic demand and gardener's ecosystemic capacity

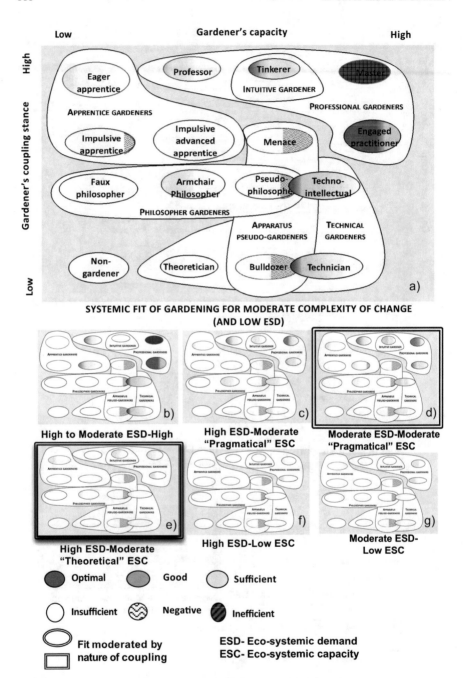

Fig. 13.6 Conceptual landscape of variations of systemic fit of gardening for different gardener profiles in conditions of moderate complexity of change, under different conditions of ecosystemic demand and gardener's ecosystemic capacity (ESC)

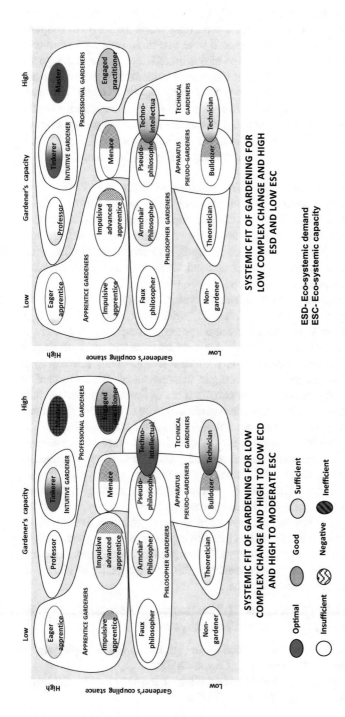

Fig. 13.7 Conceptual landscape of variations of systemic fit of gardening for different gardener profiles in conditions of low complexity of change, under different conditions of ecosystemic demand and gardener's ecosystemic capacity

cases of garden monitoring ("watch garden") the Professionals will see an improvement in their gardening. Beyond the specific conditions where the nature of coupling was a relevant moderating factor, one should note that these relata are of overall importance as they may determine the type of outcome. For example, although we have indicated that the Apparatus Pseudo Gardener's gardening fit may be insufficient and harmful, to an extent which may depend on the nature of coupling, in cases where there is low coupling from garden to garden, this risk may be decreased or the potential harm lessened. Therefore, although the nature of coupling garden-to-environment was not explicitly incorporated in lower levels of relating (cf. Fig. 13.3), it was recruited at this higher level as a moderating dimension that creates particular contexts for variations in fit.

Figure 13.6 represents the conceptual landscapes of fitness for conditions of moderate complexity of change. For moderate complexity of change one can see that Technicians have a better fit than for high complex changes. Nevertheless, in conditions of high ecosystemic demand, unless they are fully capable (theoretically and pragmatically), the fitness of their gardening will decrease. Even with moderate changes, in conditions of high ecosystemic demand, whenever there is low capacity, few gardeners will achieve satisfactory fits.

In some cases, particularly in maintenance-type changes (cf. Sect. 13.4.2.1), Eager Apprentices may achieve a sufficient fit, since their reflexivity and high coupling may help them learn enough about a system to contribute to its maintenance. As indicated by the frame in Fig. 13.6d, e there are situations where the nature of coupling gardener-garden or gardener-environment will moderate (increasing or decreasing) the fitness of gardening. For example, in situations of "Watch garden" or "Watch environment" the nature of those couplings are of special relevance as they will constitute important resources that allow gardening to be developed with a main focus on the garden while attempting to minimize risks and optimise outcomes.

In Fig. 13.7 it is possible to see that for changes of low complexity of change (requiring only low routine maintenance) several profiles can achieve minimally satisfactory fits. However, some will continue to present risks of harm when there is either low coupling, or low reflexivity, low theoretical capacity and high resourcefulness. In situations of high ecosystemic demand and low capacity, even if the change is simple there is a relevant decrease of fit for most gardeners. The ones with most integrative profiles are the only ones that will be able to achieve good levels of fit, through their ability to keep close with the garden's transformations and adapting. We have not explored other scenarios for low complexity of change as they seem less relevant in these conditions.

Consequences of Poor Fit ("Side-Effects") There are many examples of poor fit for *gardening*, in terms of unintended side effects, for example:

- Pesticides may pass up through the food chain and accumulate in higher organisms, causing wider health issues, e.g., Carson (2002).
- Single varieties for production yield ("monoculture"), leading to vulnerabilities to particular diseases/pests, e.g., Zhu et al. (2000).

- Invasive species: Alien plants introduced into new environment may outgrow (outcompete) native species and proliferate, e.g., Lockwood et al. (2013).
- Over fertilisation of soil on crop species, leading to stress to neighbouring trees (Nosengo 2003).
- Flowers bred for appearance/colour, leading to loss of scent (Rohwer 2010)

Invitations for Reflection

- To what extent is the intervenor's profile adequate considering the targeted complexity of change?
- To what extent is the level of fit acceptable or desired?
- What is known from previous experiences of interventions in the targeted system (history of that particular system) or analogous systems (general knowledge-base)?
- What are the likely consequences of a poor fit?

6 Tending the Gardening: Improving the Ecosystemic Fitness

A thing is right when it tends to preserve the integrity, stability, and beauty of the biotic community. It is wrong when it tends otherwise. (Leopold 1949)

We have explored how configurations of relations that correspond to different ways of gardening are likely to lead to different levels of fitness and corresponding outcomes. The questions now are: How satisfactory is the level of fit likely to be achieved with the current configuration? What are the likely outcomes and their implications?

Although we were able to identify broad categories of styles or approaches to gardening, and identify the relations that sustain them, the fact is that these relations (and their corresponding relata) are dynamic, therefore, subject to influence, both within and between levels. There is opportunity, and certainly need, for a continual evaluation and adjustment of gardening towards a better fit and more satisfactory outcomes.

Having explored the emergent properties of gardening and pondering the possible outcomes, we may want to re-enter the relational structure and explore its relations at different levels, looking for possibilities of change. Below we leave the reader with some additional invitations for a recursive reflection focused on exploring possibilities of change in the relations that build gardening.

Invitations for Recursive Reflection
Time and Complexity of Change

- Would a different level or type or change be acceptable or reasonable?
- Can the goals be redefined or adjusted in time (e.g., give time for capacity to develop, until aiming for the final goals while working on intermediate goals/changes)? Can different levels of complexity of change be operated sequentially or concurrently?

Intervenor's Capacity

- Can we learn more about the specific internal structure and dynamics of the intervention? What actions can be implemented to produce specific information about the intervenor's (eco)systemicity? In what timescales? Can the intervenor's theoretical orientation to (eco)systemicity be improved? Can the intervenor's available resources be used in a way that is more congruent with the system's (eco)systemicity? Can the intervenor's resources to intervene in regard to the ecosystemicity of the system be increased?

Couplings and Coupling Stance

- Can the intervenor increase the strength of the coupling with the garden? What interfaces or sources of information could support that?
- To which systems can the intervenor couple to in order to indirectly influence the garden, particularly in cases of low intervenor-to-system? Which external systems in the environment are more susceptible to the intervenor's influence?
- What kind of strategies are available to increase the intervenor's reflexivity (e.g., supervision; use of reflection diaries; reflecting peer dialogues; teaching)?

Ecosystemicity

- What other interventions are available or could be devised that meet the level of demand for ecosystemicity? What more can be explored about the natural ecological processes connecting the system with its environment and the relations within the environment that could inspire the development of novel integrative interventions?
- What new thinking strategies can be developed that are congruent with the natural complexity of the system and its ecology?

Ecosystemic Fit

- How could the systemic fits for different intervenors complement each other in a team through time? Could that complementarity be concurrent or sequential? How viable is it to increase the fit of intervention with the available intervenors for a given timescale? How can the process of change be staged in relation to the intervenor's profile?

As meta-observers, we have been gardening by adopting a meta-position on the whole of the relations, in order to identify opportunities to facilitate changes in the relata and in the relations from which they emerge. At this point the questions are: At what level of the configuration of relationships can changes be made? What are the relata (and relations) that are more susceptible to change? Where would changes have a bigger impact and to what extent do changes in one relatum contribute to adjustment in others? These are core questions for the type of meta-reflection needed for the improvement in our capacity to understand and expand our possibilities of action in relation to complex systems.

7   Harvesting the Gardening: Discussion

All models are wrong, some are useful. (Box 1979)

7.1   *Introduction*

We have explored the use of gardening, as an exemplar, to organise, in a relational way, relevant information regarding the management of change in complex systems. We acknowledge that gardening has been widely used as a perspective for exploring the world across individual, social and global levels (Marcus 1992; Cooper 2006; Pollan 2007).

We have explored gardening not just by adopting the lens of relational and systemic thinking (Bateson 1979; von Foerster 2007), but also by using gardening as a guide in developing a practice of complex thinking (Kaufmann 2000; Bar-Yam 2004; Morin 2005, 2008). The relational scheme in which we grounded our thinking, combined with the richness of the gardening culture, allowed us to approach the issue of change in complex systems in a way that builds insight and offers clues for practice. We used gardening, in a circular and recursive way, as both our starting and end points: as both the exemplar that organised the thinking, and the domain in which we applied the relational thinking framework. The framework is not a model of how to manage complex systems, it is a *metamodel* (Andrews et al. 2011), one that allows for a modelling of how different models of change may be constructed and evaluated in the face of complexity (Patton 2011). In this sense, the framework represents a *gardening of gardening*.

Figure 13.8 illustrates the steps taken in this chapter from the development of a relational framework for complex systems to its application to the domain of gardening and construction of a relational modelworld. From this modelworld

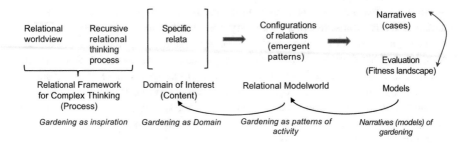

Fig. 13.8 Schematic representation of the Relational Framework and its application to generate a modelworld for a domain of interest

different models can be built and tested using different methodologies.[19] The different models can also be organised in the form of narratives, which may be prospective or retrospective narratives of the unfolding of change in real cases, or narratives of hypothetical models that can be generated and tested using methods such as simulation. The framework and its application have created favourable conditions for the development of case-based research (Byrne and Ragin 2009), and case study evaluations (Patton 2011) where different types of models can be applied and tested, developing or refining the fitness landscapes for a particular system or class of systems.

7.2 From Exemplar to Metaphor?

Pragmatically, the extent to which the gardening exemplar is successful depends upon its utility. We believe the abstractions and schema we have employed can be used in different domains, with different kinds of complex systems. By developing a framework, adopting a relational perspective, and by using concepts through an exemplar of a widely understood domain, we hope that it will be effective in scaffolding interdisciplinarity dialogue, and that by relating our different gardenings, we can expand the possibilities of understanding and action that emerge in our complex world. Further, we believe the application of our framework, along with the generality of the concepts, creates conditions for the use of gardening as a useful metaphor[20] for managing and communicating about changes in complex systems.

---

[19]We do not prescribe methodologies: although we have referred to qualitative methods, the modelworld could be used as the basis to build other kinds of models, e.g., computational models.

[20]Burke (1941) positioned metaphor as one of the "Four Great Tropes" alongside metonymy, synecdoche and irony. He noted "Give a man but one of them, tell him to exploit its possibilities, and if he is thorough in doing so, he will come upon the other three." We trust the reader will excuse this eventuality.

7.3   General and Restricted Gardening

The field of complexity has been divided into restricted complexity and general complexity by Morin (2007). A restricted complexity approach assumes a more strategic stance, neglecting the understanding of organisation and complex thinking, seeking (by "*decomplexifying*") to simplify the complex and search for general laws. A generalised complexity approach is concerned with the nature of the complex system in terms of its eco-systemic relational organisation and how we can know about it. Generalised complexity recognises opposites and differences and seeks to relate them. We hope our gardening-inspired framework is a positive contribution towards expanding a general complexity approach to study change in complex systems.

On the other hand, we could use the distinction between restricted and general complexity to classify gardening as an activity to promote change. Restricted gardening would seek some changes and focus on the technical aspects of the manipulation of the system and their interactions without a deep understanding of the processes involved and the nature of the configurations of relationships implicated in its maintenance and transformation. This would be the approach of some technical gardeners. Although useful in some cases it is a limited approach. A generalised gardening is one at the level of the professional gardeners and it may, of course, involve dimensions of a restricted gardening, but have a wider focus on understanding the nature of their relations within the system and with its ecology, and what they imply.

7.4   A Complex Web of Mutual Influence

In building our approach we considered several relata and the ways in which they relate through a build-up of relations (and relations of relations) at multiple interconnected levels. At each level, new concepts and forms of understanding emerge that recursively feed each other. In this sense, there is no privileged level of consideration or straightforward causal relationships (Macy 1991; Noble 2012), and the mutual influence of the configuration of relations is not meaningfully reducible through analysis.

7.5   The Ethics of Gardening

Huxley (1894) used gardening as an analogy for man's capacity to create gardens (a "State of Art") within the "cosmic process" (the "State of Nature"). In focusing on social systems he raised ethical issues about how this can be achieved, something that within the scope of this chapter we have not addressed. Nevertheless, our explicit inclusion of reflexivity opens the way to a consideration of the ethical dimensions of affecting change.

7.6 Complex Thinking for Complex Systems

Our recursive relational framework reflects many of the known properties of complex systems (Dent 1999). We note that other thinking approaches have been presented that also embrace both relationality and emergence, as well as reflexivity, to discover and exploit system synergies (Chenail 1995; Tsoukas and Hatch 2001; Friedman 2011; Ravetz 2014). We hope this relational framework represents a contribution towards building novel patterns of complex thinking (Morin 1992).

We look forward to the blossoming of complex thinking.

Acknowledgements We thank all the reviewers for their comments, particularly Susan Stepney for her insight and enthusiasm that encouraged us to further develop our ideas. We also thank Giulia Rispoli for the clarity of her critique and useful suggestions.

Ana Teixeira de Melo is supported by Fundação para a Ciência e Tecnologia, Portugal. This work was supported by an individual postdoctoral fellowship awarded by the Fundação para a Ciência e Tecnologia, Portugal (SFRH/BPD/77781/2011), and hosted by the Centre for Social Studies, University of Coimbra and the Faculty of Psychology and Education Sciences of the University of Coimbra.

References

Andrews PS, Stepney S, Hoverd T et al (2011) CoSMoS process, models, and metamodels. In: Proceedings of the 2011 workshop on complex systems modelling and simulation. Luniver Press, Frome, pp 1–13
Ashby WR (1958) Requisite variety and its implications for the control of complex systems. Cybernetica 1:83–99
Bar-Yam Y (2004) Making things work: solving complex problems in a complex world. NECSI, Knowledge Press, Cambridge, MA
Bateson G (1972) Steps to an ecology of mind: collected essays in anthropology, psychiatry, evolution, and epistemology. University of Chicago Press, Chicago
Bateson G (1979) Mind and nature: a necessary unity. Dutton, New York
Beer S (1979) The heart of enterprise. Wiley, New York
Begon M, Harper JL, Townsend CA (2009) Ecology - from individuals to ecosystems. Wiley, New York
Box GEP (1979) Robustness in the strategy of scientific model building. Robust Stat 1:201–236
Bradley FM, Ellis BW, Martin DL (2010) The organic gardener's handbook of natural pest and disease control: a complete guide to maintaining a healthy garden and yard the Earth-friendly way. Rodale Books, Emmaus
Burke K (1941) Four master tropes. Kenyon Rev 3:421–438
Byrne D, Ragin C (2009) The SAGE handbook of case-based methods. SAGE, London
Capra B (1990) MindWalk: a film for passionate thinkers. Atlas Leasing
Capra F (1997) The web of life: a new synthesis of mind and matter. HarperCollins, London

Carson R (2002) Silent spring. Houghton Mifflin Harcourt, Orlando, FL

Cassirer E, Swabey WC, Swabey MC (1923) Substance and function, and Einstein's theory of relativity. Open Court Publishing, Chicago

Checkland P (2000) Soft systems methodology: a thirty year retrospective. Syst Res Behav Sci 17: S11–S58

Chenail RJ (1995) Recursive frame analysis. Qual Rep 2(2):1–14

Cooper DE (2006) A philosophy of gardens. Oxford University Press, Oxford

Demakis J (2012) The ultimate book of quotations. Lulu enterprises, Raleigh

Dent EB (1999) Complexity science : a worldview shift. Emergence 1:5–19

Érdi P (2007) Complexity explained. Springer, Heidelberg

Friedman VJ (2011) Revisiting social space: relational thinking about organizational change. In: Shani AB, Woodman RW, Pasmore WA (eds) Research in organizational change and development, vol 19. Emerald Group, Bingley, pp 233–257

Glaser B, Strauss A (1967) The discovery grounded theory: strategies for qualitative inquiry. Aldine, Chicago

Goguen JA, Varela F (1979) Systems and distinctions: duality and complementarity. Int J Gen Syst 5:31–43

Guckenheimer J (2007) Bifurcation. Scholarpedia J 2:1517

Guerrero AM, Bodin Ö, McAllister RRJ, Wilson KA (2015) Achieving social-ecological fit through bottom-up collaborative governance: an empirical investigation. Ecol Soc 20(4):41

Haken H (1984) Synergetics: the science of structure. Van Nostrand, New York

Haken H (1987) Information compression in biological systems. Biol Cybern 56:11–17

Hemenway T (2009) Gaia's garden: a guide to home-scale permaculture, 2nd edn. Chelsea Green Publishing, White River Junction

Hoffman L (1993) Exchanging voices: a collaborative approach to family therapy. Karnac Books, London

Huxley TH (1894) Evolution and ethics: prolegomena. In: Collected essays. Macmillan, London

Kaufmann S (2000) Investigations. Oxford University Press, Oxford

Kegan R (1982) The evolving self. Harvard University Press, Cambridge

Kelso S (1997) Dynamic patterns: the self-organization of brain and behavior. MIT Press, Cambridge, MA

Kelso SJA, Engstrom DA (2008) The complementary nature. MIT Press, Cambridge, MA

Ladyman J, Lambert J, Wiesner K (2013) What is a complex system? Eur J Philos Sci 3:33–67

Leopold A (1949) A sound county almanac. Oxford University Press, New York, pp 224–225

Lerner RM (2001) Concepts and theories of human development. Psychology Press, Hove

Little B (2008) Companion planting. New Holland, London

Lockwood JL, Hoopes MF, Marchetti MP (2013) Invasion ecology. Wiley, Oxford

Macy J (1991) Mutual causality in Buddhism and general systems theory: the dharma of natural systems. SUNY Press, Albany

Manson SM (2001) Simplifying complexity: a review of complexity theory. Geoforum 32:405–414

Marcus CC (1992) The garden as metaphor. In: Francis M, Hester RT Jr (eds) The meaning of gardens: idea, place, and action. MIT Press, Cambridge, MA, pp 26–33

Marks-Tarlow T, Robertson R, Combs A (2002) Varela and the Uroborus: the psychological significance of re-entry. Cybern Hum Knowing 9:31–47

Maturana H (1987) Everything is said by an observer. In: Thompson WI (ed) Gaia: a way of knowing. Lindisfarne Press, West Stockbridge, MA, pp 65–82

Maturana H (1988) Ontology of observing: the biological foundations of self consciousness and the physical domain of existence. In: Donaldson RE (ed) Texts in cybernetics. American Society of Cybernetics, Washington, DC

Maturana HR, Varela FJ (1991) Autopoiesis and cognition: the realization of the living. Springer, Heidelberg

Mauthner NS, Doucet A (2003) Reflexive accounts and accounts of reflexivity in qualitative data analysis. Sociology 37:413–431

Meadows DH (2008) Thinking in systems: a primer. Chelsea Green Publishing, White River Junction

Miles MB, Huberman AM (1994) Qualitative data analysis: an expanded sourcebook. Sage, Thousand Oaks

Mitchell M (2009) Complexity, a guided tour. Oxford University Press, New York

Morin E (1992) From the concept of system to the paradigm of complexity. J Soc Evol Syst 15:371–385

Morin E (2005) Introduction à la pensée complexe. Seuil, Paris

Morin E (2007) Restricted complexity, general complexity. In: Gershenson C, Aerts D, Edmonds B (eds) Worldviews, science and us - philosophy and complexity. World Scientific, Singapore, pp 5–29

Morin E (2008) On complexity. Hampton Press, Cresskill

Nicholls R (1990) Beginning hydroponics: soilless gardening: a beginner's guide to growing vegetables, house plants, flowers, and herbs without soil. Running Press, Philadelphia

Noble D (2012) A theory of biological relativity: no privileged level of causation. Interface Focus 2:55–64

Nosengo N (2003) Fertilized to death. Nature 425:894–895

Pask G (1975) The cybernetics of human learning and performance: a guide to theory and research. Hutchinson Educational, New York

Patton MQ (2011) Developmental evaluation: applying complexity concepts to enhance innovation and use. Guilford Press, New York

Pigliucci M (2012) Landscapes, surfaces, and morphospaces: what are they good for. In: Erik Svensson E, Calsbeek R (eds) The adaptive landscape in evolutionary biology. Oxford University Press, Oxford, pp 26–38

Pollan M (2007) Second nature: a gardener's education. Grove/Atlantic, New York

Ravetz J (2014) Interconnected responses for interconnected problems: synergistic pathways for sustainable wealth in port cities. Int J Glob Environ Issues 13:362–388

Rohwer C (2010) Unintended consequences, the garden professors. http://blogs.extension.org/gardenprofessors/2010/12/22/unintended-consequences/. Accessed 4 Jun 2015

Ryan F (2011) Metamorphosis: unmasking the mystery of how life transforms. Oneworld Publications, London

Stein S (2000) My weeds: a gardeners' botany. University Press of Florida, Glainesville, FL

Sterman JD (2006) Learning from evidence in a complex world. Am J Public Health 96:505–514

Suzuki S (1973) Zen minds, beginners' mind. Weatherhill, New York

Tsoukas H, Hatch MJ (2001) Complex thinking, complex practice: the case for a narrative approach to organizational complexity. Hum Relat 54(8):979–1013

Varela FJ (1976) Not one, not two. Coevolution Q 11(Fall):62–67

Varela F, Maturana H (1987) The tree of knowledge: the biological roots of human understanding. Shambhala Publications, Boston, MA

von Bertalanffy L (1971) General system theory: foundations, development, applications. Allen Lane, London

von Foerster H (2007) Understanding: essays on cybernetics and cognition. Springer, Heidelberg

von Glasersfeld E (1984) An introduction to radical constructivism. In: Watzlawick P (ed) The invented reality: how do we know what we believe we know? (Contributions to constructivism). Norton, New York, pp 17–40

von Stackelberg P (2011) Storyworlds - what are they? In: Transmedia Digest. http://transmediadigest.blogspot.co.uk/2011/11/storyworlds-what-are-they.html. Accessed 2 Aug 2016

Watzlawick P, Weakland JH, Fisch R (1974) Change: principles of problem resolution and problem formation. W. W. Norton & Company, New York

Whitehead AN (1920) The concept of nature. Cambridge University Press, Cambridge

Whitehead AN (1929) Process and reality, Corrected edition 1978. Griffin/Free Press, New York

Wiener N (1961) Cybernetics: or control and communication in the animal and the machine. MIT Press, Cambridge

Wilden A (2013) System and structure: essays in communication and exchange, 2nd edn. Routledge, Oxon

Yin RK (2013) Case study research: design and methods. SAGE, Thousand Oaks

Zhu Y, Chen H, Fan J et al (2000) Genetic diversity and disease control in rice. Nature 406:718–722

Chapter 14
Discussion and Comment (Gardening Gardening)

Leo Caves, Ana Teixeira de Melo, and Richard Walsh

Abstract Leo Caves, Ana Teixeira de Melo, and Richard Walsh in discussion on an earlier version of "(Gardening) Gardening: A Relational Framework for Complex Thinking about Complex Systems."

RW: I'm not sure I know (yet) what complex narratives are, or how they might function as pragmatic tools. I'm also unclear about the concept of *storyworld* evoked, and about the sense in which it is "enacted" through narrative. All this might prove very interesting, but I think it needs pressing beyond the immediately apparent sense of these ideas.

LC: You ask good questions, that require various degrees of unpacking: *modelworld:* the relational thinking process applied to a domain results in configurations of relations constructed from the base relata. The configurations reflect higher order entities (e.g., relating to types of gardener, or types of change, etc.) that could form the basis of a particular model of the change process. So the process is really a model of how to build models (a metamodel), and thus the models produced constitute a world of models (modelworld) constructed from different ways of looking at relations. I also note that a particular configuration of relationships, albeit a model in its own right, can also be regarded as a framework for more detailed models. *storyworld:* the higher order entities that emerge from the relational thinking process can have particular attributes (e.g., types of gardener, types of

L. Caves
Independent Researcher, Sao Felix da Marinha, Portugal

York Cross-disciplinary Centre for Systems Analysis, University of York, York, UK

A. T. de Melo
Centre for Social Studies, University of Coimbra, Coimbra, Portugal

R. Walsh (✉)
Department of English and Related Literature, University of York, York, UK

Interdisciplinary Centre for Narrative Studies, University of York, York, UK
e-mail: richard.walsh@york.ac.uk

R. Walsh, S. Stepney (eds.), *Narrating Complexity*,
https://doi.org/10.1007/978-3-319-64714-2_14

change) and may be regarded as characters or settings that (necessarily) relate to each other. These characters, settings and change scenarios constitute a storyworld, from which particular narratives can be constructed, i.e., individual trajectories through the relational world. In this way, the potential of the characters and their settings is "enacted" through particular individual narrative trajectories. They may be termed "complex narratives" because they arise from, and reflect the characteristics of, a complex thinking process that captures the multi-level relational structure of the complex change scenario and therefore (if carefully constructed) should retain some of its "complexity."

That's the general conception. It may well need refinement.

RW: That's interesting, and I think I can see some of the potential in it. One immediate point worth bringing to your attention is that the term *storyworld* already exists in narratology with a somewhat different sense (there, it is the "world" produced or implied by a given narrative). I don't much like the concept, and I'm keen myself to think about these matters differently, but there is the potential for terminological confusion for narratologists reading this.

LC: My thought was that the storyworld once constructed affords different narratives. Thus I may have ignored its genesis, but thought I had captured its utility... If it is a real no-no, then perhaps we need to adjust the terminology.

AM: Or maybe clarify?

LC: The joys of interdisciplinary working...

AM: Our storyworld is the world that appears as constructed by particular settings, actions, characters. A world that is portrayed or constructed in that narrative. There is always an underlying narrative but to some extent it can remain in a potential state waiting to be narrated in full detail or exist in different versions.

We could say that there may not be a storyworld without narrative, but we can also say that to some extent it can exist as a sort of proto-narrative (I think this is more how we approach it): the elements are there for the construction of a narrative but it needs to be realised and it can be realised with different nuances?

RW: The source for the meaning of "storyworld" in your chapter (von Stackelberg) is rather heterodox; the standard meaning of the term derives from Herman (2004). The definition from von Stackelberg is also problematic in certain respects (see below), I think, even though it licenses your usage for the purposes of the chapter.

I need to explain my response here in three stages: (1) How the narratological concept of storyworld differs from the one proposed in your chapter; (2) Why I think the narratological concept is flawed; (3) Whether there is an alternative way of conceiving the idea of concern for this chapter, and for the prospect of narrating complexity.

(1) A story is a representation; it makes sense of its subject matter by giving narrative form to it. The form is not an inherent feature of the subject matter. A storyworld, in the narratological sense, is the product or effect of a particular story. It results from interpretation of the narrative discourse. It doesn't pre-exist the story as such, and the story only refers to it in the sense that it produces what it refers to. (It helps, perhaps, to bear in mind that the concept originates in the context of fictional stories).

(2) It's a confused and confusing concept, because it equivocates between the referential priority of "world" and the discursive priority of "story" It wants to ground story in a referent (a world), while at the same time retaining the form of story, which is a feature of the discourse but seems, in this term, to become a feature of the referent. The notion of proto-narrative actually captures the equivocation nicely: in what does the narrative quality of proto-narrative consist? Does the term merely refer to something of which we make narrative sense—i.e., simply, a feature of the world; or does it refer to something which already has the shape of a narrative—i.e., simply, a narrative (bearing in mind that narrative representations come in assorted media, including mental representations; and that any narrative may be re-narrated and re-mediated in multiple versions).

(3) The striking difference in the usage of "storyworld" in your chapter, if I understand it right, is that it wants to conceive of the concept (by analogy with "modelworld") as a kind of repository of multiple possible stories, a world of stories. I would want to say that such a notion, to be intelligible, needs to be framed as itself representational, not just as the raw material for (narrative) representations. That suggests to me the possibility that there might be a closer connection than you currently envisage between storyworld in this sense and at least one possible sense of "complex narrative." I'm certainly keen to think further about what "complex narrative" might be!

LC: Regarding (3) I think that the creation of the modelworld, which through interpretation as characters/settings is the basis of the storyworld, is itself a kind of narrative exercise. It is arrived at through a recursive relational process that involves the sense-making of the meta-observer—building a story that offers insight.

The muddying of referent and discourse is an encouraging sign for a reflexive process and appeals to the constructivist stance that Ana and I hold.

Reference

Herman D (2004) Story logic. Nebraska University Press, Lincoln

Chapter 15
The Software Garden

Julian F. Miller

Abstract It is commonplace for human beings to manipulate and control systems that they only understand at a behavioural level. Yet we expect software engineers to build software systems by assembling instructions that are extremely fragile and require extremely precise understanding of how these instructions interact. We argue that such a method of programming computers will not scale to future demand. We suggest that future software might profitably be constructed using a horticulture-inspired programming methodology. Evolved software seeds will be planted and shaped in *software gardens* for desired computational behaviour.

1 Introduction

It is self-evident that human beings routinely shape, alter and interact with systems that they have little detailed or precise understanding of. Indeed, many of these systems are not merely complicated systems but truly complex systems.[1] In human society examples of these interactions are plentiful. In fact, it is easy to argue that such interactions form the vast majority of all interactions between human beings and the physical world. We can give many concrete examples of such interactions: trading stocks and shares, animal husbandry, horticulture, sculpture, carpentry, choral singing, writing. Interactions between humans and the physical world which require precise and detailed knowledge have emerged relatively recently in human history. We know this as the development of science. Indeed, so successful has this approach been that it has transformed human society within a few hundred

---

[1]Complicated systems often have many parts that interact through precisely defined interactions. They are engineered using top-down design and analysis. On the other hand, complex systems typically have many parts interacting with each other through numerous and often poorly defined mechanisms. They show sensitivity to external environments and exhibit collective behaviour and organization, often at multiple levels of abstraction.

J. F. Miller (✉)
Department of Electronic Engineering, University of York, York, UK
e-mail: julian.miller@york.ac.uk

© Springer Nature Switzerland AG 2018
R. Walsh, S. Stepney (eds.), *Narrating Complexity*,
https://doi.org/10.1007/978-3-319-64714-2_15

years. For instance, physicists and engineers have learned how to manipulate silicon at such an exquisite level of detail that devices could be constructed that operate at an almost symbolic logical level at enormous speed. This has led to the development of computers and in turn the internet. However, at present to program computers requires humans to construct structures at an extraordinary level of precision. Such programs are extremely fragile and require humans to consciously and deliberately write thousands of instructions to achieve a desired outcome.

2 The Complexity Ceiling

We argue that there must be a natural limit to the size and complexity of human produced computer programs. We call this the *complexity ceiling*. Jaron Lanier, the pioneer of Virtual Reality, saw in 2003 that the complexity ceiling would be a fundamental problem (Lanier 2003):

> Since the complexity of software is currently limited by the ability of human engineers to explicitly analyze and manage it, we can be said to have already reached the complexity ceiling of software as we know it. If we don't find a different way of thinking about and creating software, we will not be writing programs bigger than about 10 million lines of code, no matter how fast, plentiful or exotic our processors become.

Well, he underestimated human ingenuity and since then software systems have continued to grow . . .

Software complexity is crudely measured in counts of lines of code. The list below gives an indication of how many lines of code modern software systems have (McCandless 2014):

- Linux 3.1: 15 million
- Windows 7: 40 million
- Microsoft Office 2013: 45 million
- Large Hadron Collider (total software): 50 million
- Mac OS X "Tiger": 85 million
- Average modern high end car: 100 million

It is important to realise that some of these software systems are effectively separate software packages that have some interaction. This explains why an average modern high end car has more lines of code in its software than the Microsoft Windows 7 operating system. It also calls into question a line of code as a useful measure of software complexity. However, lines of code are directly related to human effort.

Linus Torvald, the pioneering developer of the Linux operating system echoed some of Lanier's concerns and in 2011 he complained that Linux has become "too complex" and he was concerned that developers would not be would not be able to understand the software anymore. He said he was "afraid of the day" when an error occurs that "cannot be evaluated anymore" (Kehrer 2011). This brings us to an important question that is at the heart of this chapter:

Is there an upper limit to the number of lines of code in a useful piece of software that can be produced by human beings?

In Fred Brook's classic book *The Mythical Man-Month* he asserts that programmers produce about 10 good lines of code per day (Brooks 1995).[2] Let us now make some outrageous approximations. The current number of software programmers in the world has been estimated as approximately 19 million (Hilwa 2014). Assume that all these software engineers are working on the same software project. Clearly, this would be an enormous undertaking and would for many reasons be infeasible. However, if this were possible then 190 million good lines of code could be produced per day. Imagining that a single program with this number of lines of good code could actually function is wildly optimistic for many reasons. Lehman noted (Lehman and Ramil 2002)

> In every piece of real world software, there are embedded an unbounded number of assumptions. Most of the assumptions are not decisions that you have taken, but things that you have not thought about

Let us compare and contrast this with living systems and in particular a pear tree. It has been calculated that the single mature leaf of a pear tree has 50 million cells, while the entire tree has approximately 15,000 million cells (Stern 1999, p. 3). This is 150 times the number of lines of code in an average high-end car. The number of cells in an adult human body is estimated to be 10^{14}. So there are a *million* times more cells in the human body than in the largest software systems thus far constructed. A cell is an enormously complex entity itself, so equating cells to lines of code makes our argument heavily biased toward human designed programs (i.e., grossly underestimating biological complexity). In addition, living organisms are in a constant state of change and yet they maintain their overall function. For instance, in the human body it is estimated that 300 million cells die and are replaced every minute (Center for Disease Control 2013). Human engineered software resides in computer memory and if an error occurs a human being is required to re-install or re-load the software, or even replace the memory (i.e., it is very fragile).

How long would it take all the software engineers on the planet to produce a piece of software with the same number of lines of code as there are cells in a human body? The answer (using the previously discussed assumptions) is 14,500 years. Clearly there is something very special happening in biology. It implies that there ought to be another way of programming complex systems. We suggest that this methodology should not require programmers to work at the level of logical instructions, but at a *much* higher level. We suggest that this level should produce computation at a visual (or sensory) level by combining visual computational elements that always perform some form of useful computation that can shaped via visual (sensory) indicators of the computation taking place. There is a form of computing called Visual Computing

---

[2]A more recent book has reconfirmed this as a good estimate in more recent software projects (Jones and Bonsignour 2011).

where computer scientists have tried to create a programming methodology rather like this. We discuss this next.

3 Visual Programming

3.1 Introduction

Visual programming languages (VPLs) allow programmers to create programs by manipulating program elements graphically rather than by specifying them textually. VPL is also known as dataflow or diagrammatic programming. There are a large number of VPLs. One important characteristic of most VPLs is that syntax errors are impossible. The user is only allowed to manipulate graphical elements in a constrained way.

The first so-called VPL, LOGO (Papert 1980), was created in 1967 by Daniel G. Bobrow, Wally Feurzeig, Seymour Papert and Cynthia Solomon. The language included movement commands for a simple drawing "robot" called a *turtle*. However, the complete LOGO language is actually a dialect of the AI functional programming language LISP (McCarthy 1960, 1962).

3.2 Scratch

Scratch is a recently created VPL (Resnick et al. 2009) in which different visual blocks can be snapped together rather like puzzle pieces. The programming constructs are shaped so that they can only accept other constructs. Figure 15.1 shows a simple example of a Scratch program.[3]

In the development environment there is a *programming area* where the pieces are put together and an *executable area* where the program outputs are displayed. Usually programs control animated characters or shapes (which the user or programmer has previously created). Figure 15.2 shows the Scratch development environment for the crab program. When the "When clicked" piece is clicked, the crab in the executable area moves around a little at random.

The programming area acts rather like the floor of a child's playroom where Lego bricks have been used on a number of projects. The user clicks on a stack of programming pieces and this causes the execution of the program. Scratch users mainly involve children between the ages of 8 and 16, though as Resnick notes, a sizeable group of adults also participate (Resnick et al. 2009).

---

[3]Scratch is free to be used on the internet and is available at http://scratch.mit.edu/

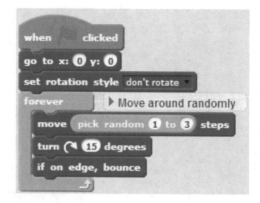

Fig. 15.1 Example program in Scratch that controls an animated crab

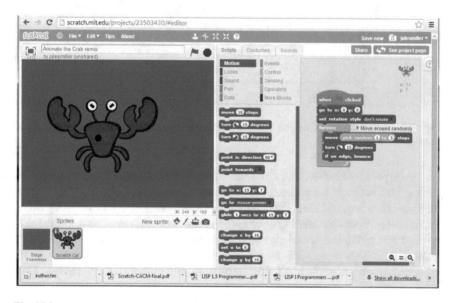

Fig. 15.2 Scratch programming development environment for the crab program

3.3   LabView

Engineers are already using forms of visual programming. LabView[4] is a well-established VPL that is used by engineers to build mixed software and hardware systems, including analysis and data acquisition, instrument control, embedded control and monitoring, and automated test and validation systems. LabView uses a visual programming language called G. G is a dataflow programming language in

---

[4]http://www.ni.com/labview

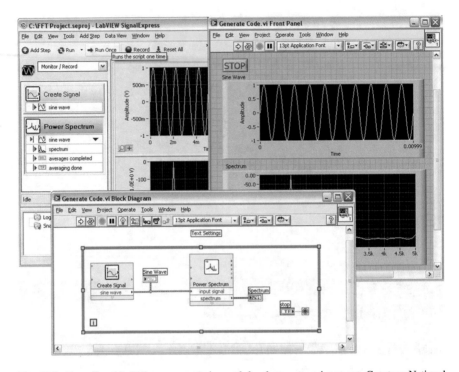

Fig. 15.3 Example of LabView programming and development environment. Courtesy National Instruments, www.ni.com

which the programmer draws, places and connects visual nodes icons together. The connections between these nodes propagate data. Nodes start executing as soon as they have their required data. Users build programs by dragging and dropping virtual instruments. However, building complex algorithms or large programs still requires detailed and extensive knowledge of the syntax behind LabView and its memory management. This means it is more like a visually assisted conventional programming system. An example of a LabView program and output[5] is shown in Fig. 15.3.

4   Nature's Way of Programming

Complex living systems are self-constructed. Single celled organisms replicate themselves and form vast collections that achieve global 'goals' that are emergent from the interactions between the cells and the environment in which they live. A classic organism in this regard is slime mould (Bonner 2009). This organism undergoes distinct and dramatic developmental stages:

---

[5]This was obtained from http://www.scilab.org

- amoebae: the cells are isolated and feed in isolation
- aggregation: when the food supply is exhausted the cells come together
- slug-like: the aggregated cells form a single creature that is capable of movement
- stalking: the cells rise up from the ground and form a stalk
- fruiting: the stalk produces a head which bears spores
- spore-dispersion: The spores are dispersed on the ground and hatch into amoebae

Multicellular organisms are built via the process of biological development in which a single event, the fertilisation of an ovum, begins a process in which cells replicate in parallel and eventually differentiate into specialist cells which co-operate in the production of a huge collection of cells. This constitutes the body of the organism. Organisms continually change during their lifetime and yet largely maintain their basic functionality.

Let us compare how organisms are 'programmed' with how computer programs are produced. Cells contain information storage mainly in the form of a sequence of *base-pairs* on a double-stranded DNA molecule. Collections of these bases form *genes*. Many cells contain collections of DNA molecules called *chromosomes*. One can think of the genes as analogous to the instructions in a computer program. The genotype (the collection of chromosomes) can be regarded as the program for a cell (Miller and Banzhaf 2003). The cell is an *enormously* complex entity. The bacterium *E. Coli* has the following components (Harold 2001). There are about 2,400,000 protein molecules (of 1850 varieties), 1400 mRNA molecules (600 varieties), 200,000 tRNA molecules (60 varieties), 20,000 ribosomes, and 2.1 DNA molecules. This list continues. The recently decoded 4,639,221 base-pair genome has 4289 protein-coding genes (Passarge 2013). Biological programs are made of this basic unit.

Human beings do not create programs from a module or entity of the complexity of a cell. Indeed, many engineers and scientists would abhor the construction of anything in which the atomic unit was anything that complex. Despite this we argue that to break through the complexity ceiling we will need a software equivalent of a cell. We think a good analogy to the software construction methodology of the future is horticulture. We call it the *software garden*. We discuss this next.

5 A Horticultural Analogy for Programming

5.1 *Introduction*

In horticulture, as in many other human activities, humans manipulate complex systems to produce desired outcomes. We manipulate plants in a variety of ways, for instance, by pruning, fertilising, spraying, training, grafting and breeding. Although recently plants have been manipulated at a genetic level, the majority of interactions between human beings and plants are phenotypic in nature.

We believe that it is useful and apposite to compare the way plants are manipulated with the way computer programs are constructed.

Fig. 15.4 Virtual organism that grows into a French flag and then stops growing

5.2 Example: An Evolved Developmental Approach to Creating Virtual Organisms

A convenient computational environment where virtual plants and other organisms can be studied and manipulated is cellular automata (CA) (Ilachinski 2001). They were invented by John von Neumann and Stanlislaw Ulam (Ulam 1952; von Neumann 1951). In CA, the world consists of cells obeying rules that depend on their discrete state and the states of their neighbours. By creating several CA maps one can simulate both the cells themselves and chemicals that interact with the cells. The chemical CAs obeyed a simple diffusion law. Miller used these ideas together with a technique called Cartesian Genetic Programming (CGP) to represent and evolve cellular programs in which "organisms" can develop from a single cell (Miller 2004). He showed that it was possible to evolve programs which caused the organisms to take on the appearance of various desired shapes (e.g., plant-like structures and national flags). Interestingly, the organisms could achieve stasis (or maturity), but when an alteration was made, the organism responded by repairing itself and in many cases eventually achieved stasis again. This characteristic was observed in a number of virtual organisms and was not explicitly rewarded by the fitness function used (i.e., it was emergent). Figure 15.4 shows a cellular program that when run develops into a French flag which subsequently stops growing.

Although the French flag organism achieves stasis, the individual cells each executing the same program are highly active. Indeed, the organism is in a constant state of rebuilding itself. This means that if the organism is damaged a dynamic period of activity starts up again until the organism becomes a French flag again. This is shown in Figs. 15.5 and 15.6. This behaviour is reminiscent of autonomous regeneration of the pond organism hydra, which can reform itself when its cells are dissociated and then reaggregated (Bosch 2007; Gierer et al. 1972).

The grafting of two different virtual organisms was demonstrated in (Miller and Thomson 2004). Figures 15.7 and 15.8 show the development of two German flag organisms.

At iteration 11 the flags were divided and joined together, so that on the left half of the German flag organisms were made of cells from organism 11 (Gf11) and the right half were made of cells from organism 0 (Gf0). When a particular cell program decides to grow it replicates its own genotype. Figure 15.9 shows the locations of the two types of cells (top) and the phenotype of the grafted organism (bottom). In the former the black region indicates the locations of Gf11 cells and the red region the gGf0 cells. The graft behaves in a stable way, with each genotype dominating on each side of the hybrid organism and mixing taking place in the region around the graft site.

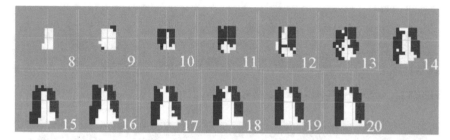

Fig. 15.5 French flag organism has red and blue sections removed. This causes rapid change until the organism recovers the French flag appearance, whereupon the organism becomes static again

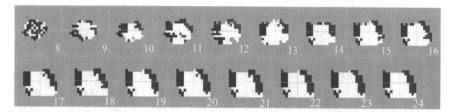

Fig. 15.6 Flag organism has cells randomly re-arranged. Rapid change occurs until the organism recovers the French flag appearance, whereupon the organism becomes static again

Fig. 15.7 Evolved growing German flag organism 0 (Gf0)

Fig. 15.8 Evolved growing German flag organism 11 (Gf11)

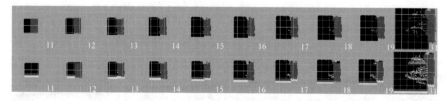

Fig. 15.9 Two different organisms Gf11 and Gf0 are grafted together at iteration 11. The upper part shows the location of each genotype over time and the lower shows the phenotype

Fig. 15.10 Evolved growing plant organism 9 (gp9)

Fig. 15.11 Evolved growing plant organism 13 (gp13)

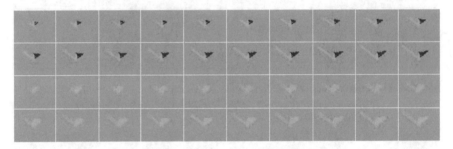

Fig. 15.12 Two different virtual plant organisms, gp13 and gp9, are grafted together at iteration 11. The upper part shows the location of each genotype over time and the lower shows the phenotype

In another example, plant-like organisms were evolved (Figs. 15.10 and 15.11). The organisms were grafted at iteration 11. Figure 15.12 shows both the location of cell types (red indicates cells belonging to organism gp13 while green indicates cells belonging to gp9).

6 The Software Garden

The software garden refers to a proposed visual developmental programming in which truly complex software is constructed by the manipulation of evolved computational developmental organisms. It is suggested that programmers of the future will manipulate (i.e., 'program') complex software by manipulating the behaviour of software, using operations that are analogous to those used by horticulturists. This form of programming will be more like a narrative. It will involve multiple parallel interactions with the software on multiple levels. Software will change in response to these interactions and new functionality will emerge rather than being engineered by design.

Human 'programmers' will observe the computational behaviour of constructed systems through a number of visual or other sensory indicators of software function and they will carry out phenotypic manipulation so that the desired computational behaviour is more closely obtained. As we saw this is rather like how Scratch programs are constructed to manipulate animated characters. In the examples of growing flags and plants the objective is visual rather than computational, however we see no reason why computational behaviours could not be represented through visual indicators (or visualizations).

In addition, we foresee that computer scientists will create computational 'seed libraries' which when planted in the appropriate computational environment will grow and develop towards certain desired computational behaviours. Analogues of many of the actions that horticulturalists perform will be created, including grafting, pruning, fertilizing, training, etc. This will allow computational systems to be programmed without the high-level programmer being aware of the internal computational mechanisms within the computational cells. We have seen by some simple examples that computational organisms can be evolved, they can repair themselves, achieve maturity, and be grafted.

References

Bonner JT (2009) The social amoebae: the biology of cellular slime molds. Princeton University Press, Princeton

Bosch TC (2007) Why polyps regenerate and we don't: towards a cellular and molecular framework for Hydra regeneration. Dev Biol 303(2):421–433

Brooks F (1995) The mythical man-month. Addison-Wesley, Boston

Center for Disease Control (2013) Human body statistics. http://www.statisticbrain.com/human-body-statistics/. Accessed 3 May 2014

Gierer A, Berking S, Bode H, David CN, Flick K, Hansmann G, Schaller H, Trenkner E (1972) Regeneration of hydra from reaggregated cells. Nat New Biol 239:98–101

Harold FM (2001) The way of the cell: molecules, organisms and the order of life. Oxford University Press, Oxford

Hilwa A (2014) Worldwide software developer and ICT-skilled workforce estimates. Technical report 244709, IDC Corporate USA, December 2013

Ilachinski A (2001) Cellular automata. World Scientific Publishing, Singapore

Jones C, Bonsignour O (2011) The economics of software quality. Addison-Wesley, Boston

Kehrer A (2011) Linux ist zu komplex geworden. http://www.zeit.de/digital/internet/2011-11/linux-thorvalds-2011. Accessed 3 May 2014

Lanier J (2003) The complexity ceiling. In: Brockman J (ed) The next fifty years: science in the first half of the twenty-first century. Phoenix, Quezon City, pp 216–229

Lehman M, Ramil J (2002) Software uncertainty. In: Bustard D, Liu W, Sterritt R (eds) Soft-Ware 2002: computing in an imperfect world, LNCS, vol 2311. Springer, Heidelberg, pp 174–190

McCandless D (2014) Information is beautiful. http://www.informationisbeautiful.net/visualizations/million-lines-of-code/2014. Accessed 3 May 2014

McCarthy J (1960) Recursive functions of symbolic expressions and their computation by machine, Part I. Commun ACM 3(4):184–195

McCarthy J (1962) LISP 1.5 programmer's manual. MIT Press, Cambridge

Miller JF (2004) Evolving a self-repairing, self-regulating, French flag organism. In: Deb K (ed) GECCO 2004, LNCS, vol 3102. Springer, Heidelberg, pp 129–139

Miller JF, Banzhaf W (2003) Evolving the program for a cell: from French flags to Boolean circuits. In: Kumar S, Bentley PJ (eds) On growth, form and computers. Academic Press, Cambridge, pp 278–302

Miller JF, Thomson P (2004) Beyond the complexity ceiling: evolution, emergence and regeneration. In: GECCO 2004 workshop (WORLDS) proceedings

Papert S (1980) Mindstorms: children, computers, and powerful ideas. Basic Books, New York

Passarge E (2013) Color atlas of genetics, 4th edn. Thieme, Stuttgart

Resnick M, Maloney J, Monroy-Hernández A, Rusk N, Eastmond E, Brennan K, Millner A, Rosenbaum E, Silver J, Silverman B, Kafai Y (2009) Scratch: programming for all. Commun ACM 52(11):60–67

Stern K (1999) Introductory plant biology. McGraw-Hill, New York

Ulam SM (1952) Random processes and transformations. In: Proceedings of the international congress of mathematicians 1950, vol 2. American mathematical society, Providence, RI, pp 264–275

von Neumann J (1951) The general and logical theory of automata. In: Jeffress LA (ed) Cerebral mechanisms in behavior: the Hixon symposium. Wiley, Hoboken, NJ, pp 1–31

Chapter 16
Emergent Causality in Complex Films and Complex Systems

Maria Poulaki

Abstract This chapter explores the complex dynamics of causality in narrative. I show that approaching the study of narrative through a complex systems framework allows us to see narrative causality as a product of dynamic transformation occurring through the interaction of causal elements connecting the intra- and extra-diegetic levels. Exploring the properties of emergence, nonlinearity and feedback in complex systems and complex narratives, with a particular focus on complex films, the chapter suggests an agent-based approach to narrative to capture the dynamics of transformation taking place in-between micro, meso and macro narrative levels, connecting the macro-causal, formal dynamics, to the micro-interactions of agents.

1 Narrative and the Principle of Causality

Causality, the way that recipients interpret narrative events as relating to each other in sequences of causes and effects (Kafalenos 2006, p. viii), is the driving force of narrative. As Edward Branigan characteristically declares: "If I were forced to use a single word to characterize a narrative organization of data, that word would be 'causality'. Creating time and place in a narrative is not as important as constructing a possible logic for the events that occur" (Branigan 1992, p. 216). The definition of narrative that he suggests is "a way of organizing spatial and temporal data into a cause-effect chain of events with a beginning, middle, and end that embodies a judgement about the nature of the events as well as demonstrates how it is possible to know, and hence to narrate, the events" (p. 3).

Narrative texts prompt recipients to formulate various causal interpretations. The function of narrative causality presupposes diegetic and character-based action, and the changes brought by it. Literary theorist Didier Coste points out the association of narrative with "'action' or 'making', if not with causality" (Coste 1989, p. 42). Although narrative causality can be distinguished and acquire different forms from

M. Poulaki (✉)
Department of Music and Media, University of Surrey, Guildford, UK
e-mail: m.poulaki@surrey.ac.uk

the intra-diegetic micro-causal level to the structural or 'macro' diegetic causal level, and also the extra-diegetic level of the recipient's interpretation, the most common conception of narrative causality is the one generated by the causal power of agents in the diegetic world. Causality in narratives operates through agents—actors or "actants"—and the "functions" they perform. According to Mieke Bal, as long as stories are constructions made by humans, involving human characters and addressed to humans, they are based on "the presupposition that human thinking and action is directed towards an aim" (Bal 1985, p. 26). Causal action is carried by agents and is most of the times oriented towards a goal. The association of causality with meaningful action is so widespread that many narratologists distinguish between narrative and other forms of texts in which causal connections through actions are not prevailing, for example descriptive passages. Narrative is a teleological construction, demanding a subject and its "will to execute his or her program" (Bal 1985, p. 33). Such "will" provides the story with the necessary energy in order for it to unfold in time. As long as we think of agency in narratives as a goal-directed activity, it is difficult to detach it from cause and effect chains at the micro-diegetic level, that of characters' actions.

Although characters are always causal agents, the actions that drive a narrative's causality are not always character-driven. Bal distinguishes between actors and classes of actors (actants) and distinctive characters in narrative texts. The former two might also be inanimate and their role is structural (always related to the overall teleology of the fabula), while the latter correspond to human beings, and from the semiological point of view, they consist in semantic units (Bal 1985, p. 79). The actantial model was introduced in narrative theory by semiotician Algirdas-Julien Greimas, who in turn borrowed the term "actant" from the linguist Lucien Tesnière. Actants may be defined as "names of roles" (Coste 1989, p. 135). The notion of actant, also becoming influential in social theory through "actor-network theory", suggests a step beyond the micro-diegetic level, by adopting a transindividual perspective. It is also helpful in order to conceive of larger patterns of causality involved in narratives, although even this notion of actant does not escape some degree of anthropomorphism. For instance, among the examples of actants that Bal provides are "The old people", "The Marxists", etc. (Bal 1985, p. 27).

What I describe as two different kinds of causal analysis in narratives, namely the analysis at the micro-diegetic level of causality (of actors) or the macro-diegetic level (of actants), correspond to different models of narrative analysis. According to film theorist Thomas Elsaesser, on the one hand "the *Aristotelian model* [by comparison to the structuralist model] seems to stress overall unity (of time, place, and action), rather than segmentation. It also centres on characters as initiating agents rather than on interpersonal transactions (functions) as the core elements of narrative" (Elsaesser and Buckland 2002, p. 30; my emphasis). On the other hand, the *structuralist and poststructuralist model* of characters and causality is "functionalist and relations-based, essentially a-causal and instead more complexly 'logical' and 'semantic'." (Elsaesser and Buckland 2002, p. 37).

I would argue that narrative causality cannot be conceived on any of these levels alone, but operates across levels and connects them in a dynamic and, as will shortly be discussed, emergent way. I would argue that neither the Aristotelian model alone nor the structuralist one can capture the dynamics linking the micro-level of characterological action to the macro-level of narrative structure. In what follows I suggest a complex systemic approach to narrative causality, which would be able to capture the complex dynamic interplay of these levels.

2   Causality and Transformation

Narrative theory is not incompatible with complex systems theory. One classical narratological model that is particularly interesting in this respect, because of its emphasis upon dynamics, is the one of narrative equilibrium. This model was suggested in 1960s France by philosopher Tzvetan Todorov, who also coined the term "narratology". Todorov considered narrative causality a dynamic process tending towards equilibrium. For him, equilibrium seems to be a fundamental structuring principle of narrative:

> The minimal complete plot consists in the passage from one equilibrium to another. An "ideal" narrative begins with a stable situation which is disturbed by some power or force. There results a state of disequilibrium; by the action of a force directed in the opposite direction, the equilibrium is re-established; the second equilibrium is similar to the first, but the two are never identical. (Todorov 1977, p. 111)

According to Todorov's model, narrative is "a causal 'transformation' of a situation through five stages" (Branigan 1992, p. 4), or five fundamental "actions": initial equilibrium, disruption of this equilibrium, recognition of disruption, repair of disruption, reinstatement of the initial equilibrium.[1] Todorov here on the one hand follows a logic derived from Aristotelian poetics, and its division of drama in a number of specific acts/stages. On the other hand, Todorov's contribution focuses on the structure of the form, thus it is more structuralist than Aristotle's model in this respect. I would add that, due to Todorov's addition of an element of dynamics in the study of narrative, his notion of narrative is systemic as well.

The complete five-stage equilibrium model is an ideal case, as Todorov himself stresses, and he recognizes the existence of cases where the narrative does not do full circle but describes "only the passage from an equilibrium to a disequilibrium, and conversely" (Todorov 1977, p. 118). Although the first two, or sometimes the last two stages might be omitted, suspending a satisfactory resolution, all narratives can be thought of as parts of the full five-stage circle (p. 39). In this respect, narrative teleological causality can be imagined as a trajectory towards equilibrium, even in cases when the latter is not finally achieved. The phase of equilibrium is considered by Todorov as static (and corresponds, at the grammatical level of predicates, to the role of adjectives), while disequilibrium is the dynamic phase, corresponding to verbs

---

[1] For an analytic description of these five stages through examples such as *The Magic Swan-Geese* fairy tale (also analyzed by Vladimir Propp) and Henry James's *In the Cage*, see Todorov (1971).

(pp. 111, 120).[2] However, if the above described "full circle" constitutes the basis of the narrative model, then narrative dynamics is overarched by a symmetrical construction—defined by the initial and the concluding equilibrium. Indeed, as Branigan notes, both Todorov's as well as Vladimir Propp's classical narrative analyses are oriented towards the "large scale symmetries" of narratives (Branigan 1992, p. 9), and, in this respect, deviate from the characterological focus of Aristotelian drama. These large-scale symmetries are not causal in the strict sense of the word, which implies a more or less direct relation between an effect and its cause (Branigan 1992, p. 27). Moreover, their function is not to drive the action forward. They rather pertain to what Todorov calls transformations, referring to larger patterns of change that do not follow strict cause and effect sequences.

Todorov's model has been tied to equilibrium, because of its emphasis upon symmetry. However, I would argue that what makes his model distinctive is exactly the opposite: its definition of narrative on the basis of change and disequilibrium. The latter seems to be for Todorov the necessary (and perhaps sufficient) condition for narrative to exist. I quote a characteristic passage from his article in *Diacritics*, where he analyzes Boccaccio's *Decameron III*:

> But what is it that *makes* this narrative? Let us return to the beginning of the story. Boccaccio first describes Naples, the setting of the action; then he presents the three protagonists; after which he tells us about Ricciardo's love for Catella. Is this a narrative? Once again I think we can readily agree that it is not. The length of the text is not a deciding factor—only two paragraphs in Boccaccio's tale—but we sense that, even if it were five times this length, things would not have changed. On the other hand, when Boccaccio says, "this was his state of mind when . . ." (and at least in French there is a tense change here from the imperfect to the aorist), the narrative is underway. The explanation seems simple: at the beginning we witness the description of a *state*; yet this is not sufficient for narrative, which requires the development of an *action*, i.e., change, difference. (Todorov 1971, p. 38)

What is incompatible with narrative, according to Todorov's description, is the stasis of non-action. Change defines narrative, either at the micro-level of characterological action, or at the macro-level of "transformation".

Narrative transformations might be "a-causal" but they still evoke causality, although not in the sense of a cause and effect sequence. No matter where the transformative agency lies, in anthropomorphic actors (with their desires, goals and internal motives) or in actants (classes of actors), the overall patterns of change make a narrative causal, as long as they reveal its status as an organization that develops in time.

---

[2]With regard to the static and dynamic nature of motifs, Todorov draws on the Russian Formalist Boris Tomashevsky.

3   Emergent Causality

The dynamics of causality in narrative do not manifest themselves only in transformation from state A to state B. They are also a matter, as already broached, of a complex interplay of the different narrative levels, that of actors and actants and that of overall formal structure. In order to explain my claim that causality in narratives can be thought as emergent out of the complex interplay of these levels, it is necessary to introduce in more detail the concept of emergence, as it has been developed first in philosophy in the beginning of the last century, and later in (complex) systems theory. The philosophical sense of emergence dates back to 1875, when George Henry Lewes used it in his work *Problems of Life and Mind*. In the late nineteenth and early twentieth century, emergence was a central concern for the cycle of British Emergentists, who participated in the debate between mechanists and vitalists about the genealogy of sciences. Emergentists occupied a moderate position, resisting the reduction of biology, and secondarily of chemistry, to physics. Life, according to them, is not just an outcome of mechanical laws, neither is it a substance itself; some of its qualities continue to be irreducible to mere mechanical processes. Among the most important figures of British Emergentism have been John Stuart Mill and Charlie Dunbar Broad. While Mill retained the attribute of causality in emergence, Broad initiated (in *The Mind and Its Place in Nature*, 1925) a "synchronic, noncausal, covariational account of the relationship of emergent features to the conditions that gave rise to them" (O'Connor and Wong 2009); his account has certain affinities with the contemporary revived interest in emergence. The "noncausal" character that British Emergentists ascribed to emergence is due to the fact that emergent laws are "trans-ordinal", as Broad called them, that is, they refer to the connection of one order (or level) with another, and do not apply in the case of elements situated within the same order. Trans-ordinal laws can only be found *a posteriori* and at the higher level, and cannot be predicted by any existent law about the composition of lower-level elements: "[. . .] we must wait till we meet with an actual instance of an object of the higher order before we can discover such a law; and [. . .] we cannot possibly deduce it beforehand from any combination of laws which we have discovered by observing aggregates of a lower order" (Broad, *The Mind and Its Place in Nature*; cited by O'Connor and Wong 2009). Trans-ordinal or emergent laws "describe a synchronic noncausal covariation of an emergent property and its lower-level emergent base" (O'Connor and Wong 2009). "Noncausal" here means that no single law of the lower level can account for the property that emerges at the higher level, thus direct cause-and-effect chains between different levels cannot be established. According to Broad's approach to emergence, "high-level causal patterns" are additional to those at the lower level, and they can exert influence upon the lower levels, in a manner that has more recently been characterized as "downward causation" (Campbell 1974).

   Other British Emergentists, and especially Samuel Alexander, have been more influential than Broad in contemporary science. Contradicting Mill and Broad, Alexander dismissed autonomous higher-level causality. Even though he emphasized the novelty of emergent qualities, he thought of emergence as an epistemological rather than an ontological category. According to the criticism, however, the "weak" emergence of Alexander cannot account for the causal properties of the whole constituted by the parts (Clayton 2006, pp. 25–26); such properties are indispensible in order for the whole to be considered as an autonomous entity.

Although the degree of connection between different orders was a point of dispute for Emergentists, what is stressed in all emergentist accounts as a central property of emergence is unpredictability: "Emergent properties are systemic features of complex systems which could not be predicted [. . .] from the standpoint of a pre-emergent stage, despite a thorough knowledge of the features of, and laws governing, their parts" (O'Connor and Wong 2009). Preoccupied with wholes that are not reducible to their parts, the concept of emergence found fertile ground in systems theory, which revived the interest in emergence (O'Connor and Wong 2009). Since Ludwig von Bertalanffy's *General Systems Theory* (GST), systems theory "was put forward as a counter to what was perceived as excessive reductionism dominating scientific discourse during much of the twentieth century" (EMIL 2007).

Different degrees of emergence, from strong (absolute irreducibility and completely "new" properties) to weak (practical but not analytical irreducibility), have been identified in the philosophy of emergence, and causality plays a crucial role in the difference between the two—strong and weak—versions.[3] Contemporary accounts of emergence in the context of complex systems study seem to favor a "weaker", or "intermediate", version of it.[4] The weak emergent approach is materialistic, according to systems scholar Mark Bedau, as it steps on the existence of microdynamics between material components of the microlevel that result in the emergence of operationally autonomous macrophenomena (Bedau 1997, p. 395). The recent complex systems theories favor these weaker versions of emergence, as the material substrate of autonomous units and their interrelations are considered to be involved in an active way in emergent self-organization.

---

[3]Strong emergence holds that the new properties of a system are not connected to the system's previous states but rather consist in ontologically novel properties. Thus, although it shares the attributes of "supereminence" and "downward causation" with weak emergence, strong emergence denies the existence of any kind of link between "the aggregation of the micro-level potentialities" and "the supervenient downward causal powers" upon them (Bedau 1997, p. 377). However, as Jaegwon Kim stresses (2006, pp. 200–201), talking about human consciousness as an emergent property (based on the complex interactions of the brain's neural network), this negative—because of the absence of causal links—definition of irreducible, "strong" emergence tells nothing about what emergence is, and about the relations that connect the different levels with each other. Thus he poses the challenge for researchers of emergence "to show that emergent properties do not succumb to the threat of epiphenomenalism, and that emergent phenomena can have causal powers vis-à-vis physical phenomena."

[4]Chalmers (2006) has suggested the term "intermediate emergence" to describe systems "in which high-level facts and laws are not deducible from low-level laws (combined with initial conditions)", and, in this case, a change of level is necessary in order to understand the emergent procedure, a level in which combinations not deducible from the basic laws but only effectuated with a change of initial conditions occur.

Complex systems are nonlinear and irreducible, in the sense that "a single high level property may be realized by more than one set of micro-states which have no lawful relationship between them" (EMIL 2007). However, as a case of weak emergence, the irreducibility of a complex system does not preclude (nonlinear) deducibility from the initial conditions, although these conditions are impossible to clearly define in open (and not isolated) systems. Therefore, the methods that are usually employed in the study of emergence in complex systems are simulation or statistical modelling (Byrne 1998, p. 62). Thus, the study of emergent causality demands a synthetic rather than an analytical approach, because synthetic approaches follow the bottom-up constitution of systems. According to Bedau, "the macrostate's behavior" could be derived "from the system's microdynamic" only by means of simulation (Bedau 1997, p. 378), or "modeling all the interactions of the realizing microstates leading up to it from its initial conditions" (O'Connor and Wong 2009).

4   Nonlinear Causality and Emergence from Cybernetics to Complex Systems Theory

Before returning to narrative and its emergent causality, I need to take another short detour through a different thread of complex systems theory starting from cybernetics (the study of regulatory systems), in order to add some further insights into the causality of complex systems. In the cybernetic tradition, nonlinear causality has been associated with the notion of feedback. Philosopher Manuel de Landa credits Norman Wiener, the "father" of cybernetics, with a nonlinear idea of causality, which broke with a tradition of "linear (nonreciprocal) causality" (De Landa 2009, p. 67). Magoroh Maruyama's study of positive and negative feedback, as well as Humberto Maturana's and Francisco Varela's "autocatalytic loops", further established a nonlinear conception of causality. This conception countered the dominant conception of causality in Western thought, according to which "similar conditions produce similar effects" (Maruyama 1963, p. 4).

The nonlinear approach to causality questions the value of negative feedback and stability, and highlights the role of non-equilibrium in the organization of systems. According to Bertuglia and Vaio, this shift to positive feedback and non-equilibrium also marked the "overtaking" of cybernetics by complexity theory:

> Cybernetics, in reality, can be considered a science that anticipated complexity in the investigation of dynamical systems, precisely because it was the first to make use of concepts such as isolated or closed systems that regulate themselves by means of internal feedback cycles. [...] complexity has overtaken cybernetics because it makes use of new concepts such as, in particular, self-organization and emergence; in other words, because it considers systems that evolve towards new states that do not have negative feedback cycles. (Bertuglia and Vaio 2005, p. 264)

When causality is conceived in nonlinear systems, it becomes the emergent product of the aggregation and "synergy" of a system's elements. Causal synergy and emergence are what differentiate nonlinear from linear systems. As complexity scientist Grégoire Nicolis explains,

> In a linear system the ultimate effect of the combined action of two different causes is merely the superposition of the effects of each cause taken individually. But in a nonlinear system adding two elementary actions to one another can induce dramatic new effects reflecting the onset of cooperativity between the constituent elements. (Nicolis 1995, p. 1)

The combination of different agents in a complex system has causal influence that again exceeds that of the sum of the combined causes taken individually. Nonlinearity in the mathematical sense of the word refers exactly to this disproportionality between starting conditions and results. To link this back to the previous discussion of the concept of emergence and its philosophical genealogy, "weaker" versions of emergence suggest that there is a connection between properties at the micro-level and those at the macro-level, but this connection is nonlinear. This, however, does not preclude some kind of causality to exist between the different levels.

In complex systems accounts, emergence is not acausal. It rather pertains to a different, "pattern-based" as it has been called, form of causality. Jeffrey Goldstein (Goldstein 1996, p. 178), following Ben Goertzel's mathematical model of "pattern dynamics",[5] rejects the view according to which complex chaotic processes are acausal—he refers specifically to the philosopher of science Stephen Kellert who expresses such a view in his book *In the Wake of Chaos*. Suggesting "a revision of causal explanation in the light of emergence" (Goldstein 1996, p. 163), instead of an abolishment of causality altogether, Goldstein distinguishes pattern-based causality (revolving around questions such as "how do the new patterns shown in emergent phenomena relate to previous patterns in the system?") from the traditional, "substantialist" causality (implied by questions such as "what is it made of?" and "how much of it is there") (p. 165). Emergence is caused when already existing systemic patterns become more complex, creating "a plurality of folds" (p. 169). Thus, either through "Boolean networks" (as Stuart Kauffman claims) or the "Baker transformation" (as does Ilya Prigogine), "emergent phenomena have [within the system] complex precursors" (Goldstein 1996, p. 170), and they do not just "pop up" out of the initial simplicity of a system. By characterizing a property as emergent, one does not imply that there is no way to explain or understand its occurrence. Causation is still an issue in emergence, but it does not happen horizontally, following the model of bowling balls hitting each other, as a classical mechanical approach to causality would imply, but vertically, between different scales and levels. Emergent events are "wholes", the causal effects of which "cannot be correctly represented in terms of the separate causal effects of [the] constituents" (O'Connor and Wong 2009).

It is complexity itself that demands some notion of causality to be preserved for emergent phenomena. There is a causal link, Goldstein argues, between increased complexity and emergence (Goldstein 1996, p. 174). The insistence upon the coupling of emergence with causality is a stance that rejects both "hard" scientific reductionism and the absolute detachment of the emergent phenomenon from its

---

[5]This mathematical model is an alternative to the thermodynamical model of Ilya Prigogine.

functional substrates (as a "strong emergence" thesis would have it). Rather, it is compatible with the combination of the "local" with the "global" level (p. 175). As Prigogine and philosopher Isabelle Stengers mention in their book *The End of Certainty*, there is "a narrow path between two conceptions that both lead to alienation: a world ruled by deterministic laws, which leaves no place for novelty, and a world ruled by a dice-playing God, where everything is absurd, *acausal*, and incomprehensible" (Prigogine and Stengers 1997, p. 188; my emphasis).

Emergence seems to require a bridge between the microlevel and the macrolevel, which allows a view over the patterns developed by aggregates of separate micro-elements. As O'Connor and Wong note: "Of central importance is to recognize that the relationship of micro-level structures and macro-level emergent properties is dynamic and causal, not static and formal (in a quasi-logical sense)" (O'Connor and Wong 2005). Especially the weak and synergetic conceptions of causality derived from emergentist approaches and second wave cybernetics can be very useful for the development of new models to approach the causality that operates between the different diegetic and narrational levels.

5 Emergent Causality and Narrative

The reader might at this point rightly wonder how this discussion of causality and emergence, coming mainly from physics, as well as philosophy, can be relevant to the study of narrative and narrative agents, who are not particles but fictive characters and situations. Narrative causality is not the mechanical and "linear" (in the strict sense) causality of Newtonian laws. It is not physical or mathematical but anthropomorphic, less precise and less tight than causality at the level of natural elements, to which complexity in sciences refers. In one sense, causality in most narratives and narrative films is *a priori* "loose". According to organizational theorists Haridimos Tsoukas and Mary Jo Hatch, narrative can be a model for all modes of thinking in which causality does not operate through strict and reductive logical sequences, but "through associ-ations that are not causal in the logico-scientific sense" (Tsoukas and Hatch 2001, p. 1006). As they point out, narrative causality operates through patterns of "co-occurrence, spatial proximity, formal similarity or metaphor" (p. 1006), features that "may help us to understand [...] the non-linearity, indeterminacy, unpredictability, and emergence of complex systems" (p. 1007). However, this conception of narrative is already made from a meta-narrative perspective, and particularly from one of complex systems theory that re-interprets narrative as a complex system, and has not always been self-evident in narrative studies, nor is it still.

In film studies in particular, narrative has been clearly differentiated from other non-narrative formal systems that are possible in film, such as the rhetorical, categorical, associational and abstract forms distinguished by film scholars David Bordwell and Kristin Thompson (2008). Certain among these non-narrative forms, and especially the associational one, which creates patterns of images related according to motifs, have similar characteristics with those that Tsoukas and Hatch mention. But this form, prominent in "experimental" films, according to Bordwell and Thompson (2008, p. 356), is downplayed in narrative films. The definition of narrative in film theory but also in narratology, sticks to the notion of causality as an organizing principle that arranges events in causal-logical sequences.

Narrative can perhaps more easily be thought of as in affinity with complex systems when conceived as a cognitive system of interpretation that retrospectively determines the sequence of events so that they can be placed in a causal-logical chain. But a complex systemic approach requires a careful examination of how any form of cognitive organization emerges from the level of the *syuzhet* (plot), and how the text and its construction complicate and even withhold the top-down establishment of causality towards which narrative tends.

To the extent that complex narratives can be conceived as complex systems (Poulaki 2011), they may still form organizations, communicate and produce meaning without putting their elements into a steady linear arrangement. As long as meaning making processes in complex films are concerned, and provided that these are emergent processes, both textually and cognitively in the different systems of the film's text and the viewer's cognitive system, a weak rather than a strong conception of their emergence can prove useful. This implies that the textual form of the *syuzhet* matters in the emergence of meaning. Adopting a weak emergent approach to the causality involved in narratives would mean to direct our attention to the actual causal role that the multiple constitution and the non-linear ordering of the *syuzhet* and the relations between its elements have in the emergence of a whole. In the opposite case, a strong emergent approach that would consider this whole to be completely independent of its units, an "order" or schema that emerges in all cases of reading and viewing being independent of the specific characteristics of each text, would tell us nothing, to paraphrase Jaegwon Kim (2006, p. 200), about the processes through which the cognitive and filmic organization is constituted in complex films.

Like physicists and organizational scientists, narrative scholars also increasingly recognize "that the presence of multilayered and changing contexts, multidirectional causalities, and feedback loops often disturb steady progression toward "equilibrium" (Langley 1999, p. 692; cited in Boje 2001), and the study of narrative organization focuses more and more on these complex processes that make narrative emerge.

6   Structure and Emergence in Networks, from Social Theory to Narrative

Let us take as an example a particular case of narrative complexity, that of the so-called "network narratives" in cinema, which are particularly interesting in terms of causality. Prominent film scholar David Bordwell in his 2006 book *The Way Hollywood Tells It* identified network narratives as an important category within the recent wave of complex narratives in popular cinema.[6] Network narratives are multiple protagonist films with parallel and interconnected stories, involving, as Bordwell further explored in *Poetics of Cinema* (2007), loose causality, connections by chance or coincidence, and repetitions of the same events from the perspective of different characters. Some of the oft-cited complex narratives in this respect are *Code Inconnu* (Michael Haneke 2000), *Crash* (Paul Haggis 2005), Alejandro González Iñárritu's *21 Grams* (2003), and *Babel* (2006). If we think of such network narratives as complex systems, then their narrative organization can be conceived as emerging from the relations between their multiple elements (narrative agents and threads) and their complex causal interactions. Adopting a complex systems framework, the number of characters in narratives, and mostly the number and entanglement of their interactions, can be seen as disrupting the classical schemata of causality in narrative.

From a complex systems perspective, the number of components of a system and their relations plays a fundamental role in the system's complexity. Complex systems scientist Stuart Kauffman has shown that complexity builds up in multi-agent and densely interconnected systems (Kauffman 1993, p. 243). These two factors, the number of agents and the density of connections, are interdependent, as the big number of individual units increases the possible interactions and therefore the complexity of the resulting system. As the anthropologist and neuroscientist Terrence Deacon notes,

> With every iterated interaction, relational properties are multiplied with respect to each other, so an increase in numbers of elements and chances for interactions increases the relative importance of interaction parameters and related contextual variables. (Deacon 2006, pp. 121–122)

By increasing the number of agents, narratives also increase the relational range and the complexity of the network that these relations form.

Complexity theory, as Russ Marion points out, "envisions adaptive systems (species, animals, plants, viruses, etc.) as neural-like interactive networks of agents and seeks to understand the dynamics of network behaviors" (2006, p. 274). Emergence happens only through such dynamic interrelations. As Marion notes, "events emerge from complex interactive dynamics involving neural-like networks of adaptive agents. That is, emergent events are products of unpredictable combinations and recombinations among interdependent agents" (p. 259). The "networked, interdependent interactions" are characteristic of every complex system. Interactions between a large number of agents/elements create increasing complexity, but these interactions between the nodes need to be dynamical and reciprocal, in order for them to transform

---

[6]This wave has attracted both popular and theoretical attention (by scholars like Thomas Elsaesser (2009), Warren Buckland (2009), Allan Cameron (2008) and others). Films like *Pulp Fiction* (Quentin Tarantino 1994), *Run Lola Run* (Tom Tykwer 1998), *The Matrix* (Andy and Lana Wachowski 1999), *The Sixth Sense* (M. Night Shyamalan 1999), *Memento* (Christopher Nolan 2000), and *Eternal Sunshine of the Spotless Mind* (Michel Gondry 2004) are among the most oft-cited examples.

into an emergent organization. A complex approach to network narratives would also be differentiated from structuralist approaches—instead of emphasizing the larger structural forms and transformations, it would place more emphasis on the emergent dynamics at the "meso-level" of unit/agent interactions, and the particular ways they give rise to "macro"-transformations.

Network theory has not always been (and still is not exactly) synonymous with systems theory. Network theory has historically been a structure-oriented approach, but *complex network theory* as a strand of systems theory moves beyond structures, focusing on the emergent dynamics that the interrelations between units release (Barrat et al. 2008). It is interesting how a similar polarity is found in the history of network theory in sociology to that between the two narrative causality models mentioned at the beginning of this chapter, the Aristotelian and the Structuralist one. Emirbayer and Goodwin distinguish between different versions of "structuralism" in network theory: the "structuralist deterministic" model prioritizes the potency of structures over that of the individual actors, while that of "structuralist instrumentalism" prioritizes actors. The former tends to work with "static 'map configurations' or relational 'snapshots' of network patterns" (Emirbayer and Goodwin 1994, p. 1426), ending up in reifying relations and considering them overarching structures that determine the units; the latter takes the theory of "homo economicus" as its starting point, attributing to individual nodes a rationalistic and utility-maximizing logic, which, even in a bottom-up direction, still pre-determines the conduct of the network's actors/nodes. Such a double "structuration" became apparent through the reference earlier in this chapter to different models of causality in narrative; on the one hand, the "characterological" (Aristotelian) construction of causality is based on anthropomorphic motives, while on the other hand the structuralist—in the narratological sense—analysis of causality succumbs the dynamics of the plot's form to overarching symmetries that preexist them. A change of theoretical context though would allow, as it did in sociology, for different properties of networks to come to the fore. Complex systems theory in sociology aims at revealing the dynamical nature of social networks and highlighting the complex links and interrelationships between the micro-level of individuals and the network macro-level. Between these two levels, a multiplicity of nested systems with their own interrelationships weaves the patterns of social complexity (Byrne 1998, p. 10).

In sociology too, as in cybernetics, systems theory initially adopted a very different approach from the one that the "new", complex systems theory takes. Even today, systems theory in sociology often refers back to the work of Talcott Parsons, who, influenced by cybernetics, developed a model of society—known as "functionalism"—as a hierarchy of nested systems always beginning from—and tending towards—equilibrium. This model can be seen as analogous to the equilibrium model of narrative in Tzvetan Todorov's narratology, since Todorov defined equilibrium in a similar way, as "the existence of a stable but not static relation between the members of a society" (Kafalenos 2006, p. 4);[7] and this conception of equilibrium, similar to that of Parsons, influenced his adaptation of structural equilibrium into his narrative theory. However, as Kenneth Bailey argues, the emphasis that functionalism placed on equilibrium gradually became incompatible with the development of the (new) systems theory in sociology. The latter saw entropy (the amount of "redundant" energy that increases during a thermodynamic process) as well as nonequilibrium as the bases for both biological and social organization. Along with the development of complex systems theory, social systems theory differentiated from functionalism, departing from the "age of equilibrium" to enter the "age of entropy" (Bailey 1994, p. 5).[8] A combination of autopoietic self-organization with complexity emphasizes evolutionary dynamics that can be observed from the macrolevel: "macro-level social order is a complex product of micro-level intentionality and the wider non-linear operation of the system" (p. 5). The nonlinear process of self-organization is described by Peter Coveney as "the spontaneous emergence of non-equilibrium structural reorganizations on a macroscopic level, due to the collective interactions between a large number of (usually simple) microscopic objects" (Coveney 2003, p. 1058). The recent rise of complex and emergent approaches to the study of social and other kinds of networks as complex systems provides new methods to bridge the micro-macro divide.

Narrative has been used as a counter-example of emergent organization in this respect. Patrick Doreian comments on how sociologists have tried to describe the formation of networks using narrative. However, the limitations of this approach, which emphasizes causality, soon became manifest, since networks cannot be represented in causal-temporal chains of events.

> A narrative as a straightforward description of a sequence of events has considerable appeal. Most network analysts who study empirical phenomena use narrative. In part, it is window dressing, but it has more than surface interest. The risk is that the narrative becomes yet another just-so story with events following each other in time under convenient stage management. Once it is recognized that the only real connection between the described events is merely temporal, the causal enterprise is shaken. If a different event could follow a given event—which happens—the coupling of the events in a narrative is loosened. And, if there could be other outcomes between two hitherto sequential events that appear in a set of narratives, the tight coupling between events is lost again. [...] The most hard-nosed assessment is that truly establishing causality in network analysis is impossible—just as it is in the realm of statistical causality. [...] There needs to be a very tight coupling of theory, mechanisms, and credible empirical information before we can delineate the actual operation of causes in the empirical world before we can tell causal stories. (Doreian 2001, pp. 110–111)

---

[7]Todorov formulated this model through his analysis of Boccacio's *Decameron* in the 1960s, a period when the popularity of functionalism in sociology had started fading, but not the interest in equilibrium.

[8]Research in the field of nonequilibrium thermodynamics contributed to a paradigm shift with regard to entropy, which was initially considered to indicate the gradual disorganization and "death" of a system. Out-of-equilibrium processes maximize entropy but also create—in open systems—an order that is different from the one of systems in equilibrium. This order is produced by the self-organization of a system in a "state of *increased complexity*" (Prigogine and Stengers 1997, p. 64). Thus nonequilibrium and entropy can be considered forms of organization.

Here the term narrative refers to the particular type of presentation of research findings in the field of social networks, a description that the writer objects. Even though in a very different context from that of film and literary theory, the function of narrative here is reminiscent of the way narrative as a cognitive process is conceived by narrative theorists, namely as a mode of data organization that constructs a causal story—and "meaning"—even from the most baffled and "anti-narrative" texts, in which causality is loosened or even broken. Our ability to construct causal stories, in the sense of tight coupling of events, is challenged by complex narratives, and at the same time a need is created to account for the organizing potential lying in a different, pattern-based causality. The multiplicity of agents that the example of "network films" involves is one of the available means through which linear causality is undermined and other types of organization become prominent. Thus, complex narratives in cinema seem to call for a development in film and narrative theory analogous to that in sociology or organizational theory. Emergent and bottom-up approaches to textual organization become pertinent when the lines of causality as traditionally conceived in narrative theory are broken, and when structuralist models of symmetry do not prove helpful. These approaches help us see how diegetic wholes emerge when narrative, along with both Aristotelian and structuralist conceptions of causality, is conceived as an emergent and not an *a priori* organization.

As organizational theorist David Boje suggests, "linear causality is a convenient fiction, an over-simplified narrative of complex antenarrative dynamics in which non-linearity (and that too is a fiction) reigns" (Boje 2001, pp. 93–94). The "chance encounters" and the "intersections of strangers" proliferating in network narratives highlight even in a way much simpler than in natural complex systems the antenarrative (from the Latin *ante* meaning "before") dynamics inherent in narratives that make their causality not just loose but nonlinear, organizing them in an emergent way. Nonlinearity characterizes the interactions of characters/actors at the representational level and also the "causal logic" of the narration itself, involved in the cognitive construction of the diegesis by the viewer.

7   Dynamics of Transformation and Narrative

As already broached, an important aspect that differentiates the complex systemic approach from older cybernetic approaches to systems has to do with a passage from the "age of equilibrium" to that of entropy, according to Bailey's expression. This passage also has to do with a shift to an "ensemble" perspective. Moreover, it is a factor that differentiates complex systemic approaches to causality from traditional narrative approaches.

Nonequilibrium and change are the basic features of self-organizing systems, according to Prigogine, the founder of nonequilibrium thermodynamics, which is considered one of the strands of complex systems theory (Bailey 1994, p. 121).[9] Unlike Newtonian dynamics, nonequilibrium thermodynamics prioritizes evolution and entropy instead of time-reversibility or equilibrium. The behaviour of systems cannot be described in terms of trajectories of individuals (in the case of thermodynamics, these "individuals" are molecules) but in terms of populations or "ensembles",[10] whose movement in time (or succession of states they are found in) is probabilistic and irreversible, leading to new, emerging properties.

In stable systems, there is no difference between the level of the individual trajectories and the one of ensembles; the ensemble can be easily understood as an additive collection of the individual trajectories. However, in unstable dynamical systems, as Prigogine and Stengers mention, "the equivalence between the individual point of view and the statistical point of view [. . .] is broken" (Prigogine and Stengers 1997, p. 83), and asymmetry is established between individuals and aggregates. What according to a Newtonian—and linear—trajectory description would appear as divergence, according to a statistical—"ensemble" and complex—description can appear as "resonance", "a coupling of events loosely analogous to the coupling of sounds by resonance" (p. 42).

It is of course not easy to draw an analogy between the behaviour of particles in physics and that of agents in narratives. However, based on the principle of isomorphism that characterizes complex systems theory as a transdisciplinary field, we could argue for a similar "ensemble approach" in complex narrative analysis. If agents/actors in a narrative are conceived as individuals in single trajectories from one event to the next, then an ensemble approach introduces an asymmetry that changes this picture. The single trajectory perspective makes events appear as the causes and effects of other events, triggered most of the time by human (or anthropomorphic) action. Complex/network narratives, as already mentioned, are structured around events that are disconnected from their causes, contingent on and divergent from the causal-logical sequence. Thus, the single trajectory perspective, or that of "lines of causality" is not particularly helpful, as it tends to reduce the causality of complex narratives to a classical Newtonian model. The ensemble perspective, however, makes events appear as emergent products of resonance between multiple threads of action, initiated by initial conditions that are different each time. Single trajectories of actions and events can only make sense as long as they are placed in an ensemble, resonating with other parallel trajectories. Complex narratives can organize themselves by means of resonance, producing complex textual organizations, and the recipient may follow them by similar cognitive resonances. Because of the multiplicity reflected in their plots, these narratives favour non-anthropomorphic—

---

[9]According to Bailey, there are four main currents in systems theory: nonequilibrium thermodynamics (established through the work of Prigogine on entropy), cybernetics, information theory and general systems theory (GST). These currents with their combined principles generate the transdisciplinary field of "new", as Bailey calls it, complex systems theory (Bailey 1994, p. 121).

[10]Albert Einstein and Josiah Willard Gibbs used the word "ensemble", although they ended up with a model of "superimposition of trajectories", as Prigogine and Stengers note (1997, p. 34).

"ensemble" in the statistical sense—descriptions, that highlight the patterns of agency emerging from the micro-level of unit interactions.

Are these statistical ensemble descriptions narrative? One of the basic problems with narrative is that it holds onto the notion of the observer. This anthropomorphic observer always judges events as probable or improbable and establishes causality between them. From the perspective of complex systems, causality can be conceived as "the outcome of a stochastic, *probabilistic* process" (Prigogine and Stengers 1997, p. 37; my emphasis), the same process that drives self-organization. However, this statistical sense of probability is different from the one based on a human observer. Prigogine and Stengers explain how probabilities are now built into the fundamental laws of the universe, which behaves probabilistically independent of an observer (pp. 5, 54 and 131). The complex interactions that take place before even narrative becomes possible, require, in the context of complex narratives, *syuzhet*-focused approaches that do not take narrative as their starting or ending point, approaches that would thus focus before or beyond narrative. Diegetic agent-based models may be one of the ways to take into account interacting agents that produce the diegetic world by means of ensemble (here not only in the statistical sense but also according to the use of the word in film/narrative theory, as in "ensemble films" that contain aggregation of agents) rather than individual trajectories.

An "agent-based" approach to film narrative analysis, following the logic of agent-based methodologies used in simulations of complex systems, would allow for a multi-directional feedback circuit to be established between the different narrational levels. "Agent-based" simulations of complex systems, also referred to as "multi-agent approaches", are used in the study of natural, economic and social systems. Referring to such simulations, computer scientist Pierre Marcenac distinguishes between "micro-agents" who lack knowledge of global constraints, "medium-agents" who model the interactions of micro-agents and who feed back (through a process called "back-propagation") upon the micro-agents' behaviour, introducing constraints to it, and lastly, "macro-agents", who observe self-organization and 'generate' the medium-agents who model it (Marcenac 1998). Applying this approach to complex narratives, the micro-diegetic level of characters and actions gives way, through complication of relations and nonlinear causality, to aggregates of agency at the meso-level. Mutual causal processes take place across levels. Higher-level "medium-agents", who are the result of (or, in simulations, who are introduced as models of) the aggregates of individual units/micro-agents, feed back into the micro-agents, who are in turn affected by the connections created between them—in complex network narratives, the characters' single trajectories are influenced by the links created between them, which also affect the overall plot's structure. The meso-level of interconnections introduces constraints to the micro-level, but at the same time contributes to the overall transformation, taking place at the extra-diegetic macro-level, of the text into an organization that acquires a causality—or agency—of its own. Causality in complex network narratives takes place across all three levels and is differentiated, by means of its emergent properties, both from the character-based causality and from a deterministic conception of narrative causal structure.

Irreversible processes create an order that is different from the one of systems in equilibrium. This ordering through nonequilibrium is produced by the self-organization of a system in a "state of *increased complexity*" (Prigogine and Stengers 1997, p. 64; emphasis in the original). Here what Todorov called narrative transformation becomes again relevant. It is not causality in the traditional sense of the word, but transformation, happening not only horizontally, as a progression from State A to State B, but also vertically across the embedded intra-diegetic and extra-diegetic narrative levels, that generates the causality of a narrative system. Transformation may be observed when the state of a system is compared at two different points in time, but the dynamics of transformation cannot be captured in such an observation of a horizontal progression. Narrative as a form of retrospective representation cannot address the process of transformation itself. It is the gradual development of the *syuzhet* that reveals the dynamics *resulting* in transformation. Transformation is an emergent process determined by contingency and impossible to attribute to a single cause or causal line.

In his article "Narrative and Emergent Behavior", literary theorist Porter Abbott argues that emergent action does not follow anthropomorphic laws of causal continuity and direct consequences of actions, laws that are indispensible in narrative (Abbott 2008, p. 237). Emergence happens in-between the micro and the macro level, and narrative according to the same writer cannot approach this area (p. 234). Thus, Abbott concludes that emergent behaviour, with its nonlinear causality, is "by definition unnarratable" (p. 233). The multiplicity of agents is for him one of the most characteristic obstacles that narrative faces when it comes to complex behaviour:

> [...] the principal reason for the incompatibility of emergent behavior with narrative understanding is its massive distribution of causal agents—a complexity of causation so acute that it disallows any perceptible chain of causation that could serve as a narrative thread. Narrative can and does play a limited role in our understanding of emergent behavior but does so only at the micro level of individual agents [...] and the macro level of the whole [...]. (Abbott 2008, p. 227)

Even though the distribution of agents in complex narratives is far from massive, as it is, for example, at the level of particles in physics, or of biological organisms such as ants, it still confronts the narrative understanding with an alternative and less anthropomorphic way of understanding. As researchers or just readers and viewers of narratives we can see emergent processes retrospectively, and then narrate them, from a macro viewpoint. However, while these processes take place they are unnarratable, and the only way to follow them is to participate in the textual and cognitive *resonances* that transgress what has traditionally been conceived as narrative *reasoning*.

References

Abbott PH (2008) Narrative and emergent behavior. Poet Today 29(2):227–244

Bailey K (1994) Sociology and the new systems theory: toward a theoretical synthesis. State University of New York Press, Albany

Bal M (1985) Narratology: introduction to the theory of narrative. University of Toronto Press, Toronto

Barrat A, Barthelemy M, Vespigniani A (2008) Dynamical processes on complex networks. Cambridge University Press, Cambridge

Bedau M (1997) Weak emergence. In: Tomberlin J (ed) Mind, causation, and world. Blackwell, Oxford, pp 375–399

Bertuglia CS, Vaio F (2005) Nonlinearity, chaos and complexity: the dynamics of natural and social systems. Oxford University Press, Oxford

Boje DM (2001) Narrative methods for organizational and communication research. Sage, London

Bordwell D (2006) The way Hollywood tells it: story and style in modern movies. University of California Press, Berkeley

Bordwell D (2007) Poetics of cinema. Routledge, New York

Bordwell D, Thompson K (2008) Film art: an introduction, 8th edn. McGraw-Hill, New York

Branigan E (1992) Narrative comprehension and film. Routledge, New York

Buckland W (ed) (2009) Puzzle films: complex storytelling in contemporary cinema. Blackwell, Chichester, pp 1–12

Byrne D (1998) Complexity and the social sciences: an introduction. Routledge, London

Cameron A (2008) Modular narratives in contemporary cinema. Palgrave Macmillan, Houndmills

Campbell D (1974) "Downward causation" in hierarchically organized biological systems. In: Ayala F, Dobzhansky T (eds) Studies in the philosophy of biology. University of California Press, Berkeley, pp 179–186

Chalmers D (2006) Strong and weak emergence. In: Clayton P, Davies P (eds) The re-emergence of emergence: the emergentist hypothesis from science to religion. Oxford University Press, Oxford, pp 244–253

Clayton P (2006) Conceptual foundations of emergent theory. In: Clayton P, Davies P (eds) The re-emergence of emergence: the emergentist hypothesis from science to religion. Oxford University Press, Oxford, pp 1–30

Coste D (1989) Narrative as communication. University of Minnesota Press, Minneapolis

Coveney PV (2003) Self-organization and complexity: a new age for theory, computation and experiment. From proceedings of the nobel symposium on self-organization held at Karolinska Institutet, Stockholm, August 25–27, 2002. Philos Trans R Soc Lond A 361:1057–1079

Deacon TW (2006) Emergence: the hole at the wheel's hub. In: Clayton P, Davies P (eds) The re-emergence of emergence: the emergentist hypothesis from science to religion. Oxford University Press, Oxford, pp 111–150

De Landa M (2009) A thousand years of nonlinear history. MIT Press, Cambridge

Doreian P (2001) Causality in social network analysis. Sociol Methods Res 30(1):81–114

Elsaesser T (2009) The mind-game film. In: Buckland W (ed) Puzzle films: complex storytelling in contemporary cinema. Blackwell, Chichester, pp 13–41

Elsaesser T, Buckland W (2002) Studying contemporary American film: a guide to movie analysis. Arnold, London

EMIL Project, Public Deliverable 2.1 (2007) Histories of the example of the emergence of open source norms: case selection and histories. Retrieved from http://emil.istc.cnr.it/

Emirbayer M, Goodwin J (1994) Network analysis, culture, and the problem of agency. Am J Sociol 99(6):1411–1454

Goldstein J (1996) Causality and emergence in Chaos and complexity theories. In: Sulis W, Combs A (eds) Nonlinear dynamics in human behavior. World Scientific, Singapore, pp 161–190

Kafalenos E (2006) Narrative causalities. Ohio State University Press, Columbus

Kauffman SA (1993) The origins of order: self-organization and selection in evolution. Oxford University Press, New York

Kim J (2006) Being realistic about emergence. In: Clayton P, Davies P (eds) The re-emergence of emergence: the emergentist hypothesis from science to religion. Oxford University Press, Oxford, pp 189–202

Langley A (1999) Strategies for theorizing from process data. Acad Manage Rev 24(4):691–710

Marcenac P (1998) Modeling multiagent systems as self-organized critical systems. In: Proceedings from HICSS-31: 31st annual Hawaii international conference on system sciences, vol 5. IEEE Computer Society Press, pp 86–95

Marion RA (2006) Complexity in organizations: a paradigm shift. In: Sengupta A (ed) Chaos, nonlinearity, complexity: the dynamical paradigm of nature. Springer, Heidelberg, pp 247–269

Maruyama M (1963) The second cybernetics: deviation amplifying mutual causal processes. Am Sci 5(2):164–179

Nicolis G (1995) Introduction to nonlinear science. Cambridge University Press, Cambridge

O'Connor T, Wong HY (2005) The metaphysics of emergence. Noûs 39:658–678

O'Connor T, Wong HY (2009) Emergent properties. In Zalta EN (ed), The Stanford encyclopedia of philosophy, Spring 2009 edn. Retrieved from http://plato.stanford.edu/archives/spr2009/entries/properties-emergent/

Poulaki M (2011) Before or beyond narrative? Towards a complex systems theory of contemporary films. Rozenberg, Amsterdam

Prigogine I, Stengers I (1997) The end of certainty: time, Chaos, and the new laws of nature. The Free Press, New York

Todorov T (1971) The 2 principles of narrative. Diacritics 1(1):37–44

Todorov T (1977) The poetics of prose. Cornell University Press, Ithaca

Tsoukas H, Hatch MJ (2001) Complex thinking, complex practice: the case for a narrative approach to organizational complexity. Hum Relat 54(8):979–1013

Chapter 17
Narrative and Cognitive Modelling: Insights from Beckett Exploring Mind's Complexity

Marco Bernini

Abstract Complex systems exacerbate a common problem for scientific enquiry: the difficulty of creating models able to discriminate fundamental elements or patterns from random behaviours or corollary components in the event or process at issue. This chapter argues that a similar tension between order and randomness has been a chief modelling problem of Samuel Beckett's narratives, tied to his interest in a specific kind of complex system (the mind) and its emergent properties (consciousness and the narrative sense of self). Bulding on narratology, complex system frameworks, cognitive theories of emergence and of scientific modelling, this chapter introduces the idea of "fictional cognitive modelling". Through this concept, the chapter analyses Beckett's treatment of narrative devices as formal tools for the creation of "exploratory models" able to atomise the emerging unity of conscious experience and of a narrative sense of self into its core components (defined as the "narrative dynamic core"). It concludes by suggesting that Beckett's narrative method shows how literature can occupy a proper position in the investigation and exploration of complex systems.

1 Modelling the Mind as a Complex System

Complex systems, despite their exceptionality, reiterate and exacerbate what is a common problem for scientific enquiry: the difficulty of creating models able to discriminate fundamental elements or patterns from random behaviours or corollary components in the event or process at issue. As James Crutchfield notes, "a key modelling dichotomy that runs throughout all of science is that between order and randomness" (2008, p. 273). In complex systems, this dichotomy is brought to the utmost limit given that randomness dominates and patterns often eschew the simplifying nature of modelling. In this respect, the resistance that complex systems pose to narrative can be regarded as one specific subset of a more general difficulty:

M. Bernini (✉)
Department of English Studies, Durham University, Durham, UK
e-mail: marco.bernini@durham.ac.uk

© The Author(s) 2018
R. Walsh, S. Stepney (eds.), *Narrating Complexity*,
https://doi.org/10.1007/978-3-319-64714-2_17

to capture complexity with formal devices. Insofar as the stake is epistemic, it is hard to gauge how much we lose of the actual dynamics of complex systems when trying to make them fit formal models—narrative structures included. As Richard Walsh neatly states in this volume (Chap. 5), "there is an important gap between our narrative talk of what a system does and how system actually does it". The same holds true, with some provisos, for the gap between scientific modelling and the modelled systems. Despite the significant divide between scientific and narrative approaches to complexity that is the very object of this volume, a shared common ground can therefore be found in the question of how we can model a (narrative) form to accommodate the chaotic behaviour of complex system and their emergent properties.

A similar question was the chief formal concern of Samuel Beckett's work throughout his career. As is famously reported, he explained in an interview with Tom Driver in 1961 that he felt that the only viable task for art was "to find a form to accommodate the mess" (Driver 1979, p. 219). This chapter argues that for Beckett this was a proper problem of modelling dichotomy tied to his interest in a specific kind of complex system (the mind) and its emergent properties (consciousness and the narrative sense of self). Within contemporary cognitive science and philosophy of mind, it is increasingly suggested that the brain should be regarded as a complex system (Gazzaniga 2012). Whether the mind and its mental properties, including consciousness and a sense of selfhood, can be interpreted through the conceptual lens of complex system theory is still a matter of debate (Vision 2011; Bedau and Humphreys 2008; Macdonald and Macdonald 2010). As it is beyond the scope of this essay to enter the controversy, I build exclusively on cognitive strands of research taking consciousness and the sense of selfhood as emergent patterns of the mind viewed as a complex system. An implicit ground of my argument, though, is that if what are called "neural correlates" of mental states exist at the brain level, human beings cannot access (narratively or not) their complex interaction. Conversely, a sustained training in introspective techniques (Hurlburt and Heavey 2001) can let us glimpse the complexity of the mental counterpart of the neural activity—the distinct and chaotically interacting components (e.g., language, time-consciousness, memory, agency, imagination), working at the edge of their emergent global coordination that gives rise to our unified feeling of being conscious and being ourselves. Modernist writers such as Beckett, as Dorrit Cohn pointed out, were arguably great introspectors (Cohn 1978, p. 89), and the phenomenal data they gathered can therefore have provided insights for deriving narrative modes (and models) of exploration into what underlies or lies beyond our (to an important extent narratively) unified feeling of subjective experience.

This unified feeling, either scientifically or introspectively, is hard to unpack into its components, and this is taken as a positive sign of its emergent nature. As Basset and Gazzaniga note, "although the material components of the physical brain might be highly decomposable, mental properties seem to be fundamentally indivisible" (2011, p. 5). Here, I suggest that Beckett was able to atomise the constantly emerging unity of conscious experience into its core components, interacting and integrating at the level of mind's complexity. He reached this difficult goal, I argue, by treating narrative elements, devices and structures as formal tools for his modelling strategy that I call *fictional cognitive modelling*. Importantly, to the extent that the unified experience of selfhood is partly the result of a narrative dynamic, Beckett's modelling of the mind as a complex system leads to and calls for a new definition of narrative (which I attempt in Sect. 4) as an emergent property resulting from the complex interaction of many levels and elements, such as those Beckett incorporates in his models.

In Sect. 2, I start by elaborating further on the problematic modelling dichotomy between order and chaos in Beckett's work. In Sect. 3, I present some preliminary arguments for why Beckett's prose overcomes the limitation usually linked to a narrative understanding of complexity. In Sect. 4, I introduce contemporary definitions of the mind as a complex system and of consciousness and the self as its emergent properties. I also elaborate on the idea that our narrative sense of self is the emergent outcome of key different components (which I call the *narrative dynamic core*) within the mind's complexity. In Sect. 5, I expand on the idea of the narrative dynamic core, by finally showing how it has been either locally or globally modelled in specific texts. In the conclusion, I argue that looking at Beckett's use of narrative as a modelling strategy can help reposition the literature as a field of exploration into mind's complexity.

2 Narrative Chaotics and the Aboutness of Complexity

In the transcript of the already mentioned interview in 1961, Tom Driver, Professor of Literature and Theology, reports how Beckett "began to speak about the tension in art between the mess and form. Until recently, art has withstood the pressure of chaotic things" (Driver 1979, p. 219). Driver then poses a question that is highly relevant to the modelling dichotomy between complexity and its formal accommodation: "How could the mess be admitted", Driver inquires, "because it appears to be the very opposite of form and therefore destructive of the very thing that art holds itself to be" (p. 219). Translating the question into the complex system terminology, the problem becomes how can narrative form approximate complexity given the (temporal, linguistic, sequential, linear) structuring nature of the former that seems refractory to chaotic behaviours? Beckett's answer is that artistic form should not "exist as a problem separate from the material it accommodates" (p. 219). More than thirty years earlier, Beckett had already formulated his stance about the necessary conflation of content and form, identifying in the writing of James Joyce the landmark example of a literary narrative where "form *is* content, content *is* form"—notoriously claiming that "his writing is not *about* something; *it is that something itself*" (Beckett 1984, p. 27). In Beckett's terms, the modelling dichotomy occurring when (narratively) tackling complexity can be redefined as how to go beyond the *aboutness* of complex systems.

In her study on what she labels "narrative chaotics", Jo Alyson Parker (2007) addresses a similar issue. She takes the lead from a 1996 article by Steven Johnson in which he restricts the possibility of literary narrative to the *aboutness* of complex systems. In this article, Johnson explains how, in his opinion, novels "may be *about* complex systems (cities, economies, ecosystems, and so on) and they are certainly the *products* of complex systems (the neural nets of the human mind), but they themselves are language-based, static, dictated from the outside..." (Johnson 1996, p. 47). Parker's objection is that the narrative works of Proust, Sterne, Woolf and Faulkner have "certain narrative structures [which] resemble chaotic nonlinear dynamical systems" and therefore can be classed as examples of "narrative chaotics" (Parker 2007, p. 21). I am very sympathetic with Parker's perceptive use of the complex system's toolbox for literary analysis. My concern here, however, is not to analyse Beckett's narrative works *as* complex systems themselves, but as *models of* the mind as a complex system. This said, the problem of the *aboutness* remains, and it is even more crucial. How can narratives targeting complexity do so without either merely representing complex systems (the *aboutness*) or becoming themselves complex systems (*narrative chaotics*)? Once again, this is a modelling dilemma and, as happens with scientific modelling, either by becoming as complex as the actual process or by distancing themselves too much towards an oversimplification of the process, narrative models can become useless.

Models of a process, in fact, never equal the process itself, but are formal simplifications enabling different kinds of analysis. As Lewandosky and Farrell synthesize in their comprehensive book on cognitive models, at its most basic "a model is an abstract structure that captures structure in the data" (2011, p. 10). This structural relation between models and processes can be directed at different scopes—descriptive, predictive, explanatory or exploratory. I return to this in the conclusion to consider how Beckett's work can be understood in relation to this variety of models. For now, it is enough to say that a model's structural relation with a process is more than mere *aboutness* and less than full identity. Thanks to the model, structures can be perceived (or hypothesized), patterns explored, processes characterized in terms of key components. It is worth repeating, though, that, as Lewandosky and Farrell constantly stress, "models are intended to be simpler and more abstract versions of the system—in our case human cognition—they are trying to explain ... Models seek to *retain the essential features of the system* while discarding uneccessary details. By definition, the complexity of models will thus never match the complexity of human cognition—nor should it, because there is no point in replacing one thing we do not understand with another" (2011, p. 11; italics mine).

With Beckett, however, it would be hard to maintain that his narrative modelling of mind's complexity has been driven by a belief in the possibility of better understanding its cognitive underpinnings. Quite on the contrary, he repeatedly insisted on the importance of accepting our ignorance about the complex chaotic behaviour of the inside and outside worlds. Given that our mind *is* a complex system itself, how can we aspire to reach an understanding of its functioning from within? As Beckett makes clear in a letter to George Duthuit in 1949, since we are enmeshed in complexity, "being in it discourages you from knowing it" (Beckett 2011, p. 131). In a similar vein, in another letter to Duthuit one year before, Beckett harshly comments on the geometrical painting technique of Antonello da Messina's St Sebastian—"pure space by dint of mathematics"—caustically concluding how "[i] n front of such a work, such *a victory over the reality of disorder*, over the pettiness of the heart and the mind, it is hard not to go and hang yourself" (Beckett 2011; italics mine). Beckett's distrust in formal means of understanding reality, of ordering its chaotic behaviour, starkly contrasts with his precocious and sustained interest in mathematics (Ackerley 1998), physics (notably thermodynamics and the idea of entropy; Duffy 2013; Harrington 1982), and science in general (Ackerley 2010), an interest that is undeniably mirrored in the formal qualities of his narrative work. The modelling dichotomy between randomness and order is therefore reflected once more in the tension between Beckett's emphasis on the chaotic nature of reality and the formal features of his narratives. As Chris Ackerley observes, while charting Beckett's interest in scientific ideas and problems, "any attempt ... to saddle Beckett with a scientific temperament, let alone a scientific methodology, runs into an impasse generated by Beckett's deep distrust of the rational process" (Ackerley 2010, p. 144).

My answer to this paradoxical tension is that, with respect to the mind's complexity, Beckett employed a formal, highly sophisticated modelling strategy in order to approach, disclose, and let the reader perceive the complex chaotic behaviour lying *beyond and before* the emergent unifying dynamic of conscious experience. What I call Beckett's *fictional cognitive modelling* of the mind's complexity can therefore be described as a formal "exploration" (a term that I return to in the conclusion of the essay) of the key components responsible for the emergent *feeling of order* in our subjective experience. As we see in the next sections, that unifying feeling is to a significant extent a narrative emergent outcome of complex interactions at the level of the mind's complexity. As such, our narrative sense of selfhood it is *an emergent property that conceals its complex origins*.

3   Beyond and Before Emergence: Experiential Art and Narratives of Centralised Control

The narrative we tell about ourselves as a unified, integrated, single, temporally consistent and causally coherent centre of experience is a specific case (we could even say the "cognitive matrix" of) what Porter Abbott defined, in his landmark article on the limits of narrative understanding of emergent behaviour, the "narrative of centralized control" (Abbott 2008, p. 231). To recapitulate the key points in Abbott's article, he suggests that there is an "incompatibility of emergent behaviour with narrative understanding" due to the "massive distribution of causal agents" (p. 227) of the former. Abbott clearly concedes that we are able to manage a certain degree of causal complexity in literary and real life narratives. Yet he proposes that, as soon as complexity increases such as in complex systems, our coping strategy is to project a "default narrative of centralised control" (p. 236) in order to explain emergent behaviour. This does not mean that we cannot narratively describe the perceptible *effects* of emergent behaviour in complex systems. We can, for instance, narratively report the story of the aerial ballet performed by a flock of birds, Abbott says; but we do so "without any reference to the emergent process that bring them into being" (p. 236). When it comes to emergent patterns and behaviours, Abbott concludes, we face a "void of unnarratibility" (p. 236) to which we respond with illusory narratives of centralised control. In other words, we are narratively stuck in the *aboutness* of complexity, of which this class of narrative provides only *a feeling of* understanding, with neither access to the actual components of the system nor to the emergent transition that leads to emergent behaviour.

Interestingly, Abbott is a foremost scholar of Beckett, whose work seems to provide a challenging counterexample to Abbott's argument insofar as it entirely resists narratives of centralised control. This resistance has to be intended both as a resistance on the part of Beckett to create centralised narratives and as a consequential impossibility for the reader to project this default narrative mode of understanding. In his more recent monograph, significantly titled *Real Mysteries: Narrative and the Unknowable*, Abbott points in this direction by classing Beckett's work as "reader-resistant" narratives, which give us "experiential knowledge of our ignorance about who we are" (Abbott 2014, p. 40). As much as I endorse Abbott's idea of Beckett's work as a "reader-resistant" narrative (a narrative opacity that, importantly, Abbott previously assigned to complex systems), my argument is that this resistance is a positive result of Beckett's modelling strategy of the mind's complexity. It is precisely because he has been able to disassemble the emergent narrative sense of self (the cognitive matrix of all narrative of centralised control) into its key components (which I address in the next two sections)—interacting and operating at the level of the mind's complexity—that we can experience what lies beyond and before this unified emergent level.

The feeling of ignorance of which Abbott speaks is due to the fact that Beckett's work presents the key components of mind's complexity *in the process of interaction*, before and beyond their emergent narrative outcome. In doing so, he models the very cognitive processes resulting in the emergent matrix of centralised control that gives us a (partly narrative) feeling of order about experience. This is why our default mode of narrative understanding fails when we encounter Beckett's work. Expecting, as readers, to be able to make sense of the events by projecting a narrative thread, we face instead the key components of our narrative understanding. If we do not recognise these components as part of our experience it is because their interaction usually goes on unperceived. In a way, our habit to succeed in casting narrative threads upon events is a precondition for Beckett's fictional cognitive models to work. It is the failure of our narrative habit that allows us to experience Beckett's narrative models as something new—something located at the level of the mind's complex interactions, which precedes (and *therefore* resists) the narrative grasp of our everyday inner experience.

Beckett's cognitive models complicate Lewandosky and Farrell's definition according to which models "retain the essential features of the system", insofar as they retain the features of the cognitive system that *at the same time they target and are shaped by*: the human mind's complex components. Put in Beckett's terms, we can say of his narrative work what he positively noted about the work of his friend and painter Avigdor Arika. When trying to explore the complex inner relations amongst the mind's components, "in his work, these intimate relations retain the specific character of the frame within which they are formed" (Beckett 2011, p. 84). To the question of how a writer can internally access these inner relations, operating before and beyond the emergent narrative that unifies and conceals their complexity, my answer is "simply" by introspecting. The limits of introspective methods have been repeatedly pointed out throughout the history of psychological and cognitive research (Butler 2013; Hurlburt and Schwitzgebel 2007). My contention is that Beckett's fictional cognitive modelling shows how narrative devices can be turned into tools for overcoming the limitations of a narrative introspective report of inner experience. And even more when it comes to modelling the elements responsible for the emergence of a narrative sense of self, which is the matrix of our everyday narrative understanding.

Together with armchair introspection, in fact, it is by the very process of creating narrative worlds (which is the novelist's business) that they can gather information about the key elements by which a narrative is formed, our narrative sense of self included. The gathered information could then be turned into a model which, more *and* less than in an analogy, retains the features of the cognitive process it addresses. As Alva Noë points out in his enactivist study on perception, "[i]t is not pictures *as* objects of perception that can teach us about perceiving; rather, it is *making pictures*—that is, the skillful construction of pictures—that can illuminate experience itself, or rather, the making or enacting of experience" (Noë 2004, p. 179). Similarly, in order to access the complex making of our narrative sense of self that is usually an emergent process transparent to us, we should not look at its products (narratives of aboutness), but rather enact the emergent process of its creation. And given the functional similarity between cognitive and literary storytelling, writers are extremely well-placed to provide insights and fictional models for exploring the complex nature of narrative emergences. Alva Noë briefly gestures at a possible role of art in accessing aspects of experience usually transparent to us—in our case the emergent unifying activity through which our (richly narrative) conscious experience is shaped. The task of this kind of art, that Noë calls "experiential art", is "not so much to depict or represent or describe experience, but rather *to catch experience in the act of making the world available* . . . The aim of experiential art and phenomenology ought to be . . . to draw attention to an activity that, by dint of the fact that we can perceive, we are very good at it" (p. 177; italics mine). In spite of our being very good at and accustomed to narrating our story to ourselves and to others, however, we are usually blind to the complexity underlying this process. This is why we need experiential art, to draw attention to this activity in order to catch the process in the making. Once we have captured the key elements of the process, its modelling can be a further step, enabling a more formal exploration of its hidden complex interactions, which is exactly what I maintain Beckett achieved in his narrative work. To better grasp the structures and elements of Beckett's fictional cognitive models, we first need a more complex definition of the processes his models are investigating.

4   A Complex Definition of Mind, Narrative and the Narrative Sense of Self

The path leading from brain activity to our subjective experience and mental states is intricate, mysterious and full of gaps in our understanding of it. How can physical interactions at the neuronal level generate mental states? This question has been (pre) occupying philosophers of mind and cognitive scientists for centuries. The problem, which harks back to Plato, found a solution (today harshly criticised) in the Cartesian dualistic view of a split between the body (*res extensa*) and the mind (*res cogitans*), which Joseph Levine more recently labelled the "explanatory gap" (Levine 1983). The inexplicability of this gap is plainly illustrated in a passage from Beckett's novel *Murphy*, in which the homonymous protagonist indulges in the pleasure of introspection: "[t]hus Murphy felt himself split in two, a body and a mind. They had intercourse apparently, otherwise he could not have known that they had anything in common. But he felt his mind bodytight and did not understand through what channel the intercourse was effected nor how the two experiences came to overlap. He was satisfied that neither followed from the other" (2009b, p. 70). Today we know there is not a single "channel", like the Cartesian pineal gland, that can explain the transition from the physical to the mental. This kind of negative knowledge, however, does not cancel out the gap, which substantially remains to be explained.

One scientific way of proceeding is to look at *correlations* between our phenomenal conscious states and neural activity at the brain level. Tononi and Edelman pioneered this kind of approach to the explanatory gap by suggesting that "analyzing the convergence between ... phenomenological and neural properties can yield valuable insights into the kinds of neural processes that can account for the corresponding properties of conscious experience" (1998, p. 1850). Their study corroborated the idea that "changes in a specific aspect of conscious experience correlate with changes in specific brain areas whether the experience is driven by external stimuli, by memory, or by imagery and dreams" (p. 1847). More specifically, they discovered that the unified nature of our conscious states is the result of a corresponding integration (that they call "functional clustering") of specific neuronal groups interacting at the level of the brain's complexity. They call this large cluster of neurons (which is not a fixed set, but nonetheless would usually include posterior corticothalamic regions), together constituting the unified neural process from which our conscious states emerge, the "dynamic core" of consciousness. The "dynamic core" is a functional cluster, a process of aggregation of key neural components whose complex global activity generates patterns that are the neural counterpart of our conscious states.

These findings are of great significance for understanding how neural complexity at the brain level gives rise to the emergent level of mental states. This said, as Philip Clayton points out, "if explanations are given exclusively in neurological terms, they will be by the nature of the case not able to specify what are the phenomenal experiences or *qualia* the subjects experience" (2004, p. 120). In other words, from the brain's complexity emerges the mind's complexity, a further level of complexity that cannot be explained in neural terms. Importantly, the mind's complexity in turn can generate further emergences, from more primitive forms of awareness to higher order emergent phenomena such as our narrative sense of self. And at the emerged level of the mind's complexity, different kinds of clustering might occur, resulting from the interaction of a variety of components in our conscious experience. The question then becomes whether we can speak of a different "dynamic core" at the mind's level, from which higher orders of cognition emerge?

If literary narratives—engaging with and building on introspective enquires into, to quote Beckett's *Molloy*, "the laws of the mind" (Beckett 2009c, p. 9)—cannot access the neural complex level of conscious experience, they can approach (and, I argue, model) what lies beyond the unified emerged level of our subjectivity. The gap between the brain and the mind, in fact, is not just difficult to bridge, but it is also hard to graduate into a spectrum of multiple and successive emergences. What we usually think of as our fully-fledged indivisible subjectivity is in reality the last emergent state in a multi-leveled trajectory rooted in the brain and continuously generating new levels of complexity and subsequent emergences. From the brain's neural complexity more primitive states of mind emerge, with a minimal sense of ownership and agency of the organism that corresponds to what phenomenologists and cognitive scientists refer to as the "minimal self" (Gallagher 2000). This minimal sense of self is far from the high-order, conceptually rich feeling of subjectivity that we habitually experience as our self. On the other side, this minimal level of awareness is a necessary complex platform in which interactions of conscious states and components generate what Neisser has called the "extended self" (Neisser and Fivush 1994), Damasio the "autobiographical self" (Damasio 1998), or more broadly it is referred to as the "narrative self" (Schechtman 2011, 2007). This description of the trajectory from the brain to the fully-fledged self as a hierarchical chain of emergences fits with the account of emergence as a new macro-level of organization of previous micro-level elements. To borrow Gazzaniga's definition, "[e]mergence is when micro-level complex systems that are far from equilibrium (thus allowing for the amplification of random events) self-organize (creative, self-generated, adaptability-seeking behavior) into new structures, with new properties that previously did not exist, to form a new level of organization at the macro-level" (Gazzaniga 2012, p. 124). The autobiographical self can therefore be seen as the last level of organisation in a sequence of progressive emergences. This level cannot be accounted for in neural terms because, as Gazzaniga clarifies, "[t]he laws are not universal to all levels of organization; it depends which level of organization you are describing, and new rules apply when higher levels emerge" (p. 130). Logically, it might be useful to look at the components and elements interacting at the previous level in order to understand something of the emergent transition. In the case of the emergence of our narrative, extended, autobiographical self, we should therefore ask which kind of elements at the minimal-self level of complexity are triggering the transition? Building on Edelman and Tononi's hypothesis at the neural level, we can ask which elements constitute what I would call the "narrative dynamic core" in the mind's complexity, whose global activity generates our rich sense of subjectivity?

Narrative approaches to the self have been proliferating (for a survey see Schechtman 2011) and sometimes bitterly criticised (Strawson 2004) in the last few decades. Daniel Dennett famously suggested that the self is no more than a narrative abstraction, a "centre of narrative gravity" that we posit as the fictional source of the stories we tell *about* our self (1991). Similarly, Bayne has suggested that the self is a virtual centre of "phenomenal gravity", around which we build (partly narrative) representations of our self (2010, p. 289). An emergent approach to the narrative sense of self, however, is still missing. For this to happen, we should probably first look for a more complex definition of narrative as an emergent property itself. My argument is that Beckett's fictional cognitive modelling, by addressing the emergent transition from a minimal self to an autobiographical self, can help on both fronts. What I want to suggest is that Beckett, by introspectively looking beyond the surface of our narratively unified sense of self, has been able to identify and then model a possible "narrative dynamic core" from which our narrative self emerges. In our everyday acquaintance with the world and with ourselves we do not perceive the complexity underlying our unified experience, and we accept our rich subjectivity as the ground (and not the emergent outcome) of experience. Our mind's complexity is usually invisible to us, and we feel narratively unified into a self even if there is no single location in our brain or mind hosting it. Moreover, none of the interacting components generating our higher subjectivity are in themselves "selfy". As Owen Flanagan explains, "[to] be sure, there is no shadowy supervisor that is your CEO, and there is no nonshadowy central head-quarters either. *You are a complex system*. Much of what makes you tick is neither "selfy" nor transparent from the subjective point of view" (Flanagan 1998, p. 210; italics mine). I want to suggest that Beckett's fictional cognitive models seem to aim precisely at exploring how non-selfy components in the mind are able to generate, by means of complex interaction, a narrative feeling of a temporally consistent and coherent self. My idea is that Beckett, building on introspective insights, appears to have singled out—a crucial moment in modelling—a restricted number of key components responsible for the emergence of a narrative self. This functional cluster, which I call the "narrative dynamic core", is, I argue, the main object of Beckett's fictional cognitive models. To anticipate the constitutive elements of the cognitive cluster that I explain in detail in the next section, I elaborate on the idea that Beckett modeled the construction of a narrative self as *the emergent property of the complex interaction between language, time, agents and imagination.*[1]

---

[1]As one of the reviewers of this essay rightly noted, a number of other authors (e.g., Proust) might be said to have 'singled out' these factors as crucial in the constitution of the Self and a variety of mental states. The originality of Beckett's manoeuvre, as the next section shows, consists rather in his 'modelling' strategy and method, i.e., in the creation of narratives *as models* (abstract, simplified forms that can be manipulated for different exploratory scopes).

5   The Narrative Dynamic Core and Kinds of Fictional Cognitive Models

To model the narrative self as an emergent process means to make hypotheses about the local elements (nodes) whose networking activity generates the self as an emergent pattern. As summed up by Evan Thompson's enactivist account of emergence—quoted by Mackenzie (2011)—"[a]n emergent process belongs to an ensemble or network of elements, arises spontaneously or self-organizes from the locally defined and globally constrained or controlled interactions of those elements, and *does not belong to a single element*" (Thompson 2007, p. 60; italics mine). In this perspective, the narrative self as an emergent process is therefore a distributed activity that cannot be identified with a single element in the system. In Varela's words, "what we call 'I' can be analysed as arising out of our recursive linguistic abilities and their unique capacity for self-description and narration" (Varela 1999, p. 61). The role of language, however, should not be overemphasized or isolated as the only element responsible for the emergence of a narrative self. The self is indeed partly a semiotic process (Pickering 1999), but language is only one of the elements involved in the complex networking activity through which the narrative self emerges. Furthermore, we can think of language itself in complex terms, as Lee et al. propose, considering it as a "multistrata of building blocks" or a "hierarchical structure of agents" in which "phonemes form syllables, which then form morphemes; morphemes form words, words form phrases, and the process continues, until we end up with speech acts, stories, and so on" (Lee et al. 2009, p. 21). As we will see in a moment, this idea that language itself might be disassembled into building blocks is the object of one kind of model in Beckett's work. Yet again, language is just one of the elements composing what I am defining as the "narrative dynamic core" that Beckett has singled out as the functional cluster generating our fully-fledged sense of self. And language alone is not enough for a narrative self to emerge. As already anticipated, the other elements that Beckett seems to have selected for and targeted in his models are time, agents and imagination. Let me cursorily outline each of these elements, before presenting concrete examples of Beckett's fictional modelling of cognition.

Firstly, language itself can take many forms within our cognitive commerce with the inner and outer worlds. It can be externally directed or internally and silently condensed in what cognitive psychologists have called "inner speech" (for a comprehensive survey see Alderson-Day and Fernyhough 2015). Since Beckett's models often portray a voice from within, and since many of his fictional worlds are isolated, closed-off mental spaces, inner speech in his work should be regarded as one of the more important aspects of language responsible for the emergence of a narrative self. Moreover, to support this choice, cognitive science is increasingly suggesting that inner speech has a fundamental role in the construction and monitoring of our self (Morin and Everett 1990).

Time is clearly also a key component in any type of narrative, the narrative of our self included. In human experience, however, we can distinguish two different types of temporal cognitive processes. The first, more basic type concerns what is usually referred to in phenomenology, from Husserl onwards, as "time-consciousness". Time-consciousness is a micro-structure of our conscious experience which allows us to perceive temporally extended objects. It does not entail reflective or self-conscious thought about the temporality of experience at issue. Rather, it is a precondition of our phenomenal experience of the world, the necessary ground for perception to occur. As Gallagher and Zahavi explain, time-consciousness is a "temporal binding" (2010, p. 73), a "temporal synthesis [which] is a precondition for the perceptual synthesis" and which explains "how consciousness unifies itself across time" (p. 79). In other words, time-consciousness is the *a priori*, low-level condition thanks to which we are living in a flow of experiences as opposed to an experiential pointillism. Time-consciousness is also the precondition of higher forms of temporal integration (Freeman 2007), such as the temporally extended narration resulting in our autobiographical self. Both types of temporality are targeted in Beckett's fictional models, and are part of the narrative dynamic core.

The third element I referred to as "agents" is a narratological subcluster—which is, as language and time, a complex one. As Jerome Bruner (2004), among others (Bermúdez 2000), puts it, the narrative of our self "is, of course, a privileged but troubled narrative in the sense that it is reflexive: the narrator and the central figure in the narrative are the same. This reflexivity creates dilemmas" (Bruner 2004, p. 693). In other words, the narratological agency in the structure of the narrative self is at the same time singular and plural. We can also add, as Beckett does, a third agent, who is the author responsible for authenticating (Doležel 1998) the narrator's and the character's existence. In the emergent process resulting in our narrative self, the paradox of a narratological singular plurality usually goes unnoticed. In Beckett's modelling, instead, the unified narration is disintegrated and disassembled, and we can therefore access the role and complexity of this narratologically nested nucleus within the narrative dynamic core.

Moving to the final element, without imagination the very hypothesis of a narrative self would be, pun intended, hard to imagine. The remembered past and the anticipated future, as well as simulations involving counterfactual situations and empathy towards other people (Goldman 2006), require a substantial degree of imagination. In this respect, memories can be considered as a particular kind of imaginative activity, closely interacting with other elements in the narrative dynamic core. For instance, memories clearly support and involve our extended sense of time, and often trigger or are triggered by our inner silent verbalizing.

Language, time, agents and imagination are, I argue, the components that Beckett singled out as the narrative dynamic core whose complex interaction produces the emergent transition leading to our narrative self. These components are either targeted individually by his fictional cognitive models, or modeled altogether in their global interaction. I would therefore class the former kind of texts as *local models*, and the latter as *global models*. I now bring some concrete examples of both types in what remains of the essay. One last important remark, however, is due before proceeding. Once created, models can be manipulated and even damaged to see what happens to the system. As Lewandosky and Farrel note: "[u]nlike people, models can quite literally be taken apart. For example, we can "lesion" models to observe the outcome on behavior of certain localized dysfunction … one can do things to models that one cannot do to people, and … those *lesioning experiments can yield valuable knowledge*" (2011, pp. 27—28; italics mine). This is precisely the kind of use of models we can see operating in Beckett's texts, which can hardly be better described than as lesioning experiments.

Within local models, the first example I would like to present, *Imagination Dead Imagine* (1996), clearly manifests already from the title a lesioning nature towards one of the elements in the narrative dynamic core. The text mainly targets the interaction between two elements in the core—language and imagination—by attempting to manipulate the former to lesion the latter. Here is the beginning of the short prose:

> No trace of life anywhere, you say, pah, no difficulty there, *imagination not dead yet, yes, dead, good, imagination dead imagine.* Islands, waters, azure, verdure, one glimpse and vanished, endlessly, omit. Till all white in the whiteness the rotunda. No way in, go in, measure. Diameter three feet, three feet from ground to summit of the vault. Two diameters at right angles AB CD divide the white ground into two semicircles ACB BDA. Lying on the ground two white bodies, each in its semicircle . . .. The light that makes all so white no visible source, all shines with the same white shine, ground, wall, vault, bodies, no shadow . . .. Emptiness, silence, heat, whiteness, wait, the light goes down, all grows dark together, ground, wall, vault, bodies, say twenty seconds, all the greys, the light goes out, all vanishes. At the same time the temperature goes down, to reach its minimum, say *freezing-point.* . .. (Beckett 1996, p. 182; italics mine)

This narrative beginning is representative of the tension between Beckett's formal modelling strategy (in this text chiefly geometrical) and the chaotic dynamics it aims to disclose. The entire text is an attempt to make the imaginative activity stall. The problem is that lesioning imagination by manipulating language is hard to achieve, since the binding of language and imagination in the narrative dynamic core is tight and constantly activated. Here is where formal modelling can become a necessity, in order to reach a use of language and narrative structures directed at reducing imagination to a bare-bones condition, then hopefully loosening its integration with language and letting both fall apart. If language functionally needs to form a cluster with imagination to generate meanings (and fictional worlds), in this text language is used to restrict the clustering by linguistically articulating the end of imagination. As the first few lines foreground, the unavoidable pitfall is that this uncoupling itself needs to be imagined. A further move is therefore to create a highly formalised narrative situation, in which the other elements in the narrative dynamic core are also reduced to a minimum of activation. The hardly imaginable image of two unnamed *white* bodies lying on a *white* ground and completely still deactivates as much as possible the "agent" element. Also the time dimension, like the temperature, approximates the "freezing point". Yet, "imagination not dead yet", and the "the absence in perfect voids" (p. 184) that later in the text is hoped for is impossible to realise because even the growing dark activates imagination. The positive outcome of this unsuccessful lesioning, however, is to discover, explore and let the reader experience the indissoluble clustering of two key elements in the narrative dynamic core.

Another case of the local model similarly aiming at lesioning the co-activation of language and imagination is the 1983 short prose *Worstward Ho* (2009a). The analogies with *Imagination Dead Imagine* are evident from the very beginning of this further lesioning experiment:

> On. Say on. Be said on. Somehow on. Till *nohow on*. Said *nohow on*.
> Say for be said. *Missaid*. From now say for be missaid.
> Say a body. Where none. No mind. Where none. That at least. A place. Where none. For the body. To be in. Move in. Out of. Back into. No. No out. No back. Only in. Stay in. On in. Still.
> All of old. Nothing else ever. Ever tried. Ever failed. No matter. Try again. Fail again. *Fail better*. (Beckett 2009a, p. 81; italics mine)

As in the previous modelling example, language is used once again to deflate imagination, this time by means of neologisms, syntactical oppositions and repeated negations of what has just been said. Neologisms and syntactical oppositions (in italics) are of particular interest here in relation to the idea, mentioned earlier in this section, of language as a complex agglomerate of building blocks (phonemes, syllables, morphemes, words, sentences). In order to understand, from a complex system perspective, the use of neologisms and syntactical oppositions in this passage, it might be worth introducing John Holland's description of complex adaptive systems as an interaction of "signals" and "boundaries" (2014).

In a complex system, Holland elucidates, "the network's nodes represent bounded entities (species, neurons, organelles) and the connections between nodes represent the flow of signals between entities" (2014, p. 7). Within what I have defined as the narrative dynamic core, all the four key elements have their own boundaries, from which they can signal each other—as in the constant signaling between language and imagination in the previous text. In complex systems, though, "because there are niches within niches, web-like hierarchies result. In signal/boundary terms, there is a hierarchy of enclosing boundaries, with matching signals at each level" (p. 16). Language, in this view, has its own internal boundaries and internal signaling. In Beckett's local model, neologisms ("missaid") and syntactical oppositions ("nohow on"; "fail better") create a mismatching signaling between words' boundaries. The resulting conflicting signals arising from the juncture of negative ("nohow"; "fail") and positive linguistic particles ("on"; "better") are then undermining the link with, and the activation of, the imagination node. With negations (e.g., "Say a body. Where none") we face a similar conflicting signaling, only at the larger boundary level of sentences. In both cases, the signals reaching the imagination boundary are in this way *almost simultaneously* cuing creative and deactivating stimuli. But once again, the production of a dysfunction in the coordination and interaction of two elements in the narrative dynamic core can disclose some knowledge about the inseparability of this cognitive coupling as well as about the nature, constitution and behaviour of the core itself.

Passing from a local to a global cognitive model in Beckett's work, *Company* (2009a) is a prime example of a text in which at issue is the global activity, the complex signaling and the interacting boundaries of all the elements in the narrative functional cluster. The text is the story of a voice coming to the only amnesic character (but not the only agent) in the dark of an unformed fictional world. The voice retells, in a non-chronological order, fifteen past scenes from the character's life, trying to force him to recognise these memories as his personal story ("To confess, Yes I remember" p. 9). Here it is how the text begins:

> A voice comes to one in the dark. Imagine.
> To one on his back in the dark. This he can tell by the pressure on his hind parts and by how the dark changes when he shuts his eyes and again when he opens them again . . .. To one on his back in the dark a voice tells of a past. With occasional allusion to a present and more rarely to a future as for example, You will end as you now are.
> Use of the second person marks the voice. That of the third the cankerous other. Could he speak to and of whom the voice speaks there would be a first. But he cannot. He shall not. You cannot. You shall not. (Beckett 2009a, p. 3).

To anticipate my interpretation, I want to suggest a reading of the text as a model of the narrative dynamic core whose global activity generates a narrative self. The "one in the dark", amnesic and endowed with just a proprioceptive sense of self ("Your mind never active at any time is now even less than ever so" p. 4) and time-consciousness (he is able to perceive a continuity in the movement of the voice), is a "minimal self" before and beyond the emergent narrative transition that would lead him into a fully fledged identity (Bernini 2014). In order for the transition to occur, all the elements in the dynamic core have to cluster and interact.

Starting from the narratological components, in the quoted passage the narratological agents (character, narrator, author) of the core are already presented through their indexical position. The character, not yet emerged into a linguistic and narrative self, still cannot speak at all, being a pure embodied indexical presence. The narrator speaks in the second person, trying to encode memories into the recalcitrant mind of the character ("To have the hearer to have a past and acknowledge it. You were born on an Easter Friday after long labour. Yes I remember." p. 22). The author ("the cankerous other"), predictably, employs the third person. The three positions, however, are continuously shifted, in order to let the reader perceive the singular plurality of the narratological agents in the creation of a narrative self. The author, we are told at a certain point, is the single yet divided source of the narrative, the "[d] eviser of the voice and of its hearer and of himself" (p. 16). In other words, "[h]e speaks *of* himself as another" (in the third person; italics mine) and, as the deviser of the voice, he speaks *to* himself (in the second person). Recalling the role of inner speech in the constantly ongoing narration in our mind, the memories retold *about* and *to* the author *as* a character can be interpreted as a modelling of inner speech in the narrative dynamic core.

As for the imagination node in the core, the retelling of memories by the voice is constantly presented as a "stretch of imagining" (p. 28) wearing and tiring the hearer, till the moment he will admit to remembering ("[b]loom of adulthood. Imagine a whiff of that. Ah you remember. Cloudless May day." p. 25). As for the time component, the encoding of memories as part of the activity in the core should reach the goal of temporally extending the self beyond his minimal sense of time-consciousness. To sum up, the text can be seen as a modelling of the emergent transition from a minimal self to an autobiographical self (Bernini 2015), operated by the interaction and co-aggregation of all the elements in the narrative dynamic core. There are actually also traces of this modelling procedure *within* the text, when the author evaluates how to ameliorate the modelling, for instance by improving the voice ("Might not the voice be improved?" p. 21) or the hearer ("Would it be reasonable to imagine the hearer quite inert?" p. 33). Like the previous local models, however, also this global model presents moments of lesioning, such as when the voice, after trying to extend the temporal existence of the character, negates to him any kind of future changes in the situation ("You will end as you now are" p. 3). Once again, this lesioning can provide valuable insights about the functioning of the building blocks (here the temporal one) in the narrative dynamic core.

In *Company*, all the nodes are active and interacting from their respective and highly formalised boundaries, casting signals that should in the end generate the flow of a narrative sense of self. As already mentioned, the elements in the narrative dynamic core operating in the mind's complexity are structurally similar to the components of a fictional narrative in general. This is why Beckett, combining introspective insights with narratological expertise, has been able to model, explore and let the reader perceive what lies before and beyond the unified integrating dynamics that gives rise to our rich subjectivity. In a sentence, he has been able to approximate the edge of mind's complexity (that is close to the "edge of sense" Walsh (Chap. 5) auspicates for narratives dealing with complexity), which usually conceals itself.

6   Conclusion

To conclude, in this essay I have tried to show how a specific kind of complex system (the mind) has been the object of exploration of what I have called Beckett's *fictional cognitive models*. Either locally or globally, Beckett's models target the activity of key elements in our mind, whose global interaction is responsible for the emergence of our narrative sense of selfhood. These models clearly do not allow prediction or scientific explanation. Rather, they can be described as what Holland calls "exploratory models", which typically "start with a designated set of mechanisms, such as the various bonds between amino acids, with the objective of finding out what can happen when these mechanisms interact" (2014, p. 43). In Beckett's case, the designated set of mechanisms he has selected is what I have called the "narrative dynamic core", the functional cluster aggregating language, time, agency and imagination. I argued that he has been able to make this modelling selection within the mind's complexity by means of introspective analysis or, as Beckett calls it in another letter to Duthuit in 1949, a "little session of autology, amid greedy sounds of suction" (2011, p. 139). If I am right, Beckett's work might constitute an exception to the limit of a narrative approach to complexity. As such, it could be regarded in itself as a model of a narrative method to be developed further, in a future where literature can occupy a proper position in the investigation and exploration of complex systems.

Acknowledgements The author is supported by the Wellcome Trust (WT098455 & WT108720).

References

Abbott HP (2008) Narrative and emergent behavior. Poet Today 29(2):227–244
Abbott HP (2014) Real mysteries: narrative and the unknowable. Ohio State University Press, Columbus
Ackerley CJ (1998) Samuel Beckett and mathematics. Cuadernos de literatura Inglesa y Norteamericana (Buenos Aires) 3(1–2):77–102
Ackerley CJ (2010) Beckett and science. In: Gontarski SC (ed) Companion to Samuel Beckett. Blackwell, Singapore, pp 143–163
Alderson-Day B, Fernyhough C (2015) Inner speech: development, cognitive functions, phenomenology, and neurobiology. Psychol Bull 141(5):931–965
Bassett DS, Gazzaniga MS (2011) Understanding complexity in the human brain. Trends Cogn Sci 15(5):200–209
Bayne T (2010) The unity of consciousness. Oxford University Press, New York
Beckett S (1984) Disjecta: miscellaneous writings and a dramatic fragment. Grove Press, New York
Beckett S (1996) The complete short Prose, 1929-1989. Grove Press, New York
Beckett S (2009a) Company, ill seen ill said, Worstword Ho, stirrings still. Faber and Faber, London
Beckett S (2009b) Murphy. Faber and Faber, London
Beckett S (2009c) Molloy. Faber and Faber, London
Beckett S (2011) The letters of Samuel Beckett 1941–1956. Cambridge University Press, New York
Bedau MA, Humphreys PE (eds) (2008) Emergence: contemporary readings in philosophy and science. MIT Press, Cambridge, MA
Bermúdez JL (2000) The paradox of self-consciousness. MIT Press, Cambridge, MA
Bernini M (2014) Gression, regression and beyond: a cognitive reading of *the unnamable*. In: Tucker D, Nixon M, Van Hulle D (eds) Revisiting Molloy, Malone Meurt/Malone Dies and L'Innommable/the unnamable. Rodopi, Amsterdam, pp 191–207
Bernini M (2015) Crawling creating creatures: on Beckett's liminal minds. Eur J Engl Stud 19 (1):39–54
Bruner J (2004) Life as narrative. Soc Res 71(3):691–710

Butler J (2013) Rethinking introspection: a pluralist approach to the first-person perspective. Palgrave Macmillan, New York

Clayton P (2004) Mind and emergence: from quantum to consciousness. Oxford University Press, New York

Cohn D (1978) Transparent minds: narrative modes for presenting consciousness in fiction. Princeton University Press, Princeton

Crutchfield J (2008) Is anything ever new? Considering emergence. In: Bedau MA, Humphrey P (eds) Emergence: contemporary readings in philosophy and science. MIT Press, Cambridge, MA, pp 269–286

Damasio AR (1998) Investigating the biology of consciousness. Philos Trans R Soc Lond Se B Biol Sci 353(1377):1879–1882

Dennett DC (1991) Consciousness explained. Backbay Books, New York

Doležel L (1998) Heterocosmica: fiction and possible worlds. Johns Hopkins University Press, Baltimore

Driver T (1979) Beckett by the Madeleine. In: Federman R, Graver L (eds) Samuel Beckett: the critical heritage. Routledge & Kegan Paul, London, pp 217–223

Duffy N (2013) Against metaphor: Samuel Beckett and the influence of science. diacritics 41 (4):36–59

Flanagan OC (1998) Consciousness reconsidered. MIT Press, Cambridge, MA

Freeman M (2007) Life and Literature: continuities and discontinuities. Interchange 38(3):223–243

Gallagher S (2000) Philosophical conceptions of the self: implications for cognitive science. Trends Cogn Sci 4(1):14–21

Gallagher S, Zahavi D (2010) The phenomenological mind: an introduction to philosophy of mind and cognitive science. MIT Press, Cambridge, MA

Gazzaniga M (2012) Who's in charge? Free will and the science of the brain. Robinson, London

Goldman AI (2006) Simulating minds: the philosophy, psychology, and neuroscience of mindreading. Oxford University Press, New York

Harrington JP (1982) Pynchon, Beckett, and entropy: uses of metaphor. Miss Rev 5(3):129–138

Holland JH (2014) Signals and boundaries: building blocks for complex adaptive systems. MIT Press, Cambridge, MA

Hurlburt RT, Heavey CL (2001) Telling what we know: describing inner experience. Trends Cogn Sci 5(9):400–403

Hurlburt RT, Schwitzgebel E (2007) Describing inner experience? Proponent meets skeptic. MIT Press, Cambridge, MA

Johnson S (1996) Strange attraction. Lingua Franca: Rev Acad Life 6(3):42–50

Lee N, Mikesell L, Joaquin ADL, Mates AW, Schumann JH (2009) The interactional instinct: the evolution and acquisition of language. Oxford University Press, New York

Levine J (1983) Materialism and qualia: the explanatory gap. Pac Philos Q 64(4):354–361

Lewandosky S, Farrell S (2011) Computational modelling in cognition. SAGE, London

Macdonald C, Macdonald G (eds) (2010) Emergence in mind. Oxford University Press, New York

MacKenzie M (2011) Enacting the self: Buddhist and enactivist approaches to the emergence of the self. In: Siderits M, Thompson E, Zahavi D (eds) Self, no self? Oxford University Press, Oxford, pp 239–273

Morin A, Everett J (1990) Inner speech as a mediator of self-awareness, self-consciousness, and self-knowledge: an hypothesis. New Ideas Psychol 8(3):337–356

Neisser U, Fivush R (eds) (1994) The remembering self: construction and accuracy in the self-narrative, vol 6. Cambridge University Press, New York

Noë A (2004) Action in perception. MIT Press, Cambridge, MA

Parker JA (2007) Narrative form and chaos theory in Sterne, Proust, Woolf, and Faulkner. Palgrave Macmillan, New York

Pickering J (1999) The self is a semiotic process. J Conscious Stud 6(4):31–47

Schechtman M (2007) Stories, lives, and basic survival: a refinement and defense of the narrative view. R Inst Philos Suppl 60:155–178

Schechtman M (2011) The narrative self. In: Gallagher S (ed) The Oxford handbook of the self. Oxford University Press, New York, pp 394–416

Strawson G (2004) Against narrativity. Ratio 17(4):428–452

Thompson E (2007) Mind in life: biology, phenomenology, and the sciences of mind. Harvard University Press, Cambridge, MA

Tononi G, Edelman GM (1998) Consciousness and complexity. Science 282(5395):1846–1851

Varela FJ (1999) Ethical know-how: action, wisdom, and cognition. Stanford University Press, Palo Alto

Vision G (2011) Re-emergence: locating conscious properties in a material world. MIT Press, Cambridge, MA

Chapter 18
Narratives for Drug Design

James Bown and Alexey Goltsov

Abstract We explore the role of narratives of complex systems in anti-cancer drug design. We set out the value of narratives relating to cancer in promoting awareness of risky behaviour and in supporting decision-making regarding treatment options. We present cancer as a dysregulated, complex system that has emergent behaviours at multiple scales, and is governed by dynamical spatio-temporal processes. We show that this system changes structure and function in response to anti-cancer drugs, and explain that these changes are sufficiently complex to impede effective drug design. We pose what narrative might offer to support the process of drug design, providing an example of work done to date that might serve as a foundation for narrating complexity. We suggest ways of using this work combined with that of others to begin to consider narrating drug design.

1 Narratives and Cancer Patients

The management of patients with long-term conditions is one of the major challenges facing healthcare systems worldwide (United Nations General Assembly 2013). A long-term condition is a condition for which there is no cure; rather, long-term conditions must be managed through a range of treatment options including drugs (King's Fund 2012). Long-term conditions include diabetes, hypertension, chronic kidney disease and cancer, and management of these conditions accounts for a substantial proportion of health service resources. For example, in the UK long-term condition patients account for 30% of the patient population and 70% of the healthcare spend (Department of Health 2012).

J. Bown (✉)
School of Design and Informatics, Abertay University, Dundee, UK

School of Science, Engineering and Technology, Abertay University, Dundee, UK
e-mail: j.bown@abertay.ac.uk

A. Goltsov
School of Science, Engineering and Technology, Abertay University, Dundee, UK

© Springer Nature Switzerland AG 2018
R. Walsh, S. Stepney (eds.), *Narrating Complexity*,
https://doi.org/10.1007/978-3-319-64714-2_18

Patients living with long-term conditions play an important role in management of their condition, and Coulter et al. (2015) provide a comprehensive review of the role of personal care planning in the management of long-term conditions. They describe personal care planning as a "collaborative process used in chronic condition management in which patients and clinicians identify and discuss problems caused by or related to the patient's condition, and develop a plan for tackling these" (Coulter et al. 2015). For personal care planning to be effective, patients must be supported in the difficult decisions they make in respect of lifestyle choices and treatment options.

Cancer is one of the fastest rising long-term conditions (Department of Health 2012) and one of the leading causes of death worldwide. There were approximately 8 million deaths recorded in 2012 and a 70% rise in new cases expected over the next 20 years (Stewart and Wild 2014).

Narrative has been shown to have value in the prevention of cancer through effective communication of risk. Janssen et al. (2013) provide a useful review of narrative in healthcare, noting that "by providing vivid information about the antecedents and the consequences of a health problem, narrative health information improves the extent to which people are able to imagine themselves developing a certain disease, which in turn may influence their risk judgments" (Janssen et al. 2013). Their own study explored the effects of risk communication to regular sunbed users in narrative and non-narrative forms. Results showed that, compared with non-narrative information forms, narrative information promoted an increased feeling of skin cancer risk with respect to sunbed use in participants, and participants could more readily imagine themselves developing skin cancer.

Narratives can also support patients when making decisions on treatment options. Shaffer et al. (2013) report on the effect of process-focused and experience-focused narratives on the patient decision-making process. Process narratives are designed to "prime participants to follow a particular decision process ... [and] would most commonly entail patients considering additional dimensions of the decision process that they might not have considered otherwise" Shaffer et al. (2013). Experience narratives are designed to "increase knowledge and the perceived ability to imagine future health states ... [which] could result in increased decisional satisfaction and an improved ability to make affective forecasts (i.e., forecasts of future feelings)" Shaffer et al. (2013). Importantly, neither process nor experience narratives are thought to bias healthcare decisions, but to promote consideration of a broader set of issues than they might have otherwise or improve understanding of treatment outcome respectively. Focusing on breast cancer treatment decisions, and through a carefully designed test with control conditions, results of the study revealed that participants exposed to process-focused narratives spent more time searching for information relating to key aspects of treatment that were discussed in the narratives. Participants exposed to experience-focused narratives were more confident in and satisfied with their treatment decisions.

We propose that narrative can also inform clinicians' understanding of cancer. We base this proposition on the following observations: (1) cancer is a complex system; (2) effective drug design depends on understanding that complex system;

and (3) narratives can inform our understanding of complex systems. The remainder of this chapter explores this proposition by unpacking these three observations in turn.

In Sect. 2 we consider cancer as a complex system. We unpack some of the complexities associated with cancer as a system of interacting cells in the context of normal tissue. We pay particular attention to one level of functioning in cancer cells – that of the intracellular signalling network that represents the biochemical interactions among different species in the cell. It is these biochemical interactions that ultimately dictate cell fate.

In Sect. 3 we explore this signalling network in the context of anti-cancer drug targets. Because of their role in cell fate, some signalling network components provide potentially useful drug targets for anti-cancer therapy. However, these drug targets are situated in the context of a topologically complex and dynamic network. We consider how anti-cancer drugs seek to restore normal functioning in cell signalling networks, and explore how therapy design is impeded by the complexity of the cellular system.

In Sect. 4 we set out what narrative might offer to support the process of drug design, both providing an example of work done to date that might serve as a foundation for narrating complexity and speculating on the contribution of narrative to anti-cancer treatment.

In the Conclusion we suggest possible ways of using this work combined with that of others to begin to consider narrating drug design.

2 Cancer as a Complex System

Cancer is not a single disease; it is a broad class of diseases of over 200 types (Cancer Research UK 2016), characterised by functional dysregulations within and surrounding affected cells, tissues and organs (Bown et al. 2012) as outlined in subsequent sections. Cancer originates from the aberrant behaviour of a single cell or region of cells that over time gives rise to an observable anomalous tissue structure in the form of a tumour, and can progress to non-local spread through the blood stream or lymphatic system.

Cancer is therefore an emergent system where local (cell) scale processes lead to system-scale patterns in local cell populations, tissue structures, organs and ultimately in the body as a whole. As explored below, those tissue patterns in turn impact cellular processes. Moreover, there is increasing awareness of the heterogeneities in cancer: tumours comprise multiple cell types; patterning in tissue is likewise heterogeneous. That cancer is emergent at multiple scales and highly heterogeneous makes treatment very challenging.

In 2000, Hanahan and Weinburg (2000) set out six biological hallmarks of cancer that have helped frame investigations and interpretation of findings; these hallmarks provide a contextual backdrop to the challenge of drug design. Here, these are briefly outlined, and indeed greatly simplified. Hanahan and Weinburg (2000) provide a rich description of all six hallmarks for the interested reader.

Normal cells regulate the processes of growth and division and pre-programmed cell death, responding to spatially and temporally structured external signals that cue the cell to grow, and to information on mechanical stresses from the environment and from other cells (note that there are a wide range of other factors involved). In effect, external signals are read in through receptors on the cell wall and processed by the cell to drive behaviour. This cellular processing enables tissue to maintain consistent and properly functioning structures.

Cancer arises from perturbations in the processing of these signals, and such perturbations can lead to cells that are not well regulated by external stimuli. This dysregulation can confer cells with one or more of the six hallmarks of cancer:

- *Increased proliferation*, where cells divide far more frequently than they should;
- *Unsuppressed growth*, where cancer cells can grow in structural forms inconsistent with normal tissue (e.g., where mechanical pressures are larger);
- *Resistance to cell death*, a natural and pre-programmed mechanism to promote cell turnover and maintain a healthy population of cells;
- *Replicative immortality*, through a combination of the above three hallmarks and through changes in the mechanisms cells use to control the number of possible divisions;
- *Sustained angiogenesis*, meaning that cancerous tissue can encourage development of structures able to supply oxygen and nutrients;
- *Invasion and metastasis*, where tumour masses can move into adjacent tissue and into distant regions by changing the physical coupling of cancer cells to their microenvironment.

Tumours thus originate from and are sustained by dysregulations within the signal processing within the cell, which confer on that cell particular ecological and/or evolutionary advantages. The resulting pattern at the tissue scale is the emerging tumour of cancer cells in the environmental context of normal tissue. An important observation is that cross-scale feedback occurs through competition for resource and space. Resource competition occurs because there is limited oxygen and nutrients yet there are increasingly more cells in the developing cancerous tissue structure. This growth is occurring in a limited space and the mechanical stresses on cells caused by too much growth in too little space are converted into biochemical signals and can actually promote further signal transduction; these stresses drive proliferation over time (see Jaalouk and Lammerding 2009 for a review).

Kreeger and Lauffenburger (2009) provide an excellent review on the challenges posed when trying to unravel both the origins and consequences of such dysregulation in cancer cells. A key observation is that cell behaviour is controlled by a mix of genetic alterations and environmental context, and that the "greatest amount of information concerning phenotypic behaviour resides in the realm comprehending both genomic and environmental effects: dynamic protein network operations" (Kreeger and Lauffenburger 2009).

These protein networks, or signalling networks, provide a mechanistic connection between external signals received at the cell surface and the cell nucleus (Cooper 2000). These signalling networks represent the biochemical species that interact to form new compounds in order to process external signals. The nodes in the network represent the compounds that are formed and broken down in space over time as the cell processes extracellular signals and it is the result of these processes that drives the behaviour of the cell.

Signals propagate through these networks, and cancerous behaviours, i.e., the hallmarks, are often associated with measurable differences in the proteins that make up these pathways. Accordingly, amongst the myriad levels of organisation of cellular, tissue and environmental factors, signalling networks are a promising route for drug design. However, signalling networks themselves attract complexities.

3 Signalling Networks and Anti-Cancer Drug Design

As noted above, signalling networks transduct external stimuli, including growth factors and anti-cancer drugs, for processing by the cell nucleus. Importantly, these networks do not operate in isolation; networks are interconnected and this complicates their study.

Figure 18.1 (from Hu et al. 2013) is illustrative of such a network, and shows two key, interconnected signalling pathways that are implicated in some of the hallmarks of cancer: pre-programmed cell death, cell proliferation and cell growth. These pathways are regulated by growth factor receptors (HER2 and HER3 in Fig. 18.1). These two receptors regulate signalling in the PI3K/PTEN/AKT and Ras/Raf/MEK/ERK pathways that control cell survival, growth and proliferation. The details of the molecular species that comprise this network are beyond the scope of this chapter. Important here are several topological features that give rise to complex, emergent behaviours. Note these features are a defining property of many signalling networks in biological sciences (Bown et al. 2012): complexity arising from network topology is prevalent and not limited to this exemplar network or indeed to cancer.

Figure 18.1 shows pathway cross-talk and feedback loops, within and between networks. Cross-talk is shown towards the centre of the network by the PP2A enzyme, a known regulator of a wide range of cellular processes. This enzyme is connected to the AKT-PIP3 complex, which drives cell survival and growth, and the MEK complex, implicated in cell proliferation and differentiation among other processes. A cell has a limited amount of PP2A at any one time, and in this particular cross-talk example an increase in signalling activity in one pathway that interacts with this limited amount of PP2A causes an inhibition of signalling activity in the other pathway. Cross-activation, rather than the cross-inhibition shown here, is also observed in other pathways.

Signalling is further complicated by the feedback loops shown in the network (Fig. 18.1, dotted lines). Feedback loops are another pervasive feature of biological networks. Feedback loops have a regulatory role in such networks, helping to keep

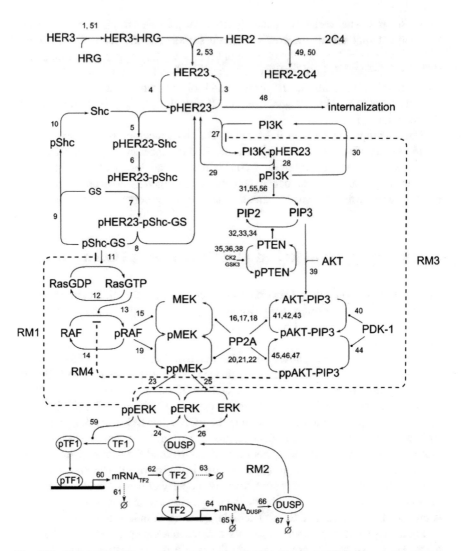

Fig. 18.1 Cellular signalling pathways (reproduced from Hu et al. 2013). The two pathways RAF/MEK/ERK (left hand side) and PI3K/PTEN/AKT (right hand side) are interconnected by element PP2A. RM1 shows a feedback loop. Additional cross-talk is shown by RM3 and RM4. Numbers refer to the underlying equation set (see discussion on interactive media below) (Hu et al. 2013)

some intracellular conditions constant in the face of any perturbation. This network describes oscillations in AKT and ERK signalling pathway outputs, and these oscillations can be controlled by varying the strengths of the feedback loops in the networks.

These topological complexities on the one hand provide signalling networks with marked robustness to external stimuli, maintaining proper functioning in the face of noisy inputs, yet on the other hand confer exquisite sensitivity to key variations in those inputs. Accordingly, networks can be either sensitive or resistant to small changes in input signals: sensitivity means that small, localised changes can have a pronounced impact on non-local network functioning; resistance means that network functioning is resilient to such change.

This emergent phenomenon has implications in anti-cancer drug design (see below) but also in cancer-associated mutations. Figure 18.2 (from Goltsov et al. 2014) shows the impact of a cancer-associated mutation on network sensitivity in the form of a heatmap. The heatmap shows the sensitivity of 19 different entities in the signalling network, where light grey indicates high sensitivity and dark grey indicates low sensitivity, i.e., resistance. In normal functioning (Column 1 in Fig. 18.2), the network sensitivity heatmap is mainly mid to light grey, indicating a network that is sensitive to change but not dramatically so. Mutations can be introduced into the model to represent biological mutations in the cell. One single mutation in a key network node results in a network that is largely insensitive to change (Column 3 in Fig. 18.2 is mainly dark grey and black), i.e., a local change results in a marked non-local change in sensitivity.

To complicate cellular signalling further still, there is an increasing awareness that the network topology itself is not fixed (Lee et al. 2012). The network topology represents the interactions among different species in the cell, and the network changes in structure over time. These changes occur because different parts of the network interconnect and disconnect as the cell responds to acquired mutations and significant changes to external stimuli such as anti-cancer drug treatments. For example, a cell can become resistant to the effect of a drug through these changes.

Anti-cancer drug treatments are typically in the form of a "targeted cancer therapy", a kind of therapy that is designed to disrupt aberrant behaviour in cellular signalling networks, either in an effort to restore normal functioning or to at least suppress cancerous behaviours in cells, by targeting a particular node in the network. Drugs are typically designed in a single-target-single-drug paradigm (Medina-Franco et al. 2013), i.e., a drug is designed to target a specific site in a network. However, single therapies have had only limited success (Singer et al. 2008), with patients either failing to respond at all, or developing resistance to the drug effect over time.

This is, in part, because the single therapies are acting in the context of a range of mechanisms that compensate for and adapt to perturbations (here, drug action): these mechanisms include cross-talk, feedback loops, differential sensitivities to change across the network and changes in network structure in response to drug action. This means that targeted therapies can impact beyond their point of application, and often in ways that are difficult to anticipate (Bown et al. 2017). These features then limit efficacy of any single therapy, and patient resistance to a drug is a key challenge in anti-cancer therapy design.

There is increasing evidence from both *in vitro* and *in vivo* studies that combination therapy, i.e., therapy comprising more than one drug and so target more than one site in the network, is a promising route to overcome the challenge of drug resistance. This evidence base is growing continually (Chandarlapaty 2012; Chong and Jänne 2013) but typically the way in which the drugs work together to deliver improved performance is not well understood (Goltsov et al. 2014). The rational

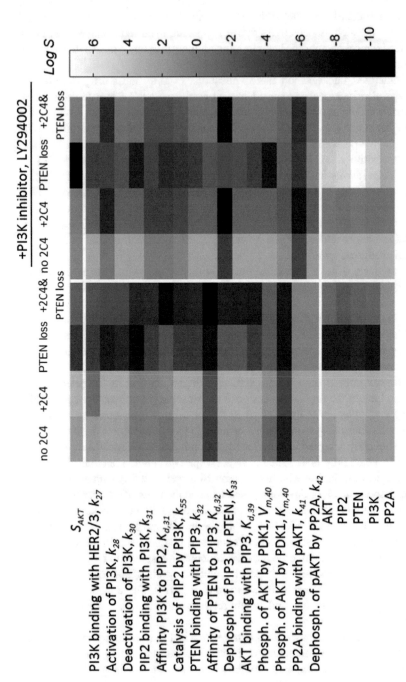

Fig. 18.2 Heatmap of sensitivity of different entities in the signalling network (adapted from Goltsov et al. 2014). Column 1 shows the network in normal functioning, and when an anti-cancer drug is applied the network increases in overall sensitivity (Column 2). When a cancer-associated mutation is introduced the network is insensitive without or with the anti-cancer drug (Columns 3 and 4 respectively). The addition of a second drug in combination with the first (Columns 5–8) restores sensitivity to the anti-cancer drug (Column 8). From Goltsov et al. (2014)

design of combination therapy depends on a mechanistic understanding of those networks in terms of the individual components and the way in which those components interact, locally and non-locally. Rational design needs ways of integrating often fragmented data that together reflect the system as a whole, or at least some representative subset of that system, and then of interpreting the results of that integration.

The complexity of that integration provides an opportunity for computational models. Models can identify signalling network states that confer drug resistance or sensitivity and shed light on how to manage the transition from one state to the other through combination therapy, e.g., Goltsov et al. (2012), and propose mechanisms of combination therapy action to explain why, in a model of drugs binding to signalling network nodes, two drugs that are applied individually are ineffective yet when applied in combination and at the same time are effective in overcoming drug resistance (Kholodenko 2015). Thus models can contribute to rational drug design and in doing so help us understand signalling pathway complexities.

This opportunity is, however, impeded by the computational–biological discipline divide. Biologists and clinicians readily understand simple models, but simple models cannot deliver value in the face of the complexities noted above. Models that represent sufficient complexity to help us understand a signalling network can be challenging for biologists to first formulate and then interpret (Janes and Lauffenburger 2013). Janes and Lauffenburger (2013) provide a review of the value of such signalling network models for experimental cell biology. They highlight that key barriers are confusion over the purpose of the model, predictions from the model, and the wide range of modelling approaches available. The purpose should be to—try to—explain specific phenomena observed in experimentation; predictions made are often in the context of assumptions especially relating to gaps in knowledge of parameter values; the selected approach needs to take account of the purpose and the available knowledge. Indeed, our own work on CoSMoS (Stepney et al. 2011) provides a framework to address exactly these barriers.

Going beyond this computational–biological discipline divide, the complexities in signalling networks run deeper than topology. Nodes, and combinations of nodes, in the network serve as switches, integrators and inhibitors, and the specific function of any given node or sub-network can be variable, contextualised by its inputs in a non-linear manner. Thus, non-linear components operate with variable function in complex networks. It then becomes impossible to describe system behaviour in linear and simple narrative. In fact, it has been suggested that rather than a node-centric view, it is likely that the dynamic features of the network itself might form the basis of drug targets (Behar et al. 2013).

4 Towards Narratives for Anti-Cancer Drug Design

We have so far established the following:

- Cancer is a complex system driven in part by aberrant cellular function;

- Signalling networks are a useful level of detail at which to study cellular function, and are themselves complex;
- Parts of those signalling networks can be targeted by anti-cancer drug therapies to seek to restore aberrant functioning;
- The signalling network is dynamic in its reaction to drugs and mutations, and its structure can change over time;
- Computational models can support our understanding of cell responses to drug action, including the various mechanisms of drug resistance;
- Computational models that are of sufficient detail to represent mechanisms of resistance can be prohibitively complex for biologists.

Here, we describe briefly an interactive visualisation technology that could provide the foundations for narratives. The use of data storytelling to communicate and stimulate insights is a growing research area (Bach et al. 2016). Segel and Heer (2010) provide a systematic review of work seeking to combine narrative and interactive visualisations, and note that while sophisticated visualisation tools might provide powerful vehicles for discovering stories, narrative communication depends on more than visualisation.

Boy et al. (2015) distinguish between two types of information visualisations: explanatory and exploratory. Explanatory information visualisations are common in journalistic contexts, are typically used to support the narrative presented in the text, and have limited interactivity. Segel and Heer (2010) categorise such explanatory information visualisations as author-driven. In contrast, exploratory information visualisations require a reader-driven approach with free interactivity (Boy et al. 2015), and are motivated by provoking discoveries in the patterns of data.

We propose that our technology is a vehicle to support reader-driven narratives, but is not in of itself a narrative. This technology, SiViT (Bown et al. 2017), turns a complex model into an interactive animation, allowing the cancer specialist intuitive access to complex systems models otherwise inaccessible. SiViT is able to represent graphically the network structure of models of cell signalling, such as that described in Fig. 18.1. The models encapsulate a system of differential equations and SiViT computes these equations and animates a simulation of the model of the system dynamics. Thus SiViT provides a 'movie' of the simulation, showing the whole system behaviour. Moreover, each node in the network can be queried and a pop-up graph of node activity over time presented.

This is a useful contribution in respect of validation: all models depend on a set of assumptions and these assumptions can be difficult to elicit, especially in the case of complex systems models. Modelling frameworks such as CoSMoS (Bown et al. 2012) have found ways of explicating and then challenging the assumption set underpinning a complex systems model and its simulation. SiViT provides a complementary explication: simulation dynamics are animated in the hope that major departures in the model (or indeed simulation) formulation are identified.

Crucially, SiViT also allows the user to add in and then visualise the effects of cancer-causing mutations and anti-cancer drugs. Mutations associated with drug resistance can be introduced by changing simulation parameters through another

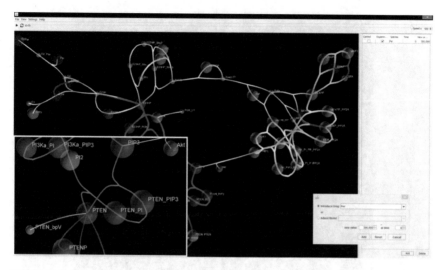

Fig. 18.3 A signalling network visualisation with a pop-up dialogue box (Inset 1, bottom right) for amending drug regime and mutational status together with an inset with magnified detail (Inset 2, bottom left) (Bown et al. 2017). For figures and related movies, see http://www.impactjournals. com/oncotarget/index.php?journal=oncotarget&page=article&op=view&path%5B%5D=8747

drop down menu. Drugs can be added in through a drop-down menu, at a prescribed dosage at a particular time. Combinations of drugs can be added to explore the effects of different doses and of dose sequencing. These combinations can be drawn from a known set of drugs. Alternatively, new drugs can be designed by changing simulation parameters directly to simulate the effect of that designed drug.

Any simulation configuration, in terms of drugs and mutations, can be compared with another (one) simulation configuration. In pairwise comparisons, the two configurations are defined as Control and Experiment and the visualisation is a mix of red, blue and white. The colour of each node and edge component is set by whether the value of the Control component is greater than, less than or equal to the value of the corresponding component in the Experiment, with colour intensity proportional to this difference. Figure 18.3 shows a signalling network visualisation using SiViT.

Figure 18.4 shows a typical set of SiViT visualisations. The network is that of the PI3K/PTEN/AKT and RAF/MEK/ERK pathways shown in Fig. 18.1 (except for the sub-network of Fig. 18.1 below the ERK—pERK—ppERK interactions). Figure 18.4a, b show the effect of an anti-cancer drug after 1 min and 10 min respectively. Figure 18.4a shows an immediate and substantial down-regulation of signalling since most of the network is blue. By 10 minutes, we observe differences in pathway dynamics: in Fig. 18.4b the lower pathway is still down-regulated and the upper pathway has similar levels of signalling to the network without the drug, i.e., the Control condition, since much of this pathway is white. Thus, the overall signalling activity in this upper pathway is the same but signalling dynamics are

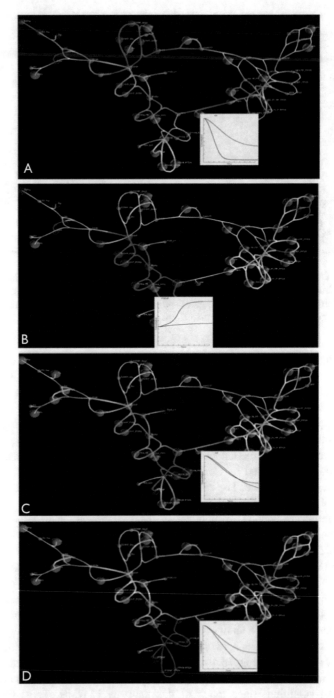

Fig. 18.4 SiViT visualisations of cell signalling (adapted from Bown et al. 2017). (**a**) the effect of an anti-cancer drug after 1 min; (**b**) the effect of an anti-cancer drug after 10 min; (**c**) a network with a cancer-causing mutation introduced at a single point; (**d**) the same network but with combination

slowed by the drug action—a different dynamic to that of the lower pathway. Areas in red show non-local, emergent phenomena: red areas represent accumulations of species concentrations as a result of drug action inhibiting nodes elsewhere in the pathway network.

Figure 18.4c shows a network with a cancer-causing mutation introduced at a single point. This single point mutation has a marked effect on the whole network functioning, where at the end of the 10-min time-course the inhibitor has a far weaker effect in reducing signalling. Figure 18.4d depicts the state of the network after the use of combination therapy to restore network sensitivity to the drug. The resistant network with combination therapy shown in Fig. 18.4d is very similar to the sensitive (normal) network with single therapy in Fig. 18.4b in respect of the overall pattern of signalling.

Note, the white insets show key biological indicators of signalling activity in the Control (black line) and Experiment (blue line) simulation conditions. In Figs. 18.4a, c and d the insets show AKT levels—a key regulator of cell survival, growth and proliferation. The intended drug action is to reduce the amount of active AKT in the network. In Fig. 18.4a levels of inactive AKT are increased following drug action as expected; in the resistant network of Fig. 18.4c inactive AKT is decreased. In Fig. 18.4d, SiViT was used to determine the minimum dose to match the key biological indicator (AKT) as shown in the overlapping blue and black lines of the pop-up inset.

Beyond this representation, the observer is currently left to construct an interpretation of the system dynamics by integrating the observed individual components; the task is of course easier than such inference from the equation set or graph-based time-series readouts. Additional layers of abstraction and perspectives could add to the explanatory power of simulation results.

5 Conclusion

SiViT can reveal system dynamics in a literal sense. A key limitation of many information visualisation systems identified by (Lee et al. 2015) is that there is no provision for the "making of a story". Where visualisations cue key events in the system dynamics, or story pieces, it is down to the user to extract and organise meaningfully those story pieces without support from the visualisation system (Lee et al. 2015). Additionally, visualisations are not typically designed to highlight key events, including system changes in functioning and—here—the invocation of compensatory mechanisms of feedback.

Fig. 18.4 (continued) therapy to overcome resistance. See http://www.impactjournals.com/oncotarget/index.php?journal=oncotarget&page=article&op=view&path%5B%5D=8747 for figures and related movies

For signalling networks, in the light of increasing understanding of the limitations of drug design targeting single nodes in the face of topological changes in signalling network architecture, Behar et al. (2013) propose that signalling hub topology, and crucially the response of that topology to differing signalling pathway inputs, i.e., drugs, has utility in advancing anti-cancer therapy. In Behar et al. (2013) the network is viewed in terms of sub-networks that provide dynamical mapping of inputs to outputs; interventions (drugs) are viewed in terms of their impact on that mapping. They combine this concept with that of a network motif (Wong et al. 2012), where a motif is a particular configuration of nodes in a sub-network that is observed regularly and pervasively in a range of biological systems. Motifs include switches, feedback loops, feed-forward loops and integrators. Behar et al. (2013) suggest that signalling networks either exhibit these motifs explicitly or may be abstracted into such a motif based on the observed dynamics of that sub-network. In taking this view the network, or at least sub-networks, in addition to the pathway nodes, has agency. Moreover, motifs and changes in network or sub-network topology may well represent key story pieces.

Thus any interactive, visual account of cell signalling in response to drugs needs to reveal both node and sub-network dynamics, in an integrated and concurrent manner. System-scale dynamics must be portrayed such that conformational changes in sub-networks, such as from e.g., a feedback into a feed-forward loop, are depicted concurrently with up- and down-regulation of nodes, and importantly how the two are connected. This interconnection is likely to be non-linear and context-sensitive: we must explore the use of concurrent accounts of signalling at different spatial and temporal scales to reveal this link, with key events in each account being cross-linked to reveal how one impacts the other.

This dynamic representation of signalling network dynamics requires communication via video, although highlighting important events is not readily translated into a narrative form. New work by Bach et al. (2016) provides a thought-provoking first study on the use of the well-established and visually rich medium of comics to tell stories about dynamic networks. Bach et al. (2016) note that comics are already used to convey information beyond entertainment in order to inform and educate in an engaging way. They founded their notational design on good practice in the existing domain of graphic comics and tested the effectiveness of designed comics to convey network changes over time. The results confirmed that with minimal textual cueing the intended dynamics were successfully conveyed.

While the comics used in this study are not as complex as required to represent signalling network dynamics, we believe that this work, combined with our own interactive and executable visualisation technology, provides a first hint towards the narrating of cellular signalling networks. In principle, and with some user direction, key switches in behaviour driven by drug action and mutation identified via SiViT could be pushed out to a comic format with panels showing key states and alternate pathways in time. The comic would then architect the key story pieces, and events leading to marked changes in signalling network functioning, into a narrative underpinned by the more detailed SiViT visualisation. This would both aid understanding of signalling network dynamics and, crucially, improve reporting in linear reporting media, in particular, in scientific journals.

References

Bach B, Kerracher N, Hall KW, Carpendale S, Kennedy J, Riche N (2016) Telling stories about dynamic networks with graph comics. In: Proceedings of the 2016 CHI conference on human factors in computing systems (CHI'16). ACM Press. doi: https://doi.org/10.1145/2858036. 2858387

Behar M, Barken D, Werner SL, Hoffmann A (2013) The dynamics of signaling as a pharmacological target. Cell 155:448–461

Bown J, Andrews PS, Deeni Y, Goltsov A, Idowu M, Polack FAC, Sampson ATS, Shovman M, Stepney S (2012) Engineering simulations for cancer systems biology. Curr Drug Targets 13 (12):1560–1574

Bown JL, Shovman M, Robertson P, Boiko A, Goltsov A, Mullen P, Harrison DJ (2017) A signaling visualization toolkit to support rational design of combination therapies and biomarker discovery: SiViT. Oncotarget 8(18):29657–29667

Boy J, Detienne F, Fekete JD (2015) Storytelling in information visualizations: does it engage users to explore data? In: Proceedings of the 33rd annual ACM conference on human factors in computing systems. ACM Press, pp 1449–1458

Cancer Research UK (2016) http://www.cancerresearchuk.org/about-cancer/what-is-cancer. Accessed 3 Aug 16

Chandarlapaty S (2012) Negative feedback and adaptive resistance to the targeted therapy of cancer. Cancer Discov 2:311–319

Chong CR, Jänne PA (2013) The quest to overcome resistance to EGFR-targeted therapies in cancer. Nat Med 19:1389–1400

Cooper GM (2000) The cell: a molecular approach, 2nd edn. Sinauer Associates, Sunderland, MA

Coulter A, Entwistle VA, Eccles A, Ryan S, Shepperd S, Perera R (2015) Personalised care planning for adults with chronic or long-term health conditions. Cochrane Database Syst Rev 2015(3):CD010523. https://doi.org/10.1002/14651858.CD010523.pub2

Department of Health (2012) Long term conditions compendium of information, 3rd edn. https://www.gov.uk/government/publications/long-term-conditions-compendium-of-information-third-edition. Accessed 3 Aug 2016

Goltsov A, Faratian D, Langdon SP, Mullen P, Harrison DJ, Bown J (2012) Features of the reversible sensitivity-resistance transition in PI3K/PTEN/AKT signaling network after HER2 inhibition. Cell Signal 24:493–504

Goltsov A, Langdon SP, Goltsov G, Harrison DJ, Bown J (2014) Customizing the therapeutic response of signaling networks to promote antitumor responses by drug combinations. Front Oncol 4:13. https://doi.org/10.3389/fonc.2014.00013

Hanahan D, Weinberg RA (2000) The hallmarks of cancer. Cell 100:57–70

Hu H, Gotlsov A, Bown JL, Sims AH, Langdon SP, Harrison DJ, Faratian D (2013) Feedforward and feedback regulation of the MAPK and PI3K oscillatory circuit in breast cancer. Cell Signal 25(1):26–32

Jaalouk DE, Lammerding J (2009) Mechanotransduction gone awry. Nat Rev Mol Cell Biol 10:63–73. https://doi.org/10.1038/nrm2597

Janes KA, Lauffenburger DA (2013) Models of signalling networks – what cell biologists can gain from them and give to them. J Cell Sci 126:1913–1921

Janssen E, van Osch L, de Vries Lechner L (2013) The influence of narrative risk communication on feelings of cancer risk. Br J Health Psychol 18:407–419. https://doi.org/10.1111/j.2044-8287.2012.02098.x

Kholodenko BN (2015) Drug resistance resulting from kinase dimerization is rationalized by thermodynamic factors describing allosteric inhibitor effects. Cell Rep 12:1939–1949. https://doi.org/10.1016/j.celrep.2015.08.014

King's Fund (2012) Time to think differently. Long term conditions and multimorbidity. http://www.kingsfund.org.uk/time-to-think-differently/trends/disease-and-disability/long-term-conditions-multi-morbidity#morbidity. Accessed 3 Aug 2016

Kreeger PK, Lauffenburger DA (2009) Cancer systems biology: a network modeling perspective. Carciogenesis 31(1):2–8

Lee MJ, Ye AS, Gardino AK, Heijnk AM, Sorger PK, MacBeath G, Yaffe MB (2012) Sequential application of anticancer drugs enhances cell death by rewiring apoptotic signaling networks. Cell 149:780–794

Lee B, Riche N, Isenberg P, Carpendale S (2015) More than telling a story: a closer look at the process of transforming data into visually shared stories. IEEE Comput Graph Appl 35 (5):84–90

Medina-Franco JL, Giulianotti MA, Welmaker GS, Houghten RA (2013) Shifting from the single- to the multitarget paradigm in drug discovery. Drug Discov Today 18:495–501

Segel E, Heer J (2010) Narrative visualization: telling stories with data. IEEE Trans Vis Comput Graph 16(6):1139–1148

Shaffer VA, Hulsey L, Zikmund-Fisher BJ (2013) The effects of process-focused versus experience-focused narratives in a breast cancer treatment decision task. Patient Educ Couns 93(2):255–264

Singer CF, Köstler WJ, Hudelist G (2008) Predicting the efficacy of trastuzumab-based therapy in breast cancer: current standards and future strategies. Biochim Biophys Acta 1786(2):105–113

Stepney S, Welch PH, Andrews PS, Ritson CG (eds) (2011) Proceedings of the 2011 workshop on complex systems modelling and simulation, Paris, France, Aug 2011. Luniver Press

Stewart BW, Wild CP (2014) World cancer report. WHO Press, Geneva

United Nations General Assembly (2013) https://www.idf.org/sites/default/files/UN%20Secretary%20General%20Progress%20Report%20on%20NCDs%20Dec%202013.pdf. Accessed 3 Aug 2016

Wong E, Baur B, Quader S, Huang CH (2012) Biological network motif detection: principles and practice. Brief Bioinform 13(2):202–215. https://doi.org/10.1093/bib/bbr033

Chapter 19
Time Will Tell: Narrative Expressions of Time in a Complex World

Leo Caves, Ana Teixeira de Melo, Susan Stepney, and Emma Uprichard

Abstract Time is intrinsic to all complex systems. Here we explore the complexity of time from three different disciplinary perspectives: the physical, the biological and the social. We do this by listing some expressions of time taken from everyday speech and idioms and relating them to complex temporal concepts that are central to these different disciplines. The result is a series of small sections that together weave a particular interdisciplinary (hi)story of time in complexity.

> *Quid est ergo tempus? Si nemo ex me quaerat, scio; si quaerenti explicare velim, nescio.*
> *(What then is time? If no one asks me, I know what it is. If I wish to explain it to him who asks, I do not know.)*
>   (Saint Augustine, *Confessions*, c.397)

> *The truth, even more, is that life is perpetually weaving fresh threads which link one individual and one event to another, and that these threads are crossed and recrossed, doubled and redoubled to thicken the web, so that between any slightest point of our past and all the others a rich network of memories gives us an almost infinite variety of communicating paths to choose from.*
>   (Marcel Proust, *In Search of Lost Time*, 1927)

> Tick. . . .tock. . . .tiiick. . . .toooock. . .

L. Caves
Independent Researcher, Sao Felix da Marinha, Portugal

York Cross-disciplinary Centre for Systems Analysis, University of York, York, UK

A. T. de Melo
Centre for Social Studies, University of Coimbra, Coimbra, Portugal

S. Stepney (✉)
Department of Computer Science, University of York, York, UK

York Cross-disciplinary Centre for Systems Analysis, University of York, York, UK
e-mail: susan.stepney@york.ac.uk

E. Uprichard
Centre for Interdisciplinary Methodologies, University of Warwick, Warwick, UK

© Springer Nature Switzerland AG 2018   269
R. Walsh, S. Stepney (eds.), *Narrating Complexity*,
https://doi.org/10.1007/978-3-319-64714-2_19

1 "Once Upon a Time ..."

We begin this chapter on time and complexity here; it could start at any number of different places. But if there are beginnings and births in complex systems, then they emerge over time, even though they are also erased through time too.

2 "Time Is a Great Story Teller"

Time is a central feature of complex systems. We are complex, and our world is complex. Everything is changing; all is process. Time is change, and change is about time. Time is here and it is there. We need to know how to talk about it, how to narrate it, so that we can deal with it.

3 "Winding Up"

Features of the *complex* world are embedded in our daily lives and will find expression in our narratives. Here we look at everyday expressions regarding time. We then look at these from three different disciplinary perspectives: *physical*, *biological* and *social*. We make no attempt to provide a comprehensive coverage of the issues relating to time within each discipline. Instead we look to bring out different disciplinary *flavours* of the conception of time in relation to complex systems. By providing different perspectives and by placing them together, we hope to throw into relief the differences in how time is viewed in different disciplines, and to explore the complementarity of these views, to see if they can provide a broader and richer view of complex systems.

The questions we address are: What can we learn from our narrative expressions of time? What do these expressions reveal about being complex and living in a complex world? How is time expressed and recognised within different disciplinary domains of complex systems research? What do the different disciplinary perspectives offer, as resources, to build a richer narrative of time?

> *I leave to various future times, but not to all, my garden of forking paths.*
> (Jorge Luis Borges, "The Garden of Forking Paths," 1941)

4 "It's All a Matter of Time"

We respond to our questions by listing some expressions of time taken from everyday speech and idioms, commonly known proverbs and sayings. We relate these idioms to temporal concepts in different disciplines with a particular focus on complex systems. The result is a series of small sections that together weave a particular interdisciplinary (hi)story of time in complexity. The story of time we present moves from the more physical notions of time, to the biological, through to more social temporal aspects. This way of delineating the physical, biological and social is artificial: they are all intertwined. Yet to explore the multiple ways that time is intrinsic to complexity, we tell the story of time and complexity in a way that both maintains some fuzzy boundaries between the physical, biological and social, and disrupts them by showing how the multiple aspects of time and temporality leak through all aspects of change. In doing so, we develop a distinctive narrative of time whilst reflexively illustrating that time shapes complex patterns of *being* and *becoming* more generally. As Lakoff and Johnson (1994) argue, metaphors shape the way we think, what we do, and how we experience the world. They also note (p. 131) that "new metaphors have the power to create a new reality". It is in this temporal spirit that we shape our chapter.

> *Time present and time past,*
> *Are both perhaps present in time future,*
> *And time future contained in time past.*
> (T. S. Eliot, "Burnt Norton," *Four Quartets*, 1936)

5 "Working Like Clockwork"

The physics of time has a punctuated history. It starts rather simplistically with Newton, who chiselled time into the bedrock of physical law and set in motion the clockwork universe of Laplace. Newton argued for an absolute time, divorced from the things existing within it. "Absolute, true, and mathematical time, of itself, and from its own nature, flows equably without relation to anything external" (Newton 1999). There is some natural underlying 'clock', ticking away regularly, independent of anything else. The Newtonian worldview is complete: the universe is out there, time is absolute, causality is straightforward; the future is predictable. If we know the system's precise location in its state-space (that is, the positions and velocities of all its particles) and the forces acting, then we can predict its future states. Newtonian physics[1] has laws that are deterministic and time-reversible, and so we can equally well retrodict, and even recreate, the past: take any given state of the system, reverse the direction of time (by reversing the direction of the velocities) and you can go back to past events. The clockwork can run backwards just as well as forwards. This, however, as we discuss below, is counter to our everyday experience of irreversible processes, ones that are not symmetric in time.

> *A clock is a little machine that shuts us out from the wonder of time.*
> (Susan Glaspell and George Cram Cook, *Tickless Time*)

---

[1] As do quantum mechanics (at least up to the point of wavefunction collapse, or many-worlds splitting, or decoherence, or whatever interpretation you prefer) and relativity.

6 "It's Just One Thing After Another"

In contrast to the Newtonian view of absolute time, the relational view of time is that it marks the order in which events occur: *time is an order of successions* (Leibnitz 1717). Time marks the order in which things happen, in which things change. Barbour (2001) states "time is nothing but change". Time does not, and cannot, pass if nothing changes. If something keeps changing, then that gives the means to measure time, and even the definition of time itself. This view of the arbitrariness of time, being merely a relational order, rather than a pre-determined ticking clock, gives us freedom to choose how we mark off the passing moments in the way that is most convenient.

> *Time is defined so that motion looks simple.*
> (Misner, Thorne, and Wheeler, *Gravitation*, 1973)

7 "Time Is Relative"

Einstein's theories of relativity also have deterministic and time-reversible equations. In contrast to Newton's clockwork time, special relativity merges space and time into spacetime (Minkowski 1918). Three-dimensional space and one-dimensional time are unified into a four-dimensional spacetime, where they are, to some degree, interchangeable. In particular, events that are remote in space that look simultaneous in time to one observer may appear to occur in different orders to other observers. General relativity allows gravitational distortions to this spacetime (Einstein 1920). So relativity brings a new view of time that is dependent on the frame of reference of the observer: time is not absolute, but relative. Relativity ushers in a strange world that has captured our imaginations: time dilation, black holes, event horizons.

> *Scientific people [...] know very well that Time is only a kind of Space.*
> (H.G. Wells, *The Time Machine*, 1895)

> *Henceforth space by itself, and time by itself, are doomed to fade away into mere shadows,*
> *and only a kind of union of the two will preserve an independent reality.*
> (H. Minkowski, "Space and Time," 1918)

8 "There's No Time"/"If We Only Had Time"

In special relativity, (space)time seems to be sitting there largely as a given quantity, not amenable or subject to explanation. Barbour (2001) takes this further, and moves from the idea of a system's trajectory through its state-space to a timeless worldline in state-spacetime. He argues that fundamental physics involves developing a model of the Universe that is devoid of time. The focus becomes one of instantaneous interactions (or configurations) that are called "Nows".

Elsewhere[2] Barbour notes, "I suggest that our belief in time and a past arises solely because our entire experience comes to us through the medium of static arrangements of matter, in Nows, that create the appearance of time and change" and "I merely want to suggest that the appearance of time arises exclusively from very special matter configurations which we find can be interpreted as mutually consistent records of processes that unfolded in a past in accordance with definite physical laws that involve time." Such a radical description of a static universe has profound implications for the way that we view the world and for the understanding of our own cognitive processes and places Time right back in the box.

> *The universe is true for us all and dissimilar to each of us.*
> (Marcel Proust, *In Search of Lost Time*, 1927)

9 "You Never Know What Will Happen"

Despite various timeless formulations, the majority of authors agree on the existence of time (Smolin 2013), if not agreeing on what it is.

One particular way of observing time through systems and understanding systems through time is *dynamical systems theory* (Strogatz 2014). Dynamical systems theory is a *deterministic* theory: given the same initial conditions, the same dynamics will unfold. There is no randomness: Laplace's demon can perfectly predict the future from the current state of the world. Even chaotic systems are deterministic. They are however *unpredictable* in all but the short term, as we can never measure the state of the world precisely enough to predict it far into the future.

In contrast, quantum systems have an intrinsic non-deterministic component. Instead of a point moving through state space, they are formulated in terms of a wave function, capturing a *probability distribution*, evolving deterministically through time. When observed, the wave function "collapses"[3] to a specific, but non-deterministic, value.

> *It is very difficult to predict – especially the future.*
> (Niels Bohr, attrib.[4])

10 "There's No Going Back"

Dropping a glass, it falling and smashing; the transfer of the heat from boiling water to a cooler mug; the diffusion of a perfume across a room; these are all natural experiences. All of these processes have an accepted and predictable direction in time. The reverse processes are, in principle, possible, but are very highly improbable: you won't observe them, unless you expend considerable work in effecting the reversal.

---

[2]Both the following quotes from an interview with Julian Barbour by John Brockman on 15/08/99 at https://www.edge.org/conversation/the-end-of-time

[3]According to the Copenhagen interpretation.

[4]For more on the origin of this quote see: https://quoteinvestigator.com/2013/10/20/no-predict/

What provides this directionality, this "arrow" of time? The Second Law of Thermodynamics is one of the few physical laws with a temporal direction: it states that the entropy, or disorder, of a system increases with time.[5] It is an *emergent property* of the underlying time-symmetric laws of motion governing the microscopic states of the system. For things to happen spontaneously there must be an increase in disorder in the universe (which, if extrapolated, inexorably leads to the heat-death of the universe).

Even if one is happy with emergent time-asymmetry, this does not solve all the puzzles of time. The current state of the universe is high entropy relative to the initial state, at the Big Bang, of low entropy, which is a highly unlikely state. Why was the initial state such low entropy? Additionally, many (but not all) cosmological models have the Big Bang as the origin of time itself: there was no "before".

An arrow of time was hypothesised early in evolutionary biology by Dollo in his Principle of Irreversibility: "An organism is unable to return, even partially, to a previous stage already realized in its ancestral series" (Dollo 1893). Modern interpretations use the same sort of probabilistic arguments that underpin the Second Law of Thermodynamics concerning the statistical improbability of systems (organisms) following exactly the same evolutionary trajectory (either forward or reverse) (Dawkins 1986). However, there is increasing evidence that organisms can revert to features thought lost in deep evolutionary time (Wiens 2011). This underpins how the organisation of biological systems, as complex adaptive systems, cannot be thought of as collections of independent particles. They are highly relational entities, whose *structure can hold their history, and this history can be revisited.*

> *Nothing in Biology makes sense except in the light of evolution.*
>   (Theodosius Dobzhansky 1973)

> *Humpty Dumpty sat on the wall*
> *Humpty Dumpty had a great fall*
> *All the king's horses and all the king's men*
> *Couldn't put Humpty together again*
>   (trad.)

11 "It's a Waste of Time"/"Time Stands Still"

Systems where all energy and matter have reached a static distribution and there is no further increase in entropy are in *equilibrium*. Equilibrium is the "natural" state of (isolated) matter. The state of matter "runs downhill" to reach equilibrium, where it is *at rest, static, unchanging*. The system may be perturbed away from equilibrium, but it will return to equilibrium once the perturbation is removed.

Complex systems dynamically exchange energy and increase order (at least locally), so they are *non-equilibrium systems*. Prigogine developed non-equilibrium

---

[5]More precisely, the entropy of a *closed* system does not *decrease* with time.

thermodynamics (Prigogine and Stengers 1985) and found a key new organising principle, the *dissipative structure*: a dynamic flow (flux) of energy or matter which maintains a stable form, such as a vortex. This provides a new physical view that supports and complements studies of complex adaptive systems. Dissipative structures allow us to make sense of how order can develop and be maintained within apparent chaos.

Systems far-from-equilibrium might *appear* static and unchanging, but such a system is actively maintaining itself in this *non-equilibrium homeostatic* state; it is constantly "walking up a down escalator". This takes expenditure of inflowing energy and produces entropy: *waste*. This apparent static nature can lead to a false sense of lack of change; a change then to inflows or outflows can have a surprisingly large effect. Restoring the inflows and outflows to their previous values may not necessarily return the system to its previous homeostatic state: a manifestation of *hysteresis*.

In Biology, evolution takes place over time. However, the notion of stasis draws attention to the fact that there can be periods where there is little evidence of change (Eldredge et al. 2005). A system's own timescale can often be defined by the period that it appears static. On longer timescales it will change: grow, develop, reproduce, die; its apparent "balance" is on a particular timescale only.

> *Now, here, you see, it takes all the running you can do, to keep in the same place.*
> (Lewis Carroll, *Through the Looking-Glass and What Alice Found There*, 1871)

> *"Is there any point to which you would wish to draw my attention?"*
> *"To the curious incident of the dog in the night-time."*
> *"The dog did nothing in the night-time."*
> *"That was the curious incident,"* remarked Sherlock Holmes.
> (Arthur Conan Doyle, "Silver Blaze," *Memoirs of Sherlock Holmes*, 1894)

12   "Any Path Will Take You There"

Although complex systems are always changing, they do so in particular ways. *State space*[6] is a fundamental concept here, as is the related notion of attractors. State space is an abstract mathematical space of many dimensions. Consider a system of many particles existing in real space and moving with time. Combine all their positions and velocities into a single point in a multi-dimensional state space. The movement of this point in the state space, its *trajectory*, describes the dynamics of the entire system (Strogatz 2014).

In some systems, the long term history of a trajectory is confined to a small region of the state space: the *attractor* of the trajectory. Some attractors are point, or simple orbits, indicating a stable history. Other *strange* attractors exhibit a complex fractal structure, indicating a chaotic history, including properties such as *sensitive*

---

[6]*State space* is also called *phase space* in Physics. See also Stepney, Chap. 3 of this volume.

dependence on initial conditions (Lorenz 1963). The trajectory may have some initial *transient* behaviour before it is confined within the attractor. Systems continually perturbed by environmental inputs may never reach an attractor, but be perpetually transient.

> *When all's said and done, all roads lead to the same end. So it's not so much which road you take, as how you take it.*
> (Charles de Lint, *Greenmantle*, 1998)

13 "Ups and Downs; Fast and Slow"

Living systems tend to be organised in hierarchies (Miller 1978). Lower levels (such as molecules, cells) can be maintained and enhanced through the emergence of higher order structures (such as tissues, organs). The system (e.g., organism) operates as a whole, with properties that emerge from the lower level subsystems, but which can in turn influence lower level behaviour (through downward causation). Such systems are not just structural hierarchies, but exhibit exquisite orchestration of events across a wide spectrum of *timescales* (Noble 2008).

A timescale might be said to be a measure of time that naturally encompasses a particular change. It forms a natural unit with which to measure the rate of that change. For example, a day, a week, a season, a year, an electoral cycle, a generation, a lifetime; social, historical, archaeological, evolutionary, geological, astronomical timescales.

A complex system necessarily has multiple timescales: at least the local timescales of the component parts, and the global timescale of the whole system. The latter is typically larger than the former. For example, the millisecond timescale of bacterial chemotaxis emerges from molecular motions on the one millionth of a billionth of a second timescale. Likewise, a country's historical change emerges from, and tends to be slower than, that of its neighbourhoods. But complex systems do not exist one within another; there will be several interacting systems nested within a higher-level system. Thus, there are several cities in a country; each city has its own particular timescale of change, and they change in interdependent ways, even if they change in antagonistic ways and in different ways.

When timescales of levels are well separated, the levels below move so fast that their motion "blurs", and the components can be treated as a relatively homogeneous blurred substrate. Contrariwise, the levels above are so slow they can often be treated as essentially static. When timescales are not so well separated, or when a system is examined over large multiples of its own timescale, such approximations are no longer valid, and fluctuations in the faster system, and changes in the slower system, become important. Extrapolations that assume a static upper (or lower) level can be badly wrong.

Additionally, in heterogeneous systems, different components at ostensibly the same "level" might have very different timescales. For example, the evolutionary timescale of viruses is similar to the individual adaptation timescale (rather than the species evolutionary timescale) of people (Zanini et al. 2015).

People in a system will tend to privilege their own timescales of experience: from about a second to about a generation. Even then, children and old people have different perceptions of time. Timescales faster and slower than these are essentially imperceptible to people, except intellectually, or by use of technology such as slow motion and time-lapse photography. Such technologies can radically alter human perception of things by viewing them at different timescales; for example, clouds viewed through time lapse photography can change in conception from relatively static *objects* to highly dynamic *processes*. Furthermore, the introduction of technology can change the timescale of part of the system (for example, automating a previously manual process), which can cause issues (for example, a trading "flash crash") if other interacting components are still working at their previous timescales.

Time goes through multiple times.
  (attrib. to Khalid Masood)

14 "Deep Time"

Complex systems can have multiple timescales, which suggests the need for multiple narratives, or at least nested narratives. How can a narrative span multiple timescales, including ones beyond natural human comprehension?

Histories clearly can encompass multi-generational timescales. There are several science fiction stories that attempt to encompass *deep time* by having "human scale" vignettes scattered along a vast timescale: Wells' *The Time Machine*, Stapledon's *Last and First Men*, Sheffield's *Tomorrow and Tomorrow*, and more. Yet even these tend to have only the two timescales: the human one, and a massively longer one.

My vegetable love should grow
Vaster than empires and more slow
  (Andrew Marvell, "To His Coy Mistress," [1681], in 1991)

The summit of Mt. Everest is marine limestone.
  (John McPhee, *Basin and Range*, 1981)

15 "Everything That Goes Around Comes Around"/"The More Things Change, the More They Stay the Same"

When patterns of change in a system persist over time in the midst of many dynamic processes, this is the signature of the coupling processes, of *feedback*. Feedback is the mechanism that affords control of a system whereby a change in level of a stock[7]

---

[7]"Stocks are the elements of the system that you can see, feel, count, or measure at any given time" (Meadows 2008, p. 17).

affects the rate of that stock's input or output processes. As Meadows puts it: "A feedback loop is a closed chain of causal connections from a stock, through a set of decisions or rules or physical laws or actions that are dependent on the level of the stock, and back again through a flow to change the stock" (2008, p. 27). Complex systems emerge from and consist of feedback. As Jay Forrester[8] notes:

> Systems of information-feedback control are fundamental to all life and human endeavor, from the slow pace of biological evolution to the launching of the latest space satellite ... Everything we do as individuals, as an industry, or as a society is done in the context of an information-feedback system. (Forrester 1961, p. 15)

> *You can drive a system crazy by muddying its information streams.*
> (Donella H. Meadows, *Thinking in Systems*, 2008)

16   "It's a Vicious/Virtuous Cycle"

Feedbacks can be balancing (negative feedback) and serve to keep stocks stable (with a given range). This is useful in maintaining the *buffering* effect of stocks, allowing more freedom in the operation of system processes. Feedbacks can also be reinforcing (positive feedback), serving to amplify the rate of change of stocks (either increasing or decreasing) (Maruyama 1963). Feedback can lead to vicious or virtuous cycles. These can be useful when you need sub-systems to grow, or replicate, or die, but if not carefully controlled they can lead to system-level instability, or destruction.

> *We are not going in circles, we are going upwards.*
> *The path is a spiral; we have already climbed many steps.*
> (Hermann Hesse, *Siddhartha*, 1922)

17   "Which Came First, the Chicken or the Egg?"

We live in a world of interlocked loops of causality, since most complex systems have *multiple feedback loops*. Here the things of interest being described in such systems are not instantaneous events, but temporally extended objects and processes. D affects E, which in turn affects D, which then affects E, contrary to a simplistic linear causal description. It might not make sense to ask if D *causes* E or *vice versa*: they mutually cause each other through feedback. *Downward causation* (Campbell 1974) is where a high level emergent property affects the low level components comprising it, for example in the case of Darwinian evolution (Ellis 2012); it can be thought of as a form of feedback causation across emergent levels.

---

[8]Jay Forrester, founder of *system dynamics*: the modelling of complex organisations through "causal loop" diagrams and their behaviour through computer simulation.

We, as organisms, are constructed from the material of the environment through myriad coupled processes that serve to orchestrate the production. We make ourselves, and continually *remake* ourselves, as we develop, maintain and ultimately decay. We exist as recurring sets of patterns of material organisation that are self-making and self-reproducing: *autopoietic systems* (Varela et al. 1974).

We are deeply coupled with the world around us: the environment we live in, with its intrinsic dynamics, affects our own dynamics; equally, we affect the environment and can change its dynamics (as we are becoming increasingly aware). A natural consequence of this deep systemic view is that we and our environment are part of one holistic system: a *dependent co-arising* (Macy 1991).

This deep coupling, the feedback loops, the downward causation, the continual remaking, this "loopiness" of time, can lead to a feeling of loss of the time dimension: there is no trivial linearisation that captures these properties of complex systems. We wonder if this may be a factor in why complex systems cannot be (trivially) narrated.

> *You cannot step twice into the same river.*
> (attrib. to Heraclitus)

> *True voyage is return.*
> (Ursula K. Le Guin, *The Dispossessed*, 1974)

> *Cosmos is a Greek word for the order of the universe. It is, in a way, the opposite of Chaos. It implies the deep interconnectedness of all things. It conveys awe for the intricate and subtle way in which the universe is put together.*
> (Carl Sagan, *Cosmos*, 1980)

18   "It Will All Come Together in the End"/"It's Not Where You Start, It's Where You Finish"

A key feature of complex systems is that they contain multiple, dynamic interactions and seemingly offer a large number of ways to change. There are myriad potential states that they could visit. However, many complex systems exhibit *equifinality*: the phenomenon that some systems, despite (and because of) their complexity, are able to consistently move towards well defined (recognisable) end states. The classic example is biological development: where the genetic regulation required for complex developmental processes is under strong feedback-driven control, and this can keep the developmental trajectory on course to its next (or end) state.

While equifinality assumes that there are many pathways to the same outcome, the *multifinality* principle states that essentially the same initial conditions can end up in very different outcomes, for example, due to the butterfly effect.

> *You can cut all the flowers but you cannot keep Spring from coming*
> (attrib. to Pablo Neruda)

19   "Things Get Worse Before They Get Better"

In complex systems, change is often non-linear and transitions occur in periods of instability, of turbulence and through critical fluctuations (Haken et al. 1985). The parameters or variables that influence or drive a system through different states may reach critical values and become unstable before the whole system can reorganize into a new state (Bak et al. 1987; Haken 1977). Disorder, then, tends to precede (new kinds of) order. It is said that for some systems the more adaptive regimes are near the *edge of chaos*[9] where there is sufficient diversity, complexity and instability for novelty to emerge through fluctuations, but also sufficient stability for some things to stay the same so we still recognise a given system as the same, even though transformed. Systems poised in critical states are thought to maximise their opportunities for change, bringing in the powerful concept of the *adjacent possible* (Kaufmann 2000).

Biology provides interesting examples of systems harnessing disorder as staging posts towards increasing complexity. In metamorphosis, developing organisms can completely change their body plan in "catastrophic" changes, such as the disintegration, digestion and reabsorption of their body in prior developmental stages (Ryan 2011). Evolution towards criticality is now associated with the emergence of collective behaviour in biological systems (Hidalgo et al. 2014), suggesting that it is an effective way of surviving in our uncertain world.

History presents many examples of how periods of instability and crises were critical for the emergence of new social orders. The progression of revolutions has been likened to a "fever" associated with different symptoms such as the breakdown of government control, the emergence of radicals, etc. (Brinton 1953). Brinton claims that revolution "in itself is a good thing ... for the organism that survives it ... The revolution destroys wicked people and harmful and useless institutions". The notion of revolution is closely associated with creativity and technology, as in *disruptive innovation* (Christensen 1997).

> *There are decades where nothing happens; and there are weeks where decades happen.*
> (Vladimir Lenin, in Friedman, 2014)

> *We are sorry for the inconvenience, but this is a revolution.*
> (attrib. to Subcomandante Marcos, 1994)

---

[9]An influential name attributed to J. Doyne Farmer, one of the original *Dynamical Systems Collective* at UC Santa Cruz.

20 "It Depends How You Look at It"/"Give It Time"/ "Things Might Look Different in Time"

How time is known and experienced individually and collectively is always and necessarily a messy mixture of (at least) three different domains of time: physical, biological and social. Whilst physical and biological aspects of time are necessarily part of human existence and are therefore relevant to social time, so much of how the social world is shaped and experienced is driven by socially constructed notions of time. Age, for example, is real in its inevitable 'arrow' of increased years, but the extent to which 'childhood' and 'adulthood' are experienced as such is dependent on the ways that these age-related phenomena are constructed socially and historically.

For example, Monday is but a moment in time, but the naming of this moment as 'Monday' gives it meaning and order which are inherently social concepts, constructed to help social order. Thus, even if we accept that 'that Friday feeling' has more to do with the social meaning of the end of the work week and the beginning of the weekend and less to do with physical or biological time, the fact that 'that Friday feeling' is experienced as real means that it is a social time that is worth exploring, since it is likely to impact on the way that everyday social life unfolds. The fact that 'that Friday feeling' may be experienced differently by a 20-year-old compared to a 70-year-old doesn't make Friday less real; on the contrary, it suggests that the social meaning and experience of 'that Friday feeling' is also shaped by the biological necessity of ageing and its impact on how we understand, live and exist *in* and *with* time all the time.

In the mix is the fascinating work on differences in time perception in human cognition (Grondin 2008). Factors such as emotional state, age, drugs, and disease can radically alter perceptions of time and tempo. Relationships can lead to interlocking and distortion of time perception in individuals. It is intriguing to wonder about larger-scale, community and societal, manifestations. Thus, a key challenge for our connected world is to gain a better understanding of the temporal coupling of our interlocking ecological, economic, social and health systems and of our perception of their timescales.

> *Time is the wisest of all things that are; for it brings everything to light.*
> (Thales, in Barker, 2001)

21 "Time Goes, Death Comes"

Decay, death and dying are intrinsic to all complex systems. If systems do not adapt, then they will die. Death is, in many ways, the ultimate state change, the final attractor. If there is nothing more to *become*, then it already became. The finality of death and dying is but another necessary rhythm of all complex systems.

22 "Winding Down"/"Looking Back in Time"

We have explored everyday expressions reflecting our embodied experience of time in the complex world, and used three lenses to understand what complex processes could be implicated or have a correspondence in the physical, biological and the social worlds.

We leave the reader with the following questions: How could narratives, as ways of not just representing and describing but of constructing the world, teach us about its complexity and its possibilities? Can we capture the necessary multiple perspectives on complex systems through multiple complex narratives? Does the essential "loopy" feedback nature of complex systems resist narrative? Are there other ways that narratives could assist science as tools or means for eliciting the kind of surprise and questioning that calls for abducting reasoning, nurturing and supporting a pathway of discovery and novel scientific exploration? Could the practice of living and enacting our world through narrative means create the playground of rehearsal and exploration that supports the kind of creativity that comes from playing and stretching the boundaries of our current constructions? Could new movements of research unfold through narrating the complex living world as experienced and enacted by our complex humanity?

Only time could tell. And that, it seemed, it disdained to do.
    (Ralph C. Glisson, "From Competition 2: Blurbs in Excess," *The Magazine of Fantasy and Science Fiction*, July 1972)

23 "All Happy Endings Are Beginnings as Well"

So, we end our beginning: a brief look at time, which we hope may catalyse some reflections and projections, in recurrent reveries, encapsulated in the recognition of this moment and its adjacent possible.

Now this is not the end. It is not even the beginning of the end.
But it is, perhaps, the end of the beginning.
    (Winston S. Churchill, 1942)[10]

Acknowledgment Ana Teixeira de Melo is supported by Fundação para a Ciência e Tecnologia, Portugal. This work was supported by a post-doctoral fellowship awarded by the Fundação para a Ciência e Tecnologia (SFRH/BPD/77781/2011), hosted by the Centre for Social Studies, University of Coimbra and Faculty of Psychological and Education Sciences of the University of Coimbra, Portugal.

---

[10]In a speech at the Lord Mayor's Day luncheon at the Mansion House, London, 10 November 1942.

References

Bak P, Tang C, Wiesenfeld K (1987) Self-organized criticality: an explanation of the 1/f noise. Phys Rev Lett 59(4):381–384

Barbour J (2001) The end of time: the next revolution in physics. Oxford University Press, Oxford

Barker W (2001) The adages of Erasmus. University of Toronto Press, Toronto

Borges JL (1941) The garden of forking paths. Penguin, London

Brinton CC (1953) The anatomy of revolution. Vintage Books, New York

Campbell DT (1974) 'Downward Causation' in hierarchically organised biological systems. In: Ayala FJ, Dobzhansky T (eds) Studies in the philosophy of biology: reduction and related problems. Macmillian, Basingstoke, pp 179–186

Carroll L (1871) Through the looking-glass and what Alice found there. Macmillan, London

Christensen CM (1997) The innovator's dilemma: when new technologies cause great firms to fail. Harvard Business School Press, Boston, MA

Dawkins R (1986) The blind watchmaker: why the evidence of evolution reveals a universe without design. W.W. Norton, New York

de Lint C (1998) Greenmantle. Orb Books/Macmillan, New York

Dobzhansky T (1973) Nothing in biology makes sense except in the light of evolution. Am Biol Teach 35(3):125–129

Dollo L (1893) The laws of evolution. Bull Soc Bel Geol Paleontol 7:164–166

Doyle AC (1894) Silver blaze. In: Memoirs of Sherlock Holmes. Newnes, London

Einstein A (1920) Relativity: the special and general theory. Penguin, Harmondsworth

Eldredge N, Thompson JN, Brakefield PM (2005) The dynamics of evolutionary stasis. Paleobiology 31(2):133–145

Eliot TS (1936) Burnt Norton. In: Four quartets. Faber and Faber, London

Ellis GFR (2012) Top-down causation and emergence: some comments on mechanisms. Interface Focus 2(1):126–140

Forrester JW (1961) Industrial dynamics. MIT Press, Cambridge, MA

Friedman SL (2014) "There are decades where nothing happens; and there are weeks where decades happen" – Vladimir Ilyich Lenin. J Hepatol 60(3):471–472

Grondin S (2008) Psychology of time. Emerald Group, Bingley

Haken H (1977) Synergetics. An introduction. Nonequilibrium phase transitions and self-organization in physics, chemistry, and biology. Springer, Heidelberg

Haken H, Kelso JA, Bunz H (1985) A theoretical model of phase transitions in human hand movements. Biol Cybern 51(5):347–356

Hesse H (1922) Siddhartha. New Directions Publishing, New York

Hidalgo J, Grilli J, Suweis S, Muñoz MA, Banavar JR, Maritan A (2014) Information-based fitness and the emergence of criticality in living systems. Proc Natl Acad Sci USA 111(28):10095–10100

Kaufmann S (2000) Investigations. Oxford University Press, New York

Lakoff G, Johnson M (1994) Metaphors we live by. In: Kollock P, O'Brien J (eds) The production of reality: essays and readings in social psychology, The Pine Forge Press Social Science Library. Pine Forge Press, Newbury park, CA

Le Guin UK (1974) The dispossessed. Harper and Brown, New York

Leibnitz GW (1717) Leibnitz's third letter to Samuel Clarke. Mr Leibnitz's third paper. http://www.newtonproject.sussex.ac.uk/view/texts/normalized/THEM00230

Lorenz EN (1963) Deterministic nonperiodic flow. J Atmos Sci 20(2):130–141

Macy J (1991) Mutual causality in Buddhism and general systems theory: the dharma of natural systems. SUNY Press, New York

Maruyama M (1963) The second cybernetics. Deviation-amplifying mutual causal processes. Am Sci 5(2):164–179

Marvell A (1991) Oxford authors: Andrew Marvell. Oxford University Press, Oxford

McPhee J (1981) Basin and range. Farrar, Straus & Giroux Inc, New York

Meadows DH (2008) Thinking in systems: a primer. Chelsea Green Publishing, Vermont

Miller JG (1978) Living systems. McGraw-Hill, New York

Minkowski H (1918) Space and time (trans: Carus EH). Monist 28:288–302

Misner CW, Thorne KS, Wheeler JA (1973) Gravitation. W.H. Freeman, New York

Newton I (1999) The principia: mathematical principles of natural philosophy (trans: Cohen B, Whitman A). University of California Press, Berkeley. Originally published in 1687

Noble D (2008) The music of life: biology beyond genes. Oxford University Press, Oxford

Prigogine I, Stengers I (1985) Order out of Chaos: man's new dialogue with nature. Flamingo, London

Proust M (1927) In search of lost time. Penguin, London

Ryan F (2011) Metamorphosis: unmasking the mystery of how life transforms. Oneworld Publications, Oxford

Sagan C (1980) Cosmos. Random House, New York

Smolin L (2013) Time reborn: from the crisis in physics to the future of the universe. Penguin, London

Strogatz SH (2014) Nonlinear dynamics and chaos: with applications to physics, biology, chemistry, and engineering, 2nd edn. Westview Press, Boulder, CO.

Varela FG, Maturana HR, Uribe R (1974) Autopoiesis: the organization of living systems, its characterization and a model. Biosystems 5(4):187–196

Wells HG (1895) The time machine. William Heinemann, London

Wiens JJ (2011) Re-evolution of lost mandibular teeth in frogs after more than 200 million years, and re-evaluating Dollo's law. Evol Int J Org Evol 65(5):1283–1296

Zanini F, Brodin J, Thebo L, Lanz C, Bratt G, Albert J, Neher RA (2015) Population genomics of intrapatient HIV-1 evolution. eLife 4(December). https://doi.org/10.7554/eLife.11282

Chapter 20
Discussion and Comment (Time Will Tell)

Richard Walsh, Leo Caves, Ana Teixeira de Melo, Susan Stepney, and Emma Uprichard

Abstract Richard Walsh, Leo Caves, Ana Teixeira de Melo, Susan Stepney, and Emma Uprichard in discussion on an earlier version of "Time Will Tell: Narrative Expressions of Time in a Complex World"

RW: There's a lot of food for thought in this draft chapter, and I think in general it does a great job of expounding a lot of difficult ideas. At the moment it suffers from its raw status as a combination of three drafts; I like the structural progression from the physical to the biological to the social, but the degree of overlap suggests that this might not be the best top-level organizing principle for the chapter: it might be better pursued within each of a number of sub-topics.

Authors: Yes, that was very much a first draft, prior to integration. We have taken those original draft sections, and woven their contents together into a more fine-grained series of time-related discussions you see here.

RW: You say that the arrow of time *"is an emergent property of the underlying time-symmetric laws of motion governing the microscopic states of the*

R. Walsh (✉)
Department of English and Related Literature, University of York, York, UK

Interdisciplinary Centre for Narrative Studies, University of York, York, UK
e-mail: richard.walsh@york.ac.uk

L. Caves
Independent Researcher, Sao Felix da Marinha, Portugal

York Cross-disciplinary Centre for Systems Analysis, University of York, York, UK

A. T. de Melo
Centre for Social Studies, University of Coimbra, Coimbra, Portugal

S. Stepney
York Cross-disciplinary Centre for Systems Analysis, University of York, York, UK

Department of Computer Science, University of York, York, UK

E. Uprichard
Centre for Interdisciplinary Methodologies, University of Warwick, Warwick, UK

© Springer Nature Switzerland AG 2018
R. Walsh, S. Stepney (eds.), *Narrating Complexity*,
https://doi.org/10.1007/978-3-319-64714-2_20

system" then "*Even if one is happy with emergent time-asymmetry ...*". So, the first statement is not the matter of fact it appears to be? It seems to assume a fundamental reciprocal relation between temporality and systemic processes.

Authors: Historically the statement caused a huge rumpus in the physics community, which may have been a factor in Boltzmann's depression and suicide. Today it is more accepted, but there is still a struggle to understand how asymmetry arises from symmetry. Some of the problem has been pushed back to the Big Bang itself: the universe must have been in a very low entropy state then, but why?

RW: And then you say: "*The reverse processes are, in principle, possible, but are very highly improbable: you won't observe them, unless you expend considerable work in effecting the reversal.*" So the issue is not one of conceptual asymmetry, but of practical feasibility?

Authors: This depends on the "level". At the micro, non-emergent level, everything is reversible in principle, yes. But it is completely infeasible in practice, except maybe in certain contrived scenarios. However, at the time-asymmetric emergent level, where the Second Law holds sway, there is no access to the individual particles in order to reverse their courses, so it is not even possible here.

RW: You say that Newtonian determinism allows us to "*retrodict the past*". Is this actually the case? For example, if you add two numbers together I can tell you with certainty what the total will be, but I can't tell from the total which specific numbers you added.

Authors: You are quite right: determinism alone is not sufficient for retrodiction. We have added "*and time-reversible laws*" to our description. Such laws mean that the system does not *lose information*: in your example enough information would be retained that you could recover the original numbers. Interestingly, this is a feature of quantum computing: it is reversible (retains enough information to run backwards) whereas classical computing is not (it loses information in the manner of your example). Systems that are deterministic, but lose information are called *dissipative systems*. Such systems end up on an attractor, but you cannot determine what their specific transient behaviour was before that.

RW: You say "*Relativity ushers in a strange world that has captured our imaginations: time dilation, black holes, event horizons.*" Some elaboration is needed to bring out the relevance of these concepts.

Authors: We would love to do this, but unfortunately the section would get too
          long and unwieldy. However, we leave in the sentence, to help show
          there is even more non-intuitive time lurking in the physics.
RW: You mention causation due to feedback in one place, and downwards
          causation in another. Is downwards causation a case of feedback
          causation, or something else?
Authors: That's a very nice way of putting it. Feedback causation is typically
          thought of as between "peer" processes, A causing B and B causing A
          in a sort of feedback leapfrog through time. Downward causation is
          between *levels*: an emergent high level influencing its lower level
          components. This statement can get physicists upset! However,
          thinking of it as a form of feedback causation across emergent levels,
          involving not instantaneous events, but time-extended processes, helps
          remove some of the controversy.
RW: *"People in a system will naturally privilege their own timescales of
          experience"*: these privileged experiential timescales constitute the
          cognitive basis for narrative logic.
Authors: That's an interesting link, thank you. This is exactly the kind of insight
          we wanted to get from this book project! So, if we are wanting complex
          narratives in order to tackle complex systems, we are going to need a
          way of handling widely differing, and non-human-level, timescales.
RW: *"We wonder if this may be a factor in why complex systems cannot be
          (trivially) narrated."* I think this is right: narration (even self-narration)
          adopts an external perspective on its object. The issue here is not just that
          of sequence *versus* loop, but that of perspectivalism. Similarly: *"Can we
          capture the necessary multiple perspectives on complex systems"* raises a
          key point of the larger book-level discussion: how to evade the
          constraints of perspectivalism. Does having multiple narratives do it?
Authors: Maybe. Probably not quite, but that's ok. If we assume that complex
          systems are always simultaneously both 'wholes' and 'parts' and that we
          may only capture 'moments', then we might also assume that like an
          orchestra of orchestras, there are always multiple partial rhythms that
          need to be narrated. Multiple narratives are certainly key to narrating
          complex systems, but they can only ever be partial.
RW: *"How can a narrative span multiple timescales, including ones beyond
          natural human comprehension?"* There is a lot of potential and
          precedent for messing around with timescales within a narrative, or
          between narratives; but does this address the presuppositions of
          narrative logic?
Authors: Perhaps that depends on the narrative logic inscribed within what we
          consider to be comprehensive and tangible timescales?

Chapter 21
Periodisation

Jason Edwards

Abstract 'Periodisation' considers the complex way in which time is experienced and described, autobiographically, historically, and epochally. It performatively lays out alongside and on top of each other numerous ways of conceiving time, some of them overlapping, some of them contradictory, some of them perspectival. Their relation may be linear, as in certain models of sequential time, and also stratigraphical, to signal a deeper time. As in a complex system, all of the elements are meant to be inter-related, and held in the mind at once. This particular system, however, is mortal, entropic, and ends in death Period.

The 18th century.
The 19th century.
The 20th century.
The 21st century.

The long 18th century.
The short 19th century.

18th-century studies.
19th-century studies.
Victorian studies.

The hungry 1840s.
The swinging 1860s.
The fin-de-siecle.
The turn of the century.
The long 1990s.

The Agrarian revolution.
The Industrial revolution.
The French Revolution.
The American Revolution.

J. Edwards (✉)
Department of History of Art, University of York, York, UK

Interdisciplinary Centre for Modern Studies, University of York, York, UK
e-mail: jason.edwards@york.ac.uk

© Springer Nature Switzerland AG 2018
R. Walsh, S. Stepney (eds.), *Narrating Complexity*,
https://doi.org/10.1007/978-3-319-64714-2_21

289

The Russian Revolution.
The Cultural Revolution.
The Velvet Revolution.
Reform.

Pre-war.
Post-war.
The Napoleonic Wars.
The Crimean War.
The American Civil War.
The First and Second Afghan Wars.
The Boer War.
The First World War.
The Second World War.
Vietnam.
The First Gulf War.
The Second Gulf War.
The War on Terror.
Perpetual War.
War? What is it good for? Absolutely nothing.

Neoclassicism. Romanticism. Historicism. Eclecticism. Realism. Pre-Raphaelitism. Aestheticism. Impressionism. Naturalism. Symbolism. Futurism. Cubism. Imagism. Vorticism. Surrealism. Abstraction. Pop. Conceptual Art.

Proto-modernism.
Modernism.
Post-modernism.
Post-post-modernism.

Chronocentrism.
À la recherche du temps perdu.

Modernism/Modernity.
Early Modernity. Modernity. Post-modernity. Late Capitalism.

The water cycle. The weather system.
The Holocaust. The Contemporary. The Anthropocene.
The capitalist world-system.

On October 14th 1971, Jason Edwards was born.
Or, historicism. Or, New historicism.

Nationalism.
Regionalism.
Imperialism.
Cosmopolitanism.
Post-colonialism.
Post-post-colonialism.
Post-feminism.

The global. The local. The glocal. The ecological.

Creation, evolution, adaptation, extinction.
The struggle for life, the survival of the fittest.
The rear guard.
The avant-garde.
Eugenics. Neoliberalism.

Humanism. Post-humanism.
The para-human. The proto-human. The peri-human.
What kind of experience of time does my cat have?
Does it know it's in 2018? Does it care?
Does it matter? Why does it matter?

Structuralism. Post-structuralism.
Marxism. Feminism. Queer theory. Deconstruction.
Theory. Theory after theory.
Theory after theory after theory, or the market.
Theory after theory after theory, or creativity.

The synchronic. The diachronic. The geocultural. The spatial turn.

Linear time, clock time, deep time, planetary time, cyclical time.
The big bang.

Men's time, women's time, queer time.
My turn, your turn.
Labour time, leisure.
Remember leisure?
Work time, guilt time.
Gin o'clock.

Birth order.
Birth, infancy, childhood adolescence, marriage.
The bildungsroman.
Apprenticeship, early career, mid career, late career, retirement.
Remember retirement?
Death.
Or, dependency, relationality, precarity, intersubjectivity, codependency, dependency, death.

The ordinary, everyday and quotidian.
Complexity, death, and nothingness.

Prefigurations. After-lives. Half-lives.
Hauntology. Futurology.
Hopes, fears, expectations, demands, disappointment.
How do you feel about time?
Daytime? Nightime? Anytime? Everytime? All the friggin' time? Contact time?

Autumn, spring and summer terms. What no winter term?
Week 1, week 2, week 3, week 4, week 5, week 6, week 7, week 8, week 9, week 10.
Reading week.
Week minus one? Week zero? Week eleven?
The 'Long vacation'?
Death.

The 37.5 hour week. The 40 hour week. Another twelve hour day.
You will be expected to work every minute that your manager wants or needs you to. Good
    luck with that.

Time well spent, time wasted.

Chronology, the anachronistic, the anachronic. The a-chronic. The anti-chronic.
Chronic and contagious diseases.

Quote: History is a nightmare from which I am trying to awake.
Sorry, what period do you work on?
Have you got your period?
How much does your period cost?
How much is your period worth?
Who cares about context when you've got the object?
Marxist history is, like, so over.
Cultural history is, like, so gay.

Why should we care about this now?
Who cares?

Russian formalism. Semiotics. New criticism. Structuralism. Post-structuralism.
Historicism. Formalism. New formalism. Novel formalisms.
The uniform. The multiform. Conforming. The deformed.

History, memory, nostalgia, camp.

Contextualisation, decontextualisation, recontextualisation.
Territorialisation, deterritorialisation, reterritorialisation.

The contemporary. The present tense.
The present, relaxed.

Close your eyes.
I'm serious.
Close your eyes.
Take a deep breath in.
Take a deep breath out.
Take a deep breath in.
Take a deep breath out.
Remember to keep breathing.
Conclusion: Death.
Period.

Part III
Analysis and Synthesis

Chapter 22
Commentary on Contributions

Richard Walsh and Susan Stepney

Abstract In this chapter we discuss each of the essays presented in Part II of this volume, under the following headings: (1) overview; (2) complexity; (3) narrative; (4) narrating complexity.

1 When Robots Tell Each Other Stories (Winfield, Chap. 4)

1.1 Overview

Winfield has designed a robot control architecture that can anticipate future events by building and running simulations of possible futures. In his chapter here, he proposes exploiting and augmenting this architecture to allow these possible futures, and other invented scenarios, to be interpreted as, and communicated as, *stories*.

1.2 Complexity

The form of complexity Winfield describes in his chapter is a social, recursive type. He describes a control architecture that allows a robot to make decisions about its future actions, and then shows how, with very minor additions, that could become an architecture for social robot learning through narrative.

R. Walsh (✉)
Department of English and Related Literature, University of York, York, UK

Interdisciplinary Centre for Narrative Studies, University of York, York, UK
e-mail: richard.walsh@york.ac.uk

S. Stepney
Department of Computer Science, University of York, York, UK

York Centre for Complex Systems Analysis, York, UK

Fig. 22.1 Red's model of the world includes itself, its environment, and other robots, possibly including the fact that itself and the others have (potentially different) internal models of the world (but not to infinite regress). Robot images © Julianne D. Halley; used with permission

The control architecture is recursive, in that it includes a model of the world that the robot can use to generate and test potential actions. That model includes a model of the robot itself (so that it can determine how it would act and respond in those scenarios), and includes models of other robots, so that it could similarly determine how they might act and respond in a joint scenario.

The model of robot selves might be quite simple, or more complex: I (robot) have a model of the world that includes myself; my model of myself might therefore include its own model of my model of the world (depending how complex my models are). Similarly, my model of the world includes models of other robots; my models of the other robots might include the fact that they have a model of the world that includes a model of myself. And so on. We readily get the possibility of a model being able to include chains of "I know that you know that I know that ..." (Fig. 22.1).

Complexity also arises from the suggested narrative process itself, and the way that impinges on the robot's internal world model. That model essentially encapsulates the robot's "beliefs" about the external world, including about itself and others. The robot can experience things in the world; it can update its internal world model based on the experience; it can remember the experience for later use; it can generate-and-test ("imagine") experiences; it can update its model based on imagined experiences; it can tell real or imagined experiences to others; it can remember real or imagined tales of others; it can update its model from the real or imagined tales of others. The task of determining precisely *why* the robot's internal world model now has the particular form it does, why it now believes what it does about the world, given the events and stories it has experienced and produced, could rapidly become complex.

1.3   Narrative

Let's assume that these robots can be programmed to make statements based on their world models: that seems relatively straightforward. Can they be programmed to *tell stories*, as opposed to uttering simple strings of declarative statements? What, from the computational point of view, is the difference in the grammatical and semantic structure of a story from that of a collection of declarative statements? If the robots can be so programmed, can they then use their stories as a part of the way they make sense of their world? If this could be done, or at the very least, experimented with, it would be an exciting first step towards getting computational experimental evidence in favour of the narrative sensemaking hypothesis about human cognition.

1.4   Narrating Complexity

The robots as described would initially be telling very simple stories: "I saw Red down by the river yesterday. I haven't seen Red since then." "Blue pushed Red in the river yesterday." But as we have seen, the essential recursive nature of the robot's architecture gives the potential for its stories to grow in complexity and sophistication, as robots imagine (run scenarios of counterfactual worlds containing robots imaging scenarios), tell stories, retell stories, embellish stories, and so on. What is compelling about this approach is the way that the robot's internal world model is somehow related to the narratives it can tell, and the fact that experimenters would have access to that internal model. This approach offers the opportunity to correlate the complexity and structure of the world model with the complexity and structure of the associated narratives. There is the potential to experiment with a variety of complex world models to discover the kinds of narratives each produces.

2   Sense and Wonder (Walsh, Chap. 5)

2.1   Overview

Walsh considers the limitations of narrative representation of complex processes to constitute a horizon of our ability to make cognitive sense, but notes the way complexity confronts us with an awareness of kinds of sense, or order, we cannot grasp. He explores, through the relation between sense and wonder, the possibility that narratives can offer an acquaintance with complexity in a sense beyond the usual scope of cognition.

2.2 Complexity

The focus here is upon emergent behaviour, and the tension between the respect in which it is readily graspable in cognitive narrative terms as a systemic phenomenon, and the respect in which it is evidently the product of interactions within the system that exceed such a mode of understanding. Definitions of emergence have sometimes sought to incorporate this tension as intrinsic to the phenomenon, with odd results; Walsh suggests that the notion of "surprise," while clearly unsatisfactory as part of such a definition, actually points in a different direction. It foregrounds the observing subject, and gestures towards a response that exceeds the bounds of cognition proper, taking on qualities of a more obviously affective character.

The larger questions at stake in this move are, firstly, that of the empirical status of emergence, and secondly, that of the nature of empirical knowledge. If emergent behaviour is constituted as such by its (narrative) intelligibility in different terms from those that apply to the micro-level systemic interactions, it seems that elements of regularity or order in the behaviour of a system may exist without being discernible as emergent, in the sense that the regularity of a pattern clearly exists even though it does not properly *become* a pattern until recognized as such. The concept of levels that informs most accounts of emergence is equivocal on this point, cultivating ambiguity between a view of the level as natural, and a view of it as an attribute of observation. Definitions invoking concepts of scale, scope and resolution refine the language of levels considerably, and make more explicit the interdependence of what belongs to the object and what belongs to the observation. This seems to be an aspect of a broader conception of empirical knowledge as not *of* or *about* the object in itself, but rather as a *relation* to the object. The evidently specific and circumscribed affordances of cognition itself dictate that knowledge is relational, and that this is a non-trivial circumstance. The connection between the particular case of emergence and the general case is apparent when we acknowledge that the same relational structure has already informed the delimitation of the system of interest itself.

2.3 Narrative

The implausible invocation of surprise in relation to emergence hints at analogous questions about our affective responses to narrative (or more specifically, to the forms of plot). This allows Walsh to refine the idea of surprise with reference to suspense, which is the most affectively powerful rhetorical exploitation of an intrinsic feature of narrative communication, its double relation to knowledge.

This doubleness recurs in different forms throughout the theorization of narrative, at different levels of scrutiny; Walsh seizes upon its operation in forms of character narration and "omniscient" narration, for the sake of the suggestive religious over-tones of the latter. The doubleness is a constitutive feature of narrative, however, precisely because narrative is a post-cognitive phenomenon, a product of cognitive activity. Hence narrative functions in semiotic terms, within the domain of meaning, whether we are talking about what is immediately present to knowledge in narrative or what is in principle available—either in retrospect, upon the narrative's resolution, or implicitly, via chains of inference. The relation is precisely between two kinds or degrees of knowledge, rather than between a knowing subject and an object of knowledge. The cognitive and affective qualities associated with narrative inter-pretation, then, offer an analogy but not an equivalence with those features of empirical sensemaking. The "real" of narrative, the "what actually happened," is itself conceptualized as already a form of knowledge, just as the religious sensibility negotiates with the universe by conceiving an absolute form of knowledge, inde-pendent of human cognition, in the form of divinity.

2.4 Narrating Complexity

This being so, the prospects for narrating complexity seem to be constrained by the fact that the complexity of narrative can only roughly approximate the ideal of a narrative of complexity. The way narrative itself elicits our cognitive and affective engagement can offer relatively little prospect, where complex phenomena are concerned, of an advance in the explicit communicative power of narrative. But does it suggest a possible route towards a cultivated practical understanding of complex processes, a kind of know-how rather than propositional knowledge? Walsh ends with Walter Benjamin's storyteller and his opposition between experi-ence and explanation, to suggest the extent to which the greatest potential of narrative may lie in its capacity to exceed the explicit, to enact and cultivate a mode of sensemaking that extends the reach of cognition by resisting the tendency to isolate and privilege information as the vehicle of knowledge.

3 A Simple Story of a Complex Mind? (Polvinen, Chap. 7)

3.1 Overview

Polvinen addresses the problems of engaging, from a cognitive humanities perspec-tive, with the manifestations of neuronal activity as cognitive processes that consti-tute the "brainmind." She considers narrative and complex systems perspectives upon the topic, and poses the twofold question of the extent to which each is able to connect with the other. She appeals to the potential for theories of enactive cognition to mediate, and examines two narrative presentations of the mind in this light to suggest the merit of narrative enaction, rather than representation, of its systemic functioning.

3.2 Complexity

In considering mind as a complex system, Polvinen contrasts computational and enactive models, arguing the merits of the latter for conceptualizing the emergence of macro-scale brain activity, and the higher-level manifestations of cognition, from the micro-scale interactions of neurons; she also champions enactive models for their emphasis upon embodiment, and hence the dynamic openness of the system to its sensorimotor environment. However, the case for such an approach to modelling the mind is of less immediate concern here than the consequent issues it raises for our ability to conceptualize the relation between the systemic relations among neurons and the forms of cognition accessible to consciousness.

Two considerations seem particularly important: the concept of agency and that of enaction. Systemic accounts of cognition inherently decompose the notion of the conscious subject as agent with which we are familiar. However, Polvinen suggests that the disconcerting appearance of this conceptual move is largely a result of the persistence of agential thinking, resulting in the equally unfounded attribution of agency to systemic elements themselves, or to the systemic brain, as distinct from "you." Enaction is important because it offers an alternative to representationalism in cognition. The latter takes a high-level cognitive concept—representation—and imposes it top-down upon lower-level processes where its applicability, even its intelligibility, become increasingly questionable. Theories of enactive cognition, on the contrary, take a concept with a very elemental role in cognition—behaviour within an environment—and extend it, bottom-up, from the neuronal micro-level to the emergence of cognition, abstract reasoning and metacognition.

3.3 Narrative

Agency and action are problematic concepts for the negotiation between narrative and systemic processes precisely because they are already invested in a narrative way of thinking. However this is itself indicative of the fundamental role of narrative, which Polvinen explores in terms of the narrative view of mind itself. The range of such approaches encompasses, at one limit, the premise that a disposition towards narrative modes of sensemaking is a characteristic of human cognition, to the hypothesis, at the other limit, that we are constituted as agents, and as selves, by such narrative processes. To the extent that narrative is not merely a vehicle for the representation of mental processes, but itself the form of mental processes, its capacity to articulate such processes appears to be enhanced, although this privileged position still remains at the level of emergent cognitive phenomena rather than their systemic neural substrate.

A sceptical question is bound to arise in response to the narrative view of mind: doesn't it extend the concept of narrative too far? Even in terms of the cognitive processes accessible to consciousness, much of mental activity seems poorly described as narrative in any very specific way; or if the term narrative is deemed to apply by fiat, then it risks losing conceptual definition to the extent that such a view ceases to mean anything specific. On the other hand, the challenge of negotiating with these dilemmas requires us to interrogate the concept of narrative itself, since it cannot be accepted as a conceptual primitive under such circumstances. That is, the explanatory power needed to clarify our ideas about the narrative quality of mind, or narrative as a mode of cognition, is not to be found in narrative itself so much as in narrative theory.

3.4 Narrating Complexity

On the basis of some version of the narrative view of mind, and of the enactive model of cognition, Polvinen suggests, the possibility arises that narrating complexity might be better understood in performative terms than representational terms. This possibility follows if it is legitimate to say in some particular sense that the mind has a narrative form which is an emergent characteristic of the enactive, systemic processes of neural interaction with an environment. That premise makes it seems plausible that, in the face of narrative texts, an interpretative attention to the process of narrative signification, as opposed to its representational product, might afford some insight into the analogous mental processes. If there are potential gains from such an approach, though, it also requires considerable circumspection. Narrative interpretation is a negotiation between the systemic interactions and the emergent narrative form of the semiotic system of narrative representation, and this may correlate in interesting ways with the emergence of narrative cognition out of systemic neural processes. But if so, it will have more to do with general properties of systems than the specific system of narrative semiotics, since this semiotics is itself an emergent *product* of the systemic micro-level of cognition, not the form of that system.

4 Closure, Observation and Coupling (Lively, Chap. 9)

4.1 Overview

The focus in Lively's chapter is on the theorization of narrative fiction in autopoietic terms, drawing upon Humberto Maturana's conception of autopoiesis as the defining characteristic of self-reproducing systems, and Niklas Luhmann's appropriation of that concept from the domain of biological systems to that of social and communicative systems.

4.2 Complexity

Lively justifies this extension of the scope of autopoiesis by showing the extent to which it was already part of the Aristotelian concept of *poiesis* upon which Maturana's theory is based. Indeed, an explicit analogy between biological organisms and works of art runs through the *Poetics*, suggesting that autopoiesis is best considered not as an idea about organic life, but more abstractly as an idea about systems. The three central ideas informing Lively's discussion of narrative and autopoiesis—closure, observation, coupling—all work at this level of abstraction.

Closure, here, is dissociated from its common literary-critical meaning in relation to the resolution of narrative, and considered instead as the foundational formal move of "operative closure," by which a system's internal operations demarcate it from its environment. The significant point is that this elementary move generates an asymmetry (following George Spencer-Brown's *Laws of Form*) and so leads to its recursive application; this is the engine of autopoiesis.

Observation is a key concept in this context because it subsumes the dual aspects of perception and communication, which provide the conceptual framework for understanding the systemic logic of autopoiesis in semiotic terms. The appropriate model for communication, on this basis, is the joint attentional situation, which triangulates the reductive model of communication as the transmission of content, and so makes communicative relations dynamically systemic. The recursive potential here is realised in a conception of the "art system" as distinctively concerned with second-order observations of observations.

The notion of coupling is already implicit in this model of the communicative situation, both in respect of the reciprocity between semiotic articulation and interpretation, and in respect of the coupling of perception and communication. The mutual constraint between systems that characterizes such structural coupling indicates the possibility of conceptualizing higher levels of systemic reciprocity, and Lively gestures in this direction by invoking such a view of the history of narrative fiction.

4.3 Narrative

The framework for the specifically narrative dimension of the chapter is provided by Mukařovský and Czech structuralism. Structuralism, along with Russian Formalism, laid the foundations for narratology, but the distinctive quality of Czech structuralism is its emphasis upon dynamic, temporal systemic process over the spatializing tendencies that are so prominent in the historically more dominant French tradition.

Mukařovský's concept of contexture articulates very clearly the way in which the sequential unfolding of narrative is distinct from the progressively emerging systemic whole of its semiotic structure. The focus of attention here is the unfolding event of the interpretative reception of a narrative, in the course of which meaning accumulates in cycles of sequential progression and retrospection.

This process of signification unfolds the polyfunctionality of language, notably in two ways that resonate specifically with narrative: the orientation of language towards subject or object, which correspond to the communicative and representational axes of narrative; and the reflexive potential opened up by this double orientation, in which both dimensions of the function of signs may themselves become the object of signification.

Mukařovský's ideas are elaborated within the horizons of a theory of art, and are oriented towards a definition of the aesthetic. Narrative fiction constitutes only part of his object, though a paradigmatic part; but it might also be said that narrative more broadly understood, beyond fiction and indeed beyond discourse as an elemental semiotic logic, might still partake of the formal dynamics that are here designated as the properties of the aesthetic function.

4.4 Narrating Complexity

The orientation of this chapter is towards the complexity of narrative rather than the narration of complexity, but its implicit consequences for the latter are significant. An autopoietic conception of narrative foregrounds the extent to which the system of narrative meaning, most especially in its fictional and artistic forms, has the capacity to extend far beyond the bare sequential logic of its formal inception. This is apparent in the reflexive movement of fictionality itself as a dissociation of narrative meaning from its informative relation to an object of representation; but it is also apparent, more inclusively, from the perspective of a (cross-)cultural history of narrative, conceived as a history of reflexive displacements of the received parameters of narrative meaning—both beyond and within the rhetoric of fictionality. Equally, it is clear that analogous reflexive negotiations with form can elaborate upon the systemic capacity of narrative meaning even within the dynamic unfolding of a particular narrative. All these considerations are highly suggestive, in principle, of the possibilities for narrating complexity.

5   The Proteus Principle (Pianzola, Chap. 10)

5.1 Overview

Pianzola's interest is a methodological concern for the future of the field of narrative studies. In considering narrative as a complex system he means to address not just the qualities of specific narratives, nor even narrative form in the abstract, but rather the concept of narrative as an object of theoretical inquiry. He invokes Meir Sternberg's Proteus Principle as the key to a comparative methodology capable of evaluating the relative merits of narrative theories of different scopes and in different contexts.

5.2 Complexity

The Proteus Principle affirms the many-to-many correlations between forms and functions in narrative. Pianzola identifies this as a systems idea with a more general methodological applicability, and relates it to a distinction between the organization and structure of systems derived from Maturana and Varela, in which structure is a particular configuration of components instantiating the more abstract organization of a system.

In the exposition of this idea and its applicability to narrative concepts and definitions on different scales, Pianzola invokes concepts of level and scope drawn from theories of emergence, and by privileging scope he lays the emphasis upon the determining role of observation. The system of concern, and the organization that it exhibits, are conditioned by the scope of our observation, such that systemic organization on other scales may be understood in terms of the target system's environment, or its sub-systems.

Form and function, as the relational concepts proposed by the Proteus Principle, can analogously be understood as products of particular determinations of the scope and context of the narrative system that a given theory takes as its object of inquiry, and equivalences of either form or function, across different instances of the other, provide for the possibility of dialogue between incommensurate narrative paradigms.

5.3 Narrative

Pianzola has in his sights the typological tendencies that continue to bear witness to the legacy of structuralism in narrative theory. Such approaches treat the semiotic function of narrative features as innate in their discursive form, rather than contingent upon the relation between discourse and audience. Importantly, though, in affirming a view of this relation as intrinsic to the intelligibility of narrative, Pianzola also recognizes that "discourse" and "audience" are themselves concepts specific to the scope of a given theoretical frame of reference (and he notes how the relation might be better expressed in other terms, for instance "stimuli" and "agent," on other scales). The pragmatist, constructivist view of narrative meaning here is therefore systemically recursive, rather than positing a foundational subject-object relation at any level. One advantage of this approach is that it accommodates a diachronic view of the development of narrative as a mode of signification, in terms of the feedback loop between discourses and audiences, or perhaps more generally between forms and occasions, that can be traced on several temporal and conceptual scales. This logic offers a purchase upon, for example, the place of narrative in individual learning and development, the cultural history of narrative forms, and even the evolutionary emergence of narrative cognition.

5.4 Narrating Complexity

The methodological orientation of Pianzola's argument is better captured by the idea of theorizing the complexity of concepts of narrative than by the specific challenge of narrating complexity, though there are implications for that challenge in his appeal to the Proteus Principle as the foundation for a consolidation of narrative studies. The argument is couched in terms of the theoretical domain of narrative studies, but it provides for dialogue not only between theoretical paradigms, but also between narrative theory and practice. Just as the diachronic study of narrative requires a recognition of the cyclical reciprocity between forms and functions, discourses and audiences, so the role of narrative theory itself is not extrinsic to the current and potential affordances of narrative. As Pianzola notes, the narrative domain continues to evolve, and the prominence of systems thinking in current thinking about narrative *and* narrative theory suggests that there are good prospects for the emergence of new affordances for narrating complexity.

6 Narrative Experiences of History and Complex Systems (Turina, Chap. 11)

6.1 Overview

Turina examines the relation between narrative and complex systems in our understanding of historical events, and in the discourse of historiography itself. She identifies the challenge to the characteristically narrative form of historiographic understanding presented by the inherently systemic nature of historical events; but she also demonstrates that such narratives, as elements of the sphere of social and political discourse, are implicated within the systemic feedback loops of history itself. She illustrates the issues with respect to the history of Trieste, and explores the potential of interactive virtual reality technologies to enhance our ability to grasp the processes involved.

6.2 Complexity

Turina makes the basic point that the events with which history is concerned are inherently complex phenomena and so are necessarily imposed upon in important ways by their subjection to narrative forms of historiographic representation. This is not the main point of her argument, however; more significant is the fact historical events are ongoing, and the public discourse of historiography is itself one of the forces in play. The feedback loops between dominant historical narratives and the political and social realities they represent have a powerful influence upon the course of events themselves. In the ideologically charged domain of events concerning the multiple conflicting social interests, there is no possibility of maintaining a distinction between what happens and representations of what happens. Turina notes that this is not just a matter of the coarse ideological power of dominant narratives, since even rigorous academic efforts to critique such narratives, and to present counternarratives, find themselves caught up in the reactive logic consequent upon the priming effect of established narratives and the antithetical status of the "silent histories" that might be pitted against them; there is no objective ground on which to stand.

6.3 Narrative

The narrative focus of this chapter is not primarily the achieved historiographical narrative that articulates a particular perspective and interpretation of evidence, but rather the "narrative matrix," the set of intersecting, complementary or conflicting micro-level narratives relating to a given historical moment. This move, while accepting that the impositions of narrative form are already present at any level of historical representation, nonetheless conceives the web of these micro-narratives as raw, systemic material relative to the order imposed upon them by any synthetic historical narrative. In response to the inescapable contingencies of historiography, Turina identifies two possible broad approaches to the narrative matrix. The first, weaker response is one that historiography routinely adopts and is already embedded in historical education; it undertakes the task of constructing a narrative reading, while emphasizing the contingencies of any single interpretation of the material. The stronger response, advocated by Turina, aims to remain in process, in an act of narrative sensemaking conscious of its own negotiation with, and intervention in, the narrative matrix rather than an orientation towards the achieved product of interpretation.

6.4 Narrating Complexity

The narrative potential of virtual reality technologies has to do with this second stance in relation to narrative matrices. Turina considers game engines as the most developed implementations of simulated interactive environments, and envisages the use of such engines for historiographic narrative matrices, enabling the interactive engagement of a player to function as an enactment of the process of narrative engagement with systemic materials. The attractions of this proposition are, firstly, that as an immersive form of interpretative engagement it can make the player's ongoing negotiation between different perspectives itself a consequential factor in the system, exhibiting priming effects and facilitating recursive meta-reflections upon the historiographic sensemaking in process; secondly, and more fundamentally, such simulations (as themselves both environments and representations) may make tangible the conflict between complexity and narrative, as a tension between systemic experientiality and the semiotic pursuit of sequential coherence. Turina maps this opposition (via the Platonic distinction between *mimesis* and *diegesis*) onto the classic pair of narratological concepts, showing and telling.

7 (Gardening) Gardening (Caves & Melo, Chap. 13)

7.1 Overview

Caves and Melo write about a novel process for building models of complex systems, focussing on the *relationships* between system components. They use a well-known complex system, the garden, to ground their description. The process supports the building of a modelworld, the basis for a predefined storyworld from which explanatory narratives may then be constructed.

7.2 Complexity

One thing that makes complex systems hard to grapple with, certainly from a science and engineering perspective, is the close coupling between the components. Something changing *here* affects something else *there*. Good engineering design tries to decouple as much as possible, and reductionist science assumes such decoupling is possible, so that components can be analysed, designed, and understood in isolation.

Complex systems also have multiway coupling: (nearly) everything is coupled to (nearly) everything else. Something changing here affects something else *everywhere*. And something changing *anywhere* else affects something here. Everything *is related* to everything else.

Caves and Melo have taken this relational view, and used it to build a process for analysing complex systems, particularly systems where there are explicit *interventions* intended to change or maintain the system. Their focus is not on the components, but on the relations. Once analysed, these relations can be considered as new components, themselves related to other parts, resulting in a growing mesh of relationships, explicitly focussed on the couplings. This allows the authors to build a modelworld not of components, but of relations. The coupling is built into the model as a first class component in its own right. The framework crucially includes modelling of interventions: the relationships between the intervenor(s) and the system.

The existence of a discipline such as General Systems Theory points to (the belief in) the existence of universal patterns across a range of disparate systems. That implies that this relational framework, illustrated through gardening, should be applicable to other domains. For gardening, interventions include processes such as weeding, pruning, planting, and fertilising. The framework will need augmentation for cases where a different complex system (that is not a garden) contains entities (that are not plants) that deserve ethical consideration in their own right, and where the intervenors are much more part of (comprise) the system under change itself. It will be exciting to see this new relational model-building process applied across a range of complex systems.

7.3 Narrative

There are two narratives exploited in this chapter: one explicit and one implicit.

The explicit part is the discussion of how the built complex relational modelworld can provide the underpinnings for a storyworld—for then building narrative(s) to explore and explain the modelworld (and, consequently, the real world). This is analogous to the considerable emphasis upon world building that underpins (some) science fiction and fantasy tales.

The focus in Caves and Melo's chapter is on narratives that help explore how to guide *change* of the world, rather than narratives of living in an unchanging, or uncontrolledly changing, world. The narrative structures discussed all assume that the Gardener (intervenor) is the protagonist, and classify the different kinds of gardeners, some of whom will be heroes, some anti-heroes, according to the circumstances. The process of intervening, coupled with self-reflection, will cause the intervenors to change, and their characters to progress. In this light, we look forward someday to reading:

> From Menace to Master: Relata Hunter intervenes on the Garden Planet of Complexus Majoris III (a science fiction trilogy)

There is also implicit narrative, in the very structure of the chapter. Unlike many impersonal accounts, it captures the process the authors went through in devising their framework. This works well, because the process of using the framework is crucial, and the narrative style helps highlight the design process itself: the decisions, the false starts, the roads not taken, the self-reflection. The style is additionally narrative in that it focuses on a single concrete example, a single story, that of the gardening domain, instead of more abstractly describing a fully generic process applicable to any complex domain.

7.4 Narrating Complexity

Scientific descriptions need some form of narrative structure to make them comprehensible. Ideas must build up in a logical manner. Goals, methods, and results must be presented clearly. Despite the somewhat narrative structure, the underlying "story" here is essentially impersonal. This can often be true in "hard" science fiction and other genres, where the phrases "idea as hero"[1], "plot as hero"[2] and "landscape novel"[3] (in contrast to the character-driven "portrait novel") have been used.

Such scientific description might be argued to be mere structured description rather than narrative *per se*. In particular, there is a timelessness about such descriptions: they are typically neither anchored in a particular time, nor have an internal temporal structure. However, complex systems are inherently dynamic. They change, develop, evolve, die. They more readily admit a narrative description. This Gardening framework chapter illustrates the value of a narrative approach to complex systems understanding: the approach highlights and foregrounds the processual nature of developing the complex modelworld: a narrative process to build a descriptive model, which may then itself be illuminated by further narratives from the associated storyworld.

8 The Software Garden (Miller, Chap. 15)

8.1 Overview

Miller proposes a new kind of approach for the difficult, intricate and error-prone task of building software. The idea is to embrace the complexity of the process by developing an explicit analogue: how people build a garden. Miller wants to plant software seeds, and visually grow, prune, and train them into complex software artefacts.

8.2 Complexity

Software is complex to build and complex to understand. This complexity seems to derive from three main aspects.

Firstly, software is incredibly *fragile*: the smallest change to the software (a single character error) can completely change the nature of its behaviour, manifesting as subtle bugs through to hanging, crashing, blue-screening, bricking or many other

---

[1]Kingsley Amis. *New Maps of Hell: A Survey of Science Fiction*. Penguin, 1960.

[2]Attributed to Edmund Crispin.

[3]Heard at a panel discussion at the 1996 British National Science Fiction Convention, April 1996.

colourful terms used by the community to describe a computer that has unintentionally stopped computing. This is sensitive dependence on initial conditions *par excellence*.

Secondly, software is *invisible*. Software has an abstract high-dimensional structure, which can be hard to discover from the textual code, or even from accompanying diagrams. And executing software is essentially *dynamic*: it has complex behaviour over time, as the consequences of executing the various algorithms unfold. This dynamic behaviour is barely reflected in the static text of the code: one can "read through" the code, but in order to deduce the route to be taken through its branching and cyclic pathways, one needs to somehow execute the statements. It becomes almost impossible to comprehend both the abstract structure and the complex dynamics together. There are diagrammatic forms that help to summarise the temporal aspects, but they are all impoverished in some way or another, due to the sheer complexity of the actual dynamic behaviours. This invisibility is one thing that makes it hard to build truly high level reusable components: it is hard for the user of such components to grasp their intended behavioural structure. Invisibility also contributes to the difficulty of *maintenance*: diving into a mature piece of software to discern where the errors are, or where new functionality can be added, is a non-trivial skill.

Thirdly, software is constructed at a very *low level*. Although programming languages such as Python, Java, and C++ are called "high level", this is only relative to the lowest level assembly languages and machine code. If using machine code is like constructing a skyscraper from individual atoms, then using "high level" languages is like constructing it from individual pebbles. But it is not a static skyscraper being constructed in software; it is a whirling, twirling, gyring, growing, adapting, *changing* complex arrangement of dynamic "pebbles". Coding is akin to trying to make a living organism by placing each individual cell.

Miller tackles all these issues in his proposal for a new way to build software: a Software Garden. He uses the concept of *horticulture* as an analogy for his process for developing robust, visible, high level software. Plants are not so fragile that minor damage to one leaf destroys that plant, let alone the entire garden. A garden is a highly visible artefact that can be viewed from many perspectives, and apprehended at many spatial and temporal scales. Gardeners do not construct individual plants, nor do they build mature gardens with fully grown plants, nor do they expect the garden to function without continual maintenance and change.

8.3 Narrative

Miller's Software Garden would support narratives for designing, constructing, running, and modifying software.

For such a dynamic artefact, there is surprisingly little focus on narrative for describing traditional software. At the stage of requirements elicitation, the Unified Modelling approach involves defining *use cases*, each use case being a description of how the system is used to achieve a particular goal. If there are many potential paths to achieving a goal, each separate one can be described using a specific *scenario*. This focus on use, or process, or dynamics, often gives way to a focus on structure once these requirements are turned into a design for satisfying them. Later in the design phase, graphical representations called *state diagrams* might be used to show the life history of a single component, and *sequence diagrams* might be used to to show how multiple components interact, leading to emergent system-level behaviours. These diagrams could be thought of as primitive narratives, capturing at least potential *linear temporal sequences* of events.

Miller's proposal changes the opportunities for narrative, raising the level from simple events to interactions and processes analogous to those in horticulture, including "pruning, fertilising, spraying, training, grafting and breeding".

8.4 Narrating Complexity

In Caves and Melo's "Gardening Gardening" (Chap. 13), they use the garden as an *exemplar* in order to make concrete their proposed design process. Miller here uses the garden as an *analogy* for proposing a novel software development process that would have many of the abstract attributes of gardening. Is gardening itself a complex system that we humans understand well enough that it can act as a starting point for developing theories of complex narratives and approaches to narrating complexity?

9 Emergent Causality in Complex Films and Complex Systems (Poulaki, Chap. 16)

9.1 Overview

The core of Poulaki's argument is the idea that certain complex films often characterised as "network narratives" resist linear, narrative ideas of causality, and provoke or require interpretation as complex systems. She examines a range of emergent and systemic models of causality, drawing upon emergentist philosophy, cybernetics and social network theory among others, showing the inadequacy of narrative understanding to such ideas and exploring their potential as ways of moving beyond narrative.

9.2   Complexity

Beginning with notions of strong and weak emergence, Poulaki shows that a narrative mode of understanding cannot capture the mechanisms involved, both because of the multiplicity of interactions and (more fundamentally) because of the categorical shift in levels that characterises emergence as such. Nonetheless, forms of determination that can appropriately be called causal are clearly involved. Poulaki explores the ways in which these effects have been theorised in terms of cybernetic models of feedback loops, the effects of mathematical nonlinearity characteristic of such models and the non-equilibrium dynamics of complex systems; she affirms a view of emergence grounded upon a "pattern-based" form of causality that disallows both reductionist causal accounts and the causal disconnect of strong emergentism.

9.3   Narrative

Poulaki notes that while the form of causality projected by narrative cognition cannot accommodate complex processes, models of narrative itself need not be incompatible with systemic complexity. She invokes the dynamic cycles of equilibrium and disequilibrium in Todorov's definition of narrative; and she traces, between the Aristotelian and structuralist traditions of narrative theory, a concern with wholes and a layered network of relations (treated somewhat statically and spatially in early structuralism, but more dynamically as it moved towards post-structuralism). The implication is that the process of narrative interpretation is necessarily a negotiation with complex systemic relations of signification. This is necessarily the case to some extent for any narrative whole, of whatever scale or degree of sophistication, but Poulaki's specific interest is in forms of "complex narrative," notably in film, that ostentatiously frustrate the linear causal paradigm privileged by narrative cognition. Here, the usual dynamics of interpretative engagement with systemic relations at the level of the represented events (in itself a prominent feature of the more elaborate kinds of realist fiction) is compounded by an analogous systemic complexity in the development of the *syuzhet*, or narrative discourse, itself.

9.4   Narrating Complexity

A complex narrative is not in itself a narration of complexity; its complexification of narration is rather a resistance to the logic of narration that enacts, in the process of interpretation, an encounter with complexity. The cultural elaboration of narrative in general can be understood as a cumulative series of efforts to break narrative, to exceed its limitations. It seems significant that many contemporary cultural narratives (Poulaki's film examples, but also a significant number of recent novels, for example) have focussed specifically upon the limitations of narrative's grasp upon complexity. Poulaki ends by noting that this systemic confrontation with narrative understanding works at the level of our interpretative negotiations with the narrative in process, the transgressive experience of which is privileged over any final achieved form, which must collapse back into the familiar mould of narrative logic. But she envisages the possibility that such modes of meaning may eventually emancipate themselves from narrative and function as new, systemic forms of organization in their own right.

10   Narrative and Cognitive Modelling (Bernini, Chap. 17)

10.1   Overview

Bernini's essay considers the mind as a complex system, and consciousness and the sense of selfhood as emergent phenomena. He proposes that Samuel Beckett's work can be understood as a sustained effort to decompose these effects into their complex systemic causes, through a strategy he calls "fictional cognitive modelling." The conflict between narrative understanding and complex systems, in this account, is mediated by a "narrative dynamic core" to Beckett's explorations of the mind's complexity.

10.2   Complexity

The challenge of complexity is framed, in Bernini's account, in terms of modelling. He notes that an adequate model must capture features of a system's complexity, rather than just representing the systemic whole, but without itself becoming a complex system as inscrutable as the target system. The differences between model and target are as important as the equivalences, and the formal simplifications involved are pragmatically justified by the particular purposes of the model. Bernini distinguishes between descriptive, predictive, explanatory and exploratory models, and it is the last of these he goes on to invoke as the orientation of Beckett's modelling strategies. There is an additional, more specific difficulty that arises when the target system is the complexity of mind, which is of course that it is the system within which our cognitive engagement is itself enmeshed. For Bernini, and for Beckett, the reflexivity this entails is both a problem and an opportunity; it provides a rationale for introspection, not in order to isolate the object of inquiry so much as to engage with it in the process. Fictional cognitive modelling, then, is a form of "experiential art" that seeks to capture something of the mind's complexity reflexively, by enacting it as much as by representing it.

10.3 Narrative

Narrative figures in this account in two mutually implicated but conceptually distinct respects. The first foregrounds the way narrative constrains our ability to make sense of complex processes, characterizing it (after Abbott) as inherently imposing a model of centralized control that fundamentally conflicts with the distributed nature of such processes. In this respect narrative always seizes upon effects of emergence, at the expense of the process by which the effects emerge. In the second sense, however, narrative (more specifically, for Bernini, the narrative sense of self) features as itself an emergent phenomenon. In this sense, the reflexiveness of the effort to understand mind is a specifically narrative reflexiveness, so that the challenge—and Beckett's strategy—is to catch narrative cognition in the process of formation. Bernini characterizes such decomposed, or precomposed, ur-narrative matter as the "narrative dynamic core," and identifies language, time, agents and imagination as its constitutive elements.

10.4 Narrating Complexity

The effort to grasp the complexity of mind does not entail the impossible task of bridging, in a single span, the "explanatory gap" between the mental phenomena of consciousness and the neurological structure of the brain. Such a binary model is itself reductive, neglecting the evident involvement of many layers of complexity and emergence in this transit. Some of this recursive layering, at least, is accessible from the perspective of introspection, and the rigorous effort to attend to processes of emergence at that level is already an important advance in understanding of the mind's complex systemic constitution. This is the light in which Bernini understands Beckett's efforts to unpick the threads of narrative representation in order to reflexively model the emergence of a narrative sense of self. The difficulty, and value, of Beckett's work in part consists in its sustained effort to push us to the threshold of narrative sense, further into the process of its emergence than we are accustomed to go. Bernini briefly illustrates two sides of this effort in examples from Beckett: an analytic strategy that isolates components of the emergent self in "local models," and a synthetic strategy that offers "global models" of the interaction between components. In both cases Beckett's exploratory models extend our understanding of the complex processes of the mind, and breach the ordinary limits of narrative sensemaking itself.

11 Narratives for Drug Design (Bown & Goltsov, Chap. 18)

11.1 Overview

Bown and Goltsov discuss the potential uses of narrative in helping drug researchers understand complex signalling pathways in cancer cells. They suggest the use of dynamic visualisation, guided by the user, as input material for building a narrative.

11.2 Complexity

Biological systems are complex. They have evolved over billions of years into highly structured, organised, exquisitely poised, and mostly incomprehensible systems. Many of our scientific understanding tools are geared towards simpler systems, where particles are identical, where variation is "noise," where averages and equilibrium hold sway. Biological systems are of a different kind: highly evolved to be far from equilibrium, and where variation is literally the driving force of their Darwinian evolution. Biological systems are complex on many levels: cells, tissues, organs, organisms, ecosystems. Moreover, where disease is concerned, these systems are embedded in a further complex socio-technical system: healthcare.

In this chapter the focus is on a single biological level: signalling pathways within a cancerous cell. This necessary simplification has not made the system simple: it exhibits emergence, downward causation (tumour tissue environmental effects), genetic mutation, cross-talk and feedback, and changing network topology.

Targeted drug design, needed to fix or kill the dysfunctional cancerous cells, requires an understanding of this dynamic complexity, and in particular of the way the system responds to different perturbations. The authors discuss ways this might be achieved, via visualisation and narrative.

11.3 Narrative

Visualisation is a powerful method for allowing people to explore and discover patterns in complex situations. A picture, even a dynamic representation, is not itself a narrative, however. The authors discuss how visualisations of complex systems might be used, interactively by the researchers, to explore the behaviour of a complex system, as a vehicle for discovering and building relevant explanatory narratives. They finish with an interesting suggestion of exploiting ideas from graphic novels to deliver the explanatory narrative so discovered.

11.4   Narrating Complexity

When conveying complex spatial relationships, diagrams help communication. When conveying complex temporal behaviours, animations help communication. So it seems plausible that in order to narrate complex systems well, some form of animated images will be needed. This increases the dimensionality of what is being presented in linear temporal sequence, from words, read or spoken, to two-dimensional or three-dimensional (holographic) images: movies. Although a moving image is not necessarily a narrative, narrating complexity might require a movie, or at least a graphic novel.

12   Time Will Tell (Caves, Melo, Stepney & Uprichard, Chap. 19)

12.1   Overview

Narrative is the semiotic articulation of linear *temporal* sequence. Complex systems are not timeless or static, but fundamentally historical and *dynamic processes*. But what *is* time? Caves, Melo, Stepney and Uprichard survey and review some aspects of time, from the perspectives of the physical sciences, biological sciences, and social sciences. From this it is clear that the time underpinning complex systems and their narration is not some uniform substrate, but is *itself* complex.

12.2   Complexity

There are several sources of temporal complexity in complex systems.

Firstly, there are *multiple timescales*. There is a natural timescale from "birth" to "death," the timescale on which a process or entity exists as a relatively stable structure. A complex system has processes and entities on multiple levels, each with their own timescales (our cells turn over on a much shorter timescale than we ourselves live). Additionally, complex systems are open, embedded in an environment which has its own natural timescales (physically realised days, months, seasons, years, geological epochs, etc; social constructs of weeks, school terms, election cycles, etc). The combinations and interplay of all these timescales leads to complexity.

Secondly, there is the *invisible* temporal activity maintaining a process or entity in a relatively stable state. In the dominant *substance* worldview, equilibrium stability is the norm, and only change requires explanation. But on taking a *process*-oriented worldview, change is the default state, and it is stability that requires an explanation. Now the far-from-equilibrium stability of a complex system, its apparent *lack* of change despite the passage of time, as it works to maintain its position by "walking up a down escalator," is in need of investigation and explanation.

Thirdly, there is *feedback*. Feedback is essential in the maintenance of a stable complex system, and contributes also to its non-linear behaviours. Complex interconnected feedback loops on different timescales mean that simple descriptions of causality do not work. This complex "loopiness" means that no simple linearisation of description and explanation is possible.

12.3 Narrative

Caves et al. suggest that the complexity of the time underpinning complex systems may be why they resist narrative. That is, the cognitive challenge that complex processes present to narrative understanding is twofold: they exceed the mind's capacity to trace and follow the complex dynamics of multiple interfering chains of interaction, but moreover, they elude the model of temporality itself presupposed by narrative.

Narrative cognition assumes, and perhaps produces, one of our basic ways of grasping temporality, but that model breaks down in the face of complex systems. However, our sense of time is not entirely narrative dependent: consider how time can be mapped onto spatial concepts in diagrams, for example. The result may be perplexity—the tendency to generate paradoxes of temporality, for example—but it may also offer possibilities for productive conceptual dissociation from our ingrained forms of cognition and representation.

12.4 Narrating Complexity

The multiplicity of timescales in a complex system presents a challenge. Interlocking timescales may make it difficult to capture the rhythm or tempo of the system. Focussing on one timescale may ignore crucial properties happening on other time-scales. Mismatched timescales may make it difficult to communicate the different parts coherently. Timescales that are outside our human comprehension (ultra-fast or ultra-slow) are difficult to communicate, even metaphorically. For example, Carl Sagan's "Cosmic Calendar" maps the history of the universe onto a year, with the totality of human history and prehistory then being a mere ten seconds or so at the end, and with modern history occupying just the last second. This provides *some* perspective, but it is still difficult to truly internalise the difference between these vastly different timescales in any essential manner: we can conceptualise a year, and also a few seconds, but rarely simultaneously.

The invisibility of complex self-organising processes can present problems and opportunities for narrative: firstly, recognising that something needs to be explained, even though nothing appears to be happening; secondly, finding a way to narrate that nothingness in an intelligible manner. Narratives of inactivity have a difficult, avant-garde quality precisely because they are refusing a basic expectation of narrative sense. This avant-garde difficulty can be compelling, however.

The feedback circularity of complex systems resists any simple linearisation. This potentially presents the major challenge for narrating complex systems: how to linearise the system for narrative in a way that does not grossly over-simplify, or worse still miss, its essential circularity? Of course, the linear structure of a narrative in no way has to map naively onto the temporal structure of the narrated, but when the two are structured so fundamentally differently, new approaches are required.

One further relevant feedback complexity not noted by Caves et al., but raised by Turina (Chap. 11) and Bernini (Chap. 17), is when the complex system (in these cases, history, and the mind, respectively) is influenced by its narratives, reflexively deepening and further complexifying the feedbacks, and enlarging the scope of the relevant system to include its own narratives and their effects (compare with Winfield's robots, Chap. 4).

The issues discussed in this book are manifold, yet tackling them is necessary to narrating complexity; that is, to the challenge of narrating some of the most pressing problems facing us today, and learning how to read and interpret such complex narratives.

Chapter 23
From Simplex to Complex Narrative?

Susan Stepney and Richard Walsh

Abstract This concluding chapter recaps the challenges to narrative understanding presented by complex systems, and speculates upon the prospects for meeting these challenges through different conceptions of "complex narrative".

The importance of understanding, explaining and managing complex systems is self-evident. They include many of the most important systems in today's world, including the environment and ecology, climate and pollution, economic and market structures, cities and transport networks, population and migration, the frameworks of democracy and political agency, information media, social and political structures, healthcare, food and water security. Our ability to grasp the way complex systems work, and so to discuss and debate these issues and arrive at judgements, is substantially dependent upon the ability to make narrative sense of them: narrative cognition is our innate means of understanding processes, and to a large extent it sets the terms for what constitutes such understanding. Yet complex systemic processes have many properties that, individually and in combination, present major obstacles to both descriptive and narrative modes of representation and understanding:

- **Feedback** and temporal "loopiness," which does not allow any simple linearisation of cause and effect
- **Emergence**, where the behaviour of the whole cannot be readily deduced from the behaviours of the parts, and where the whole affects the parts
- **Relational** nature, where the many-to-many interactions between the component parts are more pertinent to the system behaviour than are the parts themselves

S. Stepney (✉)
Department of Computer Science, University of York, York, UK

York Cross-disciplinary Centre for Systems Analysis, York, UK
e-mail: susan.stepney@york.ac.uk

R. Walsh
Department of English and Related Literature, University of York, York, UK

Interdisciplinary Centre for Narrative Studies, University of York, York, UK

- **Openness**, in that a complex system cannot be understood in isolation, because of its essential interactions with its environment
- **Reflexiveness**, in social systems, where narratives of the system are also within the system, affecting it
- **Stability** in the face of change, where the stability is not passively static, but an active self-maintenance that needs to be supported
- **Tipping points** of rapid unexpected change in the face of small perturbations, as a seemingly stable complex system is finally pushed beyond its limits
- **Multiple timescales**, fast and slow, many beyond human perception
- **Multiple spatial scales**, large and small, also beyond human perception

If we are to understand our complex world, perhaps we need more complex narratives to help us engage with its processes, and bring them into human comprehension. But what could a concept like "complex narrative" actually mean? Is it possible to envisage it? And would it help?

It should be recognised, first, that narratives *are* complex: while the fundamental logic that gives them form is hostile to complexity, its semiotic articulation necessarily proliferates meaning in implicit and open-ended ways, so that the interpretation of narrative is always to some degree a negotiation with the complexity of semiotic systems. Even as narratives harness semiotic media to impose the reductive logic of narrative form, the latent complexity of those semiotic systems is continually threatening to exceed that logic. This tension presents an opportunity, perhaps, but also a caution.

Extended and elaborate forms of narrative can offer declarative knowledge in narrative form, but also knowledge by acquaintance, in the interpretative process, with their own complexity as systems of meaning. Can this duality be harnessed? One possible avenue of inquiry is reflexiveness; indeed, the cultural history of the development of sophisticated narrative forms can be understood as a long series of reflexive moves, explicit and implicit, by which the constraints of narrative logic have been trumped and transcended. If other limitations of narrative form have been mitigated by this device, perhaps the same can be done for its resistance to complexity. The prospect seems all the more promising because reflexiveness is itself characteristic of complex interactions, and every reflexive move invites and encourages the recognition that it could be recursively applied. Reflexive moves therefore directly gesture beyond the linearity of narrative logic, allowing narratives to lead readers/audiences across the threshold from that logic to the complexity of their semiotic systems.

There are limits to the potential of such approaches, however. The constraints of narrative are more fundamental than the drag of its legacy cultural forms, and efforts to complexify it always risk subverting its sense-making capacity without generating other kinds of intelligibility. Self-consciously complexified narratives are intrinsically difficult narratives, and if a narrative purchase upon complex systems can be achieved only by reproducing the cognitive difficulty presented by the complex system in the form of the narrative itself, it isn't clear what has been gained. The problem is even more pointed in the public sphere. There the pull towards narrative complexity runs up against a fundamental reason why narrative is a privileged mode of communication, which is its directness and simplicity. It is certainly important to resist the tendency for politicians, lobbyists and decision makers to rely upon crude "sound bite" narrative explanations, which not only produce bad arguments, they also discredit good ones; but failure to communicate is not an advance upon reductive communication.

Less immediate benefits of narrative complexification may still be worth pursuing, though it is important to discriminate between the prospects of different approaches. One broad point is that there can be a cumulative effect from the proliferation of narratives that self-consciously foreground their own formal exploration of complexity. As with other kinds of innovation in the past, the gradual assimilation of such strategies amounts to a refinement of narrative literacy. There is an obvious analogy with the early history of film here: over a period of about twenty years this new medium evolved from a spectacular illusion, grasped primarily in terms of an almost magical power to reproduce life itself, into a sophisticated vehicle of narrative with its own formal idiom. Notably, this evolution was the result of communicative feedback loops between film-makers and audiences, often negotiated through highly self-conscious, reflexive filmic devices.

Such a development towards complex narrative might also offer an advance in complexity literacy, and be of value in those terms, but it does not in itself provide for a more effective narrative grasp upon complex systemic subject matter. The complexity it foregrounds is that latent in the semiotics of narrative representation itself, rather than that of any particular system with which such a narrative might engage. There is a general metaphorical or analogical relation between the two, but an encounter with semiotic and formal complexity in narrative *interpretation* is different in kind from the effort to produce adequate narrative *representations* of other kinds of complex system. And indeed, to the extent that a narrative merely reproduces complexity rather than mediating it, the result presents essentially the same challenges to comprehension as the represented system itself.

There are some complex systems that we can come to understand through continual embedded interactions; we acquire an experiential knowledge by acquaintance that exceeds the propositional knowledge of narrative cognition. This may be why gardening, as both an exemplar and an analogy, has played a significant role in this book. But we cannot engage with larger and slower, or smaller and faster, systems in such an embedded way; and here perhaps there is a productive way in which we might engage with relevant narratives instead. It is possible that the interpretative complexity of the experience of narrative can be made into a vehicle for the specific modelling of some target complex system, so that both the systemic and the emergent (i.e., narratable) behaviour of the system can be simultaneously conveyed, in a hybrid form that fuses communication and experience.

Such a hybrid mode of representation seems particularly worth exploring in interactive media, where the user's agency can itself become an instance of the dual perspective required in order to respond to the duality of simulation, as both a representation of a system and a system in its own right. That is, the user's interaction may be conceived in narrative terms, as a communicative, representational mode of engagement, or it may be conceived in experiential terms, as a form of (virtual) agency within a systemic environment; or both.

A key feature of such interactive narrative environments is the opportunity for permutation and "replayability," which provides for a cumulative acquaintance with the system distinct from any given run through it. But to become a tool of learning or intellectual engagement with complexity, this capacity needs to be conceived differently from the way it is typically exploited at present (in games, for example); that is, it needs to be dissociated from the idea of a kind of immediacy, or virtual experience of the represented system itself. This is a naïve fantasy of immersion (very similar to some early conceptions of cinema), to be contrasted with a lucid awareness that interactive agency relates to the system of the simulation itself, not its target system. The target system itself, however, is accessible through the user's creative engagement with the simulation's representational capacity, and this can be explored through the self-conscious adoption of a co-authorial stance, in interaction with the simulation itself. By such means we might use the affordances of interactivity to bring narrative form and systemic behaviour into overt dialogue with each other, and to mediate between them.

The questions provoked by the problematic encounter between narrative and complex systems are not susceptible to short answers, and remain open. The issues raised are far-reaching, not just within the domains of complexity science and narratology, but for society at large; it is encouraging, then, that these issues are attracting interest in a striking diversity of contexts, and generating considerable intellectual energy and innovation. The contributions to this volume reflect the diversity and exemplify the intellectual ferment; they testify to the productivity of this interdisciplinary dialogue, but they by no means exhaust it.